ISBN 978-1-5284-7288-3
PIBN 10095412

OMITTED CHAPTERS

OF

THE HISTORY OF ENGLAND.

VOL. II.

LONDON
PRINTED BY SPOTTISWOODE AND CO.
NEW-STREET SQUARE

HISTORY

OF THE

COMMONWEALTH OF ENGLAND

FROM THE DEATH OF CHARLES I. TO THE EXPULSION

OF THE LONG PARLIAMENT BY CROMWELL:

BEING

OMITTED CHAPTERS OF THE HISTORY OF ENGLAND.

BY ANDREW BISSET.

In Two Volumes—Vol. II.

LONDON:

JOHN MURRAY, ALBEMARLE STREET.

1867.

PREFACE.

THIS VOLUME completes the narrative of a period of English History which I think I may truly say has never before been written—the period extending from the death of Charles I. to the expulsion of the Long Parliament by Cromwell, and usually called the period of the Commonwealth. As I have shown in the preceding volume, the English Government at this time was not that which the Greeks called a democracy and the Romans a republic. It may perhaps be best described, in the language of those who carried it on, as a government differing essentially from that sort of government which the experience of that age had proved to be a bad government—" the government of a single person."[1] So strong was the conviction of those men on this point, that Cromwell himself, even after he had concentrated all the powers of government in his own person, is reported to have said, "I approve the government of a single person as little as any man."[2] Although

[1] James Harrington, the author of "The Commonwealth of Oceana," though of no authority as a practical politician, records accurately enough the opinions of the most sagacious practical politicians of that age, when he says, in his tract on "The Grounds and Reasons of Monarchy," published in his works (folio, London, 1700):

" I could never be persuaded but it was more happy for a people to be disposed of by a number of persons jointly interested and concerned with them, than to be numbered as the herd and inheritance of one, to whose lust and madness they were absolutely subject."

[2] This remark of Cromwell is reported to have been made with reference

the term " Commonwealth " may be objected to as somewhat ambiguous, for the reasons already stated,[1] nevertheless it will be convenient to entitle this work, " A History
of England under the Government called the Commonwealth,"—a Government which began on the death of
King Charles I., and ended on the expulsion of the Parliament by Cromwell.

The new materials which I have used in the composition
of this and the preceding volume are the Minutes of the
Council of State, contained in forty MS. volumes of the
original draft Order Books of that Council. It may, I trust,
not be deemed impertinent to state here that my attention
was first directed some years ago to these MS. minutes of
the proceedings of the Council of State by the kindness
of the English historian of Greece, Mr. Grote, who then
said that when, some years before, he went through
the State Paper Office, the gentlemen who showed him
these volumes of original MS. minutes told him that they

to Harrington's " Commonwealth of
Oceana," which work Harrington
dedicated " To His Highness the
Lord Protector of the Commonwealth
of England, Scotland, and Ireland." A
commonwealth in the sense of a republic with such " a Protector " is a
contradiction in terms. The Cæsars
might as well be called " Protectors of
the Roman Republic," or the boa-con-
strictor the protector of the rabbit he
has swallowed. The truth of the
assertion by which Cromwell qualifies
his disapproval of " the government
of a single person," that he " was
forced to take upon him the office
of a high constable, to preserve the
peace among the several parties of the
nation," is involved in the other assertion that Cromwell governed better
than the Long Parliament. Indeed,
one foreign writer on English History
asserts that no party could govern
like Cromwell. This remark is only
true as applied to the state of things
after Cromwell's death, when it was
found, by those who attempted to
cause the public affairs to revert to
their former channel, that, as the
writer of the preface to Ludlow's
Memoirs observes, " Oliver had so
choked the springs that the torrent
took another course;" and after a
short period of struggle among parties,
Monk performed his part, and sold the
nation to Charles II. But the remark
above cited is totally inapplicable with
regard to the Parliament and Council
of State which Cromwell expelled on
April 20, 1653, and which governed
infinitely better than Cromwell.

[1] See Vol. I. p. 33.

had never yet been examined (as far as he knew) by any English historian.

There are one or two features of the present volume to which I wish to advert. In the first place, it appears a duty to truth to make the limits of the duration of the Government called the Commonwealth thoroughly understood, inasmuch as, that Government having been confounded with the usurped military despotism of Cromwell, nearly all the English historians have thus given to Cromwell all the credit due to the good government of the statesmen of the Commonwealth, and to the statesmen of the Commonwealth all the discredit due to the bad government of Cromwell. These two volumes being devoted to the history of the Government called the Commonwealth, strictly define the limits of its duration—namely, from February 1, 164$\frac{8}{9}$, to April 20, 1653, a period of four years and somewhat less than three months. During that period, if they had done nothing else, they created a navy which defeated the most powerful navy, commanded by the greatest admirals, the world at that time had ever seen. And during the last ten months of their existence their great Admiral, Blake, besides minor achievements, such as the destruction of the French fleet under the Duke de Vendôme, fought four great pitched battles, three of which he won; and the defeat in the fourth, when he maintained for many hours, with thirty-seven ships, a fight against ninety-five, commanded by Tromp, tended rather to raise than to lower his own and his country's naval renown. So that, even by writers not favourable to the Commonwealth, this has been called " the *annus mirabilis* of the English navy." To the credit of all this, as well as to the credit of the battles won against the Dutch in June and July 1653, after his expulsion of the Parliament, Cromwell has not the shadow of a claim.

In the second place, a comparison of the preparations made by the Government of Queen Elizabeth against the Spanish Armada, with the preparations made by the Council of State of the Commonwealth against the aggression of the Dutch naval power (really far greater than the Spanish), and also against a projected invasion of England, about the time of the invasion of the Scots which led to the Battle of Worcester, by the forces of some of the Continental despots, under the command of the Duke of Lorraine (evidence of which I have found in the MS. minutes of the Council of State), leads to a clear demonstration of the vast superiority of the statesmanship of the Council of State of the Commonwealth over that of Queen Elizabeth, and her much-lauded Lord Treasurer and other councillors.

CONTENTS.

CHAPTER VII.

CHAPTER VIII.

CHAPTER IX.

CHAPTER X.

CHAPTER XI.

CHAPTER XII.

CHAPTER XIV.

CHAPTER XVI.

HISTORY OF ENGLAND

UNDER THE GOVERNMENT CALLED

THE COMMONWEALTH.

CHAPTER VII.

FROM that day in July, 1644, when the armies of the King and Parliament of England encountered each other on Marston Moor, the armies of the Parliament had marched to uninterrupted victory. Hitherto, however, they had only had to contend against enemies not very much exceeding themselves in number. But a new aspect of affairs now presented itself.

A great change had come over the scene between 1585, when the Netherlanders had shown an eager desire to become the subjects of Queen Elizabeth, and 1648-9, when the English Parliament brought their King to a public trial and a public execution; declared their Government to be a Commonwealth, or Republic, like the Government of the Netherlands, and invited the Netherlanders, or Hollanders (as they then began to be called), to enter into a close alliance—to come, as they termed it, to "oneness" [1] with them.

But the times had changed, and with the change of times a strange change had come over the minds of the

---

[1] Speech of Thomas Scot, in Richard Cromwell's first Parliament, reported in Burton's Diary.

Netherlanders.   The Netherlanders of the latter years of
the 16th century had shown themselves most anxious and
eager to obtain the aid of their fellow-Protestants of England, against the sacerdotal and royal tyranny of the Pope
of Rome and the King of Spain.   The Netherlanders of
the middle of the 17th century, so far from receiving in
a frank and friendly spirit the proffered alliance of the
Protestant English Parliament, were actually willing to
employ against England not only their own naval power,
then the greatest in the world, but to transport into England and Ireland troops, under the command of the Duke
of Lorraine,[1] one of the commanders of the army of the
Catholic League in the Thirty Years' War, just ended—
troops who had formed a portion of the disciplined brigands
of Wallenstein and Tilly, and who had shared in the storm
and sack of Magdeburg, when that unfortunate city was
given up to pillage for three days, and thirty thousand of
the inhabitants were put to the sword.   And these foreign
brigands were to be joined by large bodies of the native
Irish, according to a treaty between the Duke of Lorraine
and Viscount Taff,[2] and were thus to be enabled to accomplish that work of murder, rapine, burning, torture, and
endless abominations, which Charles I. and his Medici-
Bourbon Queen had before planned, by way of punishment,
for their rebellious English subjects, and in particular for
London, "the rebellious city," as they called it.[3]

By the treaty mentioned, the forces of the Duke of
Lorraine were to be brought by the Dutch fleet into

---

[1] The evidence of this from MS., as
well as printed documents, will be given
in subsequent pages.

[2] See Ludlow's Memoirs, vol. i. pp.
389, 390.   Second edition, London,
1721.

[3] Burnet's Mem. of the Hamiltons,

p. 212 et seq.   Wishart's Memoirs of
Montrose, p. 32 et seq.; and Appendix,
p. 422 et seq.   Baillie's Letters and
Journals, vol. ii. pp. 73, 74 (Edinburgh
1841).   Append. to Carte's Ormonde,
pp. 3, 4 et seq.   Carte's Letters, vol. i.
pp. 19, 20.   Burnet's Hist. vol. i. p. 74.

Ireland, " in order to extirpate all heretics out of that nation, to re-establish the Romish religion in all parts of it, and to restore the Irish to their possessions; all which being performed, he should deliver up the authority to the King of Great Britain, and assist him against his rebellious subjects in England : that all Ireland should be engaged for his reimbursement : that Galway, Limerick, Athenree, Athlone, Waterford, and the fort of Duncannon should be put into his hands as cautionary places.".[1]

It appears, however, from some MS. minutes of the Order Books of the Council of State, which I will quote subsequently, that a landing was to be made in England, on the coast of Suffolk, whence the foreign brigands of this Duke of Lorraine could, as they fancied, easily march upon London, which they had been given to understand was a city far more wealthy and far more defenceless than Magdeburg. If they had been told that the English were an unwarlike race—a race to be plundered and butchered more easily than the burghers of Magdeburg—and should ever chance to come to a death-grapple with the soldiers of Dunbar and Naseby, they might peradventure find themselves somewhat out in their reckonings.

The name of the Duke of Lorraine—of whose family the House of Guise was a branch—occurring here, reminds us of one significant feature of this great English Civil War ; reminds us that this war bore a certain affinity to the great conspiracy of the Pope and the King of Spain and the Duke of Guise, against the liberties, civil and religious, of all mankind. For (besides the fact of this Duke of Lorraine's having been one of the commanders of the Catholic League in the Thirty Years' War) in the preceding age,

[1] Ludlow's Memoirs, vol. i. pp. 389, 390.

when there was no hope of issue of Henry III. of France, it had been the determination of Henry's mother, Catherine de' Medici, that the children of her daughter, the Duchess of Lorraine, should succeed to the throne of France.

A branch of the sovereign House of Lorraine, which settled in France in the beginning of the 16th century, bore the title of Dukes of Guise—a name of evil omen, for it is indelibly connected in history with the Massacre of St. Bartholomew; all the preliminary details of that transaction having been arranged by Henry Duke of Guise, a man of an infamous pre-eminence, even in an age fruitful in deeds of treachery and murder. James V. of Scotland had married a daughter of the House of Guise, who after the death of James, being for a time Regent of Scotland, attempted to establish despotism and Romanism, and to extirpate heresy after the fashion of the House of Guise. His daughter was Mary Stuart, the grandmother of Charles I. And if Charles I. and his Queen (who, as well as himself, was related to the House of Guise and Lorraine), had not precisely the same relation of cause and effect with the Irish massacre of English Protestants, which Henry of Guise had with the St. Bartholomew massacre of French Protestants, the Irish massacre would certainly not have taken place if the Irish had not believed that the Queen encouraged it.[1]

[1] The Earl of Essex told Bishop Burnet, "That he had taken all the pains he could to inquire into the original of the Irish massacre, but could not see reason to believe the King was accessory to it; but he did believe that the Queen did hearken to the propositions made by the Irish, who undertook to take the Government of Ireland into their own hands, which they thought they could perform, and then they promised to assist the King against the hot spirits of Westminster. With this the insurrection began, and all the Irish believed the Queen encouraged it." (*Hist. of His Own Times*, vol. i. p. 41.) The editor of the Oxford edition (1833) of Burnet's History,

Such were some of the allies with whom the Netherlanders of 1651 thought fit to leage themselves against
the Protestant Parliament of England.

What was the cause of this great change in the conduct of the Netherlanders? There were several causes.

In the first place, by the Peace of Westphalia, concluded in October 1648—which put an end not only to the
Thirty Years' War in Germany, but to the Eighty Years'
War between Spain and the Netherlands—the United States
of the Netherlands were recognised as independent States.

In the second place, while the naval power of Spain had

in a note on this passage, merely cites
the opinion of Mr. Brodie (*History of
the British Empire*, vol. iii. p. 199,
note, Edin. 1822), that he "cannot distinguish between the King and Queen,
considering their dark correspondence
and joint plots." Mr. Morrice, the
chaplain of the first Earl of Orrery
(before Lord Broghill), in his Memoirs
of that nobleman, prefixed to the Earl
of Orrery's State Letters (2 vols. Dublin, 1743), tells the following story
respecting the commission under the
Great Seal under which the Irish professed to act: "Lord Orrery took an
opportunity one day, when alone with
Muskerry, who happened then to be
in a pleasant open humour, to ask him
how the rebels obtained that commission, which they showed, under the
King's great seal? Lord Muskerry
answered, 'I will be free and unreserved with you. It was a forged
commission, drawn up by Walsh and
others, who having a writing to which
the Great Seal was fixed, one of the
company very dexterously took off the
sealed wax from the label of that writing, and fixed it to the label of the
forged commission. Whilst this was
doing, an odd accident happened,
which startled all present, and had almost entirely disconcerted the scheme.
The forged commission being finished,
while the parchment was handling
and turning, in order to put on the
seal, a tame wolf, which lay asleep by
the fire, awakened at the crackling of
the parchment, and running to it,
seized it, and tore it to pieces, notwithstanding all haste and struggle to
prevent him : so that, after their pains,
they were obliged to begin anew, and
write it all over again.' Lord Orrery,
struck with the wickedness of this
transaction, could not refrain expressing himself to that purpose to Lord
Muskerry, who laughingly replied, 'It
would have been impossible to have
held the people together without this
device.'"—*Memoirs of Roger, Earl of
Orrery* (pp. 73, 74), prefixed to the
State Letters of Roger Boyle, the
first Earl of Orrery, Lord President
of Munster in Ireland (2 vols. Dublin, 1743). He was the fifth son of
Richard, Earl of Cork, and in 1628,
when only seven years old, was created
Lord Broghill.

been rapidly declining, the naval power of the Netherlands had been as rapidly increasing, so that at this particular time, the middle of the 17th century, it was the greatest naval power then in the world; and its masters looked upon England with very different sentiments from those of their predecessors, who had earnestly and humbly sought for the aid of England against the tyranny of Spain.

There was a third cause, the consideration of which will throw light upon a very prominent feature in the history of Modern Europe.

About a century and a half or, at most, two centuries before this time, the doctrine of the sanctity and divinity of kingship had arisen in Europe. It would delay us too long to trace here all the causes of that rise. It will be sufficient to say that the rise was sudden and rapid, and that the idea soon acquired great strength. Of both the rapid rise of this idea, and the strength which it speedily acquired, a proof is afforded in the general horror excited, about the beginning of the 16th century, by the rebellion or treason (as it was called) of the famous Constable de Bourbon against Francis I. of France; while, not many years before, the frequent conspiracies of Louis XII., when Duke of Orleans, were viewed as common occurrences of no extraordinary criminality. This idea spread itself over Europe, and of course passed into England, where it coloured the writings of the most popular writers, who were then the dramatists. Shakspeare's dramas are full of the "divinity that doth hedge a king," and Shakspeare's dramas had far more influence on the popular mind than Milton's pamphlets. A cotemporary of Shakspeare, Sir Fulke Greville, afterwards Lord Brooke, the friend and biographer of Sir Philip Sidney, has a line, of which one

of the lines oftenest quoted from Pope's "Essay on Man"
is but an alteration—a line embodying an apophthegm
pointedly expressive of the spirit of kingship of the
16th century: "Men would be tyrants, tyrants would be
gods."[1]

Under such circumstances, it is evident that the daring
men who publicly cut off a king's head, though solemnly
professing that they did that execution as an act of public
justice, were, considered merely as politicians, playing a
very dangerous game: for all their great deeds, in which
they manifested so much genius and so much valour, were
insufficient in so short a time to extirpate from the popular mind the notion that "there is a divinity doth hedge a
king,"[2]—even a king like Charles IX. of France, and
a queen like his mother Catherine de' Medici. Such force
had this notion acquired, that a Protestant archbishop
actually published at the end of his character of that com-
pound of blood and mud, that embodiment of all the vices
of Tiberius without his talents, James I., these lines,
"penned," says the archbishop, "by a learned divine":

> Princes are gods; oh do not then
> Rake in their graves to prove them men![3]

It is hardly too much to say, that this idea of the divinity

---

[1] Pope's line is, "Men would be
angels, angels would be gods." (*Essay
on Man*, Epist. i. v. 126.) What Can-
ning, in "New Morality," has said of
a very inferior versifier, may be said
here of Pope, that he "mars the verse
he steals."

[2] According to Lord Leicester, when
the Act for taking away kingly government was proclaimed by the Lord
Mayor and fifteen Aldermen in full exchange time, "the people murmured

and began to rise, but were soon suppressed by some troops of horse that
were ready in arms."—*Lord Leicester's
Journal*, May 30, 1649, p. 73, in Sydney Papers, edited by R. W. Blencowe
(London, 1825).

[3] Archbishop Spottiswood's *History
of the Church of Scotland*, vol. iii.
p. 270, Bannatyne Club edition.—The
lines quoted by Spottiswood furnish a
curious verification of the line just
quoted from Lord Brooke.

of kingship threw back civilisation more than two hundred years. It cast its ægis over the most revolting cruelties and the most hideous crimes when performed by crowned criminals. No stronger proof of its force could be afforded than the fact that, in 1584, the Netherlanders, who had been fighting so long and bravely for liberty of conscience, before they applied to Queen Elizabeth, sent an embassy to Henry III. of France, that worthy son of Catherine de' Medici, offering to him the sovereignty of their country: to that Medici Valois, of whom the English ambassador, Sir Edward Stafford, speaks in almost precisely the same terms in which the French ambassador, Count Tillieres, speaks of James the I.:—"Unhappy people! to have such a king, who seeketh nothing but to impoverish them to enrich his favourites, and who careth not what cometh after his death;" and whose court was a place of which " impiety the most cynical, debauchery the most unveiled, public and unpunished homicide, private murders by what was called magic, by poison, by hired assassins, crimes natural, unnatural, and preternatural, were the common characteristics."[1]

It is in accordance with common experience that a person of weak intellect, like James I., should give himself completely up to the dominion of this idea of the divinity of kingship. But it is not a little surprising to find a person of strong intellect, like Queen Elizabeth, fascinated[2] by it

[1] Motley's History of the United Netherlands, vol. i. p. 40.

[2] "Princes," said Queen Elizabeth. in her reply to the Netherland envoys (Feb. 7, N.S. 1587), "transact business in a certain way, and *with a princely intelligence such as private persons cannot imitate.*" (Hague Archives, MS., cited in Motley's *History of the United Netherlands,* vol. ii. p. 199.) If Her Majesty had been fated to come into contact with the intelligence of some of the statesmen and statesmen-soldiers of the English Commonwealth, she might have seen reason to change her opinion of the respective qualities of princely intelligence and the intelligence of private persons. All King

to such an extent as to contemplate a marriage with one
of the sons of Catherine de' Medici—of that abandoned

James's writings, and particularly his
"True Law of Free Monarchies" (in
which he expounds his notions of his
kingly power, and builds, on those
passages in the Book of Samuel in
which God, after condemning the
desire of the Jews to have a king,
commands Samuel to show them what
oppressions their kings would execute
upon them, conclusions in direct
logical opposition to the premisses),
discover a singular feebleness and
obliquity of understanding. It is remarkable that a person of so very
different an order of intellect from
King James as Hobbes, should have
attempted to make the same passage
of Scripture subservient to the same
purpose. Hobbes, in his "Leviathan,"
quotes the passage in even a more
mutilated shape than his royal pre-
decessor in his "True Law of Free
Monarchies." Hobbes says : "Concerning the right of kings, God himself, by the mouth of Samuel, saith."
He then quotes the verses (1 Samuel
viii.) from the 11th to the 17th, and
thus proceeds : "This is absolute
power, and summed up in the last
words, *Ye shall be his servants.*"
Again, taking care to leave out the
19th verse, which is, " Nevertheless the
people refused to obey the voice of
Samuel ; and they said, Nay, but we
will have a king to reign over us " (in
which suppression of the truth he even
exceeds James in dishonesty), Hobbes
goes on thus : " When the people heard
what power their king was to have,
yet they consented thereto, and said
thus—*We will be as other nations, and
our king shall judge our causes, and
go before us to conduct our wars.* Here

is confirmed the right that sovereigns
have, both to the *militia,* and to all
judicature, in which is contained as
absolute power as one man can possibly transmit to another." (*Leviathan,* part ii. chap. xx. p. 105, folio.
London, 1651). A strange confirmation ! In the first place, the voice of
the Jewish multitude is quoted as if it
were the voice of God, although tho
context expressly declares the contrary :
and in the second place, might not
the Jewish people choose to be governed by a king without that being
any argument whatever, either for the
divinity of the institution, or for its
being adopted by other nations ? Some
writers have of late years objected to
Hobbes being called "the apologist of
tyranny." I also at one time thought
that Hobbes had been hardly dealt
with, and the effect produced in the
way of clear thinking, on the subject
both of mental and political philosophy,
by his powerful and original understanding, not sufficiently appreciated.
But the example of flagrantly dis-
honest dealing with evidence which I
have here pointed out, appears to place
a man in almost as bad a category as
being the apologist of tyranny, or the
apologist of anything else that is bad.
The mode in which King James and
Hobbes have dealt with this passage
of Scripture is the more remarkable,
when contrasted with the use made of
it by Sir John Fortescue, Lord Chief
Justice and afterwards Lord Chancellor under King Henry VI., in his work
on the "Difference between an Absolute and Limited Monarchy" (pp. 4–6,
edn. London, 1714). Fortescue, writing before kingship had set up its

woman, half poisoner, half procuress, who had by cold
calculation plunged her sons into the deepest debauchery,
that their enervated faculties might render them the slaves
of her will in political affairs, and whose daughter, the
Medici-Valois Messalina, the Bartholomew-massacre wife
of Henry of Navarre, made the miniature Court of Pau
almost equal, in vice if not in splendour, the voluptuous-
ness and infamy of the Louvre. It is impossible that
Queen Elizabeth could have been entirely ignorant of the
character of the Court of the Louvre at that time, and
of the Medici-Valois family at the head of it; and the only
explanation of her conduct would seem to be that the
boundary-lines between vice and virtue, between good and
evil, were for the time effaced. Indeed, the cotemporary
evidence seems to lead to this conclusion. For instance,
Brantôme, who was considered one of the most accomplished noblemen and courtiers of Charles IX., while he
recounts actions that stamp the authors of them as thoroughly deserving Samuel Johnson's coarse but expressive
character of Lord Chesterfield, always begins or ends by
informing us that those personages were *très-belles et très-
honnêtes dames* or *demoiselles.* The most abandoned of the
female worthies whose lives he details, are characterised
by him as both illustrious ladies and good Christians. But
this was quite in keeping with the moral and religious
code of an age which designated Philip II. of Spain "the
most Catholic" and Henry III. of France "the most
Christian king."

claim to divinity, deals honestly with
the passage, and says that God was
greatly offended with the desire of the
Jews to have a king, and charged
Samuel to declare unto them the various oppressions and evils they would
be subjected to under a king. The
idea of turning this passage of Scripture into an argument in favour of the
divinity of kingship is one of the most
audacious perversions of truth in the
whole history of imposture.

There is an incident connected with that contemplated marriage of the English Queen with the effeminate and incestuous Medici-Valois, which stamps in strong characters the cruel and tyrannical disposition of the daughter of that Tudor tyrant—that amiable man, according to a modern historical discovery, who had the misfortune to have so many bad wives! David Hume thus tells the story : " A Puritan[1] of Lincoln's Inn had written a passionate book, which he entitled ' The Gulph in which England will be swallowed by the French Marriage.' He was apprehended and prosecuted by order of the Queen, and was condemned to lose his right hand as a libeller." " A Puritan of Lincoln's Inn!" Hume probably thought, when he branded this unfortunate gentleman with the term Puritan, that he was a religionist of the intolerant and tyrannical Presbyterian type, which in the 18th century, as well as in the

---

[1] " Puritanism—a form of religion which Elizabeth detested, and in which, with keen instinct, she detected a mutinous element against the divine right of kings." (Motley's *History of the United Netherlands*, vol. i. p. 351.) It is but justice to Leicester to add what Mr. Motley says of him in the same place : " Leicester, to do him justice, was thoroughly alive to the importance of the crisis. On political principle, at any rate, he was a firm supporter of Protestantism, and even of Puritanism." (*Ibid.*) While there can be little doubt that there was a large substratum of materials against the character of Leicester, there can be as little doubt that upon that was built a large superstructure of falsehood by the Jesuit emissaries of the Pope and the Spaniard—probably the largest, the most adroit, and the most unscrupulous dealers in falsehood in the whole history of the world. And the Jesuits themselves were outdone in their own trade by " the most Catholic king," Philip II. of Spain, whose falsehood was upon a level with his bigotry and cruelty : " To lie daily, through thick and thin, and with every variety of circumstance and detail which a genius fertile in fiction could suggest, such was the simple rule prescribed to Farnese by his sovereign. And the rule was implicitly obeyed, and the English sovereign thoroughly deceived." *(Ibid.* vol. ii. p. 311.) If Queen Elizabeth really possessed the practical ability for which she has long had credit, it seems incredible that she should have placed any faith in the words either of Philip II., or of Farnese, or of the Medici, or the Valois. Would Cromwell or Vane have been duped by them ? Certainly not.

19th in Scotland, gave the same meaning to the term
"free church" that James I. gave to "free monarchy"—
that is, free to do what they liked, and to hinder all other
people from doing what they liked. And he probably
did not know that the royal and courtly and sacerdotal
tyrants of the 16th and 17th centuries sought to brand
with the title of Puritan all men who objected to vices not
only natural but unnatural, and to wearing the attire of
women, and not of women only, but of harlots. For it
was not only in the polluted halls and chambers of the
Louvre that the degraded Henry III., the last of that
Medici-Valois brood, exhibited himself attired like a woman
and a harlot, and surrounded by a gang of "minions"
such as the world had not seen since the age of Nero and
Sporus; but a few years later, Somerset and Buckingham,[1]
with their master James, revived in the palace of Whitehall the infamies of the Louvre, the horrible crimes as
well as the revolting vices. Mrs. Turner, who was executed
for being accessory to the murder of Sir Thomas Overbury, though the real criminals, the Earl and Countess of
Somerset, were allowed to escape by "James the Just,"
shortly before her execution exclaimed against the court,
"wonders the earth does not open to swallow up so wicked
a place!"[2] Surely Admiral Blake had some ground for
the saying attributed to him, that "monarchy was a kind
of government the world was weary of!"[3]

[1] "Osborne says that Somerset and
Buckingham laboured to resemble
women in the effeminacy of their dress,
and exceeded even the worst in the
grossness of their gestures."—Note by
Sir Walter Scott, in his edition of
Somers' Tracts, vol. ii. p. 488.

[2] Conference between Dr. John Whiting and Mrs. Turner, Nov. 11, 1615.

(MS. State Paper Office.)

[3] Sir Edward Hyde to Secretary
Nicholas, Madrid, Feb. 9, 1651. (Clarendon State Papers, vol. iii. p. 27.)
Aubrey, after mentioning that Dr.
William Harvey, the discoverer of the
circulation of the blood, was wont to
say that "man was but a great mischievous baboon," continues (Letters

Such was the tyrannous force in that age of the idea of the supposed necessity of kingship, that the hardy and industrious Netherlanders, who had thrown off the yoke of one crowned tyrant, and had been fighting for sixteen years rather than return to that yoke, were willing to accept the sovereignty of a king like the last Valois, because that thing "the semblance of a kingly crown had on." Failing in their attempt to induce the Medici-Valois to accept the sovereignty of their country, the Netherlanders then applied to Elizabeth Tudor, who, albeit but the great-granddaughter of a Welsh squire and a London citizen, stood as punctiliously upon the divinity of her queenship, as if she had actually been, what Walter Scott has called her, "the daughter of a hundred kings." What between her own ill-temper and penuriousness, and the want of decision and clearheadedness of her principal minister, Burghley, "puzzled himself and still more puzzling to others,"[1] small was the benefit which the Netherlanders reaped from Queen Elizabeth. If she had sent as her Lieutenant-general a man of ability, instead of the shallow-brained intriguer and court favourite, Leicester, the Netherlanders might perhaps have reaped more benefit, even from the small assistance she sent them. But no great soldier or sailor, no Cromwell or Blake, could ever

and Lives, vol. ii. p. 381): "He would say that we Europeans knew not how to order or govern our women, and that the Turks were the only people who used them wisely. . . . He had been physician to the Lord-Chancellor Bacon, whom he esteemed much for his wit and style, but would not allow him to be a great philosopher. Said he to me, 'He writes philosophy like a lord-chancellor,' speaking in derision." Morally and socially, the court-party of that age, including some men of the highest intellectual endowments (Harvey himself, Bacon, and Hobbes), were indeed "but great mischievous baboons." If the Puritan insurrection against those moral baboons had not succeeded, Harvey might have had his wish, and England might have fallen to the moral, social, and political condition of Turkey.

[1] Motley's History of the United Netherlands, vol. i. p. 88.

flourish under the poisonous shade of a court minion, such as Leicester or Buckingham.

Besides the charge of incapacity, charges of frightful crimes were made against Leicester; and if these charges were never satisfactorily proved, it must be remembered that proof was extremely difficult in that age, in the case of a royal favourite. In the case of Somerset and the murder of Overbury, there had been less profound artifice than Leicester was master of; and, besides, the King was then tired of Somerset, and wished for an excuse to be rid of him. If Leicester was innocent of perhaps the foulest crime imputed to him, the murder of his first wife—and all that a coroner's inquest, said to be rather hostile than otherwise, could make of it was that the unfortunate lady was killed by a fall downstairs[1]—he must be considered as a deeply calumniated man; for the tale has now taken such root, that his very name calls up the phantom of a man who murdered poor Amy Robsart, that he might have the chance of marrying a red-haired, hook-nosed shrew, with

[1] In that age murder, as well as forgery of handwriting, was an art as carefully studied as the professions of law and physic. And if the unhappy Amy Robsart was killed in the manner described by Scott, in "Kenilworth," her dead body would present the same appearances which a fall downstairs would produce. What then could the coroner's jury make of it? As Mr. Motley truly says, "The secret deeds of a man placed so high can be seen but darkly through the glass of contemporary record. There was no tribunal to sit upon his guilt. A grandee could be judged only when no longer a favourite, and the infatuation of Elizabeth for Leicester terminated only with his life." (*United Netherlands,* vol. i. p. 367.) The trial of Somerset for the murder of Overbury was allowed to take its course. Why? Because the infatuation of King James had been transferred from Somerset to Buckingham. The same James, for reasons best known to himself, had murdered the Earl of Gowrie and his brother, Alexander Ruthven, and put forth a tissue of the most astounding falsehoods about a pretended conspiracy; so that the Divine Right and Jacobite writers of after-times, who profess to believe a man who was the greatest liar in Christendom after the death of Philip II. of Spain, tell us nursery-tales about an affair they call the 'Gowrie Conspiracy.'

thin lips and black teeth.   Be that as it may, it is certain
that Leicester was an arrogant, intemperate, and incapable
man—incapable, at least, in everything that constitutes a
man either a great statesman or a great soldier.   For he
was capable enough in all the base arts by which court
favourites become rich and powerful—in filling his purse
by the sale of honours and dignities, in violent ejectments
from and in the manufacture of fraudulent titles to land,
in rapacious enclosures of commons, in taking bribes for
matters of justice, and of supplication to the royal authority.
Besides the charges of poisoning (if but half of which could
be believed, neither Cæsar Borgia, nor his father nor sister,
were more accomplished in that infamous art), Leicester
was also accused, falsely or not, of forging various letters
to the Queen to ruin his political adversaries, and of plots
to entrap them into conspiracies—playing first the accom-
plice, and then the informer.

The career of this Robert Dudley, created by Queen
Elizabeth Earl of Leicester, was worthy of his origin:
for he was the grandson of that "horseleech"[1] lawyer,
who, with Empson, had been the instrument employed
by Henry VII. in oppressing and pillaging the people of
England, and who, as a reward for his subservience to
the tyrant father, Henry VII., lost his head in the first year
of the reign of the tyrant son, Henry VIII.   One principal

---

[1] Lord Bacon, in his "History of
King Henry VII.," says: "And as kings
do more easily find instruments for
their will and humour than for their
service and honour, he had gotten for
his purpose, or beyond his purpose,
two instruments, Empson and Dudley,
whom the people esteemed as his horse-
leeches and shearers—bold men and
careless of fame, and that took toll of
their master's grist.   Dudley was of a
good family, eloquent, and one that
could put hateful business into good
language.   But Empson, that was the
son of a sieve-maker, triumphed
always upon the deed done, putting off
all other respects whatsoever."—*Hist.
of the Reign of King Henry VII.*, p.
380 (in vol. iii. of Montagu's edition
of Lord Bacon's Works).

mode of oppression and plunder employed by him and
Empson, had been an abuse of that incident of the feudal
tenures, termed Escheat, by which, under certain circumstances, lands escheated or fell back to the lord who gave
them, which in the case of the tenants *in capite* would be
to the king. The officers to whom it belonged to enquire
into the escheats that fell to the crown were called escheators. The abuses to which this office was liable are
thus set forth in the preamble of the Statute 1 Henry VIII.
cap. 8, intituled "The Act of Escheators and Commissioners:"—"Forasmuch as divers of the king's subjects
lately have been sore hurt, troubled, and disherited by
Escheators and Commissioners, causing untrue offices to
be found, and sometimes returning into the courts of record offices and inquisitions that were never found, and
sometimes changing the matter of the offices that were truly
found, to the great hurt, trouble, and disherison of the king's
true subjects," &c. Thus from the abuse of this office, the
word "escheator" came to have the meaning of a fraudulent
person, and gave rise to the common words "cheat" and
"cheater." Shakspeare, in the following passage, uses the
word at once in its old and new sense : "I will be cheater to
them both, and they shall be exchequers to me." From this
escheator, cheater, or cheat descended the magnificent court
favourite, Queen Elizabeth's "sweet Robin," the husband of
the ill-starred Amy Robsart, and the husband or lover of
at least two other nearly as unfortunate women. For the
" gipsy" (as he was called, from his dark complexion) was,
to say the least, a dangerous man ; and the power which
he owed neither to genius nor to virtue, but to the caprice
of the imperious woman who then filled the English
throne, had been used for the ruin of many women as
well as many men. The infatuation of Queen Elizabeth

in favour of Robert Dudley will ever remain one of the greatest stains on her memory.　Indeed, the whole history of these Dudleys is a most instructive illustration of the government of the Tudors, under which the old nobility— who, whatever their faults, were warriors and statesmen— gave place to a nobility of pettifoggers, of horseleech lawyers, and court minions, the basest of all things wearing a human shape.　The peerages of, perhaps, the three greatest historical families in the English annals (the De Montforts, the Percys, and the Nevills) were absorbed by the Dudleys, whose cognizance was hereditary baseness; and the great historic titles of Leicester, of Northumberland, and of Warwick, as if to show into what a depth of degradation tyranny can plunge a nation, were conferred upon the brood of the horseleech of Henry VII.　If we must have a hereditary nobility, it should be distinguished by something else than the faculty of giving to the old word "escheator" the new meaning of common cheat or cheater—by something else than hereditary servility, hereditary falsehood, cruelty, insolence, and baseness. That age of transition from the old barbarism to the new civilisation presents a picture of startling contrasts: of the genius of Shakspeare, of Spenser, of Raleigh, of Bacon, side by side with the rack, the faggot, and the branding-iron; of Leicester, the gorgeous minion of court-favour, 'rustling in satin and feathers, with jewels in his ears— such was the taste of the Tudor Queen, who spoke the language and could relish the genius of Shakspeare—side by side with William the Silent, in coarse unbuttoned doublet, and bargeman's woollen waistcoat.　No wonder that, when the gorgeous courtier of Queen Elizabeth went to Holland, "everybody wondered at the great magnificence and splendour of his clothes."　The Hollanders had

not been used to consider satin and feathers, and jewels in
the ears, as essential portions of the materials that went
to make either a statesman or a soldier. And in the short
period of England's annals—namely, from February 164$\frac{8}{9}$
to April 1653, a period of less than five years—when England was governed by men who were statesmen in the best
sense of the word, neither satin, nor feathers, nor jewels in
the ears, formed a portion of the machinery of government.

This man, this Robert Dudley, owed his favour with
Queen Elizabeth—whose infatuation for him lasted till his
death, when, true to her character, she had, while drop-
ping a tear upon the grave of "sweet Robin," sold his
goods by auction to defray his debts to herself—to the
beauty of his person, and the talent which he possessed of
adroit adulation towards women. He is described by cotemporaries as "tall and singularly well-featured, of a sweet
aspect, but high-foreheaded, which was of no discommen-
dation." But when we look at his face, as the painter's art
has transmitted it to us, we see little to convey to us the
favourable impression which that face gave to Queen
Elizabeth. For though his forehead may be high, it
wants breadth; the small aquiline nose and small mouth
want the character of intellectual power; the eyebrows
are weak, and the eyes somewhat sinister; and altogether
the face and head have nothing of the grandeur, either of
resolution or of intellect, which stamps the outward aspect
of a great man, a great statesman-soldier, such as the
time and the occasion imperatively demanded, but such as
is never found lackeying either an imperious woman like the
last Tudor, or an unsexed man like the last Medici-Valois,
or the first Stuart.

And the Netherlanders—although they had known what
it was to be governed by a great man, having but just lost

William the Silent, assassinated by the hellish contrivance of the Pope and the Spaniard—were willing, from the supposed necessity of kingship, to submit to the government of such a poor imitation of a statesman-soldier as this Robert Dudley, Earl of Leicester.

Now the Rump of the Long Parliament of England, whether the fact be viewed with approbation or disapprobation, were the first in Modern Europe to change a monarchy into another kind of government, and to discard the idea of the necessity of kingship. It will be seen that the English Government of that time had, by their audacious act of declaring that kingship was not only not a necessity, but that "the office of a king in this nation was unnecessary, burthensome, and dangerous," added another solid reason to the monarchical despots of Europe for their destruction. For those accursed heretics, who by discarding the Papal supremacy had incurred the deadly enmity of the Pope, and of such tyrants and bigots as the Kings of Spain and France, had now to heresy added the frightful crime of regicide; and were therefore now more than ever to be exterminated, as being at once the enemies of God and of God's representatives on earth. The consequence was that the English Government of the middle of the 17th century had far more formidable enemies to encounter than the Government of Queen Elizabeth in 1588, when the Armada, which Spanish bombast styled "the Invincible," was ready to sail for the conquest of England.

For it seemed as if all the kings and all the nations of the earth were suddenly banded together, for the destruction of those daring men who had brought their king to a public trial and a public execution, and now called themselves the Commonwealth of England. French ships[1] made prize of all English vessels not strong enough to resist them. A fleet, under Prince Rupert, after having committed great plunder of English merchant-ships, and many atrocious acts of piracy, was protected in Portugal from the fleet of the Parliament. In Russia the English merchants were insulted and illtreated by the Government.[2] Ascham, the agent of the Parliament in Spain, was assassinated in Madrid, and the assassins were not punished by the Government of Spain. Dorislaus, soon after his arrival as the agent of the English Parliament, was assassinated in Holland, and the assassins were permitted to escape, though the Dutch Government was a republic in name. Even the Senate of Hamburg[3] ventured to make hostile demonstrations.

A glance at the state of Europe at that time will show at once that the Parliament of England stood alone; for the Senate of Hamburg, if it had been disposed to be

---

[1] I will give one or two cases from the MS. Minutes of the Council of State. On one day, the 9th of January, 16$\frac{49}{50}$, there is a statement of losses of the English merchants by French ships, to the amount of 60,260*l.* in the ship 'Talent;' of 9,838*l.* in the 'Mercury;' of 32,763*l.* in the 'Greyhound;'—for all which letters of marque or reprisal were granted, under the great seal of the High Court of Admiralty.—*Order Book of the Council of State*, Jan. 9, 16$\frac{49}{50}$, MS. State Paper Office.

[2] "That a letter be prepared to be sent to the Emperor of Russia, concerning the denying our merchants to trade in Russia as formerly; and that the merchants do give in the titles and the matter of the letter to the Council."

—*Order Book of the Council of State*, die Lunæ, Dec. 24, 1649. "That the draught of the letter to the Emperor of Russia be reported to the House by Sir James Harrington."—*Ibid.* Jan. 4, 16$\frac{49}{50}$, MS. State Paper Office.

[3] "That a letter be written to the Senate of Hamburg, to take notice unto them of the restraint which they have laid upon the heads of our merchants there, for taking the engagement, to expostulate the matter with them," &c.—*Order Book of the Council of State*, die Martis, Jan. 1, 16$\frac{49}{50}$, MS. State Paper Office. "That the Latin letter prepared by Mr. Milton, and now read at the Council, to be sent to the Senate of Hamburg, be fair-written, signed, and sent."—*Ibid.* Jan. 4, 16$\frac{49}{50}$.

friendly, was not strong enough to be an ally of any importance, and the Dutch Government, for reasons which will be mentioned presently, was far more likely to be an enemy than a friend. In all the other European Governments the principle of military despotism had by this time already acquired such force, as to regard the principle of constitutional liberty, for which the English Parliament fought, as dangerous and hateful; and all the European tyrants, from Moscow to Copenhagen, from Stockholm to Madrid, would have rejoiced to see England effaced from the list of nations, if her people could not be reduced to the servile condition of their own subjects.

Since the middle of the 15th century the progress of events had all been in the direction of absolute monarchy. Any popular liberty which had existed in the Italian Republics had been long dead. In Spain, in France, in Germany, even in Denmark and Sweden, all constitutional bulwarks against the excesses of kingly power had perished, or were perishing. The nobles were impoverished and powerless. The sword had fallen from their hands, and from those of their once warlike vassals, into those of standing armies; and the power which belonged to them, when they were a military aristocracy, had passed to the kings who were masters of the standing armies. The Free or Hanse Towns had lost their independence, and were at the mercy of the nearest robber-tyrant, who pursued his own and his family's aggrandisement with some diplomatic jargon in his mouth, and with an utter disregard of all the laws of God and man. As in the time of the Idumean Emir, "the tabernacles of robbers prospered." Except in the Parliament of England, not a vestige remained of those assemblies of freemen, in which, among the ancient Germans and Franks, the affairs of the nation were debated and settled. All authorities, corporate or individual, which had protected the people from the encroachments of their kings, lost, one after another, their power, and then totally disappeared; as, according to the Greek superstition, at the incantation of the Thessalian witches, the stars, one by one, faded from the face of heaven :—

> As one by one, at dread Medea's strain,
> The sickening stars fade off the ethereal plain ;
> As Argus' eyes, by Hermes' wand-oppress'd,
> Clos'd one by one in everlasting rest.

Throughout far the greater part of Europe the forms as well as the substance of liberty passed away, and every kingly lust had uncontrollable dominion.[1]

---

[1] Ranke's "Nine Books of Prussian History," of which an English translation (by Sir Alexander and Lady Duff Gordon) has been published, under the title of "Memoirs of the House of Brandenburg, and History of Prussia during the Seventeenth and Eighteenth Centuries," but which might be more aptly intituled a "Panegyric on the House of Brandenburg, and History of the Progress of Despotism in Europe," show how that family robbed their own subjects of their constitutional or traditional rights, as they afterwards robbed their neighbours of their property. A maxim of the Elector Frederick William was, that "no privilege should stand in the way of a needful reform." And his historian says, "We have seen how little regard he paid to traditional rights." "He was without mercy in dealing with individual opponents, as the example of Paul Gerhard sufficiently proves. His rule was by no means easy or popular. We find complaints that words were reckoned as criminal as deeds." All this, which will remind the reader of English history of Charles I. and Sir John Eliot, is defended by the plea of "the necessities of his position."—*Ranke*, vol. i. p. 72. Charles I. considered the power to raise money without consent of Parliament, and to keep a standing army with it, to oppress and insult his subjects, a "needful reform," called for by the "necessities of his position;" but he found the Englishman a rather more dangerous subject to make experiments upon than his cotemporary kings or electors found Spaniards, Frenchmen, and Germans. The sophistry by which the German writers defend tyranny may be seen by the following sentence, in which the writer, after mentioning that at this time the rights and liberties of constitutional States were "greatly abridged throughout Europe," adds: "Frederick William was compelled by his position, *and incited by the public opinion of his country*, to engage in a similar contest, and to strive to develope the idea of sovereignty as he

None of these Powers had, indeed, yet made anything like a formal declaration of war. But though the English Parliament expressed their disposition to friendly relations with all their neighbours, they had good reason to know that the intentions and feelings of the Powers of Europe were the reverse of friendly to them, and that any opportunity for effecting their destruction would be eagerly laid hold of. They were not, however, men to be taken off their guard. They had emissaries everywhere. They paid considerable sums for secret service; and they obtained intelligence of the plots of their enemies in all parts of Europe, from Stockholm to Madrid, and from Moscow to the Hague.[1]

had conceived it."—*Ibid.* p. 48. He was as much "incited by the public opinion of his country" as Charles I. was incited to levy ship-money by the public opinion of *his* country.

[1] There are many minutes in the Order Book relating to the "matter of intelligence." Thus (Feb. 27, 16$\frac{49}{50}$), "That Mr. Scot be continued in that trust for the matter of intelligence which was executed by him the last year, with the same power and salary for the year to come."—*Order Book of the Council of State*, MS. State Paper Office. "That the letter from Paris, concerning the setting out of ships at Toulon, be communicated by the Committee of the Admiralty to the Generals-at-sea, and that they give order for all expedition to be used in setting out that fleet, which is to go southward to join with those ships which are under the command of Colonel Blake." —*Ibid.* March 6, 16$\frac{49}{50}$. "That Mr. Frost do send unto Mons. Augier.so much of Langton's examination as relates to the business of Cezi, and to desire him to write over [from France]

what he knows of the said Langton's actions when he was at Beauvoir." "That Mons. Augier shall have liberty to draw Bills of Exchange upon the State to the amount of 300*l.*, to be paid at ten days' sight." "That the commands of this Council be renewed to Mons. Augier to return hither speedily."—*Ibid.* April 3, 1650. This Mons. Augier is often mentioned in the Minutes, and they had many other persons similarly employed. "That Mr. Scot be empowered for the carrying on the business of secret intelligence." Feb. 17, 16$\frac{49}{50}$. "That Mr. Challoner and Mr. Scot be appointed a Committee, to confer with a certain man which shall be brought unto them on Friday next"—*Ibid.* May 15, 1650. "That Mr. Scot, Mr. Challoner, and Mr. Martin, being the Committee of the Council appointed to receive an account from Mr. Frost concerning some business of importance, be sent unto to meet on Monday morning next, in the Inner Chambers at Whitehall." — *Ibid.* May 17, 1650. "You shall inform yourself what

The political aspect of Europe had altered considerably since the year 1588 ('88, as it was called in England for a century till another memorable '88, 1688, arrived)—the year when Spain, under the impulse partly of fanaticism, partly of ambition, had made an unsuccessful attempt to efface England from the roll of nations. In the course of the intervening sixty years, Spain had gone on declining, reaping the fruits of the despotism which destroys at once the freedom, the intelligence, and the valour of a nation. She was still, however, in a condition to be a formidable member of a confederacy against the Parliament of England. During the same period France had grown in power, chiefly under the able administration of Richelieu; and though Richelieu was now dead, and Mazarin was his successor, of a genius far inferior to Richelieu's, the power of France was likely to render her also a formidable member of a confederacy against the English Parliament. As regarded the North of Europe, the Thirty Years' War, the Peloponnesian war of Germany, had just ended.

From the day when the unfortunate Elector Palatine, the son-in-law of James I. and father of Prince Rupert, just a year after he had been chosen King of Bohemia, was defeated by Tilly under the walls of Prague, for twenty-eight

designs are on foot, and what transactions are made, in Germany, Poland, Sweden, and Denmark. and thereof give notice."—*Instructions for Richard Bradshaw, Esq., Resident from the Commonwealth of England with the Senate of Hamburg.—Ibid.* March 30, 1650. "That the letters from France, and the translation of that from Montrose [an intercepted letter], be reported to the House, and that Mr. Scot be desired to make the report."—*Ibid.* Feb. 14, 16$\frac{49}{50}$. "That a copy of the intelligence from France, concerning some ships now ready in France to come for England, be written out and sent to Colonel Deane, and the original sent to the Committee of the Admiralty, to be taken into consideration by them."—*Ibid.* June 3, 1650. "That the sum of 500*l.* be paid to Mr. Scot out of the exigent moneys of the Council, for the carrying on of the business of intelligence."—*Ibid.* Monday, August 9, 1652. There is an order also, on the 12th May 1652, for the payment to Mr. Scot of 500*l.* upon account, for intelligence.—*Ibid.* May 12, 1652.

years Swedes, Danes, Spaniards, Scots, Dutchmen, Frenchmen, Hungarians, Transylvanians, Croats, had ravaged Germany from the Baltic to the Rhine, and from the Vistula to the German Ocean.

Whatever causes may be alleged for the origin and long duration of that war—the advocates of Gustavus Adolphus alleging the defence of the Protestant religion as the moving force on his part, German writers, on the other hand, alleging that his sole object was conquest and self-aggrandisement—it will not be asserted by anyone that the defence of nations against the encroachments of kings had anything to do with it. From the German Emperor to the smallest German potentate who made pretensions to sovereignty, all that host of kings might be reckoned on as eager to join a confederacy against destroyers of kings. And, what at first sight may seem strange, the most formidable enemy that the English Parliament had was a State which called itself a Republic —a State which England had assisted to shake off the yoke of a foreign oppressor. This State was the Dutch Republic, which was more powerfully excited to hostility against England by commercial and naval rivalry, than moved to friendship or alliance by similarity of government, or remembrance of past good offices : a memorable example of the operation of the various conflicting interests that complicate the affairs and relations of nations, producing war instead of peace, contention and rivalry instead of alliance and co-operation.

But personal or family interests also entered into the question. Maurice of Nassau, son of William the Silent, Prince of Orange, had been, in 1584, elected their Stadtholder by three of the United Provinces, and from that time the Stadtholdership had continued in the House of Nassau.

William, second Prince of Orange of that name, had married a daughter of Charles I.; and, besides that he might naturally resent the death of his father-in-law, the possiblé succession of his wife and children to the English throne would be altogether shut out by the scheme of an English Republic. The Prince of Orange might therefore be expected to regard the men forming the Government called the Commonwealth of England with somewhat more than the average amount of princely antipathy.

Of these many enemies, the most formidable to England, from their being maritime Powers of the first rank, were the monarchies of France and Spain, and the so-called republic of Holland. While the hostility of the last-named was awakened by a fierce spirit of naval and commercial rivalry, that of the two former was excited by the remembrance of many defeats and humiliations, and animated with all the inspiration of hatred. And to the old causes of quarrel that had fitted out the Great Armada for the destruction of the impious and blasphemous heretics who had dared to throw off the Papal supremacy, was now added a new cause—namely, that those heretics, those enemies of God and the Pope, had become regicides, and therefore enemies of God and kings, God's representatives upon earth. Add to all this that Scotland and Ireland, at that time, stood to England in the relation much more of enemies than of friends or allies, and we shall see that England literally stood alone against the world.

Let us also remember that the Kings of Europe at that time possessed three of the greatest Generals of modern times—Condé, Montecuculi, and Turenne, any one of whom, if he had effected a landing in England with an army, even the Ironsides and their hitherto invincible leader would undoubtedly have found a far more formidable opponent than

King Charles or any of his cavalier captains. And their being prevented from effecting an invasion of England must depend on England having the command of the sea—a result which must depend on her being able to defeat the most powerful fleets, commanded by the greatest Admirals, Tromp and Ruyter, that had then ever appeared in the world. All these things being considered, will give us some idea of the work which the Parliament of England had before them about the middle of the 17th century.

A time may come again, when England may have work on her hands as heavy as that which the Council of State of 1650—1653 did so well. It will not, I apprehend, be altogether a useless labour to endeavour to show how the England of the middle of the 17th century faced and defeated her multitudinous enemies, the fleets of many kings, and of one powerful republic.

We must go back beyond modern history, to the memorable day when the great Asiatic despot sat on the rock that overlooks Salamis, and saw his mighty host—ships by thousands, and men in nations—assembled below, to find something of a parallel to the odds which the Parliament of England must now expect to meet in war. The contest with the Spanish Armada has been called England's Salamis. But England's achievements then were really as nothing to what she did now, when not merely Spain but all the kings and all the nations of Europe were arrayed against her. At that time only once in modern history had one nation been attacked by such a host of enemies; and that was when, 150 years before, the Emperor of Germany, the Kings of France and Spain, the Pope, and all the princes of Italy, formed the league called the League of Cambray, and in a week conquered all the provinces of Venice, when Venice was at the height of her power.

But there were physical as well as social and political circumstances that rendered the case of England very different from that of Venice. The English governing Council of Forty were very differently constituted from the Venetian Council of Ten: for while the latter consisted of the dregs of an oligarchy, suffered to run out its full course, the former was composed of a body of men, of whom it has been not untruly said, that they were "a set of the greatest geniuses for government the world ever saw embarked together in one common cause."[1] The social and political institutions of England, which it was the great aim of the Stuarts to destroy, had formed these men; for their genius for government, if implanted by nature, would not have produced the results it did without that practical education which such institutions alone can

[1] Bishop Warburton's Note on vv. 281, 283, 284, of Epistle iv. of Pope's Essay on Man.—I am tempted to add here some further evidence of the extraordinary care which the Council bestowed upon the most minute affairs. "That the Committee appointed to view the horses from Tutbury do appoint some fit person to expose to sale to-morrow, in the afternoon, all the colts which were brought up to the mews, excepting only those which are chosen out for the Lord-General, and that he take a note of the prices offered for every horse particularly; and, that being done, return the horses into the stable, and give an account to the Council thereof, to the end some further order may be given concerning them."—Order Book of the Council of State, July 3, 1650, MS. State Paper Office. "That the Earl of Salisbury, the Lord Howard, the Lord Lisle, the Lord Grey, Sir William Armyne, Sir Arthur Haselrig, Mr. Bond, Colonel Morley, Sir Henry Mildmay, Sir Wm. Constable, and Mr. Scot, or any three of them, be appointed a Committee, to consider how the horses and mares now in Tutbury race may be so disposed of, that the breed may not be lost."—Ibid. March 30, 1650. The Council did not think horse-races necessary for keeping up the breed of horses. "That the form of the letter written last year to the several Sheriffs, to prohibit horse-races, be brought to the Council to-morrow."—Ibid. Feb. 9, 1644$\frac{49}{50}$. "That Gregorie Julian, late yeoman of the race at Tutburie, be discharged from that employment, and the whole business of the race committed to the care of Major Edward Downes."—Ibid. June 8, 1650.

give. The physical circumstances in favour of England were that, provided she prevented invasion from Scotland, the sea, if she was master of it, would protect her from all the world.

I have already called attention to the great energy and ability with which the affairs of the Navy were conducted by the Committee of the Council of State for administering the affairs of the Navy.[1] Of this committee the most active and influential member was Sir Henry Vane, one of the ablest and most indefatigable, as well as most incorrupt, administrators recorded in history. But Vane, though a great statesman, was not, and made no pretensions to be, a fighting man. I believe I have carefully guarded myself from being understood to say, that in such times a Council of State or a Parliament could do the work that had then to be done, further than the selection of fit instruments, and the wise and economical management of the State's revenues and other resources, could be called doing the work. The work that had to be done absolutely required a great General and a great Admiral. Such men were a necessity of the time. But I cannot see how it follows that it was also a necessity of the time that the great General or great Admiral, who did the work of defeating the enemies of the Parliament of England, should turn out the Parliament from whom he had received his commission, and concentrate all their powers of sovereignty in his single person. He might do so, but it was not a necessity of the situation, further than being an incident or accident of the situation that has so often happened that it may be apt to be mistaken for a necessity.

Now, in addition to the great energy and ability with

[1] See Vol. I. (p. 49, *note* 1) for an account of the distinction between the Committee of the Navy and the Commissioners of the Navy.

which the Council of State conducted their naval affairs,
Providence sent to their assistance a man whose career, in
the conduct of their naval or foreign wars, was as singular
and wonderful as that of Cromwell had been in the conduct of their domestic wars.   This man was Robert Blake,
the greatest Admiral, save one, in the records of the world;
and his career was the more singular in this—that though
it is usually considered essential to enter the naval profession in boyhood, and though Blake set his foot on deck
for the first time as a commander at the age of fifty, he
raised in two or three years the naval glory of the English
nation to a far greater height than it had ever before attained.   The height to which he raised it may be judged
from an incident in his last action, the destruction of the
Spanish fleet in the harbour of Santa Cruz, in one of the
Canary Islands.   The Red Cross of England was descried at
daybreak from the Spanish galleons, and the well-known
red[1] flag, bearing the arms of the Commonwealth of England
embroidered in gold, visible at the maintopgallant mast-
head of one of the ships, showed that the redoubted Admiral commanded in person.   A Dutch captain, who had
seen something of the late war, happened to be lying at
that moment in the Santa Cruz roadstead with his vessel.
When he saw the English admiral's broad pendant, he
went straight to the Spanish admiral, and asked his permission to leave the roadstead with his vessel.   The
Spaniard made light of his fears, saying that with the
castles, batteries, and earthworks, in addition to his naval
force, the position was impregnable.   " For all this," said
the Dutch captain, " I am very sure that if Blake is there

---

[1] The Admiral, or General at Sea (as
he was then called) bore the arms of
the Commonwealth on a red flag,
'within a compartment: (or).'—*Order
Book of the Council of State*, March 5,
164$\frac{2}{3}$, MS. State Paper Office.

he will soon be in the midst of you." "Well," replied
the Spaniard, "go if you will, and let Blake come if he
dare!" The Dutchman returned to his ship, hoisted sail,
and left the place as fast as he could, and thereby escaped
the destruction that overtook all that floated within the
Bay of Santa Cruz on that fatal morning.

As Blake's character was as disinterested, unselfish, and
stainless, as his heart was fearless, and his genius great
and fertile, some of the details of the early life of a man
so remarkable may not only interest the reader, but may
throw light on the characters of other remarkable men of
that remarkable time.

CHAPTER VIII.

As you enter the Old Church at Delft, the first object that meets your eye is the magnificent mass of white marble, which forms the monument of Martin Harpertz Tromp,[1] and represents the Admiral lying at full length, with his head resting upon a ship's gun; and below and around him, carved in basrelief, symbols of the achievements of his stormy and valiant life. The bones of the Englishman who conquered him lie undistinguished by tomb or epitaph.

Robert Blake was born at Bridgewater, in August 1599, the same year in the month of April of which Oliver Cromwell was born; so that there were but three months between the ages of these two men, one of whom was destined to defeat all the domestic enemies, the other all the foreign enemies, of the Parliament of England. Robert Blake was the eldest son of Humphrey Blake,[2] an eminent Bridgewater merchant at a time when the Severn was the great road of England to all parts of the world, and when Bristol and

[1] The prefix *Van* to the name of the great Dutch admiral, Tromp, though used by Admiral Blake in his letter of 20th May, 1652, and also in the minutes of the Council of State of the same date, and subsequently by English writers, does not belong to his name; but it does belong to the name of his second son, Admiral Cornelis Van Tromp, created Count Van Tromp by the King of Denmark, to whose as-sistance, in his war with Sweden, Cornelis Tromp had been sent with a fleet in 1676.

[2] All the particulars that are known respecting Admiral Blake's family will be found collected with great care and industry, from family papers and other MS., as well as printed sources, in Mr. Hepworth Dixon's very interesting and valuable life of Admiral Blake, entitled, *Robert Blake, Admiral*

Bridgewater were what Liverpool is now. There is nothing very remarkable known of Blake's boyhood, as showing that early predilection for an active, particularly a seafaring life, which might help to account for his future eminence as a naval commander. On the contrary, his early bias seems to have been rather for study and meditation, than for making cruises in any of his father's merchant-ships; or, like Cromwell, robbing orchards and pigeon-houses; or, like Clive, climbing to the top of lofty steeples, or forming the idle lads of the town into a predatory army, for the purpose of exacting from the shopkeepers a tribute of apples and halfpence. Aubrey does indeed mention, on the authority of a cotemporary of Blake at Oxford, that Blake "would steal swans." But even this manifestation of an "excess of volition," or of predatory daring, if it is to be accepted as sufficiently authenticated, might have been but a resource of Blake on those occasions when his favourite mode of relieving his studies, angling, "the contemplative man's recreation," proved, as it often does, unsuccessful. The inclination of Robert Blake's mind being strongly turned to learning and scholarship, after having made considerable progress in Latin and Greek at the grammar-school of Bridgewater, while he lived in his father's house, at the age of sixteen he was sent to Oxford, where he matriculated as a member of St. Alban's Hall in Lent Term, 1615. He soon, however, removed from St. Alban's Hall to Wadham College—at the request, it is said, of his father's friend, Nicholas Wadham, a Somersetshire man, who had then recently

and General at Sea (London, Chapman and Hall, 1852). A new and cheap edition of this work, in the preface to which Mr. Dixon says, "Lord Dundonald has done me the very great honour of revising the naval parts of this narrative," was published by Messrs. Chapman and Hall in 1858.

founded the college which bears his name, and in the
dining-hall of which a portrait of the great Admiral is
still shown, as that of the greatest man who had lived and
studied within its walls.

It is a remarkable circumstance, even in a very remarkable life—particularly when we ·consider how unusual
anything like learning, in the sense of what is called
scholarship, is in the naval profession—that Blake was
probably the best scholar, the most learned man, of all the
eminent public men of his time, unless Milton be considered as one of those men.   It seems at that time to
have been a common practice to leave the university without taking a degree.   Cromwell, Hampden, Wentworth,
Pym, Vane, appear to have done so.   But Blake resided
at Oxford (first at St. Alban's Hall, and afterwards at
Wadham College) altogether about eight years, and till he
took both his degrees (B.A. and M.A.), as Milton did at
Cambridge.   Aubrey says that Blake " was there a young
man of strong body and good parts; that he was an early
riser and studied well, but also took his robust pleasures of
fishing, fowling, &c.   He would," adds Aubrey, " steal
swans."[1]   During Blake's residence at Oxford, his father
had been unprosperous as a merchant, and Blake naturally
felt a desire to turn his classical acquirements to some
account.   A fellowship having fallen vacant at Merton
College, of which Sir Henry Savile, one of James
I.'s knights, was at that time warden, Blake offered
himself as a competitor for it.   But Sir Henry Savile
chose his fellows as his master, King James, chose his

[1] Aubrey's Letters and Lives, vol. ii.
p. 241 (2 vols. 8vo., London, 1813),
printed from the MSS. in the Bodleian
Library, &c. Aubrey subjoins, in a
note, his authority for this short account of Blake at Oxford—" From
H. Norbone, B.D., his contemporary
there."

Lord High Admiral; and Blake, being only five-feet-six, fell below the Stuart and Savile standard of manhood; and lost his election, not for want of learning, but for want of stature. Napoleon Bonaparte, Nelson, and Frederic II. would have failed in the competition for a Merton fellowship for the same reason. And neither Blake nor Nelson would have been found to possess the qualities that, in the eyes of King James, fitted a man to be Lord High Admiral of England. Had Blake succeeded in his attempt to obtain a fellowship, how different a fate might have awaited him! As he trod that quiet path to a quiet grave, the words of that exquisite old English song[1] ascribed to Sir Edward Dyer, a friend of Sir Philip Sidney, might have most truly described his character and his fate :—

I feign not love where most I hate—
I wait not at the mighty's gate ;
I fear no foe, nor fawn on friend—
I loathe not life, nor dread mine end.

He could not indeed have filled a more obscure, at least a more unknown, grave than he does. But the genius and valour that made him the conqueror of the greatest admirals of his own or any past time, and the victor in a hundred storms and battles, would probably have for ever slept within him, unknown even to himself.

In regard, however, to Blake's scholarship or learning, it must be admitted to be a point about which we know very little. What we do know is that Blake passed a number of years at Oxford, which he would not have

[1] The celebrated song from which these lines are taken, is printed in several collections of poems, published in the 16th century. There are many variations in the various copies. In a MS. copy of it, in the Bodleian Library at Oxford, the poem is ascribed to Sir Edward Dyer, a friend of Sir Philip Sidney.

passed there had he not liked the place. What did he like it for? He liked it for its quiet, and for his being there able to lead the life he loved—a silent thoughtful life, with long walks, in which he often seemed absorbed in thought; as in after-years, when passing some months, before his last expedition, at Knoll, a country-house he had near Bridgewater, in his long morning walks and musings on Knoll Hill, he appeared to his country neighbours to be as if working out in his own mind the details of some of his great battles.[1] And further as to scholarship—though, when we consider that English literature then contained no historical or biographical works to be compared to those of the Greek and Roman writers, Blake would probably read with interest the narratives of Thucydides, of Xenophon, of Plutarch, as well as of Cæsar, Livy, and Tacitus—it is very improbable that a mind like his would either delight or excel in the composition of Latin verses, to say nothing of Greek. A younger brother of the Admiral, William, was also at Oxford, and furnished a Latin epigraph to the book published by the University on the death of Camden the antiquary, which, as Mr. Dixon observes, Anthony Wood falsely attributes to Robert Blake. But it is of far other stuff than that which enables a man to shine in the composition of Greek and Latin verses, or even in the solution of mathematical problems, that the men are made who fight the battles and determine, for good or evil, the fate of nations—a Blake or a Cromwell:

> A patriot hero, or despotic chief,
> To form a nation's glory or its grief.

We know further of Blake—whether or not it be

[1] Dixon's Robert Blake, pp. 266, 267.

considered as in any part due to his Oxford education, to
his having learnt "ingenuas *fideliter* artes"—that he was
emphatically what is comprehended in that untranslatable
English word *gentleman*, both in the higher and lower
significance of the term; that he was what such men as
Cromwell and Frederic II. of Prussia never were, either
as men of sincerity and honour, or as men of thoroughly
humane demeanour.   Of Frederic, Lord Macaulay has
truly said : "He had one taste which may be pardoned to
a boy, but which, when habitually and deliberately indulged
by a man of mature age and strong understanding, is almost invariably the sign of a bad heart—a taste for severe
practical jokes."   Now Cromwell had also this taste for
practical jokes, and for dirty practical jokes.   Such jokes,
which are attended with humiliation and pain to those on
whom they are practised, evince even in small things the
mind of a tyrant.   As with the Prussian tyrant, if a courtier was fond of dress, oil was flung over his richest suit.
So the English tyrant, at the marriage of his daughter
Frances to Mr. Rich, the grandson and heir of the Earl
of Warwick, amused himself by throwing about the sack-
posset and wet sweetmeats among the ladies to spoil
their clothes, and daubed all the stools on which they were
to sit with wet sweetmeats.   The Prussian tyrant had
some talent for sarcasm ; but in the war of wit against a
king, his adversary has no more chance than the wretched
gladiator, armed only with a foil of lead, against whom
Commodus descended into the arena sword in hand, and,
after shedding the blood of the helpless victim, struck
medals to commemorate his disgraceful victory.   The
English tyrant, says Cowley,[1] "was wanton and merry,

[1] Cowley's Discourse, by way of Vision, concerning the Government of Oliver
Cromwell.

unwittily and ungracefully merry, with our sufferings; he loved to say and do senseless and fantastical things, only to show his power of doing or saying anything. It would ill-befit mine, or any civil mouth, to repeat those words which he spoke concerning the most sacred of our English laws—the Petition of Right and Magna Charta. To-day you should see him ranting so wildly, that nobody durst come near him; the morrow flinging of cushions and playing at snowballs with his servants," or making his soldiers throw burning coals into one another's boots. "These things, it may be said" (observes Lord Macaulay), "are trifles. They are so; but they are indications, not to be mistaken, of a nature to which the sight of human suffering and human degradation is an agreeable excitement." If it is asked how this observation can apply to Cromwell, who has been described as " naturally compassionate towards objects in distress to an effeminate degree," I can only answer, that either his extraordinary success had corrupted him, or that his nature was made up of many and opposite elements, some good and some bad; and that at one time of his life the good, at another the bad, obtained the mastery.

After eight years' residence at Oxford, Robert Blake returned to Bridgewater, having, in consequence of his failing to obtain a fellowship, abandoned his favourite idea of a college life. In the following year his father died, leaving his property encumbered with debts. When the debts were all paid, the family property did not exceed £200 a year,[1] equivalent to about £700 per annum at the present time. Blake managed this property with prudence, as well as liberality; for, besides devoting himself to the

---

[1] Dixon's Robert Blake, p. 20.

care of his mother, who survived her husband thirteen years, he educated and enabled to make their way into the world the whole of his father's numerous family. But he showed no desire for riches ; for though he left his paternal estate unimpaired, it is said that, notwithstanding the great sums that passed through his hands, he did not leave £500 behind him of his own acquiring.

During those dark years of England's history, when Charles I. endeavoured to govern without Parliaments, and tyranny, both civil and religious, reigned triumphant, the years of his early manhood, from about twenty-five to forty, Blake lived quietly on his paternal estate, with the character of a blunt bold man, of a ready humour, and a singularly fearless temper—straightforward, upright, and honest in an unusual degree. His manners were marked by a fearless bluntness and openness, accompanied with a certain grave humour, which sometimes took the form of bitter sarcasm against the vices of those in power. This temper is described by Clarendon as " a melancholic and sullen nature, a moroseness, and a freedom in inveighing against the license of the time and the power of the Court." " They who knew him inwardly," adds Clarendon, " discovered that he had an anti-monarchical spirit, when few men thought the Government in any danger." But Blake was a man of deeds, not of words ; and it was probable enough that he would take the first favourable opportunity of doing all he could to destroy a form of monarchical government that was fertile only in vices, and in the production of such loathsome popinjays as the Somersets and Buckinghams of the First Stuart, and such savage yet imbecile tyrants as the Lauds and Straffords of the Second. Accordingly, when the civil war broke out, Blake—who had been returned as member for Bridgewater in the short

Parliament of April 1640, but was not re-elected in the Long
Parliament that met on the 3rd of November of the same
year—was one of the first in the field.   Although Pepys
and other writers foolishly talk about his "passive courage"
in his famous defence of Lyme and Taunton, Blake showed
the same military qualities at the very outset of his career
that he did in his last battle, his wonderful victory of
Santa Cruz.   He united, indeed, the indomitable courage
of the bulldog to the highest strategical genius.   While,
as James Mill has said of Clive, "resolute and daring,
fear never turned him aside from his purposes, or deprived
him of the most collected exertion of his mind in the
greatest emergencies;"[1] he at the same time acted from
first to last on the principle which, says a great authority
on such a point, Lord Dundonald, in one of his notes on
Blake's most celebrated actions, " I have never found to
fail—that the more impracticable a task appears, the
more easily it may be achieved, under judicious management," a principle judged by which "the attack on Santa
Cruz was founded on a correct estimate of the probable
result."[2]

Mr. Dixon has, with most praiseworthy industry, given
a minute and most interesting narrative of Blake's famous
defence of Lyme, from a MS. account of the Siege of Lyme,
belonging to George Roberts, Esq., of that town; and
from various authentic sources, he has furnished the details
of the still more wonderful defence of Taunton.   In the
course of this last defence, Blake sent an answer to a summons to surrender which is very characteristic both of his invincible resolution and of his peculiar humour.   After being

[1] Mill's History of British India, vol. iii. p. 376, 3rd edition, London, 1826.
[2] Preface to the new edition of Mr. Hepworth Dixon's Life of Robert Blake, pp. xi., xii.   London, 1858.

repeatedly defeated in their assaults, the besiegers sent to invite the garrison to surrender to the King, rather than die the lingering death of hunger.   Blake's answer to this request was, that he had not yet eaten his boots, and that he should not dream of giving up the contest while he had so excellent a dinner to fall back upon.

In the siege of Bristol, the fort of Prior's Hill had been entrusted by Fiennes to Blake, then only a captain.   Of this place Blake had made so resolute and obstinate a defence, that Rupert, hearing that the commander at Prior's Hill refused to admit the articles of surrender—for which the governor (Fiennes) was tried by a court-martial for cowardice, and sentenced to death, though his life was spared by Essex—threatened to hang him.   In describing the subsequent siege of Lyme, Mr. Dixon says : "How often would the thought occur to him (Maurice), If Rupert had only hung that Captain Blake at Bristol !   In London the press was filled with the wonders of this remarkable defence, and Roundhead writers used it as a set-off against their own prolonged failures at Lathom House.   Yet the Cavaliers fought before the breastworks at Lyme with the most resolute gallantry, and some of the best blood in the West of England flowed into those shallow trenches.   After the siege was raised, and the Royalists had time to count up and compare their losses, they found, to their surprise and horror, that more men of gentle blood had died under Blake's fire at Lyme, than had fallen in all the sieges and skirmishes in the western counties since the opening of the war."[1]

There is a story respecting the death of Blake's brother Samuel—who of all his brothers resembled him most in the fearlessness of his nature, and to whose son Robert,

---

[1] Dixon's Robert Blake, p. 57, cites " Lyme MS."

afterwards one of his most gallant sea-captains, the Admiral bequeathed the gold-chain bestowed on him by the Parliament [1]—which is very characteristic both of Blake and his time. Samuel, hearing at a small village alehouse at Pawlett, some four miles down the river from Bridgewater, that a captain of array and one of his followers were crossing the river to beat up recruits for the King's service, instead of carrying the intelligence to his brother, who was his commanding-officer, mounted his horse and rode after the two officers. When he came up with them a quarrel ensued, and he was killed. "When the news came to Bridgewater," says a writer who lived in Blake's family, "the officers of the regiment were seen to cabal together in little companies, five or six at a place, and talk of it very seriously—none of them being forward to tell Colonel Blake what they were talking about. At last he asked one of them very earnestly, and the gentleman replied, with some emotion, '*Your brother Sam is killed!*' explaining how it came to pass. The Colonel, having heard him out, said, '*Sam had no business there*;' and, as if he took no further notice of it, turned from the Cornhill or marketplace into the *Swan* Inn, of chief note in that town, and, shutting himself in a room, gave way to the calls of nature and brotherly love, saying, '*Died Abner as a fool dieth!*'"[2]

The difference between the ultimate positions of Cromwell and Blake—the one Lieutenant-General of the Army, Lord-Lieutenant of Ireland, Lord-General and Commander-in-Chief of the Army, and at last Lord Protector; the other only Colonel, then Admiral and "General at Sea,"—must

---

[1] Office-copy of Blake's Will, March 13, 1655, cited in Dixon's Robert Blake, p. 52.

[2] "The History and Life of Robert Blake, Esq., of Bridgewater, General and Admiral of the Fleets and Naval Forces of England," written by a gentleman who was bred in his family, cited in Dixon's Robert Blake, p. 51, London, 1852.

not be accepted as anything like a true measure of the difference between the abilities of the two men. Cromwell, though not an orator or even a passably good speaker, was from first to last eminently a Parliamentary man—in other words, a man of great Parliamentary influence. Blake had been returned for the borough of Bridgewater in the short Parliament of April 1640, but he was not re-elected in the Long Parliament. In 1645, however, he was elected as one of the burgesses for Taunton, in the place of Sir William Portman, disabled for deserting the service of the House. On this occasion Blake took the oaths and his seat at the same time with Ludlow. "When I came to the House of Commons," says Ludlow, "I met with Colonel Robert Blake, attending to be admitted, being chosen for Taunton; where having taken the usual oaths, we went into the House together, which I chose to do, assuring myself, he having been faithful and active in the public service abroad, that we should be as unanimous in the carrying it on within those doors."[1]

Blake continued to reside at Taunton, which he had so bravely defended, and of which he had been appointed Governor, and made no attempt to obtain Parliamentary influence for personal advancement. The small Parliamentary influence of Blake may be inferred from the fact that when, in November 1651, after having performed great services, he was first elected a member of the Council of State, he had only 42 votes; while, on the same occasion, Cromwell had 118, Whitelock 113, St. John 108, Vane 104, and one "John Gurdon, Esq." (whose name is otherwise unknown to history), had 103. Blake had the

---

[1] Ludlow's Memoirs, vol. i. p. 170 (2nd edition, London, 1721). The word "abroad" only means out of the House, as opposed to "within those doors," Blake at that time not having served out of England.

lowest number of votes that year of any, except Henry
Martin, who had 41.[1] In the following year, while Blake
was not re-elected, Major-General Harrison is the last
name on the list, with only 39 votes.[2] Harrison would
not appear to have been, any more than Blake, popular
with the honourable Rump. They were both bold blunt
men, likely enough to rough the sleek hides of the men
of the Rump, which Cromwell knew how to smooth down
till his time came.

It is but one more version of the old story—a story
which is as true now as it was from the beginning of time,
and as it will be to the end. The career of Cromwell
is one which has been trodden times out of number,
when the highest prizes of human ambition are in troubled
times placed within the reach of genius and valour. The
career of Blake is a less common career; but it is also a
career less dazzling to the multitude, who are naturally
dazzled by the spectacle of a man raising himself to supreme power. Blake was a Puritan as well as Cromwell;
but I do not think that Blake could have quieted his conscience, had he been rapacious, by quoting such texts as:
" He shall be called Mahershalal-hash-baz, because he
maketh haste to the spoil." And Cromwell might truly be
called Mahershalal-hash-baz, if making haste to the spoil
entitled a man to that appellation. But though, in the
eyes of those who worship the powers of good and evil
alike, the genius and valour of Cromwell have cast all
other men into the shade, there are still some—and in the
course of time there will be more—able to appreciate the
genius and valour, joined to the contempt for wealth and
all the objects of vulgar ambition, of the great Admiral,

[1] Commons' Journals, Monday, Nov. 24, 1651.
[2] Ibid. Wednesday, Nov. 24, 1652.

who has left to after-ages a truly heroic memory and a stainless name.

So far from admitting Cromwell's plea for crushing English liberty—I mean constitutionally regulated liberty—that he was forced to take upon himself the office of a high-constable to preserve the peace among the several parties in the nation, though he professed to approve the government of a single person as little as any,[1] it is, to all who steadily examine the facts, a mere sophistry, or rather a palpable untruth. The Council of State acted the part of high-constable better than he did. The Council of State, indeed, could not command armies as Cromwell could, much less could it command navies as Blake commanded them; but Blake did not make that a reason for setting up as a king on his own account, and throwing England back two centuries in her progress towards good government. When we look calmly at what the Stuarts and Cromwell did, or attempted to do, we are forced to the conclusion that there is less excuse to be made for Cromwell than for the Stuarts. Any man who sets his own or his family's aggrandisement above truth, justice, and honour, must be pronounced to be a man with a bad heart. But if such a man's brains are still worse than his heart, there is more excuse for him than if, while his heart is bad, his brains are good. Consequently, the plea cannot be set up for Cromwell which may be set up for the Stuarts—that they may be "pardoned their bad hearts for their worse brains." The really greatest and most formidable enemies of mankind have been those whose fierce and rapacious selfishness has been accompanied by ability and courage of a high order—of an order much above the average, not

[1] Biog. Brit., Art. "Harrington;" to his edition of Harrington's Works, Toland's Life of Harrington, prefixed p. xix.

by the folly and pusillanimity which so emphatically marked the Stuarts for ten generations. Harvey — the discoverer of the circulation of the blood, of whom his friend Hobbes says, in his book "De Corpore," that he is the only man, perhaps, that ever lived to see his own doctrine established in his lifetime—was wont to say that man was but a great mischievous baboon,[1] an opinion not unlikely to be formed by a thinking man whose knowledge of mankind comprehended a somewhat minute acquaintance with the Court of the Stuarts.

In the preceding volume of this History[2] I have shown that the Council of State, on their appointment, directed their first attention to the affairs of the Navy. Such attention was particularly called for, both by the importance of the navy to the ultimate success of the cause of the Parliament, and by its condition at that time. Had the Royalists become masters of the navy, it would not only have been employed in maintaining a constant communication with foreign States; but the strength thence accruing to the royal cause would have affected the conduct of foreign Powers, and strengthened and excited into activity their natural inclination to support the cause of despotism against that of constitutional liberty. In point of fact, if the Royalists had been masters of the navy, the distinction between England and Hungary, or between England and any other unhappy country which has no physical barrier against the surrounding despots, would have been destroyed; and the Parliamentary armies, after defeating the forces of their native tyrants, would have had to fight the armies of the tyrants of France, Spain, and Germany. When Lord Macaulay says that, if a

---

[1] Aubrey's Lives, vol. ii. p. 381.   [2] Page 49 et seq.

French or Spanish army had invaded England, he has no
doubt that it would have been cut to pieces on the first
day on which it came face to face with the soldiers of
Preston and Dunbar, with Colonel Fight-the-good-fight
and Captain Smite-them-hip-and-thigh, he seems to forget
that though neither France, Spain, nor Germany could produce soldiers equal to those of Dunbar and Naseby, the
genius of Condé or of Turenne might have given at least
a chance to armies composed of inferior military materials.
But, be that as it may, what has been said shows the vast
importance of the navy in preventing all foreign interference in the quarrel between the English and their Kings
—an interference which might have led to most disastrous
consequences, as regarded the independence, the freedom,
and honour of England as a nation.   I think there cannot
be a doubt that it was his conviction on this point that led
Blake—when the messenger reached his fleet, then lying
off Aberdeen, with the news that Cromwell had turned out
the Parliament by force, and when some of his captains
pressed him to declare against the usurper—to say, " It is
not the business of a seaman to mind State affairs, but to
hinder foreigners from fooling us." That Blake's private
opinion was one not only of disapprobation but of disap-
pointment is certain from all that is recorded of his
opinions and his actions.   Little more than a year before,
too, he is reported to have said openly, that monarchy was
a kind of government the world was weary of; that it was
past in England, going in France, and in ten years would
be gone in Spain.[1]   This prophecy of Blake is but one

---

[1] " That you may see how brave and
open-dealing men your friends of the
new Commonwealth are, Blake, at his
late being at Cadiz,.said openly, that
monarchy is a kind of government the
world is weary of; that it is past in
England, going in France, and that
it must get out of Spain with more

more proof, added to thousands, of the little that can be
safely predicted respecting political affairs, and of the
truth of the remark of David Hume, that the world is yet
too young to have a political philosophy. But Blake—
though, like the rest of the human race, he might miss the
mark very widely when he attempted to carry his foresight
forward for years—saw, like Cromwell and all the men of
his kind, with the unerring instinct of genius, what was
best to be done at the moment, for the hour, and for the
day that was passing over him. He thus saw that if he
declared against Cromwell, the issue of the conflict between him and Cromwell would be doubtful, while the
gain to the enemies of both would be certain. And he
saw also that if the question was of necessity between a
single tyrant like Cromwell, and a single tyrant like Stuart,
the former was infinitely to be preferred to the latter.

It is not surprising that Blake should make the mistake
he did when he said that monarchy was a kind of government the world was weary of—that it was gone in England, going in France, and in ten years would be gone in
Spain. For Blake had seen events which might well make
him think that a great change had taken place in the
ideas that had prevailed in Europe for the last two centuries or, at least, for the last century and a half. He
could remember the time in England when the very doorkeeper of the House of Lords dared to shut the door of
that House in the face of a Member of the House of Commons, with the insolent words, " Goodman burgess, you
come not here." He had also seen " Goodman burgess "
in a very different character. " Goodman burgess " had

gravity, but in ten years it would be   Madrid, Feb. 9, 1651. (*Clarendon State*
determined there likewise."—Sir Ed-   *Papers*, vol. iii. p. 27.)
ward Hyde to Secretary Nicholas,

formed and brought up the cuirassiers who turned the battle on Marston Moor. "Goodman burgess" had led the charge at Naseby. "Goodman burgess" had stormed and reduced to a heap of ruins many a feudal fortress that had baffled all besiegers, and had successfully defended places which were not fortresses, and where nothing seemed defensible but his own unconquerable will. Further, "Goodman burgess" had defeated the fleets of many kings and of one powerful republic, and had gone forth over the ocean, from the Pentland Frith to the Straits of Gibraltar, conquering and to conquer. "Goodman burgess" had sat in that old Hall in judgment on the captive heir of a hundred kings; and "Goodman burgess" had done the great execution that was to be a warning to all time. But though that execution was to be a salutary warning to after-ages—for without the ineffaceable memory of that terrible deed, so fearlessly done in the face of heaven and earth, assuredly James II. and some other royal delinquents would not have been so easily got rid of as they were—its *immediate* effect was not favourable to the cause of those who did it.

But Blake, though he was not aware of all the consequences of the King's trial and execution, was not in any degree a party to those proceedings. He wished to see the King deposed and banished. And when he found the army fanatics, of whom Cromwell—whether he really, at the bottom of his heart, desired the execution of the King or not, and *that* we can never know—was the chief leader, determined on the King's trial and execution, he loudly expressed his disapprobation of their proceedings.[1] Not that he entertained the most remote idea of the expediency,

---

[1] Dixon's Robert Blake, p. 111, and the authorities there cited.

under any circumstances, of the restoration to power of a
man who had proved himself so faithless, and so utterly
unfit to govern; but like Vane, Algernon Sydney, and
others of the more farseeing statesmen of that time, he
considered the King's trial and execution as a grievous
political blunder. The sentimentalities of the question of
the King's execution may be despatched in the words of
Casca, in Shakspeare's *Julius Cæsar*: "Three or four
wenches, where I stood, cried, *Alas, good soul!* and forgave
him with all their hearts: if Cæsar had stabbed their
mothers, they would have done no less."

At the commencement of the war between the King and
the Parliament, the bulk of the army, as well as of the
navy, had been Presbyterian. In the army the Presbyterian element had diminished, and the Independent element
had very much increased—indeed, to such an extent, that
at the time of the King's death the army might be considered as almost entirely composed of Independents, both
as regarded the soldiers and officers; though Fairfax, the
Lord-General, was a Presbyterian, to be succeeded, however, at the beginning of the campaign in Scotland, in
1650, by Cromwell, an Independent. In the navy the
Presbyterian element remained much longer than in the
army, so that, soon after the seizure of the King's person
by the army, a disposition to mutiny showed itself in the
navy in the Downs—a disposition fomented by the Royalist
intriguers of Kent; and rose to such a height, that a portion of the fleet, consisting of eleven ships, carrying
altogether 291 guns and 1,260 men, revolted from the Parliament, and, under the command of Vice-Admiral Batten,
sailed for the coast of Holland. On the 12th of June,
1647, the Earl of Warwick, the Lord High Admiral, had
written a letter to Batten, which shows that at that time

considerable doubts were entertained respecting the fleet's fidelity to the Parliament. Batten, however, instead of (as the Lord High Admiral's letter directed him to do) " improving all means to continue the mariners in a condition of obedience and service to the Parliament who have intrusted them,"[1] betrayed the trust committed to him by the Parliament; and fomenting, instead of allaying, the mutinous spirit in the fleet, finally, in June 1648, informed his partisans of his resolution to declare for King Charles, and then, with eleven ships, stood over for the coast of Holland, to consult with the Prince of Wales. The Prince received him with open arms, and conferred upon him the ignominy of knighthood, which, in all cases at the best no honour under the Stuarts, was in this case a double disgrace, as serving to affix on the man's name to all time the brand of his treachery. Batten, indeed, published in his defence a declaration, " for satisfaction of all honest seamen and others whom it may concern," in which he complains of illtreatment by the Parliament. But there is a somewhat short and simple test of the value of this complaint of Captain Batten, furnished by his own " Declaration : " for among those whom he places in the same category with himself, as having been ill-requited by the Parliament for their great services, he specifies Colonel Blake.[2] Now Batten, when he professed to be a public servant, aggrieved and ill-requited to such an extent as to be entitled to revolt from those who gave him his commission,

[1] The Earl of Warwick to Captain Batten, from the Committee, June 12, 1647, in Granville Penn's Memorials of Admiral Sir William Penn, vol. i. pp. 247, 248.

[2] Granville Penn, vol. i. p. 268. Mr. Granville Penn has printed in full the " Declaration of Sir William Batten, late Vice-Admiral for the Parliament," from a copy in the British Museum, " printed at London in the year 1648."—See *Memorials of Admiral Sir William Penn*, vol. i. pp. 266-270.

and to go over to their enemies, was in the command of a
fleet, and therefore could not have been so much ill-requited
for his former services as Blake at that time might seem
to be; for Blake had then no such command as Batten,
and Blake's defences of Lyme and Taunton were, at least,
equivalent to anything ever done by Batten. But Blake
was not one of those men who, when their own estimate
of their services is not adopted to the letter by their
Government or country, fancy that they are justified in
going over to the enemy, by way of redressing their real
or imaginary grievances. According to such a principle of
action, no Government could ever depend on its naval or
military commanders; for I believe it may be said that
there is no Government that can escape, or at least that has
yet escaped, the imputed fault of occasionally overlooking,
or at least inadequately appreciating, great services.
There is certainly, if not more excuse for, a greater tendency
in men to act as Batten acted in civil wars than on other
occasions. The revolt of those ships, however, probably
proved in the end beneficial to the Parliament; for it set
them to remodel the whole system of their navy, as they
had before done that of their army, and produced the
wonderful achievements of Blake, and an altogether new
epoch in the history of English naval affairs.

About the time of this defection of a part of the fleet
of the Parliament, a conference was held in King Street,
Westminster, between those called, says Ludlow, "the
grandees of the House and Army, and the Commonwealth's
men; in which the grandees, of whom Lieutenant-General
Cromwell was the head, kept themselves in the clouds, and
would not declare their judgments either for a monarchical,
aristocratical, or democratical government—maintaining
that any of these might be good in themselves, or for us,

according as Providence should direct us. The Commonwealth's men," continues Ludlow, " declared that monarchy was neither good in itself nor for us. That it was not desirable in itself, they urged from the' 8th chapter and 8th verse of the First Book of Samuel, where the rejecting of the Judges and the choice of a King was charged upon the Israelites, by God himself, as a rejection of Him ; and from another passage in the same Book, where Samuel declares it to be great wickedness, with divers more texts of Scripture to the same effect. And that it was no way conducing to the interest of this nation, was endeavoured to be proved by the infinite mischiefs and oppressions we had suffered under it, and by it ; that, indeed, our ancestors had consented to be governed by a single person, but with this proviso, that he should govern according to the direction of the law, which he always bound himself by oath to perform ; that the King had broken this oath, and thereby dissolved our allegiance . . . . Notwithstanding what was said, Lieutenant-General Cromwell, not for want of conviction, but in hopes of making a better bargain with another party, professed himself unresolved ; and having learned what he could of the principles and inclinations of those present at the conference, took up a cushion and flung it at my head, and then ran down the stairs ; but I overtook him with another, which made him hasten down faster than he desired. The next day, passing by me in the House, he told me he was convinced of the desirableness of what was proposed, but not of the feasibleness of it ; thereby, as I suppose, designing to encourage me to hope that he was inclined to join with us, though unwilling to publish his opinion, lest the grandees should be informed of it—to whom, I presume, he professed himself to be of another judgment."

Some time after Cromwell began again to court the Commonwealth party, and Ludlow says : "I took the freedom to tell him that he knew how to cajole and give them good words when he had occasion to make use of them; whereat, breaking out into a rage, he said they were a proud sort of people, and only considerable in their own conceits." [1] Some modern writers have adopted this view of Cromwell's respecting the Commonwealth party. Whether they and Cromwell are right or not, let the world judge, when the evidence necessary for a fair judgment is placed before it.

So large a portion of their fleet having gone over to their enemies some six months before the Council of State began their work, in February 164$\frac{8}{9}$, they had good grounds for making the setting forth an efficient navy the first business to which they should direct their attention. And in doing so they applied the same principles to the reconstruction of their navy which the Parliament had before applied to the reconstruction of their army. That reconstruction of their army the Parliament had denominated the "New Model," a term which the royalist small-wits transformed.into the "New Noddle," but soon discovered to their cost that the joke was one of those witticisms which are said to produce a laugh on the wrong side of the mouth. Miracles alone, as Mr. Motley has most ably shown in his "History of the United Netherlands,"[2] had saved England from perdition in the year 1588—miracles, and not the administrative talent displayed by the much-lauded Queen Elizabeth and her ministers. But it is not safe to trust to miracles for the safety of a Government or of a nation. And there is instruction in

---

[1] Ludlow's Memoirs, vol. i. pp. 238–241, 2nd edition, London, 1721.
[2] Motley's History of the United Netherlands, vol. ii. pp. 527, 528.

the comparison of the Council of State of the Long Parliament with the Council of Queen Elizabeth. The Council of State went about their work in a very different fashion from that of Queen Elizabeth—scolding, swearing at, and browbeating her friends, and duped by her enemies; or of her Lord Treasurer, Burghley, "puzzled himself and still more puzzling to others."[1] and "turning complicated paragraphs, shaking his head, and waving his wand across the water, as if, by such expedients, the storm about to burst over England could be dispersed."[2]

It would appear that the Government of the Commonwealth had, like that of Queen Elizabeth, found a deficiency of powder. The following minutes show the want, and their exertions to supply it:—" That it be reported to the House that the Council upon the despatch of provisions for Ireland finds a great want of powder." The Council recommend that the manufacture of petre (saltpetre) be forthwith set on foot in England.[3] And another minute orders, " That a letter be written to Mr. Pennoger, to deal with the East India Company for their proportion of saltpetre which is now come in by the East India fleet from those parts."[4]

The "New Model" was, in fact, merely the application to the armies and fleets of a State of the same principle which all men of common sense employ in the conduct of their ordinary business. The year 1649 was not a time when any Government, unless brained like the oligarchy composed of Stephano, Trinculo, and Caliban, would have thought of advancing men with family interest over the heads of men who had nothing to recommend them but

[1] Motley's History of the United Netherlands, vol. i. p. 88.

[2] Ibid. vol. ii. p. 299.

[3] Order Book of the Council of State,

9th July, 1649, MS. State Paper Office.

[4] Ibid. 11th September, 1649.

their skill and courage. But the Government of which the
Council of State was the executive was brained very differently, not only from the three worthies above mentioned,
but from the English Governments which went before and
came after them—Governments that gave the command of
armies to such men as Leicester and Buckingham, and
commissions to such men as Ensign Northerton and the
captain in Hamilton's Bawn.

There is nothing that more strikingly shows the condition of England under the Tudors than Queen Elizabeth's
habitual treatment of her soldiers and seamen. She does
not treat them half or a quarter so well as à man of
average humanity treats his horse or his dog. " They
perish for want of victual and clothing in great numbers."[1]
And such was the carelessness of the much-lauded Government of Queen Elizabeth, that after the defeat of the
Spanish Armada, the English sailors were dying by
hundreds, and even thousands, of ship-fever, in the
latter days of August 1588. They rotted in their ships, or
died in the streets of the naval ports, because there were
no hospitals to receive them.[2]

How different from the condition of the troops of the
Commonwealth was that of Queen Elizabeth's, " shoeless,
shivering, starving vagabonds "[3] will appear from what follows. One of the first things to which the Council of State
directed the most minute attention was the quality and
quantity of the food supplied to the seamen on board their

---

[1] Leicester to Burghley, 15th March, 1586, MS. State Paper Office, cited in Motley's United Netherland, vol. i. p. 448, *note.*

[2] Lord Howard to the Queen; to Walsingham; and to the Privy Council, 22nd August to 1st September, 1588. MSS. State Paper Office, cited by Mot-

ley (vol. ii. p. 524).

[3] Motley's History of the United Netherlands, vol. i. p. 438.—The abundant evidence of the miserable condi-
tion in which Queen Elizabeth was not
ashamed to keep her troops, quoted by
Mr. Motley, furnishes a striking but
most painful picture.

ships. They found that the food was bad in quality, often
unfit to be eaten, and deficient in quantity. Those persons
who, like the prize-agents who keep the soldiers and
sailors' prize-money for a series of years in order to make
fortunes by the interest of it, supplied the provisions for
the navy had no objections to starve or poison the seamen, provided they made fortunes by the proceeding. The
result of the indefatigable exertions of Sir Henry Vane
and his colleagues on the Committee of the Admiralty,[1]
aided by such an admiral as Blake—who, like his cotemporary Turenne to his soldiers, was a father to his seamen
—was similar to that produced some years before by the
"New Model" of the army on the food as well as the discipline of the soldiers.

I have stated in the preceding volume[2] that on the
20th of February, 164$\frac{8}{9}$, the Council of State ordered "that
it be reported to the House as the opinion of the Council
that the ordinance of Parliament constituting the Earl of
Warwick Lord High Admiral be repealed;" that on the
same day it was resolved by the House, "that the House
doth agree with the Council of State as to the repeal of
the ordinance constituting the Earl of Warwick Lord
High Admiral;" and that, on the 26th of the same
month, the Council of State ordered, "That the names
of the Commissioners who are appointed to command at
sea shall be ranked in this order, viz.—Colonel Popham,
Colonel Blake, and Colonel Deane." The commission " to
Colonel Edward Popham, Colonel Robert Blake, and
Colonel Richard Deane, nominated and appointed by this

---

[1] There are numerous minutes evinc-
ing the most anxious care of the seamen's food. Some of these have been
already given as to the observation of
Lent, as likewise the half allowance
on Friday night (see Vol. I. p. 51).
Others will be given in subsequent
pages of this volume. (See Chapter
XII.)

[2] Vol. I. pp. 49, 50.

present Parliament to be Commissioners for the immediate
ordering and commanding of the fleet now at sea, and
which shall be set forth for the year ensuing, 1649," bears
date "February 27, 164$\frac{8}{9}$;" and empowers the said Commissioners, or any two of them, "to hold and execute the
place of Admiral and General of the said fleet, and to give
commissions, with the seal of. the anchor, unto the Vice-
Admiral and Rear-Admiral of the said fleet, the Admiral of
the Irish seas, and all other officers of the said fleet; and
further to appoint and empower any one of themselves to
command-in-chief the said fleet, or any part thereof."
The powers of the commission are to continue to the first
day of March, 164$\frac{9}{0}$. The multifarious business of the
Council of State obliged them to have different seals for
their various functions. Accordingly this commission
thus ends—" And for the present, this shall be your warrant. Given under the Admiralty seal of this said Council
of State, this 27th day of February, 164$\frac{8}{9}$.

" Signed in the name and by order of the Council of
State appointed by authority of Parliament,

" DENBIGH,

" Preses pro tempore."[1]

On the 22nd of the same month of February, 164$\frac{8}{9}$, the
Council of State ordered, "That the ships at sea in the
service of the State shall bear the red cross in a white
flag;[2] and that the engravings upon the stern of the ships

---

[1] "That the Commission engrossed
and brought in for the three Commissioners to command the fleet at sea, be
signed by the Earl of Denbigh, as
being Preses .pro tempore." — *Order
Book of the Council of State*, 27th
February, 164$\frac{8}{9}$, MS. State Paper
Office. The Council at this time appointed a President at each meeting;
but on the 10th of March next, they
made an order "that Mr. Serjeant
Bradshaw shall be President of this
Council."—See Vol. I. p. 38.

[2] A proclamation of Charles I., in
1634, prohibits any but King's ships
from carrying the Union flag in the
maintop, or elsewhere—that is, Saint
George's cross and Saint Andrew's

shall be the arms of England and Ireland in two escutcheons, as is used in the seals."[1]   And on the 5th of
March the Council of State ordered, " That the flag that is
to be borne by the Admiral, Vice-Admiral, Rear-Admiral,
be that now presented with the arms of England and
Ireland in two several escutcheons, in a red flag, within a
compartment: (or)."[2]   This ensign of the red flag borne
by the Admirals of the Government called the " Commonwealth of England" was for the next seven years to be as
widely known and as victorious as the famous red flag,
which was displayed on a spear from the top of the Præ-
torium, the tent of the Roman general, as the signal to
prepare for battle.   It was first displayed against an adversary whose career bears a resemblance to that of Blake,
in so far as he had fought with some distinction on land
before he fought at sea.   In other respects, this man differed from Blake, both in his character and his exploits, as
widely as it is possible for one human being to differ from
another.

If high birth and great bodily strength and activity

cross joined together; and orders the
English subjects to carry the red cross
commonly called Saint George's cross,
and the Scotch subjects to carry the
white cross, commonly called Saint
Andrew's cross.

[1] Order Book of the Council of
State, 22nd February, 164$\frac{8}{9}$, MS. State
Paper Office.

[2] Ibid. die Lund. 5th March, et
Meridie, 164$\frac{8}{9}$.—Mr. Granville Penn,
who in his valuable memorials of his
ancestor, Sir William Penn, gives a
few extracts from the Order Book of
the Council of State, gives the first of
the orders transcribed above, which
was for all the State ships except the
Admiral's, Vice-Admiral's, and Rear-

Admiral's; but he does not seem to
have been aware of the existence of
the second order, which was only for
the Admiral's, Vice-Admiral's, and Rear-
Admiral's. It appears further, from
the List of the Commonwealth's fleet
at sea in 1653 (London: printed by
M. Simmons, and sold at his house in
Aldersgate Street; and by Thomas
Jenner, at the south entrance of the
Royal Exchange, 1653; and reprinted
in Mr. Granville Penn's Memorials of
Sir William Penn, vol. i. p. 491), that
the first squadron of the fleet carried
the arms of the Commonwealth embroidered in gold on a red flag; the
second squadron on a white flag; the
third squadron on a blue flag.

could make a great man, Prince Rupert would have been
a great man.   But it is hardly necessary to go beyond the
periwigged face of this cavalier hero to see that he was
not a great man; for it is a face which has little or nothing
to distinguish it from those of the "round-faced peers, as
like each other as eggs to eggs, who look out from the
middle of the periwigs of Kneller."   No one can look on
the face of Cromwell—marked though it be, as Macaulay
has eloquently and truly said, "with all the blemishes
which had been put on it by time, by war, by sleepless
nights, by anxiety, perhaps by remorse"—without seeing
"valour, policy, authority, and public care written in all its
princely lines."   Yes, the lines in this man's face—this man,
by birth but a private gentleman, by occupation a brewer—
were princely, were grand[1] and commanding; while those of
this son of an English princess and a German potentate
whose pedigree the heralds might, perhaps, attempt to carry
back to Charlemagne or Attila, were as commonplace as
those of any of Kneller's round-faced periwigged peers.
Even in this age of heroes, "when every year and month
brings forth a new one," it needs something more than
cruelty and rapacity, though backed by bodily strength and
activity, to make a hero of whom "one would care to vaunt."
And in that troubled time there was no room for heraldic
heroes and heraldic princes, however long and fine might be
their hair, their pedigrees, or their periwigs.   Necessity
at such times is sure to find out the men who are princely
by nature, whether or not they are so by birth : and then,
when the hollow image

> Is found a hollow image and no more,
> The power returns into the mighty hands
> Of Nature, of the spirit giant-born.

---

[1] Sir William Napier repeatedly expresses himself as much struck with the
"grand face," as he calls it, of Soult, the greatest of Napoleon's Marshals.

By one of those strange caprices of fortune by which retribution is so often escaped upon earth, this German adventurer had always escaped from those fields of battle on which the vengeance of an outraged nation had taught the Stuart tyrant, and his French wife, and his German nephews, that Englishmen were not to be oppressed with impunity, like French and German serfs.   Long before he fled from Naseby, with Cromwell's horse-hoofs thundering close behind him, Rupert had endeavoured to secure some part of the plunder (which, and the power of plundering the English people for ever after, was all he fought for) by freighting one or two vessels with it.   But these ships fell into the hands of the Parliament.   After the fall of Bristol—which Rupert, after a defence forming a strong contrast to Blake's defence of Lyme and Taunton, surrendered to the army of the Parliament—the King signified his pleasure to the Lords of the Council, that they should require Prince Rupert to deliver his commission into their hands.   He likewise wrote a letter to Rupert, dated " Hereford, September, 1645," in which he says : " I must remember you of your letter of the 12th of August, whereby you assured me that, if no mutiny happened, you would keep Bristol for four months.   Did you keep it four days ? Was there anything like a mutiny ? More questions might be asked; but now, I confess, to little purpose : my conclusion is, to desire you to seek your subsistence, until it shall please God to determine of my condition, somewhere beyond the seas—to which end I send you herewith a pass."   Rupert went first to Holland, then to France, where, in July 1646, he was made Maréchal-du-camp, and had a regiment of foot, a troop of horse, and the command of all the English in France.[1]

[1] Rupert MS. in Warburton, iii. 237.   *Maréchal-du-camp* has sometimes been   translated Field-Marshal. But Field-Marshal is a much higher rank, though

It is probable that Rupert's arrogance made him as disagreeable to his own party as his cruelty and rapacity
rendered him hateful to his enemies.   Clarendon says
he had the misfortune "to be no better beloved by the
King's party than he was by the Parliament." As he had
before fled from Cromwell, he was now to have to fly before
another Parliamentary officer, as terrible by sea as Cromwell was by land.   For when the seamen of that part of
the fleet which had revolted from the Parliament mutinied
against Batten, who had brought them over to Prince
Charles, Rupert obtained the command, though some of
the chief seamen refused to " sail under Rupert, a foreign
prince."   And the same cotemporary document (" From
the Hague, 2nd November, 1648 ") adds :—" The seamen
desert daily; the chief that stay are very debauched,
which produces duels every day."[1] It is evident that ships
manned by such seamen would be fit enough to become
pirates; and pirates they became.   It is also remarkable
that, though we hear enough of their depredations upon
merchant-ships, not sufficiently armed to offer any effective
resistance, we do not hear of a single instance of their attacking any ship of war—at least any ship of such strength as to
make anything like a good and equal fight.   This is, indeed,
the nature of pirates and robbers generally, who, though
they may, when forced to it, fight as men fight with the hal-
ter about their necks, have really little or nothing at all of
that high and adventurous courage which has been falsely
ascribed to them by those modern writers, who have done
their utmost to corrupt public morals, by making, or at

when Turenne, in his twenty-third year,
obtained the appointment of *Maréchal-
du-camp*, that appointment was then
the next in rank to that of Maréchal-
de-France.   The French term, equivalent to the German term Field-Marshal, is Marshal of France.

[1] Proceedings in Parliament, &c.
Granville Penn, vol. i. p. 277.

least attempting to make, heroes of tyrants, robbers, and villains of every description, small and great.

Though there may be very much doubt about the heroism of this German adventurer, there is very little about his rapacity and cruelty. The cotemporary narratives of the events of this English Civil War abound with instances of the outrages perpetrated by him, upon the persons, property, and dwellings of the English people. Admiral Penn, in his Journal, relates several cases that place his tyrannous and cruel nature in a strong light. He says, under date 24th July 1651, that there came on board one of his ships, "to serve the State, four of Rupert's men (but pressed by him since the revolt), who ventured their lives in attempting their escape from him at Toulon."[1]   And the Admiral tells a story of Rupert's cruelty, so atrocious, that, as Mr. Granville Penn remarks in a note, it is to be wished that Rupert's reputation were such as to give the lie to this dreadful statement, which I would not venture to give in any words but Admiral Penn's own : "30th October, 1651.—About noon Captain Jordan came aboard, and informed me of a Genoese he stopped two nights since, who came from the island Terceira . . . . The lieutenant of the said ship, who was brother to the slain captain " [killed by a shot from Captain Jordan's ship], " with others of the ship's company, gave us intelligence of Rupert's being, about six weeks since, at Terceira ; and how cruelly he murdered the gunner of this ship, being an Englishman, and refusing to serve him. He commanded him from the town of Terceira aboard the *Reformation,* wherein he is Admiral; and, having him aboard, commanded his ears to be cut off; which being done, he caused his arms to be bound together, and flung

---

[1] Admiral Penn's Journal, July 24, 1651, in *Granville Penn,* vol. i. p. 353.

him overboard into the sea, where the poor creature
perished.   The Lord forgive this bloody wretch, and con-
vert him, if he belongeth unto him; otherwise, if His
Holiness please, suddenly destroy him! " [1]   So prays the
Admiral, a prayerful man even for that time.   If Rupert
had ventured his person in Drogheda or Wexford, or if
Blake had ever fairly fallen in with him, his life would not
have been worth much.   But his powers of escaping pursuit, both by-land and sea, appear to have been very
extraordinary.   At this very time Penn was cruising in
search of him, after he had escaped from Blake, who had
captured or destroyed all his pirate squadron—the whole
of the revolted fleet, with the exception of the *Reformation* and the *Swallow*, the two ships in which Rupert and
his brother Maurice sailed, and the *Marmaduke*, a ship
they had recently taken.   Clarendon mentions, as a proof
of Rupert's bodily strength, as well as " notable vigour,"
that in one of the mutinies which he suppressed, " he had
been compelled to throw two or three seamen overboard
by the strength of his own arm."

During the whole of the year 1649, Rupert, with his
fleet of revolted ships, carried on a war of piracy against
the merchant-ships of all nations.   The Dutch suffered
from his depredations no less than the English.   According to the Rupert MSS. (published by Mr. Elliot Warburton)
the Court of the exiled Prince Charles subsisted on these
robberies.   This, however, is denied by Clarendon, who,
though neither his nor Rupert's testimony can be accepted
as very conclusive, is at least as trustworthy a witness as
Rupert, and who says: " Sure when it is known that Prince
Rupert, instead of ever giving to the King one penny
of those millions which he had taken, demanded a great

[1] Admiral Penn's Journal, 30th Oct., 1651, in *Granville Penn*, vol. i. p. 380.

debt from the King; that he received £14,000 since his
being in France, and took no more notice of it to the King
then if he were not concerned; and that he went away
discontented, because the King would not approve of all
he did, or desired to do, it cannot be wondered that the
King did not importune him to stay."[1]   But whether he
gave one penny to the King or not, it is certain he took
many pennies from the English, who had then a Government which at least had this virtue—that it was one which
would not suffer its subjects to be robbed or maltreated in
any way by any but itself.   There are many minutes in the
"Order Book of the Council of State," during the year 1649,
relating to the depredations committed by Prince Rupert
on English ships.   The town and castle of Kinsale being
in the hands of the Irish rebels, Rupert found the harbour
of Kinsale a convenient place for refuge, as well as for disposing of some of his prizes; though the greater part were
probably sold in French, Dutch, and other continental ports.[2]
. But Blake, with his division of the Parliamentary fleet,
shut up the pirate and his fleet in Kinsale Harbour, and
established a strict blockade; while Cromwell, by his
storm of Drogheda and Wexford, showed that Ireland
was not, at that particular time, a very safe abode for any
whom the Parliament of England designated pirates or
rebels.

Under these circumstances, towards the end of October,
Rupert, with his usual good fortune in running away from
formidable enemies, contrived to make his escape, with a

---

[1] Clarendon State Papers, 26th June,
1654.

[2] "That a letter be written to Sir
George Ayscue, now in the Downs, to
inclose unto him the case stated by
Dr. Walker (of the Admiralty Court)

of the injuries offered unto the English
nation by the French, in suffering
prizes to be brought into and sold in
Dunquerque."—*Order Book of the
Council of State*, 29th September,
1649, MS. State Paper Office.

considerable part of his pirate fleet; Blake — as the winter and the strong north-east winds set in, and as it was an extremely dangerous lee-shore, and entirely without safe anchorage—being forced to ride out at a greater distance from the mouth of the harbour.[1]

It appears from an original letter[2] (which has never been printed) among the Tanner MSS. in the Bodleian, from Blake to Cromwell, that in the beginning of November, Blake was in Cork Haven. This letter is dated " Cork Haven, November 5, 1649," and thus commences: " Right Honourable,—By God's good providence on Saturday last, in the morning, we came safe into Cork Haven, notwithstanding we were shot at divers times from a fort, at the entering of the harbour, held by the Irish." The writer then goes on to state that he finds, by the expressions of several officers, " now aboard with me, and by the relation of two other officers who were yesterday in Cork," that there is a great deal of cordial and unanimous resolution among them, with a firm and sincere affection, as far as I can judge, to the English interest and army." It

---

[1] Even in the preceding June, as appears from a letter to the Speaker of the 'House of Commons, " From aboard the *Triumph* in Milford Haven, June 18, 1648," and signed " Robert Blake, Ric. Deane," the weather had driven the blockading fleet to take refuge in Milford Haven. "We have now," the letter says, " been 13 days absent from Kinsale, from whence we were forced by extremity of weather, and driven hither where we now are with 8 ships. We shall, God willing, with the first opportunity, endeavour to get to Kinsale Bay again, and pursue our former resolution, if we shall find them there, or otherwise follow them whithersoever they shall go."— See the letter in Dixon's *Robert Blake*, new edition, pp. 104, 105, London, 1858.

[2] I am indebted for a copy of this letter to the kindness of Mr. F. K. Lenthall, Recorder of Woodstock, a lineal descendant of the Speaker of the Long Parliament. Mr. Lenthall himself copied the letter from the original in the Tanner MSS. in the Bodleian. I am also indebted to the same gentleman for a most graphic account of Cromwell's dissolution of his last Parliament, which he also copied from an original letter among the Tanner MSS.

would be extremely interesting, as well as important, to
know Blake's real opinion of Cromwell, about three years
or a little more after this point of time, though such
opinion could hardly be expected to be found in a letter
from Blake to Cromwell himself.   But when we consider
what an unusually frank, fearless, and plainspoken man
Blake was, and that, in an official letter to his Commander-
in-Chief, he was under no necessity to pay him compliments,
it may, I think, be fairly inferred, from the following
sentences in this letter, that at this time Blake placed full
and hearty confidence both in Cromwell's ability and his
fidelity to the Parliament.   "I look upon it," the letter
continues, "as an extraordinary and very seasonable mercy
of God, in stirring up and uniting so many resolute spirits
to a work of so great consequence, and which, by God's
further blessing and *your management*, may be a means of
reducing, in a short time, the greatest part of Munster.
The gentlemen that were chief actors in this business had
penned certain propositions, to be tendered to your Excellency, in behalf of themselves and others; but they are
willing to decline that way, and to put themselves upon
your goodness, of which I have made bold to assure them
that they shall receive more satisfaction than if they
should insist upon any conditions, they professing themselves all resolved to live and die in defence of the Parliament and army of England, under your command.
To-morrow, God willing, I intend to go to Cork, to do my best
to confirm (if need be) the resolutions of the soldiers and
townsmen, they being now upon their duty, and expecting
every day some relief from your Excellency.   I purpose
to stay here till then, and till some other ships of fire[1]
come hither, and then I wait on your Excellency.   In the

[1] Fire-ships.

meantime, having nothing to add but my hearty prayers unto God for you and your army and undertakings, I remain, your Excellency's most affectionate and humble servant,

Robert Blake." [1]

On the 20th of November, 1649, Kinsale surrendered to Blake.[2]

Rupert directed his course southward, and his movements appear now to have attracted more of the attention of the Council of State than they did before.   On the 1st of December 1649, the day following that on which the Council received Blake's letters concerning the surrender of Kinsale, they directed a letter to be written to Colonel Popham, the like to Colonel Blake and Colonel Deane, "to inclose unto them the informations which are sent hither concerning the spoils which are made by Prince Rupert about the Straits [of Gibraltar], and to desire them to hold a serious consultation thereupon, and to consider in what way some prevention may be given unto him, and to return their opinions therein to the Council." [3]   On the 3rd of December, the Council of State directed "a letter to be written to the Generals at sea, to give them the state of the winter fleet, and to desire them to think of taking a squadron out of the winter guard to go to seek out Rupert's fleet; and, in such ships as shall need it, to desire them to increase their number of men, not exceeding the proportion of the winter guard." [4]

---

[1] This letter is endorsed in Cromwell's hand, " Coll. Blacke's letter to " (" me " erased and substituted) " the Ld.-Lnt. of Ireland."

[2] "That the letter from Colonel Blake of the 20th November, concerning the rendition of Kingsale, be reported to the House; and Sir Henry Vane is desired to make this report."— *Order Book of the Council of State*, 30th November, 1649, MS. State Paper Office.

[3] *Ibid.* 1st December, 1649.

[4] *Ibid.* 3rd December, 1649.

On the following day, the 4th of December 1649, the Council of State made an order, " That Colonel Blake shall be the person who shall be appointed to command the squadron which is to go towards Cales [Cadiz] to seek out Prince Rupert." [1]   And on the same day they ordered, " That a letter be written to Colonel Blake, to let him know that this Council hath pitched upon him as the person whom they intend to send against Prince Rupert; to let him know that he is to reside at Plymouth until all things shall be ready for his setting forth; and in the meantime the Irish squadron may do service in the station to which they are appointed." [2]   On the same day they ordered a letter to be written to Colonel Popham, to let him know that they had pitched upon Colonel Blake to command the squadron which is to go against Prince Rupert; and in this letter, as well as in that to Blake, they say, " which the Council hath done to prevent the delays which may be occasioned by appointing a consultation."   In this letter to Popham they also say, " That this Council leaves it to him and the rest of the Generals at sea, to appoint such number of ships, and of such quality as they shall think fit, to go forth in the squadron; that the Committee of the Admiralty will take care for the providing of all supplies which may be necessary for the expedition, and will likewise advise with such as are traders to the Straits for their judgment in the business." [3]

On the same day the Council made an order, " That it be referred to the Committee of the Admiralty, to advise with some merchants, traders to the Straits, to know of

---

[1] Order Book of the Council of State,   [2] Ibid.
4th December, 1649, MS. State Paper   [3] Ibid.
Office.

them their opinions concerning the sending of a fleet against Prince Rupert, now about the Straits, who are to report to the Council what they shall receive from the said merchants concerning this affair." [1]

On the 8th of December the Council of State made the following orders: " That £14,000 be lent to the Committee of the Navy out of the money laid aside for the use of the emergent affairs of this Commonwealth, to be made use of by them for the setting out of the squadron which is to go against Prince Rupert." " That some part of the summer fleet may be sent as a reserve after this squadron that is now to go out." [2]

The Council of State were, as I have before observed, manifestly anxious for peace with foreign States, though when attacked or insulted they showed themselves not unprepared for war. On the 13th of December they determined that two persons should be sent into Spain (one as agent, the other as counsel or consul), "to keep a good correspondence between the two nations." [3]

On the 31st of December, 1649, the Council ordered a letter to be written to the Committee of the Navy, to acquaint them with the former vote (appointing Blake Admiral of the fleet against Rupert), and to enclose unto them the vote of the Council, whereby Captain Moulton is

---

[1] Order Book of the Council of State, 4th December, 1649, MS. State Paper Office.—On the 28th of December, 1649, a petition was presented to the Council of State from the Company trading into Turkey, representing the great losses they have sustained by piracies, and craving redress therein. (*Ibid.* 28th December, 1649.) On the same day (the 28th December, 1649), there is a warrant to Mr. Willoughby to transport into foreign parts forty couple of English hounds. On the 5th of February, $16\frac{49}{50}$, there is an order of the Council of State, "That the Lord Ambassador of Spain shall have liberty to ship 20 horses, of which 12 are coach and the rest saddle horses."

[2] *Ibid.* 8th December, 1649.

[3] *Ibid.* 13th December, 1649.

made Vice-Admiral to the fleet now to go to the south, and likewise to enclose unto them the opinion of the Masters of the Trinity House concerning the sending of the fleet to the South."[1]

On the 5th of January, $16\frac{49}{50}$, the Council of State sent formal notice to the Spanish Ambassador "yet remaining in England," that "because they find that the trade between the two nations is like to be very much disturbed by the means of the revolted ships commanded by Prince Rupert, who, with others their adherents, have betaken themselves to piracy, they [the Council of State] have thought fit to appoint a considerable fleet to go into those seas in pursuit of the said revolters and pirates, who they hear are now at Lisbon, but do presume will have no maintenance nor protection from any that are allies to this State."[2]

On the 7th of January, $16\frac{49}{50}$, the Council of State made the following important minute relating to the increase of the navy: "That it be reported to the Parliament that the Council is of opinion that it is necessary that some more ships should be built for the service and safety of the Commonwealth, and that it may at this time be more conveniently done in regard of the great stores of timber that is now cut down." There are three orders of the following day, the 8th of January, which, though not relating to naval affairs, I venture to transcribe: "That £100 be paid to Mr. Thomas Waring, for a book containing several examinations of the bloody massacry (*sic*) in Ireland." "That Mr. Milton do confer with some printers

---

[1] Order Book of the Council of State, 31st December, 1649, MS. State Paper Office.

[2] "Instructions from the Council of State for Sir Oliver Fleming, Knt., to the Spanish Ambassador yet remaining in England."—*Ibid.* 5th January, $16\frac{49}{50}$.

or stationers, concerning the speedy printing of this book."
"That Mr. Milton do prepare something in answer to the
Book of Salmatius (*sic*), and when he hath done it, bring
it to the Council." [1]

The following order of the 12th of January, $16\frac{49}{50}$,
confirms what has been said in the preceding volume respecting the pressing of seamen: "That it be referred to
the Committee of the Admiralty to give order for the
victualling of the ships that are to go southward, for six
months from the 20th of January instant; that they also
give orders to the Commissioners of the Navy to *press* 150
men, and send them down to Portsmouth for the service of
the fleet now going south." On the same day they ordered,
"That it be referred to the Committee of the Ordnance to
contract with Mr. Browne, the gunfounder, for ordnance for
the winter fleet of the next year." [2]

On the 16th of January, the Council of State ordered a
letter to be written to the Committee of the Navy, "That
in regard Colonel Blake is to go General of the fleet that
is to go to the southward, to desire them that order be
presently given for the pay of his last year's salary, that he
may be thereby the better fitted for this service." On the
same day they also ordered " an instruction to be prepared
for Colonel Blake, to send for the merchants of this nation
who are in such places abroad as he shall have occasion to
apply himself unto with his fleet, and to tender unto them
the engagement; and to let them know that as this State
gives protection unto them in their trade, so this State
expects that they should be faithful unto them, and that
they should not own or apply themselves unto any persons

---

[1] Order Book of the Council of State, 7th and 8th January, $16\frac{49}{50}$, MS.
State Paper Office.   [2] *Ibid.* 12th January, $16\frac{49}{50}$.

whomsoever who come as ambassadors from Charles Stuart, and have no character from this State." [1]

On the 17th of January, 16$\frac{49}{50}$, the Council of State sent Blake his instructions. " You shall," say the instructions, " if you find yourself strong enough, not spare the revolters, but fight with them, and by God's assistance prosecute their destruction; and in case any foreign ships shall thereupon assist the said revolters, or fight against you, you likewise shall fight against them, and destroy or surprise them as God shall enable you; but so that after the fight ended, in case you happen to take any foreigners, there be not made any slaughter of them in cold blood, but that they be kept and used civilly as prisoners of war. And in case that you find occasion, by reason of any unexpected assistance given to the said revolters, or any power of ships set forth by any for the surprising of our merchant-ships or prejudicing of this Commonwealth, that then and in such case you shall be and are hereby enabled, according as the Lords Admirals of England in such cases formerly were, to call unto your assistance, and embargo, arrest, and make use of any English merchants'[2] ships to join with you, to fight or make defence for the safeguard and benefit of this Commonwealth. And they are hereby enjoined to yield obedience. Furthermore, if the said

---

[1] Order Book of the Council of State, 16th January, 16$\frac{49}{50}$, MS. State Paper Office.

[2] As I have before shown, the merchant-ships were, at that time, all more or less armed. See note at p. 107 of the preceding volume, where it is shown that even colliers' ships of 160 tons carried as many as eight guns. Consequently, merchant-ships were easily made available as ships of war, and were frequently bought for the use of the State, of which the following minute furnishes an example: "That the opinion brought in from the Committee of the Admiralty, concerning the buying of the merchant frigate for the use of the State, at the rate of £2750, be approved of."—*Ibid.* 9th January, 16$\frac{49}{50}$.

revolted fleet, or any of them, should happen to be sold by
their Commander-in-Chief, or any of their captains, or other
persons whatsoever, to any foreign Prince or State, or any
of their subjects, or stayed there under any colour or pretence, you are not for all that to forbear to seize, burn,
destroy, or surprise them wheresoever you can do it; and
to signify to them that these ships are part of the navy
of England, and the Parliament's own ships, and were
treacherously carried away by those perfidious revolters,
who have no property in them nor power to sell them; and
that your commission from the Parliament enjoins you to
demand them wherever they be, and to seize upon them
and send them home. And whereas the dominion of these
seas hath anciently and time out of mind undoubtedly
belonged to this nation, and the ships of all other nations,
in acknowledgment to that dominion, have used to take
down their flags upon sight of the Admiral of England, and
not to bear it in his presence, you are—as much as in you
lieth, and as you find yourself and the fleet of strength
and ability—to do your endeavour to preserve the said
dominion of the sea, and to cause the ships of all other
nations to strike their flags and not to bear them up in
your presence; and to compel such as are refractory therein,
by seizing their ships, and sending them in to be punished
according to the law of the sea, unless they submit and
yield such obedience as you shall approve of: yet we would
not that you should, in this expedition, engage the fleet in
any peril or hazard for that particular. There are special
letters of credence delivered to you, to make use of as you
may have occasion." For the use of the fleet there were
provided £3,000 in Spanish money—pieces of eight, bought
at 4s. 10d. per piece, and £1,000 in English money. There

were also letters of credit in Spain, Italy, &c., to the amount of £10,000.[1]

On the 23rd of January, the Council of State gave " Instructions for Anthony Ascham, Esq., Agent from the Commonwealth of England to the King of Spain," by which Ascham is directed " to signify to the King of Spain that the Parliament of England hath received information that there are arrived at the Court of Spain the Lord Cottington and Mr. Edward Hyde, calling themselves ambassadors from the late King's eldest son, pretending himself King of Great Britain, who have presumed to write to the merchants of the Commonwealth residing in Spain, requiring them to acknowledge them, the said Cottington and Hyde, as public ministers of the said Pretender." Ascham is, by his instructions, further directed " to desire the said King of Spain, that if any ships or goods belonging to the people of this Commonwealth shall be brought into any of the ports, by Rupert or any other pirate, that they may be put in safe custody, and without breaking bulk be delivered to the owners thereof."[2]

On the same day instructions, to the same purport, were given to Charles Vane, Esq., " Agent from the Commonwealth of England to the King of Portugal."[3]

On the 24th of January, a letter was ordered to be written to Colonel Popham and Colonel Blake, " to give them what information the Council hath received of the preparation of frigates by the enemies in Dunkirk for the infesting of the seas"; and Colonel Popham is therefore desired to have an eye to those seas, " when that squadron is gone

[1] Order Book of the Council of State, 17th January, 16$\frac{49}{50}$, MS. State Paper Office.

[2] Ibid. 23rd January, 16$\frac{49}{50}$.
[3] Ibid. same day.

southward which is now to go forth with Colonel Blake." [1]
On the following day, the 25th, an order is made, " That
the General of the fleet (Blake) shall land Mr. Ascham in
such port of Spain as shall be thought most convenient for
his journey to Madrid." [2] Next day (26th of January), it is
ordered " that a messenger be sent down to Gravesend, to
hasten away the ships that are to go to the southward." [3]
It would appear, however, that Blake's fleet had not sailed
by the 8th of February; for on that day Blake is directed
to give Mr. Ascham accommodation suitable to his quality,
and, in case he shall not be received as ambassador, to receive him on board again. [4]

On Saturday, the 16th of February, $16\frac{49}{50}$, an order
was made, " That all whose names are in the new Act for a
Council of State for the year to come be desired to be here
on Monday in the afternoon, for the putting in execution
of the powers given them by the new Act; and that all
orders concerning Standing Committees formerly made be
written out, with the persons that are of those committees."
Of these Standing Committees, the principal were—

" Admiralty,

" Ordnance,

" Ireland,

[1] Order Book of the Council of State, 24th January, $16\frac{49}{50}$, MS. State Paper Office.

[2] *Ibid.* 25th January, $16\frac{49}{50}$.

[3] *Ibid.* 26th January, $16\frac{49}{50}$.

[4] *Ibid.* 8th February, $16\frac{49}{50}$.—It would seem from the following order that some members of the Council of State were not members of the Parliament: "That notice be given to all the members of this Council who are *not of the Parliament*, that the corpse of the late Earl of Pembroke is to be carried out of town on Wednesday next, to the end that they may accompany it two or three miles onwards the way, the Parliament having ordered that all their members do accompany the corpse out of town." —*Ibid.* 4th February, $16\frac{49}{50}$. On the same day the Council made an order, "That a coach with seven horses shall be bought for the service of the State, for the receiving of Agents from abroad, and likewise liveries for six footmen, and a coachman and a postilion, &c."—*Ibid.*

" Private Examinations,

" Foreign Negotiations." [1]

On Monday the 18th of February, $16\frac{48}{50}$, the Council reappointed Mr. Serjeant Bradshaw President of the Council, with the like provisions as in the preceding year.[2] They then voted the reappointment of Mr. Milton, Mr. Frost [father and son], and all the clerks employed the preceding year, at the same salaries.[3]

On the 23rd of February, the minutes contain the following rather important construction of the Council's oath of secrecy : " That any of the Council shall have liberty to reveal whatsoever is debated, resolved, or spoken of, if they be not forbidden to reveal by the major part of those present at the said debates, resolutions, and speeches." [4]

On the 27th of February the Council of State proceeded to make " Orders for regulating the Proceedings of the Council ; " some of which I will transcribe, that the reader may be better enabled to form an opinion of the character given them by Bishop Warburton—" a set of the greatest geniuses for government the world ever saw embarked together in one common cause ":—

" That after the reading of the letters " [which included the letters received that morning or since the last meeting of the Council, and those ordered at the last meeting to be

---

[1] Order Book of the Council of State, die Saturni, 16th February, $16\frac{48}{50}$, MS. State Paper Office. On the 1st of February, the Council made an order, " That Mr. Serjeant do speak unto Colonel Goffe for the furnishing of 20 men every afternoon, well and full armed, to be placed in the chamber commonly · called the Guard Chamber, there to attend until the rising of the Council." " Lamps to be set up in the galleries about Whitehall for making the passage convenient for the members ´of the Council."—*Ibid.* 1st February, $16\frac{48}{50}$.

[2] Vol. i. p. 38.

[3] Order Book of the Council of State, die Lunæ, 18th February, $16\frac{48}{50}$, MS. State Paper Office.

[4] *Ibid.* 23rd February $16\frac{48}{50}$.

written by the secretaries], "*if there be nothing of present danger that must be instantly despatched,* then all the Committees of the Council that have any business stand referred to them shall make their report thereof to the Council."

"That the letters sent to the Council be opened at the place of the Council's sitting, in the presence of *three* at the least of the Council, and then be delivered to the Secretary."

"That if letters shall arrive when the Council is not sitting that are known or supposed to be of importance, and to require a more speedy despatch than to attend the ordinary meeting of the Council, the President and any two of the Council shall have power to open them, and, if necessary, to give order for the present summoning of the Council, to take it into consideration and make a despatch."

"That whatever is propounded, seconded, and *thirded,* be put to the question, if none of the members of the Council speak against it."

"That when a business is resolved by the question, the Secretary shall enter the said votes into the books, and *nothing of any debate or argument shall be entered,* but only the results thereof declared in the said votes."

"That when there shall be but nine members of the Council, none of them shall depart the Council Chamber without leave, during the time appointed for sitting of the Council." [1]

Although at other times the Council, as has been stated in the preceding volume, had morning sittings (namely, at 7 or sometimes 8 in the morning), as well as afternoon sittings, at this time the order was, "That the Council shall sit every day, except Lord's-days" [as we shall

---

[1] Order Book of the Council of State, 27th Feb. 16$\frac{48}{50}$, MS. State Paper Office.

see they sat on Lord's-days when the business was urgent, as during the march of the Scots into England before the Battle of Worcester, and during the Dutch war], "at 3 in the afternoon, and shall not sit after 6 when the House sits, unless for business that cannot bear delay till next day." [1]

On the 2nd of March the Council of State made the following orders :—

"That the paper now sent from the Parliament, containing the increase of wages to the seamen, be sent to the Committee of the Navy."

"That the Council doth declare that in the framing of the new Militia they will have no such officer as a Lieutenant-Colonel of Horse ; and that commissions granted to any to be Lieutenant-Colonels of Horse be revoked, and commissions for Majors given in lieu of them."

"That the whole Council, or any five of them, be appointed a Committee for Trade and Plantations."

"That Sir Henry Vane, Colonel Wauton, Mr. Challoner,[2] Colonel Popham, Colonel Stapeley, Colonel Purefoy, Earl of Salisbury, Mr. Luke Robinson, or any three of them, be appointed a Committee to carry on the affairs of the Admiralty and Navy, and to exercise the same powers as they have formerly done." [3]

The following minute of the 25th of March 1650 shows the stringency of their *press* warrants: "Whereas the Council of State hath contracted with Mr. Pitt, gunfounder,

---

[1] Order Book of the Council of State, 27th February, 16$\frac{48}{49}$, MS. State Paper Office.—On the same day the following order was made: "That when any Members of Parliament shall come to the Council, there shall be chairs set for them, and they shall be desired to sit down."

[2] Of Chaloner (Thomas Chaloner,

Esq.) Aubrey says : "He was as far from a Puritan as the east from the west. He was of the natural religion, and of Henry Martyn's gang, and one who loved to enjoy the pleasures of this life."—*Aubrey's Letters and Lives*, (2 vols. London, 1813), vol. ii. p. 282.

[3] Order Book of the Council of State, 2nd March 16$\frac{49}{50}$, MS. State Paper Office.

for new casting of some ordnance for the service of the State, in which he is to make use of Edward Lane, these are therefore to will and require you not to press the said Edward Lane, servant to Mr. Pitt, for any other service of the State during his employment in the said service of the Commonwealth.—Given 25 Martii 1650." The warrant is addressed "to all Constables, *Pressmasters*, and all others whom it may concern." [1]

By this time symptoms of the Dutch quarrel began to manifest themselves. A Dutch man-of-war having refused to be searched, the Council of State ordered that efficient assistance be given to the searchers to do their office.[2] By this time also the Council began to be fully aware that they would have to encounter more enemies than the Dutch and the German pirate Rupert. In their instructions of the 30th of March 1650, "for Richard Bradshaw, Esq., Resident from the Commonwealth of England with the Senate of Hamburg," they direct him to inform himself, and give them notice, "what designs are on foot and what transactions are made in Germany, Poland, Sweden, and Denmark;" and in regard to the Senate of Hamburg their instructions run thus—"You shall demand of them, in the name of the Commonwealth of England, that justice may be done upon those offenders that assaulted and attempted to assassinate the minister of the company of English merchants resident there; and also upon those pirates who took away the deputy of that

[1] Order Book of the Council of State, 25th March, 1650, MS. State Paper Office.

[2] *Ibid.* 28th March 1650.—The following minute has reference also to the same subject: "That the Company trading to the East Indies do take care that, as soon as the ship's company shall come to this town which brings the tidings of the injury offered to their trade by the Dutch, they put the thing into a way of proof and attestation in the Admiralty, to the end that complaint may be made thereof to the States."—*Ibid.* 6th May, 1650.

company and some other merchants—against whom there hath been no proceeding for those crimes." [1] On the 22nd of March they ordered a letter to be written to Mr. Strickland, to inform himself what English, especially persons of quality, are with the Scots' king at Breda. [2]

On the 12th of April the Council made an order, "That Colonel Popham be desired to go forthwith to Portugal, with a fleet to consist of eight ships." [3] On the 20th of April the Council despatched "additional instructions to Colonel Robert Blake, appointed General of the first fleet that is gone to the southward." In these "additional instructions," the Council state their case with a force and clearness which form such a remarkable contrast with some of the other writings of him who drew them (for I believe them to have been drawn by Sir Henry Vane), that they may serve as an instructive elucidation of the remark of Lord Macaulay, that while any time might have produced George Fox and James Naylor, to that time alone belonged the frantic delusions of such a statesman as Vane, and the hysterical tears of such a soldier as Cromwell :—

"You shall remonstrate forthwith to the King of Portugal, that those ships now in his ports, *de facto* commanded by Prince Rupert, are of a nature not capable of neutrality ; for that they were part of the Navy of England, in the real and actual possession of the Parliament, armed, equipped, and furnished by them in their own ports; the mariners being also their own servants, hired by them, and placed in those ships in the immediate service of the Parliament, from which service, and from their duty, the said mariners have perfidiously apostatised and made defection; and as

---

[1] Order Book of the Council of State, 30th March 1650, MS. State Paper Office.

[2] *Ibid.* 22nd March, 16⁴⁹⁄₅₀.

[3] *Ibid.* 12th April 1650.

fugitives and renegades have run away with the said ships, and in the same as pirates and sea-robbers they have made depredations, and by adding to their number the ships by them taken were growing to a strength like to prove dangerous, to the interruption if not the destruction of all trade and commerce. That they are such fugitives and renegades as have not place in the world which they can pretend to be their own, nor have any port of their own whither to carry their prizes, and where to make show of any form of justice; but whatever they can by rapine take, from any whomsoever, like so many thieves and pirates, they truck the same away, when they can get admittance for that thievish trade. And being, as they are, *hostes humani generis*, they may neither use the law of nations, nor are capable of protection from any prince.

" You shall signify the strict charge laid upon you by the Commonwealth of England to surprise [1] or destroy those revolted ships wherever you can find them.

" If the King of Portugal shall refuse or neglect to do you right in the premisses, then, for default of justice from him therein, you shall seize, arrest, surprise, or destroy in the way of justice, all such ships, either merchant or other, belonging to the King of Portugal or any of his subjects, and secure the same and all the goods therein, and all the writings, in the same manner and form as by the instruction given you concerning the French, to be kept till the Parliament shall resolve what further directions they will give concerning them." [2]

The " Instructions for Colonel Edward Popham,

---

[1] It will be observed that the word "surprise" is, in these and the other instructions to the same effect, used in its primary sense—"to take unawares, to fall upon unexpectedly."

[2] Order Book of the Council of State, 20th April 1650, MS. State Paper Office.

appointed to command the second fleet ordered to go to the southward," dated "Whitehall, April 25, 1650," are for the most part the same as those before given to Blake. It will, therefore, only be necessary to give the following portions of them, which are, in fact, to be instructions for Blake as well as Popham :—

"Whereas all particulars cannot be foreseen, nor positive instructions for each emergent so beforehand given, but that many things must be left to your prudence and discreet management, as occurrences may arise upon the place, or from time to time fall out; you are, therefore, upon all such accident, or any occasion that may happen, to use your best circumspection, and, advising with your Council of War, to order and dispose of the said fleet, and the ships under your command, as may be most advantageous for the public, and for obtaining the ends for which this fleet was set forth—*making it your special care, in discharge of that great trust committed unto you, that the Commonwealth receive no detriment.* [1]

"You are, upon your coming into the Bay of Weires,[2] or any other place where you shall meet with Colonel Blake, to show him these your instructions, who is hereby authorised and required to put the same in execution jointly with you, if you shall continue together, or severally and by himself if you find it for the service to divide yourselves,

[1] Order Book of the Council of State, 25th April 1650, MS. State Paper Office.—It is not unworthy of notice that these last words are a translation of the words by which, in critical times, the power of the Roman Consuls was made unlimited by the decree of the Senate,—" Videant consules ne quid respublica detrimenti capiat."

[2] Oeiras. It is spelt "Oeyras" in the Wellington Despatches (vol. viii. p. 228). The Council of State dealt with Spanish or Portuguese names somewhat as Charles James Fox did, who, says Lord Brougham, " preferred Cales and Groyne to Cadiz and Corunna."—*Historical Sketches of Statesmen of the Time of George III.*, third series, p. 203, London, 1843.

as well as if the same had been directed particularly to himself." [1]

On the 29th of April the Council gave an additional private instruction to Blake and Popham, to the effect that if they should find they were like to come to a breach with the King of Portugal, by any acts they should be necessitated to put in execution in pursuance of their instructions, they should first send for Mr. Vane, the Resident there, to come on board, and show him their instructions, and declare their resolution, that he may give order for securing his papers, and that his person may be in safety with them, against any wrong might be done to him, or advantage made of him against the public service. [2]

Rupert, in the course of his flight from Kinsale to Portugal, captured four ships, which, having been fitted out by him as men-of-war, made up his fleet to nine vessels. The goods captured in these four ships he sold to the Portuguese merchants for £30,000. "These prizes," says Rupert, in one of his letters to Charles, "being considerable, and being fearful of some disaster, having near three hundred prizemen aboard us, it was generally thought fit to secure and sell them with the first convenience, to do which no place was thought more convenient nor safe than Lisbon." [3] Accordingly, Rupert sailed into the Tagus, and John of Braganza, the first Portuguese king of the House of Braganza, who had been placed on the throne of Portugal by the nobility in 1640, undertook to protect him in that river against all his enemies. At the approach of spring, Rupert—having, as before mentioned, fitted out his prizes as men-of-war—dropped down the river to Belleisle, with the

---

[1] Order Book of the Council of State, 25th April 1650, MS. State Paper Office.

[2] Ibid. 29th April 1650.

[3] Fitzroy MS. in Warburton, iii. 295.

intention of renewing his piracies; but, before he could get clear of the river, Blake with his fleet of five ships was at its mouth, and Rupert, though he had nine ships against Blake's five, anchored under the guns of the fort. Blake, having sent an officer to ask the King's permission to attack the revolted ships at their anchorage, and having met with a refusal, affected not to comprehend the King's answer, and ordered his boats to cross the bar. A few shots were fired at them from Belim Castle. Blake sent a boat to enquire the reason for this show of hostility against a friendly Power, there being no war at that time between Portugal and England. The officer in command replied that he had received no orders to allow Blake's ships to pass. Blake then sent a remonstrance to the King of Portugal, according to the instructions he had received from the Council of State, that the ships to which the King of Portugal gave protection were a part of the English navy, which had revolted from the Parliament of England; that their commanders had acted as pirates and sea-robbers, and, by adding to their fleet the ships they captured, were growing into a power likely to prove dangerous to the lawful commerce of all civilised nations; that therefore they were unable to appeal to the law of nations, or ask the protection of any prince in their revolt and piracy, without thereby creating a cause of war between that prince and the Commonwealth of England.[1]

Blake's remonstrance, strong as it was, produced not more effect than any words, however strong, usually do; for the battle which the Parliament of England had now to maintain against the world was to be fought by other weapons than the arguments even of such a statesman as

[1] Rupert MS. in Warburton, iii. 135-137, London, 1852; new edition, 300, 301; Dixon's Robert Blake, pp. pp. 110-112, London, 1858.

Vane. In the meantime, the weather growing foul, Blake entered the river with his fleet, and anchored in Oeyras Bay; but weeks passed on, and he could obtain no satisfactory answer from the King of Portugal. During this time an incident occurred which exhibits two bad features that characterised the proceedings of the Royalist party— assassination and falsehood. An attempt to destroy Blake, not certainly in fair fight, was defended by the partisans of the German robber and pirate by a false statement, to the effect that some persons from the English fleet went on shore at Belleisle to attack a hunting-party, including Rupert, Maurice, and several other cavaliers; the fact being that the men were sent on shore, in the ordinary way, to obtain fresh water, and while getting it were assailed by Rupert's party, who killed one of them, wounded three others, and made five prisoners. Towards the evening of the same day, a bombshell placed in a double-headed barrel, with a lock in the middle so contrived that on being opened it would give fire to a quick-match and cause the whole to explode, was sent by Rupert to Blake's flag-ship in a Portuguese boat, manned by two negroes, and a sailor dressed as a Portuguese tradesman, who was instructed to say he was an oil-merchant come with a present for the seamen. When these men arrived with their boat at the ship's stern, they found the ports there closed; and while they were rowing round to the transom-port, some of the crew recognised the pretended Portuguese tradesman as one of Rupert's men, whom they had frequently met on shore at Belleisle; and he was immediately arrested, and this honourable Royalist device for getting rid of Blake discovered and baffled.[1]

Dixon's Robert Blake, p. 140; Thurloe, i. 145, 146.--In the "First Rupert MS. in Warburton, iii. 305; Paper of Demands, in the name of the

The time consumed in these proceedings against Rupert shows that the Parliament of England was not yet by any means strong enough at sea to encounter all their enemies; and the indefatigable exertions made by Sir Henry Vane and the Committee of the Admiralty to build new ships of war, as well as to furnish their present fleet [1] with all needful provisions and materials of war, form one of the most important features in the history of that which has been truly called " the Sheet-anchor of the British Empire," the British Navy.   If the navy of the Parliament of England had been as strong, or half as strong, at the beginning of Blake's career as it was at the end of it—when the great Admiral, "who would never strike to any other enemy, struck his topmast to Death," soon after his most brilliant victory, the action at Santa Cruz—Blake would have made very short work of such enemies as this King of Portugal and this German pirate; but the Parliament was entering on a new career in their naval wars, and it was natural enough that they should make some miscalculations in the adaptation of means to ends.   Accordingly Blake, even when strengthened by the arrival of Popham's squadron of eight ships, still only continued to demand permission to take vengeance for the outrages perpetrated by the German pirate, instead of proceeding (as he did afterwards in the case of the Barbary pirates) at once to destroy him

Parliament, made to the Public Minister of the King of Portugal," one article is, " That justice be done upon those that murdered our men in Portugal, being on shore, and upon those that attempted the burning of the Admiral's ships in the river."— *Order Book of the Council of State,* 10th Feb. 1651, MS. State Paper Office.

[1] " That the Committee of the Admiralty confer with Mr. Vane" [Mr. Charles Vane, the brother of Sir Henry Vane, who had been recalled from Portugal by a letter of the Council of State, 21st June 1650, MS. State Paper Office] " concerning the present condition of the fleet riding at the bar of Lisbon, to the end for the speedy supplying of them with such things as are needful."—*Ibid.* 3rd July 1650.

and his fleet. Instead of granting the permission demanded by Blake, the King of Portugal put some of the English merchants under arrest. Upon this Blake seized the whole of the Brazil fleet, of nine sail, coming out of the river. He also threatened to seize the American fleets on their return, if the revolters were not immediately compelled to quit the Tagus. A squadron of thirteen Portuguese men-of-war was then equipped, and ordered to join the force under Rupert. But it is remarkable that the veteran admirals of Portugal did not consider it prudent to attack the English fleet, commanded by a man who had never held a naval commission till about a year before, when he was fifty years of age ; and who, in spite of the approach of winter, continued to cruise at the river's mouth, where he attacked a Brazil fleet of twenty-three sail as it was about to enter the Tagus, sank the Portuguese flag-ship, destroyed three other ships, and captured the Vice-Admiral and eleven large ships laden with the most precious cargoes. The King of Portugal now began to perceive that his sympathy for the cause represented by Prince Rupert was too expensive. It was accordingly intimated to the German princes, that the Crown of Portugal could no longer protect them against the power of the Commonwealth of England. Rupert therefore, while Blake was at sea in search of the dispersed fleet of Brazil, dropped down the river, and got clear away with his ships.

The King of Portugal then despatched an envoy to London. The Council of State insisted upon the following conditions :—the immediate restoration of ships and goods seized; justice upon those that murdered our men in Portugal when on shore, and upon those that attempted the burning of the Admiral's ships in the river; repayment of the charges in fitting out the several fleets sent to Portugal, for reducing the revolted ships protected by the King of Portugal; restitution of, or reparation for, all English goods taken by Rupert or Maurice, or any of their ships, and brought into Portugal and disposed of there.[1] The Portuguese envoy, venturing to dispute some dates and details, was ordered to quit the country. The King of Portugal then sent a nobleman of high rank as his ambassador to the Parliament of England. But delays again arose, and it was not till January 1653 that the treaty of peace was concluded between England and Portugal.[2] Towards the end of 1652, the King of Portugal had agreed to pay £50,000 to the Commonwealth, as appears from the following minute of 24th December 1652: "That Sir Oliver Fleming and Mr. Thurloe do receive from the Portugal Ambassador the Bill or Bills of Exchange, which he shall give for the payment of £20,000 at Lisbon, part of the £50,000 which is to be paid in whole by the King of Portugal to this Commonwealth."[3]

Rupert with his pirate fleet, after leaving Lisbon, passed through the Straits of Gibraltar and entered the

[1] "First Paper of Demands, in the name of the Parliament, made to the Public Minister of the King of Portugal."—*Order Book of the Council of State*, 10th Feb. 165½, MS. State Paper Office.

[2] "At the close of the dispute with the Court of Lisbon, the owners of the nine ships seized and detained by Blake at the mouth of the Tagus were allowed to present a statement of their grievances to the Judges of the Court of Admiralty. Blake's conduct in the matter was minutely investigated; Admiral Popham was called on to give evidence as to the facts; and after a full enquiry, the Judges decided that the General-at-sea had acted in the spirit of his instructions. But they acknowledged the private losses which the owners might have suffered by the forcible detention of their ships, and decided that the same compensation should be awarded to them for the service, as in cases where ships had been hired by the State."—Dixon's *Robert Blake*, p. 146, cites *Judges MS. Reports*, March 24, State Paper Office.

[3] Order Book of the Council of State, Friday, December 24, 1652, MS. State Paper Office.

Mediterranean.   A manuscript memoir, found among
Rupert's papers, thus expresses the spirit that animated him
and his companions : " Misfortune being no novelty to us,
we plough the sea for a subsistence ; and being destitute of
a port, we take the confines of the Mediterranean Sea for our
harbour : poverty and despair being our companions, and
revenge our guide."   Coasting the shores of Andalusia,
they fell in with the Malaga fleet during a dark night,
and captured two ships.   Rupert then stood in for Malaga,
and sent forward one of his ships (the frigate *Henry*), with
instructions to take up a position between the vessels
lying outside the port and the mole, so that, when attacked
in the night, they might be prevented from retreating into
the harbour.   But the design was defeated by the desertion of some of the *Henry's* men, who informed the
Spaniards of the intended night-attack ; and a signal
from the batteries warning the ships of their danger, they
stood safely in while it was yet broad day.   Rupert, finding
his plan defeated, sailed for Velez-Malaga, higher up the
coast, where some English merchant-ships were lying.
The Governor of Velez-Malaga, on hearing of the appearance of Rupert on the coast, had despatched a courier to
Madrid for instructions ; but, on the ground that this
messenger had not returned when Rupert arrived, he refused
to interfere, and six English ships were fired and burnt
by Rupert under the guns of the Spanish batteries.

Spain was now destined to learn that a change had
come over the scene, since that dark time in England's
annals when her minister Gondemar had declared that
" there were no men in England."   Blake was waiting the
arrival of a supply of stores sent by the Council of State,
when the news reached him of this act of hostility committed in a friendly port.   He at once turned his bows

towards the entrance of the Mediterranean, and passed the
Straits with all his fleet[1]—the first English Admiral who
had sailed in those seas since the time of the Crusades.
When he reached Malaga, he found that Rupert had left
that part of the coast.   At Capo Palos, near Carthagena,
the revolted ships had last been seen in a tremendous
squall, when Rupert and his brother separated from the
rest, and ran out to sea.   The other revolted ships ran
into Carthagena for shelter ; and when the weather cleared,
the English fleet was seen riding before the harbour.
Blake sent a messenger to inform the governor of the
town that enemies to the Commonwealth of England had
taken refuge in that port; that he, as Admiral, carried
instructions from the English Council of State to pursue
and destroy them; and that, the two nations being then at
peace, he hoped to be allowed to execute his orders without
interference.   The Spaniard sent an answer, which was
tantamount to a refusal to recognise the Parliament as
the supreme power in England.   Besides this, Anthony
Ascham, the minister sent by the English Parliament to
the Court of Spain, had been basely assassinated not long
before at Madrid, by some of the servants of Hyde and
Cottington, as Dorislaus had been assassinated in Holland
by some servants of Montrose ; and the Spanish Government
had, like the Dutch, taken no effective steps to punish the
assassins.   Blake therefore lost no more time in messages
to the Spanish governor, but, attacking the revolters,
boarded the *Roebuck*, set fire to another ship, and drove
the remainder on shore.   Their guns, stores, and ammunition were saved, and delivered up by the Spaniards to the

---

[1] This was in 1650. Hume, in relating Blake's entrance into the Mediterranean in 1654, says : "No English
fleet, except during the Crusades, had
ever before sailed in those seas."

Admiral's agent.[1]   The whole of the revolted fleet were now captured or destroyed, with the exception of the *Reformation* and the *Swallow*, the two ships in which Rupert and Maurice sailed, and the *Marmaduke*, a ship they had recently captured.

The cotemporary correspondence, as given by Whitelock, furnishes characteristic sketches both of Rupert and Blake: "December 20, 1650.—Letters that Prince Rupert came to Malaga and other ports, and fired and sank divers English merchant-ships, and demanded the master of a London ship, saying that he would boil him in pitch; but the Governor of Malaga refused to deliver up the master to him."[2]   But the avenger of blood was behind him, for the next entry in Whitelock is this: " December 21.—Letters that Blake fell upon Prince Rupert in Malaga Road,[3] sank two or three of his ships, ran on shore and exposed to shipwreck the rest of his fleet; only two ships escaped, wherein it is conceived Prince Rupert and his brother Prince Maurice were, and Blake in chase of them."[4]

There is something strange in Rupert's luck in escaping from Cromwell on land, and from Blake at sea. How came it that Rupert always managed to get away unscathed—at Marston Moor, at Naseby, and elsewhere, where so many valiant Royalists went down before the Parliamentary cuirassiers and pikemen—and that now his and his brother's ships alone escaped?   Rupert was a " tall black man," strong of body, and cruel and fierce of

---

[1] Dixon's Robert Blake, pp. 155–161; Rupert MS. in Warburton, iii. 313–318.

[2] Whitelock's Memorials, p. 485.

[3] There is a minute of the Council of State of Friday, 13th December 1650, "That the letter from Colonel Blake of the 30th of October 1650, dated from aboard the *Leopard* in Malaga Road, be reported to the Parliament."—*Order Book of the Council of State*, Friday, 13th December 1650, MS. State Paper Office.

[4] Whitelock's Memorials, p. 485.

heart. His bodily strength and, perhaps, superior horse-manship may have enabled him to escape on land, without making the supposition that he managed to get the credit of being a dashing cavalry officer without much exposing his own person. But that explanation will not extend to a naval fight: and the two ships, in which he and his brother were, must have escaped by being less exposed to the enemy's fire than the rest of the fleet. Rupert by this time knew Blake too well to wait for his onset. Blake's height of 5 feet 6 inches, though too short for a Merton fellowship, was far more than a match for the 6 feet odd of the "fiery Rupert," as his admirers love to call him. To fight Blake was a very different thing from cutting off a defenceless man's ears, or boiling him in pitch.

It is incorrect to infer from a man's good horsemanship that he is a man of courage. Good horsemanship depends on the conformation and disposition of the muscles. In some persons what is called the riding muscle (the muscle on the inside of the thigh) is not only undeveloped, but incapable of strong development; while the muscle on the outside of the thigh, on which walking depends, is well developed. To call a man who rides well "a dauntless rider" looks like brag ; though it may be quite true that the man is a fearless rider. But the "fearlessness" is only the confidence arising from the feeling that the muscular power gives a security unattended with risk; and is a totally dif-ferent thing from the fearlessness which faces death, where no strength of muscle can be of any avail. A man who exposes himself to a shower of shot, as Blake constantly did, shows courage. A man who, trusting to his thews and sinews, and the power they give him of managing his horse, attacks men of far less muscular force, and worse-

mounted than himself, merely shows the confidence a
strong animal has in his strength.   This latter quality
was the sort of courage possessed by Prince Rupert—very
different from the sort of courage evinced by Blake, and
also from the sort of courage evinced by Harrison and by
Cromwell.   The courage of Harrison, indeed, was of that
fiery and enthusiastic nature, which made him have
sowmehat the relation to Cromwell that Murat bore to
Bonaparte.   Harrison's fate, too, bears some resemblance
to that of Murat; so that it may be said of Harrison, as
it has been said of Murat :

> Was that haughty crest laid low,
> By a slave's dishonest blow?
> Little didst thou deem, when dashing
>   On thy war-horse through the ranks,
>   Like a stream which burst its banks,
> While helmets cleft and sabres clashing,
> Shone and shiver'd fast around thee,
> Of the fate at last which found thee.

Indeed, if ever man in his warlike enthusiasm resembled
the war-horse in Job, it was Harrison.   "He mocketh at
fear, and is not affrighted; neither turneth he back from
the sword.   He saith among the trumpets, Ha! ha! and
he smelleth the battle afar off, the thunder of the captains,
and the shouting."   The very first time that Rupert
came into conflict with Cromwell and Harrison, namely at
Marston Moor, he was defeated in less than half an hour;
and he and his Life-Guards, the picked men of the Royalist
cavalry, were driven off the field in irretrievable confusion
and headlong flight.

On the 2nd of November, 1650, the Council of State wrote
a letter to Blake, informing him that they had ordered
Captain William Penn (afterwards Admiral Sir William
Penn), " with as many ships as could be fitted out, to sail

southward, both for the prevention of Rupert, as much as he is able with this strength, from doing further mischief on the good people of this nation; and for the surprisal or destruction of as many of the Portugal's fleet as he can make attempt on, in their return homeward from Brazil." In this letter the Council also say: "We desire that you, with the rest of the fleet, will repair home with all the speed conveniently you may; that we may, upon conference with you, the better understand the state of affairs in those parts where you are and have been; and also may give timely orders for fitting out those ships with you, against the next spring, if there should be occasion for their service."[1]   On the 25th of the same month, Penn received a commission to command the *Fairfax*, a new frigate of 50 guns lately built at Deptford, and also another commission, to command-in-chief a squadron of eight ships for the service specified above.

Penn sailed on the 30th of November from Spithead, in the *Centurion*.   On the 17th of January 165$\frac{0}{1}$, he made the island of St. Michael, in the Azores, where, on the 22nd, he was joined by Lawson, who brought him out the *Fairfax*. After cruising for some weeks between the Western Islands, the Rock of Lisbon, and Cadiz, Penn entered the Mediterranean, with his whole fleet, on the 29th of March. Penn's Journal from the time of his setting sail from Spithead, on the 30th of January 165$\frac{0}{1}$, to the time of his return to England, in March 165$\frac{1}{2}$, has been published by Mr. Granville Penn from the papers in the possession of his family.   On the 18th of March there is this entry: "I went to Pendennis Castle; having not put foot on land since my departure from this place outward-bound, which

[1] The Council of State to General Blake, Thurloe's State Papers, vol. ii. p. 93.

was in last December was twelve months." [1]   And on the
1st of April there is this entry: "About 4 afternoon,
we anchored in the Downs, (praised be the name of our
Heavenly Father!) where I met with the Right Hon.
General Robert Blake." [2]   His pursuit of Rupert, however,
was unsuccessful.   There is an entry in Penn's Journal,
which mentions the foundering at sea of two of Rupert's
three ships: "26th November, 1651.—I received a letter
from Mr. Hill at Cadiz, in which he informs me that the *Reformation* and the *Revenge*, formerly called the *Marmaduke*,
were sunk between the islands St. Michael and Terceira;
of which ships' companies none were saved but Prince
Rupert and nine more, in the *Reformation's* pinnace." [3]
It would seem from this that Prince Rupert considered
it the duty of a commander to be not the last but the
first to save himself when his ship was sinking.   This is
in accordance with a character that has come down from
those times linked, if not with one virtue, with many
crimes.   He and his brother, after pursuing their piracies
for some time in the West Indies, parted company in a
storm.   Maurice was never heard of again; but Rupert
lived to enjoy the spectacle of the ignoble revenge executed, by command of his royal cousin, on the remains of
his conquerors; and of the great nation, which Blake
had raised to the height of power and glory, reduced to
the lowest depth of discomfiture and disgrace.

On the 11th of January, 165$\frac{9}{1}$, the Council of State
ordered "that Mr. Frost do prepare a letter of thanks to
be sent to Colonel Blake, in pursuance of an Order of

[1] Granville Penn's Memorials of Sir
William Penn, vol. i. p. 393.

[2] *Ibid.* p. 394.
[3] *Ibid.* p. 387.

Parliament, for the good services done by him against Prince Rupert." [1]

I have already mentioned the seizure of many English merchant-ships by French privateers, and the issuing by the English Admiralty of letters of marque or reprisals to the English merchants. Hitherto the English admirals had avoided attacking French ships. But the revolters having been protected by the French authorities at Toulon, Blake, on his voyage homeward, captured four French prizes. One of these was a frigate of 40 guns, respecting the capture of which the following story is told. Blake signalled for the captain of the French frigate to come on board his flag-ship, which the Frenchman did. The Admiral told him he was a prisoner, and asked him to give up his sword. The Frenchman refused; upon which Blake told him he might go back to his ship, and fight it out as long as he was able. The French captain thanked him, returned to his ship; and, after two hours' hard fighting, struck his flag, and being brought again on board Blake's ship, made a low bow, kissed his sword, and delivered it to Blake. A somewhat similar story is told of Monk, whose character, except in courage, bore little resemblance to Blake's. In one of his campaigns in Scotland, Monk having arrived one day at the house of a certain Scotch laird, found it fit for the reception of a small garrison. But the laird refused to grant Monk's request to that effect. "Well," said Monk, "I will not violate hospitality," and he immediately commanded the officers who accompanied him to evacuate the house. "Now," said he to the laird, "look to the defence, for we are about to attack." The laird, however, though

---

[1] Order Book of the Council of State, 11th Jan. 165$\frac{0}{1}$. MS. State Paper Office.

surrounded by a great number of his friends and relations, thought it wise to make terms, and consented to receive a garrison, on condition that a portion of his house should be set apart for his own use.

Though the Parliament of England had now got rid of the two German pirates, Rupert and Maurice, they had still upon their hands the work of ridding themselves of a strong force of English pirates, who from the Scilly Isles and Jersey infested the English Channel. Rupert, at the commencement of his piratical career, had fixed on that .... remarkable group of small rocky islets lying off the Land's End in Cornwall, known as the Scilly Isles,[1] as a convenient situation for the establishment of one or more strongholds for the reception of his plunder. Nature and art seemed to have combined to adapt these islands for such a purpose. Intricate channels with dangerous sunken rocks, and the frequent occurrence of the most sudden and violent storms, were the obstacles opposed by nature to the approach of hostile ships; and the art of man had erected block-houses and batteries, connected with each other by lines and breastworks, at those places where a landing seemed most likely to be attempted. It has been observed, by those who have kept journals, that not more than six days of perfect calm occur in the course of the year. This violent and almost constant action of the sea renders the opinion not improbable, that these islands have, at some period antecedent to authentic history, been separated from the mainland. From the same cause the islands, though for the most part composed of granite,[2] are undergoing a gradual

[1] In the "Order Book of the Council of State" they are described as "the islands of Scillyes or Sorlings, anciently a part of the territories belonging to the Commonwealth of England."— Instructions for the Ambassadors with the States-General of the United Provinces, *Order Book of the Council of State*, 2nd April 1651, MS. State Paper Office.

[2] A Guide to Mount's Bay and the Land's End, by a Physician (Dr. Paris):

diminution. At present there are more than 140 islands, of which six are inhabited, containing altogether a population of about 2,500. The area of the islands varies from St. Mary's, the largest, about 1,500 acres, to less than one acre. The islands form a compact group, rising for the most part abruptly, with rugged sides, from the deep sea around them. In the channels which separate the islands the depth of the sea is much less; some of these channels being dry at low water, and others only kneedeep. The employments of the inhabitants of the Scilly Isles are agriculture, fishing, making kelp, and pilotage.[1]

St. Mary's, the most important island, consists of two portions; the smaller of which, called "The Hugh," is joined to the other part by a low sandy isthmus, on which stands "Hugh Town," the principal place in the island. This island is about 2½ miles long, 1½ mile broad, and about 8 miles in circumference. The Hugh is a steep hill rising about 110 feet above the level of the sea, and was then fortified by lines, having a circuit of more than a mile, with 18 bastions or batteries, and enclosing a small fort called Star Castle. Tresco, the island next in importance, is inhabited chiefly by pilots and fishermen. Most of the houses are on the north-east side, near the beach, opposite a harbour called Old Grinsey Harbour; and form a village called Dolphin Town, which may perhaps be an abbreviation of Godolphin Town, the Godolphin family having been long the lessees of the islands. A stone tower, called Oliver Cromwell's Castle, now deserted, commands the harbour of New Grinsey, on the west side of the island; and near it are the ruins of a fortress, called King Charles's

London, 1824.—The granite is, according to Dr. Paris, a continuation of the Devonian range.

[1] A View of the Present State of the Scilly Islands; by the Rev. George Woodley, London, 1822.

Castle. St. Martin's, nearly 2 miles long and about 6 miles in circumference, is chiefly inhabited by pilots and fishermen. About the middle of the 17th century, this island was uninhabited, but there are indications of its having been peopled at an earlier period. St. Agnes is a mile in length, half a mile in breadth, on an average, and 4½ miles in circumference. St. Agnes is very irregular in outline, and is surrounded by rocks. Though the soil is the most fertile, and now the best cultivated, in the whole group, the shore is rocky and almost inaccessible, which may be the cause of its having apparently at that. time been considered the most important of the islands after St. Mary's.

In these islands 2,000 men were placed as a garrison, and with them was a considerable number of Royalist gentry, all under the command of Sir John Grenville, designated " Governor of the Islands of St. Mary's and St. Agnes, in Scilly, on the behalf of His Majesty."[1] Before Blake drove him into Kinsale, Rupert had carried the plunder he got by piracy into these islands; and, in a letter to Sir John Grenville, in April 1649, he says he " doubts not ere long to see Scilly a second Venice."[1] This shows that Rupert, if neither a great commander nor a great statesman, possessed at least a bold imagination. In March 1649 he sent to Sir John Grenville, from Ireland, some ships laden with corn, salt, iron, and steel. And in April, in the letter to Grenville quoted above, he says: " You will receive, if these ships come safe, such provisions as we can spare here, and also some men, which I was fain to send out of my own regiment. ' They are all

[1] In the Articles of Surrender, of 23rd May 1651, cited by Mr. Dixon (*Life of Robert Blake*, p. 169, note), between Admiral Blake and Sir John Grenville, the latter is styled " Governor of the Islands of St. Mary's and St. Agnes, in Scilly, on the behalf of His Majesty."

armed, and have some to spare. The officers have formerly served his Majesty. You may trust them. I doubt not ere long to see Scilly a second Venice. It will be for our security and benefit; for if the worst come to the worst, it is but going to Scilly with this fleet, where, after a little while, we may get the King a good subsistence; and, I believe, we shall make a shift to live in spite of all factions." [1] It is observable, however, that between April 1649 and the end of 1650, Rupert had altered his opinion about the Scilly Isles as a place of security and benefit; for, after his utter discomfiture by Blake, he did not return thither, but sailed for the West Indies.

But, though Rupert did not join them again, the Royalist pirates in the Scilly Isles became so active as to call for the particular attention of the Council of State in the beginning of the year 1651. In February of that year we meet with notices, in the "Order Book of the Council of State," of "losses by pirates upon the west coast." [2] On the 26th of March following the Council of State ordered a letter to be written to Major-General Desborowe, to let him know " that the Council is informed that Sir John Greenvill, Governor of Scillie, doth, contrary to the law of arms, detain and keep in strict imprisonment divers persons who are merchantmen and traders; to desire him to seize the persons of the relations of the said Sir John Greenvill in Cornwall, and to keep them in safe custody until he shall dismiss the said merchantmen, now prisoners with him; and he is to give notice thereof to Sir John Greenvill before his doing of it, and to expect [wait for] his answer; and upon his writing back, to certify to the Council what effect it hath had with him, and to desert therein [to do

---

[1] Fitzroy MS. in Warburton, vol. iii. pp. 289-295. [2] Order Book of the Council of State, 18th Feb. 165$\frac{0}{1}$, MS. State Paper Office.

nothing further therein] till further order from the Council." [1]

On the 31st of March 1651 leave is given by the Council of State, to certain petitioners, to buy their ship, taken by two Jersey men-of-war [2]—that is, by two Royalist pirate-ships having their stronghold in the isle of Jersey, as others had in the Scilly Isles. But on the 18th of the same month the Council of State ordered, "That it be returned in answer to the petition of George Dickens, that this Council cannot treat with Rupert for any exchanges, but the Council will be ready to grant letters of reprisal." [3]

On the 1st of April 1651, the Council of State ordered, "That a letter be written to Colonel Blake, to inclose him a copy of the Order of Parliament, to let him know that the Parliament is informed that Van Tromp [sic] is before Scilly, and hath refused to give an account of his being there to some of the Commonwealth ships that have demanded an account of him; to desire him therefore to repair thither with the ships bound for the Barbadoes, and likewise with the three ships under his command appointed for the Irish Seas; [4] and demand of him the cause of his being there, and not to depart from thence until he hath received such an answer as may be for the honour and interest of the Commonwealth; and he is to give such orders for the guard of the Irish coast as he shall think fit, during the time he shall be detained in this service." [5]

---

[1] Order Book of the Council of State, 26th March 1651, MS. State Paper Office.

[2] Ibid. 31st March 1651.

[3] Ibid. 18th March 165$\frac{0}{1}$.

[4] On the 15th of March 165$\frac{0}{1}$ an order had been made by the Council of State, "That Colonel Blake command the squadron designed for the Irish Seas."—Ibid. 15th March 165$\frac{0}{1}$. On the 13th of February last £1,000 had been ordered to Colonel Blake by the Parliament. (Ibid.) The warrant for payment of this sum is dated 18th March 165$\frac{0}{1}$.

[5] Ibid. 1st April, 1651.

On the same day it was ordered, " That a letter be written to Sir George Ayscue, that the force appointed to go with Colonel Blake to Van Tromp must be made up with the ships under his command." [1]

The complication produced by the piratical proceedings of Rupert is shown by the instructions given by the Council of State to Blake on this occasion. For while Blake is directed, by these instructions, to require Tromp to desist from any attempt prejudicial to the honour or interest of the Commonwealth of England, he is " to signify to the said Van Tromp, that by requiring him to desist it is not the intention of this Commonwealth to protect those who are now in possession of Scilly in the wrongs they have done the Dutch, or to hinder them from righting themselves upon them, so as they act nothing to the prejudice of the honour or interest of this Commonwealth, but shall be ready to give them all assistance therein, and expect the like from them in what you are there to execute." [2]

A satisfactory account of Tromp's fleet having been received from the States-General of Holland, Blake proceeded with his fleet against the Scilly Islands. Having summoned the Governor, Sir John Grenville, to surrender the islands to the Parliament of England, and not receiving a satisfactory answer, he ordered 800 men, under the command of Captain Morris, to land in Tresco, the island, as we have seen, next in importance to St. Mary's. A garrison of nearly a thousand men were posted behind a line of breastworks to oppose them. But Blake's troops threw themselves into the water, waded on shore, and, as soon as they were formed, attacked the entrenchments. The

[1] Order Book of the Council of State, 1st April 1651, MS. State Paper Office.

[2] Instructions for Colonel Robert Blake.—*Ibid*.

Royalists made a stout resistance, but when night came on
they withdrew to their boats, and passed over to St. Mary's.
At daybreak Blake erected a battery on Tresco, so placed
as to command the roadstead of St. Mary's; but seeing that
his battery produced little effect on the castle and fortifi-
cations, he brought his frigates through the intricate and
dangerous channels, and planted them in the roadstead
under the castle guns—a feat which has been achieved so
often since, that, as Mr. Dixon justly observes, " it is not
easy now to estimate the daring which it then implied.
Up to that day it had been considered a fundamental
maxim in marine warfare, that a ship could not attack a
castle or other strong fortification with any hope of success.
Blake was the first to perceive and demonstrate the fallacy
of this maxim; and the experiment, afterwards repeated
by him in the more brilliant attacks on Porto Farino and
Santa Cruz, was first tried at the siege of St. Mary's." [1]
Notwithstanding a furious cannonade from the castle, the
guns of the frigates having made a practicable breach,
Blake ordered an assault to be made.   But Grenville then
sent to beg a parley, which ended in an engagement on
his part to surrender the islands, with their garrisons,
stores, arms, ammunition, standards, and all other imple-
ments and materials of war, on condition that the lives of
the officers, soldiers, and volunteers should be spared.   The
soldiers and sailors were allowed to enter the Parliament's
service.   Sir John Grenville and the Royalist gentlemen
taken with him were put on board Sir George Ayscue's
squadron, and carried into Plymouth Sound.   The Parliament, acting in the lenient spirit of Blake's articles, permitted Grenville to enjoy his forfeited family estates without

---

[1] Dixon's Robert Blake, p. 168; and p. 138 of the new edition.

molestation.[1] Under date 9th August 1651, there is the following entry in the rough draft of the Order Book of the Council of State—" Mem. : Colonel Blake to leave two ships about Scilly."

There is a minute of the Council of State of the 22nd March of this year, relating to a ship taken by Sir George Ayscue, which I will transcribe, as throwing light on the nature and effect of the Government of England at that time : "That a letter be written to Sir George Ayscue, to let him know that the Council, since the receipt of his letter, have had notice that there is more money in the ship *Lemmon* than is expressed in his letter; to desire him to make an effectual search in the ship, and to compare the bills of exchange with the inventory taken of the goods, and to give an account to the Council."[2] The tact of the statesmen who formed the Council of State is manifest in the careful wording of this minute, which, it will be observed, does not contain the slightest insinuation of any intention (which it may be hoped did not exist) on the part of Sir George Ayscue to appropriate to himself a part of the money referred to without the knowledge of the Council, but yet adopts an effectual course for securing an exact account of the money.   One decided advantage of a Government like this Council of State, was its capability of appreciating the pure honesty and honour of a man like Blake, who would have received no credit, but on the contrary discredit, for his honesty from any of the Stuarts; would have been set down as an "impracticable fool" (that is the favourite phrase), not only by the Government of Charles I. and Charles II., but by many a Government since. This result was, I apprehend, produced, in part

---

[1] Dixon's Robert Blake, pp. 166–169, and the authorities there cited.

[2] Order Book of the Council of State, March 22, 165$\frac{0}{1}$, MS. State Paper Office.

at least, by the large number of persons composing the
Council of State.   For though that Council, like other
Councils, doubtless contained several unscrupulous men, it
also had its own public opinion, which would be in favour
of such a man as Blake; whereas if a man cheated or
robbed the public, and gave half of his plunder to the
Stuart, the Stuart approved of the proceeding.[1]   But such
a proceeding was difficult or impracticable with a Council
of State consisting of 41 members, of whom as many as
38 (as appears by the MS. minutes) were sometimes
present together.

[1] The Lord Cottington, Chancellor
of the Exchequer, to the Lord Deputy
of Ireland, January 27, 1635 : "When
William Raylton first told me of your
Lordship's intention touching Mount-
norris's place for Sir Adam Loftus, and
the *distribution of monies for the
effecting thereof*, I fell upon the right
way, which was *to give the money to
him that really could do the business*,
which was the King himself; and this
hath so far prevailed, as by this post
your Lordship will receive His Majesty's letter to that effect; so as there
you have your business *done without
noise* : and now it rests that the *money
be speedily paid*, and made over hither
with all expedition."—*Strafford's Letters and Despatches*, vol. i. p. 511.

CHAPTER IX.

THE fate of Dorislaus and of Ascham showed that the post of ambassador from the English Parliament to foreign Powers was a post of more danger than honour. For a death like that of Dorislaus and Ascham was worse than a soldier's death on the field of battle, and was unattended by the circumstances that to a victorious soldier may take from death all its bitterness. Notwithstanding, however, the sad fate of Dorislaus, the Parliament of England resolved to send another envoy to the States of Holland; for, as has been said, they were desirous not only of friendly relations but of close alliance with the Dutch Republic, which in its form of government they considered as bearing a close resemblance to that form of government which they had established in England, and according to which they had styled themselves "The Parliament of the Commonwealth of England." They had accordingly appointed Walter Strickland, one of their members, as their agent to the United Provinces.

On the 21st of June 1650, the Council of State had recalled Walter Strickland, by the following order, which explains the reason of his recall : " That a letter be written to Mr. Strickland, to recall him from his residence with the States-General, the State being very sensible of the slight put upon them by not receiving of him."[1]

---

[1] Order Book of the Council of State, June 21, 1650, MS. State Paper Office.

The Council of State did not, however, yet give up the hope of peace instead of war with the Dutch; and they resolved to make another attempt, and to send this time two ambassadors, instead of one agent or envoy. Accordingly, on the 22nd of January 1650, they made the following orders: "That such persons as shall be sent from this Commonwealth to the present Assembly of the United Provinces be sent in the quality of Ambassadors. That the number of persons who are to go as Ambassadors shall be two—Walter Strickland, Esquire, and the Lord Chief Justice St. John."[1] St. John presented a petition to the House, praying to be excused from this embassy. But, upon a division, it was resolved, by 42 against 29, that he should go.[2]

The opinion of the Council of State as to the importance of the mission may be inferred from the fact of their appointing Lord Chief Justice St. John one of the ambassadors.   John Thurloe, whose patron through life St. John had been—and who soon after, on the death of Walter Frost the elder, became Secretary of the Council of State, and subsequently the secretary of Cromwell—accompanied St. John and Strickland as their secretary.

Oliver St. John, a barrister of Lincoln's Inn, had argued the case of ship-money in the Exchequer Chamber as one of Hampden's counsel. This would naturally bring him into frequent communication with Hampden.   With Cromwell he was connected by family ties (having married a cousin of Cromwell) as well as by political and religious opinions.[3] It is not improbable that St. John was indebted

---

[1] Order Book of the Council of State, Jan. 22, 165⁹⁄₀, MS. State Paper Office.

[2] Parl. Hist. vol. iii. p. 1362.

[3] The admission of Richard Cromwell to Lincoln's Inn bears, after the names of the sureties, " Ri. Graves, John Thurloe," the words "Admissus pr. Ol. St. John."—*Admission Book of Lincoln's Inn.*

for his introduction to professional business to the
powerful interest of the Earl of Bedford, whose great
landed possessions would give him much influence with
attorneys, and " to whom," says Clarendon, " St. John was
allied (being a natural son of the House of Bolingbroke),
and by him brought into all matters where himself was to
be concerned." [1]   St. John, like Hampden and Cromwell,
was a man whose power in the Parliament was not to be
measured by his power as a Parliamentary speaker. At
the first opening of the Long Parliament, Pym appeared
to be far the most powerful man in the House of Commons:
but he was, observes Clarendon, " much governed in private
designing by Mr. Hampden and Mr. St. John." [1] Clarendon
describes St. John as " a man reserved, and of a dark
and clouded countenance; very proud, and conversing
with very few, and those men of his own humour and
inclinations." [3]

To St. John, as Solicitor-General, had fallen the duty
of carrying up to the Lords the Bill of Attainder against
the Earl of Strafford, and there is one passage in
particular, in his speech on that occasion which has been
often quoted and much criticised : " My Lords," he said,
" he that would not have had others to have a law, why
should he have any himself? Why should not that be
done to him that himself would have done to others?
It is true we give law to hares and deer, because they be
beasts of chase : it was never accounted either cruelty or
foul play to knock foxes and wolves on the head as they
can be found, because these be beasts of prey. The
warrener sets traps for polecats and other vermin, for
preservation of the warren." [4]

---

[1] Clarendon's Hist. vol. i. pp. 324, 325.
[2] Ibid. vol. iv. p. 437.
[3] Ibid. vol. i. p. 243.
[4] Rushworth, vol. viii. p. 713.

Notwithstanding the censure which has been bestowed on this argument of St. John, while the argument of Pym has escaped such censure, it will be observed that St. John really argues the case as a statesman, and Pym as an orator, but neither as a statesman nor a lawyer. As all the laws against treason in England had down to that time been made to protect the King and not the subject,[1] it was not to be expected that the English law of treason should contain any power to punish an aggressor who strove, as Strafford unquestionably had done, to make the English king absolute and Englishmen slaves. Consequently, when Pym says that " nothing can be more equal than that he should perish by the justice of that law, which he would have subverted ; " that " there are marks enough to trace this law to the very original of this kingdom ;" and that " if it hath not been put in execution for 240 years, it was not for want of law," [2] he speaks rhetorically, and assumes the existence of a law which did not exist : whereas St. John put the case upon its true basis—

---

[1] Hobbes—who, though the slave of fear, was not, like most men, the slave of words—saw this with his usual clearness. " And for those men," he says, "who had skill in the laws, it was no great sign of understanding, not to perceive that the laws of the land were made by the King to oblige his subjects to peace and justice, *and not to oblige himself that made them.*"—*Behemoth*, part iii. pp. 254, 255, London, 1862. The constitutional timidity of Hobbes, which in his Latin autobiography he at once admits and accounts for—he was born April 5, 1588,

Atque metum tantum concepit tunc
  mea mater,
Ut pareret geminos, meque metumque
  simul,—

explains much of his aversion to all resistance to constituted authority. His timidity made him shrink from and even abhor the very idea of resistance ; for resistance implied war, and in Hobbes's mind war implied all that was most detestable—" no arts, no letters, no society, and, which is worst of all, continual fear and danger of violent death."—*Leviathan*, part i. c. 13. But with all Hobbes's intellectual power, this defect in his organisation would have reduced his countrymen to the condition of Hindus. Luckily, England produced in that age organisations very different from his.

[2] Rushworth, vol. viii. pp. 669, 670.

that he whose proved purpose had been to reduce Englishmen to the condition of serfs, who should have no law but the will of an absolute king, should be destroyed as a public enemy, or a dangerous and noxious beast of prey.

It will be perceived, then, that when the Council of State of " The Parliament of the Commonwealth of England " of 1651 resolved to send Oliver St. John as their ambassador to the States of the Netherlands, they made a very different selection from that made by Queen Elizabeth (who has obtained much credit for her choice of ministers at home and abroad), when, in 1588, she despatched as her envoys to the Netherlands two doctors of law—" very slow old gentlemen," one of whom valued himself above all things upon his Latinity, and the other was " a formalist and a pedant, full of precedents and declamatory commonplaces which he mistook for eloquence," [1]—to be duped and laughed at by Alexander Farnese. " A very slow old gentleman, this Doctor Dale," wrote Parma to Philip II. ; " he was here in the time of Madam my mother, and has also been ambassador at Vienna." [2] " If Valentine Dale," says Mr. Motley, " were a slow old gentleman, he was keen, caustic, and rapid as compared to Daniel Rogers," [3] the other egregious doctor selected for that difficult work by the wisdom of Elizabeth. It is enough to read the account, so ably given by Mr. Motley, of the conferences between those men and Farnese, to enable us to see the full force of Blake's remark about preventing " foreigners from fooling us."

Whatever else might turn up out of the mission to their High Mightinesses the States of the Netherlands of Oliver St. John, it may be pretty safely concluded that that dark

---

[1] Motley's History of the United Netherlands, vol. ii. pp. 373–375.

[2] *Ibid.* p. 373.

[3] *Ibid.* p 374.

and subtle spirit—the familiar (though how far the confidant we know not, and can never know) of a darker, a more powerful, and more subtle spirit—would not be "fooled" by them, as Queen Elizabeth's envoys had been fooled by Alexander Farnese.

To prevent such another outrage as had been perpetrated upon the unfortunate Dorislaus, forty gentlemen were appointed to attend the ambassadors St. John and Strickland, at once for their security and honour; "ten thousand pounds," adds Ludlow, "being delivered to the Lord Ambassadors' steward, for the expense of the embassy."[1] In the sum here mentioned Ludlow, however, is in error, as appears from the following minute of the Council of State, under date 30th January 165$\frac{9}{1}$:—"That £3,000, besides the £1,000 already paid, be furnished to the ambassadors to Holland."[2]

But though the forty gentlemen appointed as a guard to the ambassadors of the English Commonwealth proved sufficient to protect them from actual assassination—which was still the grand weapon of the successors in Europe, in the 17th century, of those who, in the 16th century, had assassinated De Coligny and William the Silent, making Louisa de Coligny an orphan and twice a widow—they were not sufficient to protect them from repeated affronts and insults, and from repeated attempts at assassination, by the Royalists. Thus, Mr. Strickland's coachman and another of his servants were attacked by six cavaliers at their master's own door; the former of whom received a cut upon his head, and the latter lost his sword in the fray.

[1] Ludlow's Memoirs, vol. i. p. 344, 2nd edition, London, 1721.

[2] Order Book of the Council of State, Jan. 30, 165$\frac{9}{1}$, MS. State Paper Office.

The threats of the Royalists ran so high that the Ambassadors' domestics were obliged to keep constant watch by turn. A design was formed to assassinate Lord Chief Justice St. John, and an attempt was made to break into his chamber. Prince Edward, one of the Queen of Bohemia's sons, and a brother of the pirates Rupert and Maurice, walking in the Park at the Hague with his sister, and meeting the ambassadors in their coach, called out to them, " O you rogues, you dogs ! " with many other similar expressions. There is another story of a sort of rencounter in the Park at the Hague, between the Duke of York and Chief Justice St. John, told by a French writer, who gives it on the authority of a gentleman resident in Holland, when the affair happened. St. John, taking a walk in the Park at the Hague, met the Duke of York, also walking, and was grossly insulted by him—so grossly that, says the writer who relates the story, " in all probability, the dispute would not have ended without bloodshed, had not the company upon the walk interfered and parted them."[1]

And truly the dispute did not end without bloodshed. It might seem a small matter to a weak-minded and petulant boy (the Duke of York was at this time about 18), who, when he attained all the manhood he ever had, was only remarkable for the hardness of his heart and the softness of his brains,[2] to insult the Ambassador of the Government which was to make England famous and terrible over the world ; but for the insults of such repre-

[1] Parl. Hist. vol. iii. p. 164, and the authorities there cited.

[2] According to Horace Walpole (*Reminiscences*), Catherine Sedley, one of James the Second's mistresses whom he made Countess of Dorchester and Baroness of Darlington, was accustomed to wonder what James chose his mistresses for. "We were none of us handsome," said she; "and if we had wit, he had not wit enough to find it out."

sentatives of the divinity of kingship, the Dutch were to
pay very dearly.

There can be little doubt that the Dutch Government
could have prevented all this, if they had been fully resolved to do so.   For William II. of Nassau, Prince of
Orange, who had married Mary, daughter of Charles I., King
of England, had died just before this time; and his post-
humous son, born in 1650, William III. of Nassau, Prince
of Orange, and ultimately King of England, was then a
helpless infant, whose youth was destined to suffer, from
the jealousy and hostility caused by his father's infringe-
ment of the constitutional rights of the States of the
Netherlands.   It could not therefore be said that the
Dutch Government was at that time in the hands of a son-
in-law of Charles I., who might be expected to look with
no friendly eye upon a Government formed of the men who
had brought his father-in-law to the block.   But the
Dutch Government, though at that time calling itself a
republic, was a republic with a very narrow basis.   The
election of the magistrates or councillors of the cities, who
with the nobles formed the Provincial States, the deputies
chosen by which formed the States-General, had been
originally in the burghers at large.   But during the confusion of the great struggle against Philip II. of Spain, it
was found convenient to invest the magistrates with the
power of filling up vacancies in their own number.   This
irregularity continued when the necessity for it had ceased,
and the consequence was that the Government, though in
form a republic, was a narrow oligarchy; and probably did
not feel itself attracted towards the Government calling
itself the Commonwealth of England, either by admiration of the constitution of the English Government, or by
approbation of its proceedings.   The Dutch Government,

moreover, had passed from the condition in which a Government is content with defensive strength, to that in which its strength is apt to become aggressive. For the Dutch Government of that time possessed the most powerful navy and the greatest admirals then in the world —a navy compared to which any navy they had yet seen possessed by England, they looked upon but as a collection of small privateers and corsairs, which they could easily sweep from the face of the sea. They were destined, in the course of two short years, to find themselves somewhat out in their reckonings. Yet it is not surprising that they should not have then known what England was capable of; for at that time England did not know herself what genius and valour could accomplish when they have freed themselves from the withering spell of tyranny combined with imbecility.

There was no inconsiderable amount of baseness as well as of shortsightedness in the conduct of the Dutch at this time. The baseness was in some degree the cause of the shortsightedness; for it was the cold, calculating, and nevertheless shortsighted baseness of commercial avarice, which pursues its ends with a reckless rapacity, as blind to all consequences, but the glutting of its own appetite for what it calls wealth, as the ravenous fury of a hungry tiger. Thus the Dutch, while valuing themselves on being a republic, were willing to lend their aid to the tyrants of Europe to destroy the English Commonwealth, shutting their eyes to the fact that their own destruction would be the next object those tyrants would aim at. This is established on the testimony both of royalist and republican writers. According to Hobbes, " the true quarrel on the Dutch part was their greediness to engross all

traffic, and a false estimate of our and their own strength." [1]
Ludlow's testimony is to the same effect, and is strengthened by his actual experience of the Dutch, in purchasing
an agreement with England, after the Restoration, with the
price of blood, in delivering three of King Charles's judges
into the hands of their enemies, which made him decline
the offer made to him from Holland, of the command of a
body of land-forces to be shipped on board the Dutch
fleet. "All men knew," says Ludlow, "they preferred
the profits of trade before any other thing in the world:[2]
choosing rather to see a tyranny than a commonwealth
established in England, as knowing by experience that
they could corrupt the former, and by that means possess
themselves of the most profitable parts of trade."[3]

On the 1st of April 1651, the Council of State despatched
a letter, "demanding satisfaction for the affront offered to
the English ambassadors in Holland by Prince Palatine
Edward." [4] On the following day it was ordered, "That
the letters and instructions now read to the Lords Ambassadors in Holland be fair-written, signed, and sent away
this night by an express, and that duplicates be sent to-
morrow by the post."[5]

[1] Hobbes's Behemoth, p. 287 (London, 1682).

[2] Ludlow's Memoirs, vol. iii. p. 166.

[3] Ibid. p. 203.

[4] Order Book of the Council of
State, Tuesday, April 1, 1651, MS.
State Paper Office.

[5] Ibid. April 2, 1651.—The following
order shows that Scott performed the
duties now performed by the Secretary
of State for Foreign Affairs: "That
Mr. Scott do hold a constant intelligence with the Lords Ambassadors
who are now to go over into the Uni-

ted Provinces." (Ibid. Feb. 28, 165 9/1.)
The following minute further shows
that particular members of the Council
of State were, from their personal pre-
eminence, considered as Ministers, or
Secretaries of State. : "That it be referred to the Committee for Irish and
Scottish Affairs, to consider of the particulars desired in a letter from Scotland, written to Sir Henry Vane, and
in his hands, and thereupon to give
order for the speedy providing." (Ibid.
April 17, 1651.) By a subsequent minute of May 8, it appears that this

In these instructions for St. John and Strickland, the Council of State say:—"Admiral Van Tromp is arrived at the islands of Scillyes or Sorlings, anciently a part of the territories belonging to the Commonwealth of England, with a fleet under his command consisting of ten or fifteen men-of-war; in some of which are great number of men and some persons of quality not usual in men-of-war only designed for sea-service: which said Admiral declined to have a boat of our fleet to come on board to him; and does continue his abode with his said fleet near those islands and the western parts of England, without discovering his clear intentions therein, pretending that it is to procure satisfaction for the injuries done by the garrisons in those islands, and ships belonging thereunto, unto the ships of their [the United Provinces'] subjects; but with instructions, as we are informed, to compel such satisfaction without any limitation of means, either by possessing himself of those islands or otherwise, and to seize upon all ships whatsoever going in or coming out from that place, whereby just cause of jealousy is given to the Parliament. And that until the intentions of the States-General in this expedition be clearly made manifest to the Parliament, and assurance given to them that the said fleet may act nothing to the prejudice of this Commonwealth in honour or interest, the instructions and commission given to Van

letter was from the Lord-General Cromwell. Sir Henry Vane had entered the Council-room just before. He probably then read the letter to the Council. Thus, while Scott might be considered as Secretary of State for Foreign Affairs, Vane might be considered, in regard to his connection both with the Committee of the Admiralty and Navy, and with the Committee for Irish and Scottish Affairs, as Secretary of State for War. Sir Henry Vane's name stands first, both in the list of the Committee for carrying on the Affairs of the Admiralty and in that of the Committee for the Affairs of Ireland and Scotland.—*Order Book of the Council of State*, Saturday March 1, 165$\frac{0}{1}$, MS. State Paper Office.

Tromp in reference to the said islands may be recalled, to avoid all occasions of disputes and differences between the two States; the Parliament having thought fit to give order to their fleets not to suffer the said Admiral Tromp, or any other, to act anything to the prejudice of the State in honour or interest." [1]

On the 10th of April the Council of State ordered, " That it be reported to the Parliament that the Council of State received letters from the Lords Ambassadors from Holland, relating to a paper put in by them concerning an affront offered to them by Edward, the son of the Queen of Bohemia; and that the Council of State have again by this post received letters from the said ambassadors, and some papers, relating further affronts offered unto them." [2]

It would appear from the following minute that the Dutch gave a satisfactory account of Tromp's fleet at Scilly, so that for the year 1651 the war with Holland was avoided, that war which was to break out with such fury in the following year, 1652 : " That a letter be written to Colonel Blake, to enclose him a copy of the paper of the States of Holland, in answer to a paper of the ambassadors of England, concerning the going of Van Tromp towards Scilly ; and to let him know that he is so to carry the matter, that the honour of the Commonwealth may be preserved, and a good correspondence between the two nations." [3]

The following minute of the same date confirms what has been said respecting the disposition of the Kings of Europe towards the Parliament of England : " That it

---

[1] "Instructions for the Ambassadors with the States-General of the United Provinces."—*Order Book of the Council of State*, April 2, 1651, MS. State Paper Office.

[2] Order Book of the Council of State, April 10, 1651, MS. State Paper Office.

[3] *Ibid.* April 17, 1651.

be referred to the Committee of the Admiralty to inform themselves concerning the truth of the intelligence given of the preparation of men and shipping in Sweden; and thereupon so to appoint the fleet of the Commonwealth, that prevention may be given to any attempts which may be made by them upon any parts of this nation to the prejudice thereof." [1]

The following minute further shows that some designs were on foot of effecting a landing in some parts of England, with a view of making a diversion in favour of the King of Scots and the Royalists, who had probably by this time (the end of April 1651) formed the design of their invasion of England which led to the Battle of Worcester : " That such of the letters intercepted in Holland as refer to designs against this Commonwealth be referred to the consideration of the Committee for Examinations ; " " the Committee of the Admiralty to consider of some fit ships for those parts designed upon, as shown by the intercepted letters." [2]

At this particular time the ability and vigilance of the Council of State were tasked to the utmost. Besides the threatened invasions from the Continent and from Scotland, they had also received intelligence of an intended diversion in Scotland from Ireland: "That a letter be written to the Lord-General [Cromwell], to acquaint him with the propositions made concerning the making of a diversion in Scotland from Ireland ; and that they have written to the Lord Deputy [Ireton], to hold intelligence with his Lordship concerning the same; to enclose the copy of the Council's letter to the Deputy to him, and to lett [sic, i.e. leave], the whole business to his Lordship's considera-

---

[1] Order Book of the Council of State, April 17, 1651.   [2] Ibid. April 28, 1651, MS. State Paper Office.

tion."[1] And with regard to the invasion from the Continent, the Council received intelligence, in the beginning
of June, "of the enemy's designs to land at or near Yarmouth."[2]

On the 11th of April, several papers from the Parliament's ambassadors in Holland, and two intercepted
letters, were read in the House, upon which the House
passed the following resolutions : "1. That the Parliament doth approve of what the Ambassadors Extraordinary
to the General Assembly of the States of the United Provinces have done upon the affronts offered to them.—2.
That the Parliament doth approve of the direction given by
the Council of State, to the said Ambassadors Extraordinary, touching their return.—3. That it be referred to the
Council of State, upon the debate now had in the House
on this report, to give such orders and directions as they
shall think fit, for the honour of this Commonwealth and
safety of the Ambassadors.—4. That the debates of the
House this day, and the votes thereupon, *be not made
known to any person : and that the members of the House,
and the officers thereof, be enjoined secrecy therein for* 21
days."[3] This injunction of secrecy would appear to refer
to intelligence contained in the intercepted letters, and in
the ambassadors' despatches, respecting some designs to
land foreign forces on the east coast of England, near Yarmouth, under the command of the Duke of Lorraine ; and
the injunction of secrecy would also appear to have been
continued for a considerable time beyond the 21 days specified above. For, on the 5th September of this year,

---

[1] Order Book of the Council of State,
April 22, 1651.

[2] "Intelligence the Council have had
of the enemy's designs to land at or
near Yarmouth."—*Order Book of the*

Council of State, June 3, 1651.

[3] Commons' Journals, April 11,
1651; Parl. Hist. vol. iii. pp. 1363,
1364.

just two days after the Battle of Worcester, there is this
minute entered in the "Order Book of the Council of State:"
"That the injunction of secrecy laid upon the business of
the Duke of Lorraine be taken off." [1]

It also appears, from the following minute of 12th
August 1651, that the Council of State had reason to
expect the foreign forces to sail from Dunkirk or Ostend,
and the attempt at invasion to be made at or near
Yarmouth: "That Colonel Popham should send some
ships from the Downs to lie before Dunkirk and Ostend, to
prevent any forces coming out from thence from the Duke
of Lorraine to make any diversion; and should also send
some ships to Yarmouth, to prevent the landing of any in
England."[2]   There are various subsequent minutes to the
same effect.

All these minutes and the resolutions of Parliament,
taken together, afford strong confirmation of the statement
of General Ludlow, and also show that the Council of
State had information of designs of attempting a landing
of foreign forces in England, as well as in Ireland.   Ludlow states that the Council of State had reason to think
that the Dutch had a design to transport some foreign
forces by their fleet to the assistance of the Irish, who were,
says Ludlow (and, as then commanding in Ireland, he
had the best means of knowing), " not only still numerous
in the field, but had also divers places of strength to
retreat to."[3]   Ludlow then goes on to give the account
which has been quoted at the beginning of this volume
of the designs of the Duke of Lorraine, who was a

---

[1] Order Book of the Council of
State, Friday, Sept. 5, 1651, MS.
State Paper Office.

[2] Order Book of the Council of

State, Tuesday, August 12, 1651.

[3] Ludlow's Memoirs, vol. i. p. 389
(2nd edition, London, 1721).

near relation of Henry of Guise, one of the principal authors of the Massacre of St. Bartholomew, and also a relation of the Stuarts. It was within the Lorraine territory that the conferences were held, among the chiefs of the "Sacred League," some 60 years before, at which it was resolved to require of the last Valois the immediate extermination of heresy and heretics, and the formal establishment of the "Holy Inquisition," in every province of France.

Here then was a repetition, in the 17th century, of the story of some memorable years of the 16th. "It will not take much time to put down the heretics here," wrote Philip II.'s ambassador at Paris on the 7th of June, 1585; "nor will it consume much more to conquer England with the forces of such powerful princes, there being so many Catholics, too, to assist the invaders. If your Majesty, on account of your Netherlands, is not afraid of putting arms into the hands of the Guise family in France, there need be less objection to sending one of that house into England, particularly as you will send forces of your own into that kingdom, by the reduction of which the affairs of Flanders will be secured." The Spaniard adds, with characteristic modesty, "To effect the pacification of the Netherlands the sooner, it would be desirable to conquer England as early as October."[1]   The difference,

---

[1] Letter from Mendoza to Philip II. from the MS. in the Archives of Simancas, in Motley's History of the United Netherlands, vol. i. pp. 128, 129. The Spanish ambassador also insists on the want of disciplined forces in England to oppose an invasion. It is remarkable that so late as the year 1849 a French vice-admiral, by name Dupetit-Thouars, gave a similar opinion in his evidence in the French "Enquête Parlementaire" of 1849, respecting the facility of conquering England. Between Mendoza and Dupetit-Thouars, however, two men, Blake and Nelson, had lived, who had made it necessary for Vice-Admiral Dupetit-Thouars to assume a landing made. The landing having been effected, Vice-Admiral Dupetit-Thouars assumes that the

however, between 1585 and 1651 was important. For in 1585 England had at least the Netherlands on her side, whereas in 1651 she had the Netherlands leagued with the rest of Europe against her.

But if the tyrants of Lorraine, of France, of Spain, imagined that they could extinguish in England religious and civil liberty in a 'sea of blood, shed by assassins and not by honourable soldiers, as they had extinguished it in France, they little knew the spirit of the people they undertook to subdue and massacre : they little knew that the arts of Italian falsehood would be no match for such statesmen as Vane, and the arms of Lorraine, of Spain, of Holland, no match for such soldiers as Blake and Cromwell.

When the States of the United Provinces received the letters of the English Council of State, demanding satisfaction for the affronts offered to the English ambassadors in Holland, they remonstrated with the Queen of Bohemia and the Princess Dowager of Orange, against the behaviour of the two princes. They also offered a reward of 200 guilders (£20) for discovery of the other offenders, and published a proclamation for the punishment of all such as should offer any violence to the persons or privileges of ambassadors or agents from foreign Powers. The smallness of the sum offered looked like an aggravation of the insult. And such the English Parliament felt it to be, for they soon after recalled their ambassadors.[1]

The speech which St. John made, or, as Hobbes says,

English would be driven before the invaders like a flock of sheep. However the case might have been in 1585 and 1849, whoever expected to find England an easy conquest in 1651 would have found he had made a slight mistake; and that the Parliamentary cuirassiers and pikemen were a morsel by no means easy of digestion.

[1] Parl. Hist. vol. iii. p. 1365.

the " compliment which he gave," to the Dutch commissioners at taking leave, is a curiosity in diplomacy, and,
as Hobbes observes, worth hearing.   " My lords," said
St. John, " you have an eye upon the event of the affairs
of Scotland, and therefore do refuse the friendship we have
offered.   Now, I can assure you that many in the Parliament were of opinion, that we should not have sent any
ambassadors to you before they had put an end to the
contest between themselves and that King; and then
expected your ambassadors to us.   I now perceive our
error, and that those gentlemen were in the right.   In a
short time you shall see that business ended ; and then
you will come to us, and seek what we have freely offered,
when it shall perplex you that you have refused our prof-
fer."[1]   As Hobbes observes after quoting these words, St.
John guessed well, as we shall see in subsequent chapters.

On the 2nd of July, 1651, the ambassadors took their
seats in the House, when the Lord Chief Justice St. John,
Mr. Strickland standing by him, gave an account of their
negotiation, beginning with the particulars of their reception at the Hague, and relating the several occurrences
which passed between them and the Assembly of the
States ; and presenting the several papers delivered in on
either side, in the business of the Treaty, and the letters
re-credential from the said Assembly, in French, directed
thus : " *Au Parlement de la République d'Angleterre.*"
These several papers having been read, it was resolved,
" That the Parliament doth approve of all the proceedings
of the Lords Ambassadors in this negotiation, and that
they have the thanks of the House for their great and

---

[1] This parting speech of St. John is
given, in almost the same words, in
Hobbes's "Behemoth," pp. 285, 286;
and in Heath's "Chronicle of the Civil
Wars," p. 287.

faithful services therein;" which the Speaker gave them accordingly. The same compliment was also paid to the gentlemen that attended them abroad, for their services to the Parliament, and the respect shown to their ambassadors.[1]

[1] Parl. Hist. vol. iij. p. 1367.

CHAPTER X.

It is a remarkable fact, that among the members of the Council of State and of the Parliament, at the time when the Government called itself the Government of the Commonwealth of England, were some peers, who or whose fathers had been the especial favourites of the first of the Stuart kings who reigned in England. William Cecil, Earl of Salisbury, the son of Robert Cecil, who had been created Earl of Salisbury, by King James, in 1605, and Philip Herbert, created Earl of Montgomery by King James, also in 1605, and who succeeded his brother as Earl of Pembroke in 1630, were both members of the Rump, and also members of the first Council of State. Among the peers who sat as members of the Rump, was Edward Howard, a younger son of Thomas Howard, who had been created Earl of Suffolk, by King James, in 1603. This Thomas Howard—who had, in the early part of King James's reign, filled the post of Lord Chamberlain, and upon the death of the Earl of Salisbury had been made Lord High Treasurer—was the father of Lady Frances Howard, known, among other things, for poisoning Sir Thomas Overbury; and also of Edward Howard, created by King Charles, in 1628, Baron Howard of Escrick, whose son, also Lord Howard of Escrick, is known, among other things, as the single witness against Algernon Sydney, who was condemned and executed, to borrow the words of Evelyn, " on the single witness of that monster of a man, Lord Howard of Escrick, and some sheets of paper taken in Mr. Sydney's study."[1]   In the early part of this year (1651), a complaint had been exhibited in Parliament against this Edward, Lord Howard of Escrick, now a member of the House of Commons for the city of Carlisle.   The witnesses against him had been examined strictly by a Committee of the House appointed for that purpose.   The particulars of the charge are not given in the Journals of the House; but Ludlow, in his Memoirs, gives the following account of it :—

" Before I left the Parliament " [to go to Ireland], " some difference happening between the Countess of Rutland and the Lord Howard of Escrick, Colonel Gell, who was a great servant of the Countess, informed Major-General Harrison, that the Lord Edward Howard, being a Member of Parliament and one of the Committee at Haberdashers' Hall, had taken divers bribes for the excusing delinquents from sequestration, and easing them in their compositions ; and that, in particular, he had received a diamond hatband, valued at £800, from one Mr. Compton of Sussex, concerning which he could not prevail with any to inform the Parliament.   Major-General Harrison, being a man of severe principles, and zealous for justice, especially against such as betrayed the public trust reposed in them, assured him, that if he could satisfy him that the fact was as he affirmed, he would not fail to inform the Parliament of it : and upon satisfaction received from the Colonel touching that matter, said in Parliament, 'That

[1] It would seem the Earl of Salisbury, mentioned above as a member of the first Council of State, had married a sister of this Lord Howard of Escrick, respecting which marriage, see the despatches of La Boderie, the French ambassador at the Court of James (tom. iv. p. 100).

though the honour of every member was dear to him, and
of that gentleman in particular (naming the Lord Howard),
because he had so openly owned the interest of the Commonwealth as to decline his peerage, and sit upon the
foot of his election by the people; yet he loved justice
before all other things, looking upon it to be the honour
of the Parliament and the image of God upon them; that
therefore he durst not refuse to lay this matter before them,
though he was very desirous that the said Lord might
clear himself of the accusation.' The Parliament, having
received this information, referred the consideration of the
matter to a committee, where it was fully examined; and,
notwithstanding all the art of counsel learned in the law,
and all the friends the Lord Howard could make, so just
and equitable a spirit then governed, that the Committee
represented the matter to the Parliament as they found it
to be."[1] It was therefore resolved by the House : " That
upon consideration of the several charges against Edward,
Lord Howard of Escrick, and the proofs reported, and his
answer and defence thereupon, the Parliament doth, upon
the whole matter, declare and adjudge him guilty of
bribery : that the said Edward Lord Howard be discharged
from being a member of this Parliament, and for ever disabled to sit in any Parliament, and from bearing any
office or place of trust in this Commonwealth : that he be
fined £10,000; committed to the Tower during the pleasure of the Parliament; and that he do attend at the bar
of the House, and, upon his knee there, receive this judgment."[2] The Lord Howard was released, from his imprisonment in the Tower, on the 6th of August following;
and on the 5th of April, 1653, the fine of £10,000 imposed

---

[1] Ludlow's Memoirs, vol. i. pp. 334,   [2] Commons' Journals, June 25,
335 (2nd edition, London, 1721).   1651.

upon him was ordered to be discharged.[1]   His son, when thirty years after he brought Algernon Sydney to the scaffold, might think that he then paid back upon the Republican party the humiliation which on this occasion they had inflicted on his father.   The history of this family would be an instructive illustration of the sort of virtues which recommended men to the favour of the Stuarts, and of the depth of infamy to which the Stuarts reduced nobility in England.

The fact of this Lord Howard of Escrick's sitting as a member of this assembly may be explained easily enough, on the ground that such men as he are ever ready to side with that party, whatever its principles may be, which is the strongest for the time being.   But there is a far deeper significance in the fact that Philip Earl of Pembroke, and Philip Lord Viscount Lisle, the eldest son of the Earl of Leicester, were members of this Parliament, and also of the Council of State ; and that Algernon Sydney, another son of the Earl of Leicester, was a member of the Parliament, and an officer of the army of the Parliament, and also a member of the last Council of State elected in November 1652.   These two brothers were related by blood to the Earl of Pembroke, whose mother was the sister of Sir Philip Sydney, and also of Robert Sydney, their grandfather, created Viscount Lisle in 1605, and Earl of Leicester in 1618, by James I.   No one, therefore, had better means, than they had, of knowing what was the price of King James's honours.   Whether all the wickedness of the Court of the Stuart was known to all those who called themselves Cavaliers, and fought for the Stuarts like Falkland, or wrote for them like Hyde, I cannot say.   If they did not know for what the Earl of

---

[1] Parl. Hist. vol. iii. pp. 1366, 1367.

Gowrie and his brother had been murdered, they could hardly miss knowing why the murderers of Sir Thomas Overbury escaped punishment, and retired with a pension of £4,000 a year. However that might be, this Earl of Pembroke knew the wickedness of that Court too well; and Viscount Lisle knew enough of it to take an active part in the business of the Council of State, for his name appears often in the MS. minutes, showing that his attendance was as regular as that of most of the members. But the case of Lord Lisle's brother, Algernon Sydney, is still more significant.

Algernon Sydney was not a member of the Council of State till November 1652. He was again elected a member of the Council of State, on the restoration of the Long Parliament, in 1659. But in 1646 he was returned Member for Cardiff; and in 1647 he received the thanks of the House of Commons for his services in Ireland, and was appointed Governor of Dover. In April 1645 Fairfax had raised him to the rank of Colonel, and had given him a regiment. On the 2nd of July 1650, there is this minute in the " Order Book of the Council of State":—" That Colonel Algernon Sydney be desired to repair down to Dover Castle and take care of the place, the Council being informed that the enemy have some design upon the place."[1]

Of Algernon Sydney's qualities as a soldier, there could not be a stronger testimonial than this—that when Cromwell, after his return from Ireland in 1650, proposed to Ludlow that " some person of reputation and known fidelity might be sent over to command the horse in Ireland, and to assist Major-General Ireton in the public

[1] Order Book of the Council of State, July 2, 1650, MS. State Paper Office.

service," and desired Ludlow to propose one whom he thought sufficiently qualified for that station, Ludlow told him that, in his opinion, " a fitter man could not be found than Colonel Algernon Sydney;" and the only exception Cromwell made against him was " his relation to some who were in the King's interest."

The character of Algernon Sydney has been a favourite theme with writers, great and small; and, as is usual, the small writers have been harder upon him than the great. For it is a source of wonderful self-complacency to a small man to pass judgment, from an imaginary judgment-seat, on what he terms the narrow-minded obstinacy, the utter impracticability, the infatuated helplessness, of a shipwrecked faction. The man fancies that, by such lofty denunciations, he establishes his·own title to vast practical ability. But sometimes he is undeceived before he dies. Algernon Sydney, in one of his letters to his father, seems to forebode this part of his sad fate, when he says: " I wander as a vagabond through the world, forsaken of my friends, poor, and known only to be a broken limb of a shipwrecked faction." In another letter to his father, first published by Mr. Blencowe in 1825, from the original in Mr. Lambard's collection, Algernon Sydney pleads, as it were by a voice from the grave, against Jeffreys, who pronounced upon him the judgment of death,[2]· as well as against those who, after death, pronounced him to be a narrow-minded, opinionative,

---

[1] Ludlow's Memoirs, vol. ii. p. 320 (2nd edition, London, 1721).

[2] At Algernon Sydney's trial, Finch, the Solicitor-General, a far more adroit legal sophist than Prideaux, the Attorney-General at John Lilburne's trial, maintained that one witness to one fact, and another witness to another fact, were the two witnesses required by law. It is remarkable that Sydney was destroyed by the very same falsification of law by which the *Rump*, of which he had been a member, had attempted, though in vain, to destroy John Lilburne.

fanatical egotist.   Let us hear Algernon Sydney's defence
of himself.

He thus writes to his father from Hamburg, August
30, 1660: " Sir John Temple sends me word, your Lordship is very intent upon finding a way of bringing me into
England, in such a condition as I may live there quietly
and well.   I acknowledge your Lordship's favour, and will
make the best return for it I can; but I desire you to lay
that out of your thoughts; it is a design never to be accomplished.   I find so much by the management of things
at home, that it is impossible for me to be quiet one day,
unless I would do those things, the remembrance of which
would never leave me one quiet or contented moment
whilst I live.   I know myself to be in a condition that, for
all circumstances, is as ill as outward things can make it.
This is my only consolation, that when I call to remembrance, as exactly as I can, all my actions relating to our
civil distempers, I cannot find one that I look upon as a
breach of the rules of justice or honour.   This is my
strength, and, I thank God, by this I enjoy very serene
thoughts.   If I lose this, by vile and unworthy submis-
sions, acknowledgment of errors, asking of pardon, or the
like, I shall from that moment be the miserablest man
alive, and the scorn of all men.   I know the titles that are
given me, of fierce, violent, seditious, mutinous, turbulent,
and many others of the like nature; but God, that gives
me inward peace in my outward troubles, doth know that
I do in my heart choose an innocent quiet retirement,
before any place unto which I could hope to raise myself
by those actions which they condemn.   If I could write
and talk like Colonel Hutchinson, or Sir Gilbert Pickering,
I believe I might be quiet; contempt might procure my
safety; but I had rather be a vagabond all my life, than

buy my being in my own country at so dear a rate : and
if I could have bowed myself according to my interest,
perhaps I was not so stupid as not to know the ways of
settling my affairs at home, or making a good provision
for staying abroad, as well as others, and did not want
credit to attain unto it; but I have been these many years
outstripped by those that were below me, whilst I stopped
at those things that they easily leaped over.   What shall
I say ? It hath been my fortune from my youth, and will
be so to my grave, by which my designs in the world will
perpetually miscarry.   But I know people will say, I strain
at gnats, and swallow camels ; that it is a strange conscience, that lets a man run violently on, till he is deep in
civil blood, and then stays at a few words and compliments ;
that can earnestly endeavour to extirpate a long-established
monarchy, and then cannot be brought to see his error,
and be persuaded to set one finger towards the setting
together the broken pieces of it.   It will be thought a
strange extravagance for one, that esteemed it no dis-
honour to make himself equal to a great many mean
people, and below some of them, to make war upon the
King; and is ashamed to submit unto the King, now he is
encompassed with all the nobles of the land, and in the
height of his glory, so that none are so happy as those
that can first cast themselves at his feet.   I have enough
to answer all this in my own mind ; I cannot help it if I
judge amiss; I did not make myself, nor can I correct the
defects of my own creation.   I walk in the light God hath
given me; if it be dim or uncertain, I must bear the
penalty of my errors.   I hope to do it with patience, and
that no burden shall be very grievous to me, except sin
and shame.   God keep me from those evils, and, in all
things else, dispose of me according to his pleasure ! I

have troubled your Lordship very long, but it is that I might ease you of cares that would be more tedious, and as unfruitful. I do not know whither the course of my fortune doth lead me, probably never to return to see your Lordship or my own country again. However, if I have offended your Lordship, transported by folly or the violence of my nature (I have nothing else that needs your forgiveness), I beseech you to pardon it; and let me have your favour and blessing along with me. If I live to return, I will endeavour to deserve it by my services; if not, I can make no return but my prayers for you, which shall never be omitted by your Lordship's

ALGERNON SYDNEY."[1]

In another of his letters to his father, first published by Mr. Blencowe in 1825 from Mr. Lambard's collection, and dated Venice, October 12, 1660, Algernon Sydney gives the following account of his conduct with regard to the King's trial, which shows that he had clearer notions on the illegality of "High Courts of Justice" than either Cromwell or Bradshaw. He says :—" The truth of what passed I do very well remember. I was at Penshurst, when the Act for the trial passed; and coming up to town I heard my name was put in, and that those that were nominated for judges were then in the Painted Chamber. I presently went thither, heard the Act read, and found my own name with others. A debate was raised how they should proceed upon it; and after having been some time silent, to hear what those would say who had the directing of that business, I did positively oppose Cromwell, Bradshaw, and others, who would have the trial to go on, and drawing rea-

---

[1] Sydney Papers, pp. 195–198, edited by R. W. Blencowe (London, 1825).

sons from these two points :—First, the King *could be tried* by no court; secondly, that *no man* could be tried by that court. This being alleged in vain, and Cromwell using these formal words, ' I tell you, we will cut off his head with the crown upon it,' I replied: ' You may take your own course, I cannot stop you, but I will keep myself clean from having any hand in this business ; ' and immediately went out of the room, and never returned.[1] This is all that passed publicly, or that can with truth be recorded, or taken notice of. I had an intention, which is not very fit for a letter.''[2]

This last sentence has given rise to some discussion. Sir James Mackintosh, in a note[3] printed at the end of Mr. Blencowe's volume, expresses an opinion that the intention to which Sydney alludes, was to procure a concurrence of both Houses of Parliament in the deposition of the King. The Lords had passed an ordinance, making it High Treason *in future* for a King of England to levy war against the Parliament, a measure which of itself declared the judicial proceedings against the King illegal. " Sydney, we know from a letter to his father," says the note of Sir James Mackintosh, " approved that ordinance, and blamed the resolutions of the Commons which were

[1] The Earl of Leicester's Journal agrees with this account: " My two sons, Philip and Algernon, came unexpectedly to Penshurst, Monday 22nd, and stayed there till Monday, 29th January, so as neither of them were at the condemnation of the King ; nor was Philip at any time at the High Court, though a commissioner; but Algernon (a commissioner also) was there sometimes, in the Painted Chamber, but never in Westminster Hall."—*Journal of the Earl of Leicester,* p. 54, in Sydney Papers.

[2] Sydney Papers, edited by R. W. Blencowe (London, 1825), p. 237.

[3] In that note Sir J. Mackintosh says, " what this intention was it is no longer possible to ascertain ; but we may with tolerable certainty affirm that it was one which he wished not to be known to the Government of Charles II., who were pretty sure to read his letter, and yet was willing to communicate to his father in conversation."

founded on other principles. The design of deposition seems perfectly reconcileable with the known opinion of Sydney and his connexions at the moment." Sydney, in the letter just quoted, also says that his opposition to the trial, and to the subscription of a paper declaring approbation of the order for the King's execution, "had so ill effects as to my particular concernments, as to make Cromwell, Bradshaw, Harrison, Lord Grey, and others my enemies, who did from that time continually oppose me." In regard to the supposition that the words of Sydney's letter referred to private assassination, Sir James Mackintosh says:—" Even the enemies of Sydney's memory cannot surely think it probable that a man of so frank and fearless a character should have preferred expedients which had no other recommendation than their tendency to provide for the personal safety of the actors. But it is altogether incredible that, if he had been a partisan of secret regicide, he should have needlessly alluded to such a disposition, in a letter written to supply his father with every fair means of procuring his secure admission into England." [1]

In another letter beginning " Sir, " and without date or address, Algernon Sydney says :—" I confess we are naturally inclined to delight in our own country, and I have a particular love to mine ; I hope I have given some testimony of it. I think that being exiled from it is a great evil, and would redeem myself from it with the loss of a great deal of my blood. But when that country of mine is now like to be made a stage of injury, the liberty which we hoped to establish oppressed ; the Parliament and army corrupted, the people enslaved ; all things vendible, no man safe, but by such evil and infamous means

[1] Sydney Papers by Blencowe, note I. pp. 281-284, London, 1825.

as flattery and bribery; what joy can I have in my own
country in this condition?   Shall I renounce all my old
principles, learn the vile court arts, and make my peace by
bribing some of them?   Better is a life among strangers,
than in my own country on such conditions. * * * Let
them please themselves with making the King glorious,
who think that a whole people may justly be sacrificed for
the interest and pleasure of one, and a few of his followers.
Nevertheless, perhaps they may find their King's glory is
their shame, his plenty the people's misery."[1]

Now let it be observed that in all this Algernon Sydney
—one of that body of statesmen whom a modern writer has
thought fit to term "a small faction of fanatical egotists,
more important from their passionate activity than from
their talents,"—was right, and they who again brought in
the Stuarts upon the English nation were wrong, as the event
fully proved, when, after twenty-eight years of crimes and
follies, those Stuarts were expelled for ever.   In estimating
the conduct of Sydney, it must also be remembered that his
experience had not furnished him with any remedy for the
evils of which he had seen and heard so much, and which
seemed inherent in monarchical government, except a republic, or, at any rate, some form of government like that
which had been established after the death of Charles.
For he could hardly be expected to know that a remedy
might be found such as the Government established in
England after the final expulsion of the Stuarts.   He had
seen the evils of the monarchical government brought very
near to him; for Leicester, the unworthy favourite of Elizabeth, was as bad a man, and as incapable a minister and
general, as Buckingham, the unworthy favourite of James

[1] Sydney Papers, pp. 199-201, edited by R. W. Blencowe (London,
1825).

and Charles.   It so happened that Sydney was peculiarly situated for observing both the old and the new nobility. The Sydneys belonged to the new nobility.   But Algernon Sydney was descended from Hotspur and the old warrior nobility, through his mother, the Lady Dorothy Percy, eldest daughter of the Earl of Northumberland ; and he was also descended from the new or court-lackey nobility, his great-grandmother being the sister of Robert Dudley, the Earl of Leicester of infamous memory.   Moreover, his aunt, the Lady Lucy Percy, having been married to one of James's favourites, was the Countess of Carlisle, a woman celebrated for her beauty, but whose reputation was not likely to meet with the approbation of Algernon Sydney, any more than it would have been likely to meet with the approbation of her ancestor, Hotspur—a proud rough man, who hated the "vile court arts," which Algernon Sydney, a proud rough man also, hated.   Further, the two nephews of Sir Philip Sydney, the Earl of Pembroke and his brother Philip Herbert, had been favourites at James's Court; and of that Court it may be said that its favour was even worse than its enmity, and that none ever escaped with honour from its deadly embrace.   Now, when all this is taken into account, and when it is remembered that Algernon Sydney was a thoughtful and observing as well as a proud and conscientious man, one can understand that, as he could see no other remedy but a republic for those intolerable evils of a monarchical government, he was willing to take help wherever he could get it—to take help even from a despot like Louis XIV.   And if we are bound to consider the papers of Barillon as sufficient evidence that 500 guineas were paid to Algernon Sydney on the part of Louis XIV., the only explanation of such a circumstance, which can in the least reconcile it with Sydney's character, is that he considered the situation of affairs so desperate as to warrant a desperate remedy; as his cotemporary, Thomas Hobbes, defended his retaining a friend or two at court, to protect him, if occasion should require, by saying, "If I were cast into a deep pit, and the Devil should put down his cloven foot, I would take hold of it to be drawn out by it."

The folly of the attempt to represent that assembly of " the greatest geniuses for government the world ever saw embarked together in one common cause," as " a small faction of fanatical egotists, more important from their passionate activity than from their talents," will be made abundantly manifest in the present chapter, from the minutes of their proceedings which happily exist.

During the winter of 165$\frac{0}{1}$, which Cromwell passed in Scotland, he had an attack of illness, which would seem to have been very severe. In a letter to the President of the Council of State, dated Edinburgh, March 24, 1650$\frac{0}{1}$, he says—"I thought I should have died of this fit of sickness; but the Lord seemeth to dispose otherwise." And in May, Cromwell sent word that the air of Scotland did not agree with him, and desired to remove himself to some part of England for the restoration of his health. Leave was granted to him; but he appears to have recovered his health so much as not to need to make use of it.

It is extremely difficult to get at the truth respecting powerful men—I mean men powerful from their position. The truth, if likely to be distasteful to them, cannot be published during their lifetime, or even, in many cases, till long after their death. Thus some persons who attempted to publish a version of what James I. called the Gowrie Conspiracy, different from King James's version, were punished with torture and death. And even after James's accession to the throne of England, any expression of dissent from the doctrine of the royal wisdom and virtue brought ruin and death on the unhappy dissenter.[1] The common accounts say that Cromwell's illness on this occasion was an attack of ague. But Aubrey, in his account of Jonathan Godard, M.D., tells the following story, which may be taken for whatever it is worth: " He [Godard] was one of the College of Physicians in London; warden of Merton College, Oxon; physician to Oliver Cromwell, Protector; went with him into Ireland. Qu. if not sent to him into Scotland, when he was so dangerously ill there of a kind of calenture or high fever, which made him mad, that he pistolled one or two of his commanders that came to visit him in his rage."[2]

The Scottish Parliament, which after the Battle of Dunbar had retired beyond the Forth, still maintained a show of decided opposition to those whom they called the English sectaries. The moderate Presbyterians, who desired monarchical government, resolved on the coronation of Charles, with a view of conciliating him, having been alarmed by a proceeding of his called the *Start*, the nature

[1] May 5, 1619. "Relation of the Execution of Williams, a Counsellor at Law, as a Traitor, for writing a libelling Book against the King, called ' Balaam's Ass.' "—*MS. State Paper Office.*

[2] Aubrey's Letters and Lives, vol. ii. pp. 357, 358 (London, 1813).—Aubrey was right as to Dr. Godard, as appears from the following minutes:—" That Dr. Goddard shall have the sum of £100 given unto him for his care and pains with the Lord-General in his sickness. That Dr. Goddard be recommended to the Committee for the Universities, to be made master of a college in one of the Universities; and Sir H. Vane is desired to acquaint them that the Council have, in consideration hereof, given him a smaller sum than otherwise they would have done, for his care and pains with the Lord-General in his sickness." (*Order Book of the Council of State,* June 13, 1651, MS. State Paper Office.) It appears from a minute of May 23, 1651, that the Council also despatched two other physicians, Dr. Wright and Dr. Bates, " to give his Lordship advice for the recovery of his health."—*Ibid.* May 23, 1651.

of which was not fully known. The ceremony of the coronation was performed at Scone, on the 1st of January 165$\frac{0}{1}$ with such solemnities as the circumstances of the times admitted. Charles, in royal robes, walked in procession from the hall of the palace to the church; the spurs, sword of state, sceptre, and crown being carried before him by the principal nobility. The crown was carried and placed on the head of Charles by the Marquis of Argyle, who was beheaded immediately after the Restoration in 1660, and said upon the scaffold, "I placed the crown upon the King's head, and in reward he brings mine to the block."

This coronation spectacle, at this particular time, is well fitted to give rise to some grave reflections. We have here two aristocracies in presence of each other —a natural and an artificial aristocracy, or, employing the words in their strict meaning, an aristocracy and an oligarchy. The natural aristocracy consists of an army composed of the best soldiers, commanded by the best officers that the world had ever seen—"an army to which," as Clarendon has truly and eloquently said, "victory was entailed, and which, humanly speaking, could hardly fail of conquest whithersoever it should be led; an army whose order and discipline, whose sobriety and manners,[1] whose courage and success, have made it famous and terrible over the world." But then, says Mr. Denzil Holles, all of these men, from the General to the meanest centinel, were not able to make £1,000 a year lands; most of the

---

[1] See the testimony of Baillie (*Memoir*, p. 63), as to Cromwell's "sojours doing less displeasure at Glasgow, nor [than] if they had been at London, though Mr. Zacharie Boyd railled on them all to their very faces in the High Church"—a strong contrast with some other "sojours," in times that might be thought more civilized.—See *Wellington's Despatches* (particularly Gurwood's Selections), p. 375, No. 426; p. 449, No. 507; p. 919, No. 1013.

colonels and officers being mean tradesmen, brewers, tailors, goldsmiths, shoemakers, and the like—" a notable dunghill," adds this son of one of James I.'s notable peers, " if one would rake into it to find out their several pedigrees." [1]

Nevertheless, if it be true, as nowadays some persons are presumptuous enough to think, that men's deeds are their best pedigrees, such persons might be disposed to say that this army of the Parliament of England constituted a real aristocracy, while the coronation procession, with all its symbolical paraphernalia, was but a phantom. If this heraldic aristocracy dreamt that war was an art the knowledge of which was their birthright, and which the herd of burghers and mechanics could never learn, they were suddenly startled from this dream by the trumpet-blast of an enemy more terrible than any they had ever encountered through all the dark centuries of their reign upon earth ; though that enemy's ranks were, in part, composed of " mean mechanics," and in part officered by " mean tradesmen,"—by men who, when they had done their work of war, returned to their former peaceful and industrious occupations, only noticeable thereafter by their superior skill in their various trades, and their superior sobriety, honesty, and good conduct.

The Royalist writers, who strive to make it appear that their King was not only a gallant soldier but a prudent commander—though they have never been able to show, upon any good evidence, that he displayed even the humblest private soldier's virtue of steadiness and personal courage under an enemy's fire, or indeed that he was ever under an enemy's fire at all on any one occasion—

---

[1] Holles's Memoirs, p. 149.

inform us that after his coronation the King assumed the command of the Scottish army in person, and took up a position to the south of Stirling, having in his front the River Carron. This particular tract of country had witnessed some of the most desperate struggles for the independence of Scotland, when the Scots fought under leaders very different from this Stuart king. On the banks of the Carron had been fought the bloody Battle of Falkirk, in which Wallace had been defeated, in consequence, partly at least, of the treacherous defection, during the battle, of some of the Scottish nobility with their retainers. On the banks of the Bannock had been fought the still bloodier Battle of Bannockburn, in which Robert Bruce had given England the greatest overthrow recorded in her annals. The strong position now taken up by the Scottish army was no doubt the work, not of the King— who never showed a genius for war or anything else (according to the authority of his friend the Duke of Buckingham, who ought to have known his gifts), " but ducks, loitering, and loose women," [1]—but of David Leslie, who still acted as Lieutenant-General ; though his prudence and military skill were rendered of small avail under the control of this " dull blockhead," as Buckingham calls him, as they had been baffled before by the incapacity and folly of the Scottish oligarchy.

[1] " Nay, he could sail a yacht, both nigh and large,
Knew how to trim a boat, and steer a barge :
Could say his compass, to the nation's joy,
And swear as well as any cabin-boy.
But not one lesson of the ruling art
Could this dull blockhead ever get by heart;
Look over all the universal frame,
There's not a thing the will of man can name,
In which this ugly perjur'd rogue delights,
But ducks and loit'ring," * * *
— The Cabin Boy, by George Villiers.
Charles was learned in the mechanism of ships, but his knowledge in them and their uses did not extend beyond that of a child in some huge new toys.

Here, as when, before the Battle of Dunbar, the Scots occupied a strong entrenched position between Edinburgh and Leith, Cromwell could neither with prudence attack them in their lines, nor find means of inducing them to hazard a battle, unless at a great disadvantage to himself. Now, as in the preceding summer, the Scottish army remained in their fastnesses, carefully and pertinaciously avoiding an engagement, though Cromwell continued to use his utmost efforts to provoke them to it. Here, again, the generalship of David Leslie is for the last time manifest. Cromwell himself pays a high compliment to Leslie's skill in taking up strong positions. "The enemy," he says, "is at his old lock, and lieth in and near Stirling, where we cannot come to fight him except he please, or we go upon too manifest hazards : he having very strongly laid himself, and having a very good advantage there. Whither we hear he hath lately gotten great provisions of meal, and reinforcements of his strength out of the north. under Marquis Huntly. It is our business still to wait upon God, to show us our way how to deal with this subtle enemy; which I hope He will."[1]

When the armies had faced each other for more than a month, Cromwell despatched Lambert into Fife, to turn the left flank of the Scottish army, and intercept their supplies. Lambert attacked a detachment of the Scots, commanded by Holborne and Brown, and totally defeated them.[2] Cromwell also proceeded with his army to Perth, which was surrendered after one day's siege.[3] These

---

[1] Cromwell to the Speaker, Linlithgow, July 26, 1651, printed in Mr. Carlyle's Cromwell, from the Tanner MSS.

[2] Parl. Hist. vol. iii. p. 1369; Cromwell to the Speaker, Linlithgow, July 21, 1651, in Old Parl. Hist. vol.

xix. pp. 494, 495; Cromwelliana, p. 106.

[3] Cromwell to the Speaker, August 4, 1651; Balfour, vol. iv. pp. 313, 314; Lord Leicester's Journal, p. 110, in Sydney Papers, edited by R. W. Blencowe (London, 1825).

operations speedily had the effect which Cromwell intended; for on the 31st of July the Scottish army broke up their camp near Stirling, and moved to the south-westward by rapid marches.[1]

Mrs. Hutchinson represents the Council of State as very much surprised at hearing that the King of Scots was passed by Cromwell, and was marching southward; and as not only very much surprised, but very much frightened and disturbed in their counsels, till Colonel Hutchinson encouraged and put heart into them, " as they were one day in a private council raging and crying out on Cromwell's miscarriages." [2] Modern writers, in the weight they have attached to this statement, have overlooked the fact, that Colonel Hutchinson was not at that time a member of the Council of State, as I will show presently. But I will first say, in reference to Mrs. Hutchinson's statement respecting the very great surprise of the Council of State at hearing of the King of Scots' march southward—that, so long before as the 14th of January of this year, several extracts of letters from Cromwell and Lambert to the Council of State, dated from Edinburgh the 4th and 8th of that month, intimating a design of the Scots to attempt an invasion of England, had been read in the House.[3] So that the idea of the invasion of England would appear to have been entertained by the Scottish leaders for some time, though the fact of Cromwell's having turned their position probably hastened the execution of the project.

In reference to another statement of Mrs. Hutchinson, that the Council of State " scarce had any account of

[1] Cromwell to the Speaker, Leith, August 4, 1651 ; Lord Leicester's Journal, p. 110.

[2] Memoirs of Colonel Hutchinson, p. 356, Bohn's edition, London, 1854. [3] Parl. Hist. vol. iii. p. 1362.

Cromwell, or of his intention, or how the error came about to suffer the enemy to enter England, where there was no army to encounter him,"[1] it is fair to hear Cromwell's account of the matter. "This is our comfort," he says, "that in simplicity of heart, as towards God, we have done to the best of our judgments; knowing that if some issue were not put to this business, it would occasion another winter's war, to the ruin of your soldiery, for whom the Scots are too hard, in respect of enduring the winter difficulties of this country, and to the endless expense of the treasure of England in prosecuting this war. It may be supposed we might have kept the enemy from this by interposing between him and England, which truly I believe we might; but how to remove him out of this place without doing what we have done, unless we had had a commanding army on both sides of the River of Forth, is not clear to us, or how to answer the inconveniences afore-mentioned we understand not."[2]

In the preceding volume I have given an account of the election of the first and also of the second Council of State. As the time drew near for the election of a Council of State for the third time—namely, for the year 1651, the third year of the new Government called the Commonwealth—an opinion manifested itself in the Parliament, that a different principle should be adopted from that on which the election had been made in the preceding year, when all the members of the first Council of State were re-elected except three and two, who had died, so that only five new members were chosen. Accordingly, on the 5th of February 165$\frac{0}{1}$, the Parliament decided that the Council of

---

[1] Memoirs of Colonel Hutchinson p. 356.

[2] Cromwell to the Speaker, Leith, August 4, 1651.

State for the ensuing year should consist of 41 persons as before, but that only 21 of those who were now of the Council should be allowed to be re-elected.[1]   An inattention to this important fact has led some writers, generally accurate and careful, into erroneous conclusions.   Thus Mr. Brodie says, in reference to some remarks of Mrs. Hutchinson on the Council of State about the time of the Battle of Worcester, "her husband, though a member of the Council, appears to have been absent on employment."[2] The fact, however, is that Colonel Hutchinson was a member of the Council of State for the first two years, but not afterwards.   Consequently, he was not a member at the time of the Battle of Worcester; and this explains Mrs. Hutchinson's expression, " private council."   With her usual exorbitant self-assertion, she charges everybody but her husband, and one or two other persons whom she honoured with her approbation, with cowardice and folly ; and attributes all the vigour and energy which the Council of State displayed on that occasion, to the magical influence exercised on them by Colonel Hutchinson "in a private council."   As Mrs. Hutchinson's book has obtained far greater authority on this important period of English History than it deserves—for her account of this and many other matters is very untrustworthy, and written with all the conceit of knowledge without the reality—I will transcribe here what she says on this point, that the reader may have an opportunity of comparing it with the record of the proceedings of the Council of State, preserved in their own minutes :—

" The army being small, there was a necessity for

---

[1] Commons' Journals, February 5, 165$\frac{0}{1}$.

[2] History of the British Empire, vol. iv. p. 305, *note.*

recruits; and the Council of State, soliciting all the Parliament men that had interest to improve it in this exigence of time, gave Colonel Hutchinson a commission for a regiment of horse. He immediately got up three troops, well armed and mounted, of his own old soldiers, that thirsted to be again employed under him, and was preparing the rest of the regiment to bring them up himself; when he was informed, that as soon as his troops came into Scotland, Cromwell very readily received them, but would not let them march together, but dispersed them, to fill up the regiments of those who were more his creatures. The Colonel, hearing this, would not curry him any more; but rather employed himself in securing, as much as was necessary, his own county, for which he was sent down by the Council of State, who at that time were very much surprised at hearing that the King of Scots was passed by Cromwell, and had entered with a great army into England. Bradshaw himself, stout-hearted as he was, privately could not conceal his fear; some raged, and uttered sad discontents against Cromwell, and suspicions of his fidelity; they all considered that Cromwell was behind, of whom I think they scarce had any account, or of his intention, or how this error came about, to suffer the enemy to enter here, where there was no army to encounter him. Both the city and country (by the angry presbyters, wavering in their constancy to them and the liberties they had purchased) were all amazed, and doubtful of their own and the Commonwealth's safety. Some could not hide very pale and unmanly fears, and were in such distraction of spirit that it much disturbed their councils. Colonel Hutchinson, who ever had most vigour and cheerfulness when there was most danger, encouraged them, as they were one day in a private council raging and crying out on Cromwell's miscarriages, to apply themselves to councils of safety, and not to lose time in accusing others, while they might yet provide to save the endangered realm, or at least to fall nobly in defence of it, and not to yield to fear and despair. These and suchlike things being urged, they at length recollected themselves, and every man that had courage and interest in their counties went down to look to them."[1]

Upon this passage the Reverend Julius Hutchinson, the editor of Colonel Hutchinson's Memoirs, has this note— "The trepidation of the Council of State is well described by Whitelock." Now, so far is Whitelock from saying anything of the kind, that his account—written at the time, and when he was in daily conference with the Council of State, of which he was a leading member—particularly describes the *courage*, as well as the diligence and prudence, exhibited by the Council of State in this trying crisis. Under date August 19, 1651, he says : " The Council of State during this action [the advance of the Scots' army] had almost hourly messengers going out and returning from the several forces, carrying advice and directions to them, and bringing to the Council an account of their motions and designs, and of the enemy's motions.   It could hardly be that any affair of this nature could be managed with more diligence, courage, and prudence than this was ; nor, peradventure, was there ever so great a body of men so

---

[1] Memoirs of Colonel Hutchinson, pp. 355, 356, Bohn's edition, London, 1854.—Colonel Hutchinson, of whom we seldom hear in the records of that time, though his wife's interesting Memoirs have made his name well known, might be, and on his wife's showing was, a very respectable country gentleman ; but there needs some corroborative evidence, in addition to his wife's testimony, to prove that he saved the Commonwealth on this occasion. From the terms in which Mrs. Hutchinson speaks of Monk, it may be inferred that Ludlow's charge against Colonel Hutchinson, of co-operation with Monk, is groundless. The reader has seen, in a preceding page, Algernon Sydney's opinion of Colonel Hutchinson—certainly not a complimentary one.

well armed and provided got together in so short a time as were now raised, and sent away to join with the rest of the forces attending [*i. e.*, watching the movements of] the King."[1]

Mr. Brodie says, "Ludlow corroborates Mrs. Hutchinson's account."[2] As far as I can see, Ludlow does not corroborate Mrs. Hutchinson in the least. Ludlow says: " They [the Scots] passed the River Tweed[3] near Carlisle, there being a strong garrison in Berwick for the Parliament, and were considerably advanced in their march before our army in Scotland were acquainted with their design. Major-General Harrison, with about 4,000 horse and foot, somewhat obstructed their march, though he was not considerable enough to fight them; and being joined by Major-General Lambert, with a party of horse from the army, they observed the enemy so closely as to keep them from excursions, and to prevent others from joining with them. The Scots, who were in great expectation of assistance from Wales, and relied much upon Colonel Massey's interest in Gloucestershire, advanced that way. Few of the country came in to them; but, on the other side, so affectionate were the people to the Commonwealth, that they brought in horse and foot from all parts to assist the Parliament, insomuch that their number was by many thought sufficient to have beaten the enemy, without the assistance of the army; some even of the excluded members appearing in arms, and leading regiments against the common enemy."[4] Not a word here that seems in the least to corroborate the aspersions cast by

[1] Whitelock, pp. 502, 503, August 10, 1651.
[2] History of the British Empire, vol. iv. p. 305, *note*.
[3] Ludlow's geographical knowledge was evidently not extensive. However, the Scots did pass the border near Carlisle.
[4] Ludlow's Memoirs, vol. i. pp. 362, 363: 2nd edition, London, 1721.

Mrs. Hutchinson upon the Council of State, of which her husband was *not* then a member, in which fact may perhaps be discovered the cause of her imputations of cowardice.   Ludlow's account of the zeal of the people in all parts of England " against the common enemy"—for such the Stuarts and their adherents might be most truly called at all times, in 1745 as well as in 1645 and 1651— is fully supported by Whitelock as well as by the MS. minutes of the Council of State ; and many will be of the opinion stated by Ludlow, that the forces suddenly raised and got together by the Council of State, particularly with such soldiers as Lambert and Harrison to lead them, would have been quite sufficient to have beaten the enemy, without the assistance of Cromwell and his army.

But the best defence of the Council of State against the aspersions of Mrs. Hutchinson is afforded by their own Order Book.   The fair-copy of the minutes of the Council of State for this particular time is lost, but, happily, the original rough drafts have been preserved ; and the hasty almost illegible writing, the interlineations, marginal jottings, and memoranda, present what may be not untruly called a graphic picture of the rapid and energetic action with which they encountered the danger that threatened them—with no trace of the " very pale and unmanly fears " which Mrs. Hutchinson has thought fit to impute to them. There is not, in fact, in the whole of this graphic record of their proceedings, one trace of ground for this malicious imputation.[1]

---

[1] It is remarkable how fond Mrs. Hutchinson is of imputing cowardice and baseness. Some of her imputations of this sort are ludicrous—as, for instance, where she charges the Scots with cowardice for killing Colonel Thornhagb, who made such speed to set upon a troop of Scotch lancers, that he was somewhat in advance of his regiment ; and the lady is wroth because the Scots did not wait, and let him kill a few of them before his

152 COMMONWEALTH OF ENGLAND. [CHAP X.

In the first place, there are some circumstances recorded in the MS. minutes of the proceedings of the Council of State, which are at variance with Mrs. Hutchinson's statement that when the Scottish army entered England, there was no army there to encounter them. On the 12th of March of this year we find, in the Order Book of the Council of State, a minute respecting the " discovery from Scotland of a plot of some gentlemen in Cheshire and Lancashire."[1] On the 15th of March, three days after, the Council of State ordered, " That a letter be written to the Lord-General [Cromwell], to take notice of the receipt of his letter ; to let him know that the Council look upon the discovery made by the late letters sent from his Lordship as a very great mercy, and bless God for it, and for the good news of his Lordship's recovery ; to desire him to send the person lately apprehended there, to this town in a ship of war ; to desire his

regiment came up. And then, because the Scots naturally defended themselves when they could, and asked quarter when they could not, this just and merciful woman thus characterises the barbarity of Thornhagh's regiment— the Scotch lancers, be it repeated, were only a troop: "Deaf to the cries of every coward that asked mercy, they killed all, and would not a captive should live to see their colonel die ; but said the whole kingdom of Scotland was too mean a sacrifice for that brave man." When the Battle of the Metaurus was lost, Hasdrubal spurred his horse into the midst of a Roman cohort, and there fell sword in hand— fighting, says Livy, as became the son of Hamilcar and brother of Hannibal. But who talks of the cowardice of the Roman cohort for killing him ? Though there it was a whole cohort against one man, who possibly might have

been saved (though Mrs. Hutchinson, as the wife of a colonel, and not an absolute fool, though not quite so wise as she imagined herself to be, ought to have known that in the heat of action such a thing is always difficult and often impossible), whereas in the case of Colonel Thornhagh, he was followed (if at a little distance) by his regiment. Consequently, how could it prove cowardice, in a troop attacked by a regiment, that the troop killed the colonel of the regiment instead of saving his life, when they only killed him as being the first man of his regiment who attacked them?

[1] Order Book of the Council of State, March 12, 165⁰⁄₁, MS. State Paper Office.—On the same day there is a proclamation to " all officers and soldiers who have come into England, some with leave and some without leave, forthwith to repair to their colours."

Lordship to give intelligence to this Council of anything which may occur to his Lordship there, which may relate to the public peace, and the Council will take care to do the like to him."[1] In consequence of this discovery, Major-General Harrison was, on the 19th of March, sent down to the northern counties—Derby, Nottingham, Lancaster, York; and Sir Arthur Haselrig was desired, with the forces and garrisons under his command in the four northern counties, Northumberland, Durham, Westmoreland, and Cumberland, to give assistance to Major-General Harrison.[2] On Monday the 24th of March, an order is made by the Council of State, "That an Adjutant-General be allowed to Major-General Harrison for his expedition into the North, and that he be allowed the pay of 14s. per diem for himself and two men; which pay is to be satisfied unto him out of the incidents of the Council."[3] On the 7th of April an order was made "for raising 4,000 horse and dragoons for the safety of the Commonwealth." And on the same day "a petition of many godly and well-affected persons in the county of Norfolk, concerning the associating of honest men there for the defence of the public"—a petition which shows that the Government was by no means generally unpopular at that particular time—was referred

---

[1] Order Book of the Council of State, Saturday, March 15, 165$\frac{0}{1}$, MS. State Paper Office.

[2] *Ibid.* March 19, 165$\frac{0}{1}$.

[3] *Ibid.* March 24, 165$\frac{0}{1}$.—On the same day there is a minute of the Council of State, which still further confirms what I have before said as to the erroneous statement of Roger Coke, that the Parliament never pressed "either soldiers or seamen in all these wars."—*Detection of the Court and State of England,* vol. ii. p. 30. The following is the minute of the Council of State:—"That it be reported to the Parliament that the Council find great difficulty to get recruits for Ireland, of which the regiments there have great need. And therefore offer it to the consideration of the Parliament, that 2,500 recruits may be raised by way of press within the county of Cornwall, from whence the Council conceive they may be sent much cheaper and more conveniently than from other places." —*Order Book of the Council of State,* March 24, 165$\frac{0}{1}$, MS. State Paper Office.

to a committee, " who are to speak with the gentlemen that attend that business, and give them thanks for their good affection, and consider with them what use may be made of what they offer, and report the same to the Council."[1] On the following day an order was made, " That a letter be written to the Lord-General, signifying the present state of those forces in Lancashire, and the danger that threatens the Commonwealth in the parts adjacent; and to desire his Excellency to order his intended expedition upon the enemy, so that he may be able to attend their attempts for the invasion of this Commonwealth."[2] On the 24th of April it was ordered, " That the report concerning the business of the gentlemen who were secured in Cheshire upon the discovery of the conspiracy be made to-morrow in the afternoon."[3] And we find, by the minutes of the 9th of May, that the Council of State were making great exertions to send troops to Major-General Harrison in the North—six troops of horse of 100 each, and " 100 dragoons of Captain Okey's troop of dragoons," in all 700[4] men despatched: and it was ordered, " That a troop of dragoons be sent to attend the demolishing of Nottingham Castle, and the two companies of foot now there are to march to Major-General Harrison." [5] On the 30th of May a letter from Major-General Harrison from Lancaster, of May 27, was referred to the Committee of Irish and Scottish Affairs.[6] It appears, then, that the forces drawn northwards under

[1] Order Book of the Council of State, April 7, 1651, MS. State Paper Office.

[2] *Ibid.* April 8, 1651.

[3] *Ibid.* April 24, 1651.

[4] This further shows the numerical proportion of dragoons to horse, already stated, namely, about one to six.—See Vol. I. p. 44.

[5] Order Book of the Council of State, May 9, 1651, MS. State Paper Office.—The following order of the 13th of the same month has reference to what was needed at that critical time—secret service: "That £100 be paid by Mr. Frost unto Captain Bishop, to be by him paid unto a certain man for a special service."— *Ibid.* May 13, 1651.

[6] *Ibid.* May 30, 1651.

Major-General Harrison were intended not only to suppress the intended insurrection in Cheshire and Lancashire, but to resist any invasion of England by the army of the King of Scots; and that therefore the Council of State was by no means taken by surprise, and altogether unprepared, by the invasion that ended in the Battle of Worcester.[1]

When Cromwell wrote to the Speaker on the 4th of August, the army of the King of Scots had not entered England. On the 6th of August the Scots' army marched into England over the border about three miles from Carlisle; and on the same day Cromwell, with about 10,000 horse and foot, and a light train, that he might move the swifter, marched from Leith, having despatched Major-General Lambert the day before (the 5th of August), with about 3,000 horse and dragoons.

In the afternoon of the 9th of August, the Council of State received by an express a letter from Mr. George Downing, dated from Newcastle on the 7th, containing the news that the King of Scots, with what forces were left with him, to the number of 14,000 men, had invaded England, and was advancing southward by rapid marches; part of the Parliament's forces, consisting of the cavalry under Major-General Lambert, being in his van, and the Lord-General Cromwell with the rest following in his rear. The House being adjourned for four days, the Council of State thought this intelligence so important that they met the next morning,[3] the 10th, though a Sunday, and passed the following orders:—

[1] See further evidence of this in the Order Book of the Council of State, March 26, 1651, MS. State Paper Office.

[2] Lord Leicester's Journal, pp. 110, 111, in Sydney Papers, edited by R. W. Blencowe: London, 1825.

[3] This meeting is headed "Sunday, August 10, 1651."—*Order Book of the Council of State*, MS. State Paper Office.

" To write a letter to the Lord Grey to come forthwith
to town ; to give him notice of the Scottish march."

" That the letter now read be sent to the Lord Mayor,
with a copy of the letter from Scout-master-General
Downing, to be published at Paul's " [the next two words I
cannot decypher, but I think they are " this forenoon ; "
" this fore—" is legible].

On the afternoon[1] of the same day, the Council of State
again met, and made the following orders :—

" That a warrant be sent to the Lieutenant of the Tower,
that the prisoners in the Tower are to be kept close prisoners till further order."

" That a letter be written to General Blake, to desire him
to take care of the West, in the absence of Major-General
Desborowe ; and to send two ships of those with him
toward the Isle of Man and those parts, to prevent the
landing of any forces from the Isle of Man."

" That letters be written to the several militias forthwith,
to bring the forces of their counties together, without any
delay, to some place where they are to be ready to execute
such orders as shall be sent them from the Parliament,
this Council, or Lieutenant-General Fleetwood."

" That letters be written to all the militias in the way
toward Staffordshire, to get together all their forces, and
furnish them with a fortnight's pay, and have them ready
to receive the orders of the Parliament, this Council, Lieutenant-General Fleetwood, or Major-General Harrison."

" To write to Major-General Harrison, to give him an
account of what posture things are put into in respect of
forces in these parts ; and that he goes on to raise the

---

[1] The heading of the afternoon's
meeting is, instead of the old form " a
meridie," " the afternoon of the same
day."—*Order Book of the Council of
State*, Sunday, August 10, 1651, MS,
State Paper Office.

honest men he speaks on, and that the Council will move the Parliament for pay for them."[1]

Now, as the express from Scout-master-General Downing only arrived on Saturday afternoon, and by Sunday afternoon—that is, in the course of twenty-four hours—all these energetic proceedings were taken by the Council of State; couriers, mounted on the fleetest horses, despatched with letters to Lord Grey, to General Blake, to Major-General Harrison, and to all the militias of the several counties; and such expedition used that satisfactory answers to their letters were received by Tuesday the 12th of August—that is in forty-eight hours, as appears by the Council's report to the Parliament, to be quoted presently —it will be observed that Mrs. Hutchinson's assertions respecting the Council of State's having been paralysed by fear to such an extent as to be incapable of efficient action, till, "*one* day in a private council, Colonel Hutchinson encouraged them" (she does not say the evening of Saturday, the 9th of August, the only portion of time between the receipt of the news of the Scottish invasion and their energetic action to resist it when what she asserts was possible) are to the last degree improbable, not to use a stronger word. In fact, Mrs. Hutchinson's words, according to their most obvious construction, imply that Colonel Hutchinson was in Nottinghamshire at the time the express from Downing reached the Council of State.

On that Sunday, the 10th of August 1651, "the broad place at Whitehall" (it is in these words that the minutes of the Council describe the space in front of Whitehall) presented an extraordinary spectacle. The ordinary staff consisted of twelve[2] mounted messengers, who waited the

---

[1] Order Book of the Council of State, Sunday, August 10, 1651, MS.

[2] State Paper Office. " That the twelve messengers

orders of the Secretary of the Council of State in " the broad
place at Whitehall," which, though we pass that spot now
without emotion, possessed at that time a strange and
terrible interest, associated with that transaction which,
even Hume admits, " corresponded to the greatest conception that is suggested in the annals of human kind—the
delegates of a great people sitting in judgment upon
their supreme magistrate, and trying him for his misgov-
ernment and breach of trust."[1]   But on this memorable
Sunday, the 10th of August, 1651, a large addition was
necessarily made by the Secretary of the Council to his
staff of mounted messengers.   And one by one, as they
received their despatches, courier after courier set spurs to
his fleet horse, and galloped off from the door of the
Council Chamber.   In this case the couriers must have been
far more numerous, as their business was far more momentous, than Sir Walter Scott's

who
> Ten squires, ten yeomen, mail-clad men
> Waited the beck of the warders ten.

But the speed with which the Council's couriers galloped
off from the front of Whitehall, in various directions, may
recall the scene so graphically described in the "Lay of the
Last Minstrel :"—

> And out! and out!
> In hasty route,
> The horsemen gallop'd forth;
> Dispersing to the south to scout,
> And east, and west, and north.

---

hitherto attending the Council be entertained still in the service of the Council,
to be at the direction of the Secretary.
And shall have 5s. per diem [each] for
their salary, and 6d. per mile for riding,
in the same manner they formerly had
at Derby House." "That Mr. Frost

shall entertain one servant to keep the
office and to be at his command to call
messengers, &c., and that he shall have
2s. per diem for his salary."—*Order
Book of the Council of State*, June
5, 1649, MS. State Paper Office.
[1] Hume's Hist. of England, chap. lix.

On Monday the 11th of August, the Council of State ordered :—

" That a letter be written to the Lord Mayor of London, to desire him that a Common Council may be warned to meet this afternoon, at 2 of the clock, to be in readiness to receive some members of this Council, in order to communicate something unto them in order to public safety."

" That Mr. Bond, Mr. Chaloner, Mr. Darley, Colonel Purefoy, Lord-Commissioner Whitelock, Lord Grey, Colonel Fielder, Lieutenant-General Fleetwood, Mr. Goodwyn, Mr. Scot, Mr. Carew, or any three of them, be appointed a Committee, to consider of what is fit to be done at this time for the safety of the Commonwealth, and to report their opinion to the Council from time to time, as they shall think fit."

Another Committee is appointed " to go to the Common Council of London at 4 P. M. this day, to inform them of the invasion of this land by the King of Scots, the time and manner thereof; and also of the posture of the forces of this Commonwealth both in Scotland and England, as to prevention of the danger to the Commonwealth thereby; and to move the City to do their best for raising some considerable forces for the defence of the Parliament and City, in case the enemy should pass our forces. And that they also take care for the quiet of the City within itself, and to prevent any assistance to be sent to, or any correspondence to be held with, the Scots' King, or any of his party."

" That the Lord Grey be desired to repair into Leicestershire, to do there what shall occur to him to be for the prevention of the Scots' army in their march."

" That a warrant be forthwith issued, to stay the 1,500

backs, breasts, and pots[1] that are now shipped to go to Scotland, and that they be brought back to the Tower till further order."

At the afternoon meeting of the Council of State, the Council made two orders, relating to a subject not connected with the invasion of the Scots; which circumstance is of itself sufficient proof that, so far from the Council's being in that state of trepidation alleged by Mrs. Hutchinson, they not only took all the requisite steps for resisting the invasion, but attended also to ordinary business. The two orders referred to are as follows : —

"That a declaration be published, that all those that come to drink the waters at Lewisham in Kent do behave themselves peaceably, without tumult."

"That Lieutenant-General [Fleetwood] be desired to send a fit party of horse, to prevent tumults and miscarriages at the waters at Lewisham."

Then comes the following order :—"That Mr. Rushworth [2] and Captain Bishop maintain intelligence between the Council and the armies" [namely, 1, the army under Cromwell: 2, that under Lambert: 3, that under Harrison] ; "and that the sum of £200 be paid to Captain Bishop by Mr. Frost, out of the monies in his hands for the use of the Council."[3]

On the following day, Tuesday the 12th of August, the House passed three Acts for the support of the Commonwealth against the present danger—namely: 1. An Act

---

[1] "Backs" are the back-pieces of the defensive armour; "breasts" are the front pieces, i.e. the cuirasses or corslets ; "pots" are helmets.

[2] John Rushworth, the great historical collector, who appears from this minute to have by this time returned to

London, having been secretary to Cromwell at the time of the Battle of Dunbar, at which he was present.

[3] Order Book of the Council of State, Monday, August 11, 1651, MS. State Paper Office.

empowering the Commissioners of the Militia to raise forces and money; and for reviving all commissions formerly granted by Ordinance of Parliament, or the Council of State, to any Colonels and other officers.—2. An Act containing instructions to the Commissioners of the Militia. —3. An Act for declaring it High Treason to hold any correspondence with the King of Scots.

On the same day, Tuesday the 12th of August, the Council of·State made the following orders :—

"That a letter be written to the Lord Fairfax, to desire his Lordship to use his best endeavours for the raising of forces in Yorkshire."

"That the 1,000 backs and breasts, the 1,500 pots, the 1,000 long[1] pikes, the 1,000 snaphance [flintlock] muskets, the 500 matchlock muskets, which were shipped on board the *Thomas* of London, Jonathan Gibbs, master, be returned back into the Tower."

"That it be reported to the Parliament, that the Council of State, taking into consideration the present state of affairs upon occasion of the Scottish army marching into England, and finding that their march is not upon confidence, with which, when it was whole and unbroken, they could not be provoked to give battle to our army, or come out of their straights to save their own country, which they saw broken in one part after another; despairing of their own country, which they have deserted as lost, they are marched into England with their last hope, that from their own party of the traitors to this Commonwealth, there will be a great conflux unto them for their recruits and assistance, in which, if they should be disappointed, they will soon come to nothing, though they should have but weak

---

[1] This shows that the pikes were of various lengths.

opposition. And although the Council find also, that by the great diligence and care of the Lord-General and his officers, the forces of the nation are disposed so as they conceive they will not be able to advance far before our forces will be with them, and that there will-be (through God's goodness) a speedy and thorough end of the work; yet they have thought fit, for the better prevention of any such resort and recruit to them, and also for the better preserving the peace of these parts, humbly to offer the ensuing particulars to the consideration of the Parliament, if they shall so judge fit, viz. :—

" 1. All persons joining or giving any aid whatever to the Scottish army shall be tried by the Council of War, and upon due proof of the fact shall suffer death and forfeit, as in case of treason, and be executed accordingly.

" 2. One-third part of the estate of offenders to all who shall discover them." [1]

The rest of the articles relate to disarming suspected persons, and police regulations. The Lord Mayor and the rest of the Committee of the Militia of the City, and also the Commissioners of the Militia of Westminster, the Hamlets, and Southwark, are to sit daily.

On the same day a letter is ordered to be written to the commander of the 2,000 foot at Weymouth, to march them with all expedition to Reading. A warrant is ordered to be prepared, to be sent to the several Postmasters in London and elsewhere upon the roads, to require them to keep a certain number of horses constantly in the house, to be ready upon all occasions. Letters are ordered to be written to the militias, to apply some horses towards the post-roads ;

[1] Order Book of the Council of State, Tuesday, August 12, 1651, MS. State Paper Office.

and also to the Commissioners of the Militias of the
several counties, " to enclose the Act against correspondence with Charles Stuart (which was, as we have seen,
passed that day—and this circumstance shows the rapidity with which the Council acted) ; and that they take
care to deliver it to the Sheriffs, who are to cause the
same to be proclaimed forthwith in every market town,
and at their County Courts, and that it be also sent to
every parish."[1]

On the same day a report is ordered to be made to the
Parliament of the various proceedings they have taken
upon the first notice received of the Scottish army marching
towards England.

The Council of State on the same day also made the fol--
lowing orders :—

" That six blank horse-commissions be prepared, to be
given to the Lord Grey,[2] for the raising of voluntarie
[volunteer] horse in the counties of Northampton, Leicester, and Rutland."

" That the Lord Grey have a commission to command
the forces of Leicester, Northampton, and Rutland, and to

[1] Order Book of the Council of
State, Tuesday, August 12, 1651, MS.
State Paper Office.

[2] The Lord Grey of Groby. The
Lord Grey of Werke, who had been a
member of the Council of State in the
two former years, was not re-elected in
February 1651. Henry Grey, second
Baron Grey of Groby, was created
Earl of Stamford in 1628. The person
here mentioned as Lord Grey of Groby was Thomas Grey, the eldest son
of the Henry Grey above mentioned ;
and as he died during the life of his
father, he never became either Earl of
Stamford or Baron Grey of Groby;
but his son, Thomas Grey, succeeded
his grandfather, in 1673, as second
Earl of Stamford and third Baron
Grey of Groby. The Lord Grey of
Werke had been Sir William Grey,
one of King James's baronets, and
was created Baron Grey of Werke in
1624. Though the name of Grey, as a
baronial name, is nearly as old in
England as that of Plantagenet, these
peerages of Groby and Werke were,
it will be observed, only Stuart peerages, the least honourable in the
English annals.

receive his orders from the Parliament, the Council, and the Lord-General."

" That £200 be paid unto the Lord Grey, for his incident charges in his journey and expedition which he is now sent upon." [1]

On Wednesday the 13th of August the Council of State continued their labours, as the following orders show :—

" That Barnet be appointed for the place of rendezvous for the forces which are to be gathered together in these parts, and Tuesday next is to be the day when the forces are to rendezvous."

" That the Commissioners of the Militia of Leicester, Rutland, and Northampton do draw the forces of their respective counties to several rendezvous, and send a month's pay with them, who are to receive orders from the Lord Grey."

" That the Lord Grey shall have power to list what volunteer horse will offer themselves, and to assure them pay, from the time they are in actual service, for so long as they continue in service." [2]

The free constitutional spirit of the Council of State—a spirit in strict accordance with the ancient English principles of constitutional liberty, self-government, and self-defence—is strongly marked, even at this critical time, by the following directions to Lord Grey, to receive advice from the County Militia Commissioners ; and is in manifest contrast with the more centralised but not more efficient action of the Government, when Cromwell concentrated the sovereignty in his single person :—

" That whereas there was yesterday an order made for the giving unto the Lord Grey six blank horse-

---

[1] Order Book of the Council of   Paper Office.
State, August 12, 1651, MS. State   [2] Ibid. August 13, 1651.

commissions, for the raising of so many voluntary troops for the defence of those parts, the Council doth now declare that their intention is that the officers of the said troops, as also the soldiers, are to be appointed and enlisted by the Lord Grey *with the approbation of the Commissioners of the Militia for that county in which any of the said troops shall be raised.*"[1]

On Thursday, 14th August 1651, the Council thus continued their labours :—

" That 1,000 dragoons be mounted to go towards the army."

" That the Commissioners of the Militia of London, Westminster, Hamlets, and Southwark do make a return to the Council, by 3 P.M., what horses they have of those which they have seized that are fit for dragoons, except those that are already listed in troops for the service of the Parliament."

" That it may be reported to the Parliament, that Mr. John Claypoole [*sic*] may be authorised to raise a troop of horse, such as shall come voluntarily[2] unto him, in the counties of Northampton and Lincoln, or elsewhere; and that they may be paid according to the establishment of the army."[3]

On Friday morning, 15th August 1651, the Council ordered :—" That a letter be written to the Commissioners of the Militia of Salop, to quicken them, and take notice of their slow proceeding, and to [desire them to] certify who

---

[1] Order Book of the Council of State, Wednesday, August 13, 1651, MS. State Paper Office.

[2] Another example of the English voluntary principle, in marked contrast to that of the centralised despotisms already widely spread over Europe, and which the English Council of State was even now exerting itself to keep out of England.

[3] Order Book of the Council of State, Thursday, August 14, 1651, MS. State Paper Office.

of the Commissioners do not appear and act vigorously in this time."

" That answers be given to the letters from Staffordshire, Cheshire, Lancashire, to approve their diligence, to desire them to proceed with the greatest vigour to break bridges and stop passes, and receive orders from Major-General Harrison."

" That it be reported to the Parliament, that it is the humble opinion of this Council that the regiment of Colonel Gibbons may be forthwith mounted and sent toward the army; and that for that purpose the Parliament will give power to the Council, out of the horses now seized about London and the parts adjacent, or otherwise, to take up horses to mount the said regiments; and that the said horses be prized with the names of the proprietors of them, listed, and tickets given to them for payment of them, if any of them shall be lost or spoiled, if the Parliament shall so think fit." [1]

Friday afternoon, 15th August, 1651.—" That the proposition of Sir Michael Livesey, for the raising of a regiment of horse and a regiment of foot volunteers in the county of Kent, be accepted of, and he desired to repair into the country to press the same into execution.

"That the Parliament be moved that the regiment of Colonel Gibbons may be paid as so many dragoons, for so long time as they shall be continued to serve in that condition." [2]

Saturday, 16th August, 1651.—" That a letter be written to the Commissioners of Kent, to let them know the Council expects that they should send up their two troops of

---

[1] Order Book of the Council of State, Friday morning, August 15, 1651, MS. State Paper Office.

[2] *Ibid.* Friday afternoon, August 15, 1651.

horse to the rendezvous on Tuesday next; and that they should proceed to the raising of their regiments of foot in full numbers." [1]

Monday morning, 18*th August,* 1651.—" That a short letter be prepared, to be sent to the several militias of this nation, to give them a brief account of the state of the armies."

" That the letter from Colonel Blake of the 15th inst. be referred to the Committee of the Admiralty." [2]

Monday afternoon, 18*th August,* 1651.—" That a letter be written to the Lord Grey, to be by him communicated to the Commissioners of the Militia for Northampton, Leicester, and Rutland, to desire his Lordship to cause the whole forces of Northampton, Leicester, and Rutland to march to Daventree, the 23rd of August."

" That a letter be written to the Commissioners of Militia for the counties of Leicester, Rutland, Lincoln, Northampton, Warwick, Oxford, Bedford, Huntingdon, Buckingham, and Worcester, to draw what forces they can possibly together, and to send them to Daventree on Saturday the 23rd of August, to a rendezvous;·to desire them to put a week's pay into the pockets of the private soldiers, and to send the other three weeks' [pay] to the field-officers, or, in defect of them, to the captains of companies; and they are to take care that none be armed who have been in arms against the Parliament."

" That Lieutenant-General Fleetwood be appointed Commander-in-Chief of all the forces which are now

---

[1] Order Book of the Council of State, Saturday, August 16, 1651, MS. State Paper Office.—It may be proper to state, that the minutes here extracted by no means represent all the business transacted by the Council at that time, but only that part of it which appears of the greatest historical interest.

[2] *Ibid.* Monday morning, August 18, 1651.

appointed to rendezvous at Barnet, Daventree, and St. Albans." [1]

Admiring as I do the great political ability, as well as the spotless integrity, of Sir Henry Vane, I might be disposed, if I were writing in the spirit of an advocate, to keep back the minute which follows. But, as I have said before, I am anxious to ascertain the truth, if possible, whatever it may be :—

"That a letter be written to Sir H. Vane, to let him know that, in the present state of affairs, the Council are of opinion that his presence is necessary here ; to desire him, therefore, to repair up hither with all convenient speed." [2]

It appears, by the subsequent proceedings of the Council in which Vane's name appears, that he obeyed this summons. But why did he not come up sooner ? It is impossible that he should not have heard of the Scottish invasion. I can see no solution of the question but the acceptance of the authority of some of Vane's cotemporaries on this point of Vane's character—that he was naturally a timid man, and that he was at this critical time keeping out of the way, though the courage he displayed at his trial and execution seemed to be at variance with that character. It is, moreover, due to Vane's memory—which was assailed by the malignity of Hyde, who himself never risked a scratch of a finger in the cause, while he never scrupled to impute cowardice to others, an imputation which veteran soldiers, really brave men, are always slow to make—that the veteran soldier Ludlow, who had proved his courage in so many battles, says that to Vane's other great and estimable qualities, "were added a resolution and courage, not to be shaken, or diverted from the public service." [3]

[1] Order Book of the Council of State, Monday afternoon, August 18, 1651, MS. State Paper Office.

[2] *Ibid.* same meeting.

[3] Ludlow's Memoirs, vol. iii. pp. 110, 111: 2nd edition, London, 1721.

The philosophy of courage is indeed a dark subject, in regard to which few men are willing to give the evidence of their actual experience, and consequently many difficulties lie in the way of a complete elucidation of it.　There is a sort of courage which has been called " orator courage," which such men as Vane and Strafford possess, and which is distinct from that sort of courage which leads men to face death on fields of battle.　This latter sort of courage I do not think Strafford possessed, whether Vane possessed it or not, though some modern writers have spoken of the " valour " as well as the " capacity " of Strafford.　That Strafford did not possess what is commonly understood by " valour," I think is proved by his letting the Scots pass the Tyne at Newburn, when he commanded the English army for Charles I.　At the same time, though Strafford behaved bravely, as well as Vane, both at his trial and execution, there was a fundamental distinction between them. There was in Strafford a spirit of insolence, tyranny, and cruelty of which there is no trace in Vane.　Strafford was, in one word, a bully.　Vane was nothing of that.　It is also a very remarkable psychological fact, that while, both at his trial and execution, " though timid by nature "—according to Hume, who of course follows Hyde in the imputation of timidity against such a formidable enemy of the Stuarts—" the persuasion of a just cause supported Vane against the terrors of death, " [1] Lambert, who had faced death on a hundred fields of battle, having been tried and condemned at the same time as Vane, obtained, by throwing himself abjectly on the royal mercy, a reprieve at the bar, and thus sacrificed, to the fear of death on the scaffold, all those principles he had so long and so bravely fought and bled for.　There was probably a constitutional or organic

---

[1] Hume's History, chap. lxiii.

distinction between the courage and fear of Vane and
Lambert. Yet, when we look at these two men at the time
of the Scottish invasion, and see Vane keeping himself
absent even from his ordinary duty at the Council of State,
and Lambert gallantly leading the Ironside cavalry, ha-
rassing the march of the Scots, and then thoroughly
defeating them at Worcester; and then look again at the
trial of the same two men for their lives, and see Vane
bravely facing death, and Lambert abjectly shrinking from
it: when we remember, moreover, the remark of Sir William
Temple, " some are brave one day and cowards another,
as great captains have often told me from their own experience and observation "—the reported saying of Napoleon,
that " no man is brave at two o'clock in the morning "—and
the fact that there were occasions on which even Nelson[1]
was subject to fear, we must feel strongly the rashness
and presumption of dogmatising, either generally or
specially, on the subject of courage and cowardice.

On Tuesday, 19th August 1651, the Council made
the following orders, among many others :—

" That such arms shall be taken out of the Tower as
shall be necessary for the soldiers."

" That authority be given to the several Postmasters
upon the road, to press horses upon this exigent for the
despatching of intelligence."

" That a commission be sent to Colonel Blake, to command-in-chief, in the absence of Major-General Desborowe,

---

[1] I have seen it stated, on the authority of a friend of Nelson, that
Nelson, having one day been taken by
him into his phaeton-and-four for a
drive, in a few minutes became uneasy;
and then, with evident marks of ner-
vousness, requested that he might be
set down, expressing his fears of being
run away with, of which there was no
danger, since the horses, though lively,
were perfectly broken in. But the
situation was novel to the man of the
Nile and Trafalgar.

all the forces raised and to be raised in the counties of Cornwall, Devon, Somerset, and Dorset; and that letters be written to those four counties to obey his orders."

" That power be given to the Lord President of the Council, in case that any packets shall arrive here in the night-time, to open the said letters, and, according as he shall find they do import, he is to give order for the summoning of a Council immediately."[1]

Wednesday, 20th August, 1651.—" That letters be written to the Commissioners of .the Militia for the counties of Wilts, Gloucester, Hereford, and South Wales, to bring what forces they can with all speed to a rendezvous at Gloucester, for the security of those parts; and this rendezvous to be at Gloucester on Monday next."[2]

Thursday, 21*st August,* 1651.—" That Major Winthrope do appoint a troop of horse to be in readiness, to observe such directions as shall be given to him from the Treasurer at War."

" That a letter be written to the several counties through which the army is to march, to desire them to furnish them with all provisions necessary for them of all kinds."

" That Mr. Waller and Mr. Cromwell be desired to repair into the county of Huntingdon; and that they and the Commissioners of the Militia do take care that the forces of that county may be drawn together to a rendezvous."[3]

On the same day a committee was appointed, " to draw a proclamation for the proclaiming of Charles Stuart traitor, according to the debates had this day."

On the same day, the 21st of August, the House received

---

[1] Order Book of the Council of State, Tuesday, August 19, 1651, MS. State Paper Office.

[2] *Ibid.* August 20, 1651.

[3] *Ibid.* August 21, 1651.

intelligence, that the Scots' army lay on the 17th at North-
wich, and the next day advanced between Nantwich and
Chester; and that Major-General Lambert and the forces
with him were cheerfully followed by the officers and soldiers of the Cheshire and Lancashire militia of foot; who
upon this emergency, though their harvest was ready to
cut, promised not to leave them till they either should be
properly dismissed, or the Lord put a seasonable issue to
the business.[1]   Under the same date, Whitelock mentions
" an account of forces raised in Salop and the neighbouring counties, and breaking of bridges, and endeavouring to
divert the course of the Scots' army;" " that the Governor
of Stafford went to Harrison with 700 men;" "that
4,000 of the General's foot march in their shirts 20 miles
a day, and have their clothes and arms carried by the
country."[2]

All this sufficiently shows that a Stuart, or any other
claimant of the Crown of England, had mighty small chance
of success in his attempt, when made by the help of a
foreign army, whether that army was Scotch, French, or
German.   In fact this, as well as the attempt of 1745,
shows that it was a blunder of the Stuarts to think that
the English would allow a foreign army (for such, in fact,
the Scottish army then was) to impose a King upon them.
The zeal of the Parliamentary soldiers, and of the country
generally, is forcibly expressed in the fact last quoted from
Whitelock, that the soldiers' upper clothes and arms were
" carried by the country," in order that the soldiers might
march with more speed.   As the Scots' army with their
King advanced in that direction, " the Forest of Dean rose
for the Parliament, and there was great resort of people to

---

[1] Parl. Hist. vol. iii. p. 1369.   [2] Whitelock, August 21, 1651.

Gloucester and Hereford to defend those places.''[1] In all places, on the march of the King's army southward, the garrisons were summoned in the King's name to surrender, but without any success.   And when, in the more eminent places, *Charles II.* was proclaimed by heralds, the people returned no approving shouts, but, on the contrary, as the Royalists admit, preserved a gloomy silence, or exhibited— as if they truly foreboded what was to come to pass in after-years, under the King then proclaimed—the consternation of persons stricken by some great calamity.[2]

It is strange indeed to turn from this spectacle to that described by Pepys and Aubrey, as seen in London some nine years after this month of August 1651. What was the cause of the great change that took place, or at least that appeared to take place, between 1651 and 1660? Was it that the Government of the Long Parliament was popular, and that of Cromwell unpopular? I think not. I think that the Government of the Long Parliament and the Government of Cromwell were both unpopular; for both were arbitrary, and both imposed, of necessity perhaps, a very heavy taxation. It might indeed at first sight appear, as it at one time appeared to me, that this zeal of the country, manifested on this occasion, against the King of Scots, contrasted with the zeal manifested in 1660 for the return of that same King of Scots as King of England, showed that the Government of the Long Parliament was popular, and that of Cromwell unpopular. But I think that the zeal of August 1651 only expressed the determina-tion of the English people not to have a King imposed on them by a foreign army, and not the approbation of the Government of the Rump; though that Government, as

[1] Perf. Diur. August 25 to Septem-ber 1, in Cromwelliana, p. 110.   [2] Bates, part ii. pp. 120, 121.

compared with the Government of Charles II., might
well be called an assembly of gods as compared with an
assembly of baboons. No one can deny this who compares
Charles II.'s Council, as described in Pepys's Diary, with the
Council of State of the Long Parliament, as described in
their own minutes ; which happily exist, to vindicate their
memory to all after-ages against the scurrility not only of
the Royalist writers, but of Cromwell, who destroyed them,
and of Cromwell's parasites and worshippers. If I were
an advocate of this Rump and its Council of State, as some
men are advocates of Oliver Cromwell, it would be easy to
say that, by 1660, things had altered greatly—that Cromwell
had succeeded in so digusting all men, that they were willing to try once more even the Government of the Stuarts.
But though it can be clearly proved that Cromwell's
Government was unpopular, I think more unpopular than
that of the Long Parliament—for Cromwell's usurpation
had taken away all hope of what both the army and the
people wanted, namely, " a free Parliament "—it can at the
same time, I think, be proved that the Rump was unpopular
also. In fact, in the saturnalia of the Restoration, the
most obtrusive exhibition was the roasting of rumps ; there
was no burning of Oliver Cromwell in effigy. But there
was also a significant fact, which, though not noticed by
Pepys, is particularly mentioned by Aubrey : " Mem. that
Threadneedle Street was all day long, and late at night,
crammed with multitudes, crying out, ' *A free Parliament !
—a free Parliament !* " [1] I have never seen any completely
satisfactory answer made to the question why the Rump

---

[1] Aubrey's Letters and Lives, vol.
ii. p. 455 : London, 1813.—" Bells
ringing, and bonfires all over the city
  . . They made little gibbets, and
roasted rumps of mutton ; nay, I saw
some very good rumps of beef. Health
to King Charles II. ! was drunk in the
streets by the bonfires, even on their
knees."—*Ibid.*

put off so long the petitions presented to them for a free Parliament. Scot, one of their ablest members, made this answer : " The Dutch war came on—when Hannibal is *ad portas*, something must be done *extra leges*—we stayed to end the Dutch war." But the answer to this answer is, that they were petitioned to dissolve, and make way for a free Parliament, long before the Dutch war was thought of. In fact, their conduct must be admitted to form the best excuse, though far from a satisfactory excuse, for the conduct of Cromwell.

On Friday the 22nd, Mr. Scot and Mr. Salwey were sent by the Council of State to the Major-Generals, with instructions " to let them know what course the Council have taken for raising and ordering of forces for the present occasion, besides those with them; and thereupon to confer and debate with them, at Councils of War or otherwise, in what manner the forces of this Commonwealth may be best employed against the enemy, with consideration to all emergencies that may thence arise." [1]

On the same day the following orders were made :—

" That a letter be written to Major-General Lambert, to let him know that it is the opinion of this Council that a considerable force of horse and dragoons should wait upon the enemy, whereby he may be impeded in his march, kept from refreshing his men, and the people discouraged from coming in to them."

" That a letter be written to the Lord-General, to acquaint him with the resolutions of the Council taken this day—both of the letter written to Major-General Lambert,

[1] Order Book of the Council of State, Friday, August 22, 1651, MS. State Paper Office : " Instructions for Thomas Scot and Richard Salwey, Esqrs.; sent by the Council unto the Major-Generals of the Forces of the Parliament employed against the Scots' army now in England."

and likewise of sending Mr. Salwey and Mr. Scot to the Major-Generals."

"That a letter be written to the Commissioners of the Militia for the four northern counties, to desire them to have their militia forces speedily in readiness, and to apply themselves to the public service, that they may be assistant to the Governors of Berwick and Carlisle, for the prevention of any correspondence between Scotland and the Scottish army in England."

"That the Lord-Commissioner Whitlocke do report to the Parliament, that it hath pleased God to take out of this life Colonel Edward Popham, late one of the Generals of the fleet of this Commonwealth."[1]

The following minute of the same date shows that by this time, the 22nd of August, Sir Henry Vane had returned to his duty at the Council of State:—" That the Lord-Commissioner Whitlocke and Sir Henry Vane be desired to go to Mrs. Popham from this Council, to condole with her the loss of her husband; to let her know what a memory they have of the good services done by her husband to this Commonwealth; and that they will upon all occasions be ready to show respect unto those of his relations which [sic] he hath left behind him."[2]

"Saturday, 23rd August, 1651.—" That the Lord-Commissioner Whitlocke, Lord-Commissioner Lisle, Mr. Attorney, Mr. Say, or any two of them, be appointed a committee,

[1] Order Book of the Council of State, Friday, August 22, 1651, MS. State Paper Office.—The Earl of Leicester thus notices in his Journal the death of Colonel Popham: "Wednesday, 20th August, 1651.—We had news out of Kent of the death of Colonel Popham, one of our Admirals, a person of much honour and eminent fidelity, who was taken away by a fever at Dover, the 19th instant."— Lord Leicester's Journal, p. 115, in Sydney Papers, edited by R. W. Blencowe, London, 1825.

[2] Order Book of the Council of State, Friday, August 22, 1651, MS. State Paper Office.

to consider of the draught of a proclamation now brought in for the proclaiming of Charles Stuart traitor, the declaration of the said C. Stuart upon his entering into the Commonwealth of England with a Scottish army, and the letter of the said C. Stuart to the City of London; and upon consideration of the whole, to draw up something in the nature of a proclamation, whereby he may be proclaimed traitor; and this to be done so that it may be offered to the Parliament on Monday morning."[2]

By the middle of August the Parliament had got together so many troops, under those able commanders, Lambert and Harrison, that it was believed, on good grounds, that even had Cromwell remained in Scotland, the enemy could easily have been defeated.

Upon Tuesday the 12th of August, the Scots' King came to Lancaster, and set all the prisoners in the Castle at liberty. Upon Wednesday the 13th he lodged at Myerscoe, Sir Thomas Tildesley's house, and from thence marched through Preston. On Thursday night he lodged at Euxten-burgh, six miles on this side of Preston, Sir Hugh Anderton's house, who was prisoner at Lancaster, but set at liberty by the Scots. "This Anderton," says a cotemporary Parliamentary newspaper, "is a bloody papist, and one that, when Prince Rupert was at Bolton, boasted much of being in blood to the elbows in that cruel massacre." On the night of Friday, the 15th, the Scots' King

---

[1] Order Book of the Council of State, Saturday, August 23, 1651, MS. State Paper Office.—On the 26th of August the letter of Charles Stuart to the Lord Mayor was burnt upon the Old Exchange by the hangman; and the Parliament's declaration against him, wherein he was called " son of the late tyrant," and declared rebel and traitor, and public enemy to the Commonwealth of England, and against all his abettors, &c., proclaimed there and at Westminster by beat of drum and sound of trumpet. —*Lord Leicester's Journal*, p. 116.

lodged at Brine, six miles from Warrington, the house of Sir William Gerard, a papist.

On Saturday the 16th of August, there was a sharp skirmish, at Warrington, between the army of the King of Scots and the forces of Lambert and Harrison. The fullest account of this skirmish which I have met with is that quoted, in Lord Leicester's Journal, from a cotemporary newspaper. It is commonly stated that Lambert and Harrison were "pressing hard on the rear" of the Scottish army, whereas this account, written apparently by a Parliamentary officer who was present, mentions "the present posture of *flanking and fronting* the enemy;" and their retiring to Knutsford Heath also shows that they kept on the south of the enemy—that is, between the enemy and London :—

"*Saturday, 16th August.*—About noon the enemy's scouts came into Warrington, and presently after a forlorn hope of horse and dragoons, we having left one company of foot to dispute the pass at the bridge and fords, and to amuse the enemy; for the said passes, and several other passes upon the river, were not tenable, by reason of the enclosed grounds, whereby our horse could not have room to charge, in order to the security of the foot. Yet that single company of the Cheshire foot disputed the bridge and pass with the enemy above an hour and a half; and then he that commanded the foot drew them off, when the enemy began to press hard upon him. Presently after the enemy marched over the pass, with horse and foot, towards our rearguard. We[1] marched to Knutsford Heath, being a convenient place for our horse to engage, expecting

[1] The special correspondent of Politicus, who sent this relation of the skirmish at Warrington, was probably an officer of the Parliamentary army; many of the officers of which could, like John Lilburne, wield the pen as well as the sword.

the enemy would have advanced thither; but the van of their army came that night about five or six miles on this side Warrington. It is conceived best to continue in the present posture of flanking and fronting the enemy, till we have a conjunction with other forces, unless they press hard, and force an engagement; and then (God willing) our forces are resolved on some open plain to fight them, we having 9,000 horse and dragoons, and between 3,000 and 4,000 foot, to give them battle."[1]

It may here be observed, that the large proportion of horse to foot in the army of Lambert and Harrison (9,000 to 3,000), and the enclosed nature of the ground, "whereby our horse could not have room to charge," as well as Cromwell's orders *not to risk a battle*, may explain why such soldiers as Lambert and Harrison, the best perhaps (not even excepting Cromwell) whom that war had produced, did not fight a battle with the invading army at Warrington. If they had done so, and won the battle, which was probable, Cromwell would have been stripped of that "crowning mercy" which, though it did not actually give him a crown, gave him a power greater than that of most wearers of crowns.

On the 23rd of August, the House received intelligence from the Major-Generals, Lambert and Harrison, dated the 22nd, that the Scots' army lay the night before at Tonge, a village in Shropshire, on the borders of Staffordshire— near to which are White Ladies' Priory and Boscobel House, known in connection with the escape of Charles

[1] Journal of the Earl of Liecester, pp. 112-114, in Sydney Papers, edited by R. W. Blencowe, A.M. : London, 1825.--In regard to the passages extracted by Lord Leicester from the newspapers of the day, Mr. Blencow observes, in his preface, that "it may be presumed, from the care with which Lord Leicester has copied them, that he considered them faithful accounts of the transactions which they record."

after his defeat at Worcester—and that they inclined towards Worcester; that Colonel Danvers, Governor of Stafford, with some few horse, fell in upon some of their quarters, killed five of their men, and gave an alarm to their whole army. In another letter, it was stated that the Scots had, of horse and foot, 120 columns; that their horse were poor and harassed out; that their foot were miserably ragged, and sick creatures a great number of them; that their King was found, with cap in hand, desiring them yet a little longer to stick to him—persuading them that, within two days' march, they should come into a country where all things would be plentifully provided for them, and shortly thence to London. It was also stated that the Parliament's forces were at Tamworth, and from thence had sent several parties to attend the enemy's motions; and intended to dispose their own marches, in order to a conjunction with the Lord-General, and the other forces lately sent from London.[1]

On Friday the 22nd of August, the Scots with their King reached Worcester[2]; where the country forces made a gallant resistance, and beat back the enemy several times. But the townsmen having laid down their arms, and some of them shooting out of the windows at the Parliament's soldiers, that had been sent by Harrison and Lambert to secure Worcester, the latter removed their ammunition and withdrew to Gloucester, 30 of them keeping the enemy in check while they were so employed.[3] The Council of State took measures for punishing the townsmen of Worcester for their conduct on this occasion, as appears by the following minute, made on the afternoon

---

[1] Parl. Hist. vol. iii. pp. 1369, 1370; Whitelock, August 23, 1651.

[2] Letter from Lieutenant-General

Fleetwood, in Cromwelliana, p. 110.

[3] Whitelock, August 25, 1651.

of the 29th of August: "That a letter be written to the Lord-General, to desire him to send a commission of martial law into Yorkshire, for the trial of such persons as have assisted Charles Stuart, some of which [sic] are there in restraint. And his Lordship is 'also to be put in mind, that in case the city of Worcester, or any persons, inhabitants of the same, who have been instruments in the betraying of that town to Charles Stuart, do fall into his hands, that he proceed to try all of them according to the late Act." [1]

The Earl of Derby, who had held out the Isle of Man for the King, at this time made a descent on Lancashire, for the purpose of creating a diversion. He had got together 1,500 men, when Colonel Robert Lilburne (the brother of Lieutenant-Colonel John Lilburne), with not half that number, fell upon him near Wigan. After a hot dispute, for near an hour, the Earl's forces were routed. The Earl himself was wounded, but escaped and fled, to seek refuge in the royal army at Worcester. The Lord Widdrington and 80 officers and persons of quality were slain. Four hundred prisoners were taken, of whom many were officers and gentlemen. Three cloaks with stars of the Earl of Derby, his George and Garter, and other valuables, were taken. The Parliament ordered £500 to Colonel Lilburne, £200 per annum as a mark of honour for his faithful services, and £100 to his lieutenant, that brought the news from him; and thanks next "Lord's-day in the London churches for the surrender of Stirling Castle and the defeat of the Earl of Derby," and prayers "for a blessing upon the Parliament's forces, *now near an engagement*." [2]

---

[1] Order Book of the Council of State, August 29, 1651 (afternoon), MS. State Paper Office.

[2] Whitelock, August 29-30, 1651.— About the same time, the Parliament ordered to Colonel Mackworth a chain of gold with a medal, as a mark of their favour "for his faithful and gallant refusal of the King's summons to render Shrewsbury Castle."—*Ibid.*

The Council of State relaxed not their exertions. On Tuesday, the 2nd of September, they wrote to the Commissioners of Yorkshire, to hasten their forces towards Colonel Lilburne; to Sir Arthur Haselrig, to send some forces into Scotland, to prevent the levies of the enemy; and they referred to the Committee for the Admiralty a letter of Colonel Blake, from aboard the *Victory* in the Downs, dated the day before (September 1, 1651).[1] On Wednesday the 3rd of September 1651, the day on which was fought the Battle of Worcester, much business of various kinds—some of it of great importance—was transacted by the Council of State; the numbers present in the morning being 19, in the afternoon 20. But many members of the Council of State were at Worcester—Scot and Salwey and Lord Grey of Groby being there, besides the military officers, Cromwell, Fleetwood, Harrison, and others. Of the minutes of their proceedings on that day I will mention two as especially deserving of attention. The first is this: "That thanks be returned to the sick and maimed soldiers living about this town, for their free offer to be a guard to the Parliament; and to let them know that, through the goodness of God, the state of affairs is such at present that they have not need of any other guards than what are already appointed to that service."[2]

same date. On August 27, the Council of State made the following order:—"That Mr. Alderman Allein [who was a member of the Council of State, and then present] do prepare a chain of gold and a medal [he was, I suppose, a jeweller and goldsmith—one of Denzil Holles's "mean tradesmen"] for Colonel Mackworth, to the value of £100, in pursuance of an Order of Parliament."—*Order Book of the Council of State*, Wednesday, August 27, 1851, MS. State Paper Office. On Saturday, August 30, the Council of State ordered, "That Lord-Commissioner Whitelock be desired to report to the Parliament the letter from Colonel Lilburne, and also the narrative prepared of the success of the forces of the Commonwealth in Scotland and England, in pursuance of an Order of Parliament."—*Ibid.* Saturday, August 30, 1651.

[1] *Ibid.* Tuesday, September 2, 1651.
[2] *Ibid.* Wednesday, September 3, 1651.

The other minute is a very remarkable one, and confirms what I have before stated—that foreign nations were eagerly watching the issue of the present attempt of the Stuarts and their adherents, with a view to seize any favourable opportunity of crushing the English Commonwealth. The minute states that " the Council have received information of some designs from Holland to land foreign forces on the coast of Suffolk ; " and they order letters to be written to the Commissioners of Norfolk and Suffolk, to furnish between them one regiment of foot to the guard of those parts, and Suffolk to send one troop of horse ; and to Colonel Wauton and Colonel Jermie, to desire them to take especial care of that part of the coast.[1] On the following day (Thursday, the 4th of September, 1651), they order a letter to be written to Colonel Blake, to give him an account of the state of affairs at Worcester ; to acquaint him with the intelligence concerning the coast of Suffolk, and to desire him to give order that a fitting strength of ships may be applied to those parts.[2] On the day after that—namely, Friday, the 5th of September—there is

[1] Order Book of the Council of State, Wednesday, September 3, 1651, MS. State Paper Office.—I give these two minutes in full : " That a letter be written to Colonel Wauton and Colonel Jermie, to desire them to take especial care of the safety of the Island of Lothingland ; to let them know the Council have received information of some designs from Holland to land foreign forces there, and therefore have thought fit to write to the Commissioners of Norfolk and Suffolk, to furnish between them one complete regiment of foot to the guard of the island, and Suffolk to furnish one troop of horse ; to desire them to confer with the Commissioners of the two counties concerning the business, and to give orders for the marching of the forces."—"That a letter be written to the Commissioners of Norfolk and Suffolk, to furnish between them one complete regiment of foot to the guard of the Isle of Lothingland, and Suffolk to send one troop of horse." By the " Isle of Lothingland " is here meant the Hundred of Lothingland, the part of Suffolk, nearest to Yarmouth, on the border of Norfolk. There are various subsequent minutes, which show that the Council had reason to expect that some attempts would be made to land forces on the coast near Yarmouth.— *Ibid.* July 2, 1652 ; July 14, 1652.

[2] *Ibid.* Thursday, September 4, 1651.

this remarkable minute: "That the injunction of secrecy laid upon the business of the Duke of Lorraine be taken off." [1]

I earnestly hope that the fullness with which I have, in this chapter, given the proceedings of the Council of State, as recorded in their own minutes, may not have appeared tedious.   And when it is considered that the occasion was the actual invasion of England by an army from Scotland, under the King of Scots, and the expected invasion by another army from Dunkirk and Ostend under the Duke of Lorraine, it will be admitted that all the details of the preparations made, by the English Government of the year 1651, to meet such a crisis must form a study both interesting and instructive to the English people.   It is no compliment to any Government to say of it, that it is a better Government than the Government of Charles II., or indeed than the Government of any of the Stuarts.   But we have the means of comparing the Government of this Council of State of 1651 with an English Government, in circumstances so far similar as regarded danger from powerful foreign enemies—the Government, namely, of Queen Elizabeth in 1588, and the two or three preceding years.   The fullness with which Mr. Motley has given the proceedings of the English Government of that time, from original records, enables us to compare it with the Government of the Council of State of the Parliament of the Commonwealth.   And if the Government of the Commonwealth be pronounced to be a sort of despotism as well as the Government of Elizabeth, the despotism of the Commonwealth must also be pronounced to be a despotism that evinced a great genius for government, while the

[1] Order Book of the Council of State, Friday, September 5, 1651, MS. State Paper Office.

despotism of Elizabeth must be pronounced to be a despotism that evinced no genius for government at all.

To pass over the indecent exhibitions in Elizabeth of a temper at once violent, savage, and capricious, all her proceedings in the affair of the Netherlands and Spain; her violent and vituperative language to the States of the Netherlands; her negotiations with Parma, in which she was so signally duped; her tardy and inefficient preparations for the Spanish invasion; her treatment of the poor men she sent from England as soldiers to the Netherlands— whom, by her inhuman neglect, she changed from brave soldiers into brigands, or famishing half-naked vagabonds, and many of whom, maimed and wounded, begged their way back to England, and even at the very gates of the palace of the " good Queen Bess, the mother of her people," begged for a morsel of bread in vain—displayed as great a want of real political ability as of humanity : and formed the strongest contrast with the statesmen of the Commonwealth, whose despotism, if despotism it is to be called, was, as compared with such despotism as that of Elizabeth Tudor, a humane, an energetic, and a sagacious despotism. Its humanity was shown by its provision for the welfare of its soldiers and sailors, as well as in its anxious care to protect the people from any possible military outrage: ordering that in their march their soldiers " shall quarter in inns and alehouses only, and not in private men's houses; and in case of necessity, where there are not inns or alehouses, that they agree with people where they come to quarter, and duly pay for what they have." [1]

[1] Order Book of the Council of State, February 21, 165½, MS. State Paper Office.—The concluding words of the above order are also indicative of an estimate of the people of England, very different from the estimate taken of them by either the Tudors or the Stuarts, with whom the English people were "the rude and rascal commons:" "And that the Parliament, if they

Queen Elizabeth's reputation for ability must have been obtained by the talent, which she really displayed, as a speaker and writer. Her speeches certainly have the show of talent—even of sagacity. And, as compared with the Stuarts, she may be looked upon as a ruler of even some practical ability. But when compared with that of the statesmen of the Commonwealth, her Government appears, on a close and minute examination, to be at once imperious and feeble: and the ruler who appointed Robert Dudley, Earl of Leicester, to oppose such a general as Alexander Farnese, must be regarded as, while by such delegation of her office admitting her own incapacity to command armies, also incapable of selecting those who could. No one who reads the evidence can refuse to agree with Mr. Motley, in his conclusion respecting the attempted invasion of England by Spain in 1588, that " very little credit can be conscientiously awarded to the diplomatic or the military efforts of the Queen's Government;" and with the opinion of Roger Williams, cited by Mr. Motley, that " miracles alone had saved England on that occasion from perdition." [1] But as miracles cannot be trusted to with safety in human affairs, the Government that needs the aid of miracles to accomplish its first and most essential duty—the defence from foreign invasion of the country it professes to govern—must be pronounced to be a very bad and a very incompetent Government.

---

think fit, will give order the same may be *made public, for the better satisfaction of the people.*" When the nobility, who looked upon the people as little better than the sweepings of the kennel, and the doorkeeper of whose house insulted even members of the House of Commons (see Vol. I. p. 13), were but the lackeys of the Tudors and the Stuarts, it may be inferred that the Tudors and the Stuarts would not look with much respect upon those their lackeys trampled on.

[1] Motley's History of the United Netherlands, vol. II. pp. 527, 528.

CHAPTER XI.

ANOTHER great and decisive battle was now to be added to
the list of those which have made the Severn, and its tri-
butary the Avon, famous in the English annals. For at
Evesham, on the Avon, had been fought the battle which
determined whether a Plantagenet or a De Môntfort, and
at Shrewsbury, on the Severn, that which determined
whether a Plantagenet or a Percy, should rule in England :
while at Tewkesbury, where the Avon joins the Severn,
had been fought the battle so disastrous to the House of
Lancaster, where Queen Margaret and her unhappy son
Prince Edward were taken prisoners, and the latter was
savagely murdered in cold blood after the battle. And in
this civil war of the 17th century—a war far greater and
more momentous than any of the former wars—the Battle
of Edgehill, the first battle of the war, had been fought in
the Vale of the Red Horse,[1] through a part of which the
Avon[2] flows ; and at Naseby, where the Avon[3] rises, had

---

[1] "Not far from the foot of Edgehill
was a broad plain called *The Vale of
the Red Horse,* a name suitable to the
colour which that day was to bestow
upon it ; for there happened the greater
part of the encounter."—*May's Hist.
of the Parliament,* b. iii. ch. i.

[2] Washington Irving, in his "Sketch
Book," in giving an account of his walk
from Stratford-on-Avon to Charlecot,

"through some of those scenes from
which Shakspeare must have derived
his earliest ideas of rural imagery,"
particularly describes the windings of
the Avon "through a wide and fertile
valley, called the Vale of the Red
Horse."

[3] The spring which forms the source
of the Avon rises in the village of
Naseby.

been fought that battle which may be said to have determined the fate of Charles I.

As you trace the course of these two famous rivers, the
Severn and the Avon, the latter linked with associations of
another and a very different kind—with Shakspeare and
his youth, his scenery, and his burialplace—you trace
at the same time many of the great battles, which tell the
story of the struggles by which the great English people
attained that settled government, and that regulated
liberty, denied as yet to all the other nations of the world.
For on the Avon and the Severn were fought some of the
most decisive battles of this great Parliamentary war :
and though at Evesham Simon De Montfort "with all
his peerage fell," his cause did not perish with him; for
he had before won the great Battle of Lewes, and, as the
fruit of that battle, had founded Representative Government
in England, thence to spread in the course of time over
the world.   He may thus be truly said to have achieved,
if ever man achieved, something that is more than a vain
shadow—something truly excellent and great :

> Something, indeed, that may for ever live
> In honour where'er man is most divine.

· The length of the course of the Avon, to its junction
with the Severn, may be estimated at about 100 miles.
The whole length of the course of the Severn, from its
source in Montgomeryshire to the Bristol Channel, is
about 200 miles.   And it would be difficult to name any
rivers in the world associated with events of greater his_
torical importance than these two English rivers.   The
horrors of war are a topic easy to dilate upon.   But he
who studies carefully the history of all those sanguinary
conflicts on the banks of these two English rivers may,

when any voice is raised to say that those fields were bedewed with blood in vain, and that man should never engage in so dangerous a game as war, be reminded of the remark of Hotspur, made shortly before that day when he determined

> to abide a field,
> Where nothing but the sound of Hotspur's name
> Did seem defensible,

—" I tell you, out of this nettle, danger, we pluck this flower, safety." For it appears that man will be satisfied with no decision of certain great questions but the decision of the sword.

Soon after his arrival at Worcester, King Charles, by proclamation, commanded all from 16 to 60 years of age to come in to him at Worcester. According to a statement in Whitelock, none came—that is, the proclamation or summons produced no effect.[1] According to other accounts, this proclamation brought him about two thousand men, who with those he had with him made in all 14,000—two thousand Scots having dropped off by the way.[2] These 14,000 consisted, according to a statement in Whitelock, of 7,000 horse and 7,000 foot. According to the same authority, their discipline was very strict; and some prisoners brought before their King were courteously treated by him, and having kissed his hand were discharged.[2] The Scots' foot were mostly Highlanders. The Lowlanders had had enough, for the present, of their covenanted oligarchy and covenanted King. These poor Highlanders were much harassed by excessive marches and insufficient food; insomuch that they " did importune the King to take pity on them," who in reply gave them all he ever gave in return for such

---

[1] Whitelock, August 27, 1651.   [3] Whitelock, August 28, 1651.
[2] Bates, part ii. p. 122.

service—"good words." The Scots proceeded to refortify Worcester, and to that end summoned in the country to repair the works, and that which was called the Royal Fort.[1]

On the morning of Thursday, the 28th of August, Cromwell, advancing from the Evesham side, arrived before Worcester. He encamped on Red Hill, about three-quarters of a mile south-eastward of Worcester, on the London road, having with him upwards of 30,000 men. The cotemporary authorities say that he " came before Worcester having about 17,000 horse and foot, with Major-General Lambert and Major-General Harrison."[2] The meaning of this statement, which is not very clear, probably is that the forces he brought with him from Scotland, and those under Lambert and Harrison, amounted altogether to about 17,000 horse and foot. But, in consequence of the exertions of the Council of State—which have been described in the preceding pages, on the authority of their own minutes— bodies of militia were flocking to him from all parts. Bates, who is not a very great authority, says that " those who from all parts came flocking in, made up an army (if some be not mistaken in their reckoning) of fourscore thousand men and more, whom he posts round the city of Worcester."[3] Hobbes says that Cromwell, joining with the new levies, environed Worcester with 40,000 men.[4]

Worcester is on the left bank of the Severn, with a

---

[1] Letter from Lieutenant-General Fleetwood, in Cromwelliana, p. 110; and in Whitelock (the substance of letters from Lieutenant-General Fleetwood), August 26, 1651.—Under the same date, in Whitelock, it is stated that they have very few English horse among them; their foot Highlanders. That a messenger from the army brought an account that the Lord-General, the Lieutenant-General, the Major-Generals, and the Lord Grey of Groby, met at Warwick.

[2] See Proc. in Parl. (August 28 to September 4), in Cromwelliana, p. 110.

[3] Bates, part ii. p. 123.

[4] Hobbes's Behemoth, p. 282: London, 1682.

suburb on the other side of the river, connected with the city by a bridge. Fort Royal, mentioned above, is on the south-east of the city, towards Cromwell's lines. At Upton, seven miles below [1] Worcester, there was a stone bridge over the Severn. Colonel Massey had broken down this bridge, but had accidentally left a foot-plank from one arch to another; and lay secure with 250 horse in the neighbouring town, leaving no guard to defend the pass. On the morning of Thursday, the 28th, the same day on which Cromwell came before Worcester, Lambert marched, with a party of horse and dragoons, from Evesham towards Upton. The dragoons,[2] straddling upon the plank, passed over, one after another, and then fired upon the enemy in the town, who had taken the alarm; while the horse partly forded, partly swam, their horses across the river, about pistol-shot from the bridge. The dragoons, about eighteen in number, then advanced, and took possession of the church, upon a little hill near the bridge-foot. The enemy drew up to the church, and fired their pistols, and thrust their swords in at the windows; but the dragoons fired upon them, killed three or four of their men, and eight or nine of their horses, and took one prisoner, who was shot in the arm. By this time a small party of Lambert's horse were come up, at whose appearance the enemy faced about without a charge. Lambert then sent for Fleetwood, who, being four miles behind with his brigade, mounted about 300 of Colonel Cobbet's

---

[1] Bates (part ii. p. 124) makes the strange blunder—which several modern writers have copied, to the inextricable confusion of themselves and their readers—of placing Upton *above* instead of *below* Worcester.

[2] The operations here described are a good illustration of the primary character and use of the sort of troops called "dragoons," showing precisely the sort of service for which they were fitted and intended. As to the difference between "horse" and "dragoons," see Vol. I. pp. 44, 45.

foot behind troopers, and hastened to the bridge, the rest of his brigade following. In the meantime Lambert used all diligence to make up the bridge for the party to march over, he and Major-General Deane themselves working at it; and receiving no interruption from the enemy, the work was speedily accomplished, and the troops all marched over. In illustration of the small execution at that time done by firearms, it may be mentioned that, although at least forty carbines were fired within half pistol-shot at Massey, " who brought up the rear of his party very stoutly," when they faced about, the only result was that Massey's horse was killed, and himself badly wounded in the hand.

By the end of August, Cromwell's forces had gotten within half musket-shot of the enemy's works, on the south side of Worcester, and his cannon played daily into the city, in which the enemy had planted some great guns. On Sunday, the 31st of August, the Earl of Derby went wounded into Worcester, having with him not above thirty horse left of all his levies in Lancashire. The King of Scots, according to a cotemporary account, seeing all his hopes in the Earl of Derby frustrated, would have marched away with his horse; whereupon his infantry began to mutiny, protesting their horse should not desert them, but, since they must suffer, they should all fare alike. At length, with fair words and large promises of supplies from the King and their officers, they were somewhat appeased.[2]

On the right or west side of the Severn, the River Teme runs into it about three miles below Worcester, and four

---

[1] King's Pamphlets, large 4to, No. 54, article 15. The same account—a special express from Major-General Lambert—in Cromwelliana, p. 111; Bates, part ii. p. 124.

[2] King's Pamphlets, large 4to, No. 54, article 14; Cromwelliana, pp. 111, 112.

miles above Upton. On this River Teme, at Powick, about
a quarter of a mile from the place where it joins the
Severn, there was a bridge. This bridge the Scots took
possession of on Monday the 1st of September. Cromwell, having resolved on an attack on Wednesday the 3rd
of September, the day on which the Battle of Dunbar
had been fought twelve months before, ordered Fleetwood
to advance in the morning with his brigade from Upton.
The plan was (and preparations had been made accordingly) to lay a bridge of boats across the Severn close to
the mouth of the Teme, and also a bridge of boats across
the Teme within pistol-shot of the other bridge; and, by
this means, to connect the two parts of his army on the
two banks of the Severn. Accordingly, the forces under
Fleetwood began their march from Upton, between 5 and 6
o'clock on Wednesday morning, September 3. But, in
consequence of some delays, probably connected with
the bringing-up of the boats for the making of the bridges,
they did not reach the River Teme till between 2 and 3
in the afternoon. The boats came up much about the same
time, and a bridge was presently made over the Severn,
and another over the Teme. The right wing of Fleetwood's forces then crossed the bridge of boats over the
Teme at its junction with the Severn, while the left wing
attacked the bridge at Powick, a quarter of a mile up the
Teme. The dispute here lasted a long time, and was very
hot, the Scots having drawn out a considerable body of
their forces to oppose Fleetwood here. Cromwell led
some regiments of horse and foot, across the bridge of
boats, over the Severn at the mouth of the Teme, to act in
conjunction with Fleetwood's forces, "His Excellency
leading them in person, and being the first man that
set foot on the enemy's ground." The ground was so

encumbered with hedges that the horse had not much liberty to act. The Scots on that side of the Severn having been driven into Worcester, then drew out all their forces that remained from the conflict on the right bank of the Severn, and made a furious attack upon Cromwell's forces on the other side of the river.

Cromwell had recrossed the bridge of boats, and was ready to receive them. Although the Scots at first gained some advantages—forced some of Cromwell's troops to retreat with disorder, and made on that side (to use Cromwell's own words) "a very considerable fight with us for three hours' space," [2] in the end they were totally beaten, and driven back into the town. Fort Royal was then taken, and their own cannon were turned against them. The fight and carnage were then continued in the streets of Worcester, till the Scottish foot were all killed or taken. The Duke of Hamilton had his thigh broken with a shot, and died four days after the battle. The King and David Leslie, with most of the horse, and several noblemen and persons of note, fled. Many noblemen and persons of rank were. taken. The King and some few of the cavalry escaped. The wounded Earl of Derby was taken, tried for treason against the State, and executed at Bolton. The Earls of Lauderdale and Cleveland and others were sent to the Tower.

Clarendon and other English writers have represented the Scottish army as making little resistance at this Battle of Worcester. Yet Cromwell's own words testify that the Scots fought so well, that for a time it was doubtful

---

[1] Cromwell to the Speaker, September 3 and 4, 1651; Letter from Robert Stapylton, 10 at night, September 3, 1651, in Cromwelliana, pp. 112, 113.

Newspapers in Cromwelliana, pp. 114—116.

[2] Cromwell to the Speaker, September 3, 1651, 10 at night.

on which side success would fall. " This battle was
fought with various success for some hours, but still hopeful on your part, and in the end became a complete
victory." [1] " Indeed, this hath been a very glorious mercy,
and as stiff a contest, for four or five hours, as ever I have
seen." [2] And again, " indeed it was a stiff business," and
" the slain are very many " of the enemy, " and must
needs be so, because the dispute was long and very near
at hand ; and often at push of pike, and from one defence to another." [3] He does " not think the Parliamentary forces have lost two hundred men." And Cromwell
uses that remarkable expression :—" The dimensions of
this mercy are above my thoughts. It is, for aught I
know, a crowning mercy." [4] But, as Sir Walter Scott
says, well or ill disputed, the day was totally lost. Three
thousand men were slain in the fight, ten thousand were
taken prisoners ; and their fate formed a melancholy contrast to that of His sacred Majesty, and his councillors,
the Duke of Buckingham, the Earl of Lauderdale, and
other noble persons, who had dragged those poor men
from their homes and families, and who lived and flourished
in after-years, " a spectacle for the angels."

The covenanted King of the Scots—exhausted, it is said,
by want of rest, having been, according to Clarendon,
upon his horse most part of the night—retired a little
before noon to his lodging, to eat and refresh himself,
under the impression that the enemy meant to make no
attempt that night. [5] He had fallen asleep, and slept till
the most terrible of all earthly sounds, that of his flying

<hr />

[1] Cromwell to the Speaker, September 4, 1651.

[2] *Ibid.* September 3, 1651, 10 at
night.

[3] *Ibid.* September 4, 1651.

[4] *Ibid.*

Clarendon's Hist. vol. vi. pp. 510,
511 : Oxford, 1826.

troops driven pellmell through the streets of Worcester—
the sound of rapid footsteps, like that of a great river
bursting a barrier—footsteps rendered swift by fear, but
unsteady on streets slippery with blood—the shouts of the
victors, and the cries for quarter of the vanquished—broke
his slumbers. He started up, mounted his horse (which
stood ready at the door), and fled instantly, surpassing even
David Leslie in the faculty of flight.   He immediately took
his natural place here, which place was the van in flight;
as that of Robert Bruce, as whose representative he claimed
to be King of the Scots, had been the rear in retreat, and the
van in onset.   The first time that day that this "heir of a
hundred kings" was seen by the enemy, was as the foremost of his cavalry in headlong flight. "They make no resistance when any of ours overtake them," says the officer
in command of the pursuing cavalry—a man whose back no
enemy ever saw—"but ride post and in great confusion,
the King being the foremost." [1]

It is remarkable that this is the first time the King is
mentioned by any of Cromwell's officers as having been
seen during the affair. He is before mentioned, indeed, in
these words: "Their King (it is said) went out very
meanly, with only 12 horse" [2] And here it is only, "it is
said." If the King had shown himself, much more if he had
exposed himself to danger, would Cromwell's despatches
and the other letters from the army have said nothing
of it?   Clarendon, after saying that "a little before noon

---

[1] Letter from Major-General Harrison, in   Whitelock, p. 508.—The
course and extent of Harrison's pursuit are indicated in the following
minute of September 12: "That the
letters from Major-General Harrison
and the Committee of Yorkshire, with
the list of the prisoners enclosed, be
reported to the Parliament."—*Order
Book of the Council of State*, September 12, 1651, MS. State Paper Office.

[2] *Cromwelliana*, p. 115.

he retired to his lodging," goes on to relate that "he had not been there near an hour when the alarm came; and though he presently mounted his horse, which was ready at the door, before he came out of the city he met the whole body of his horse running in so great fear that he could not stop them." Lord Clarendon has also the courage to assert, that "in no other part, except where Middleton was hurt and Duke Hamilton's leg broke with a shot, was there resistance made; but such a general consternation possessed the whole army, that the rest of the horse fled, and all the foot threw down their arms before they were charged." [1]

Now, it has been shown that the battle commenced towards 3 P.M., and lasted, according to Cromwell's own words, "as stiff a contest for four or five hours as ever he had seen." But, according to Clarendon, the battle ended about two hours before it began. Clarendon then suddenly, without any intimation that the King had left the town to fight the enemy, begins his next sentence thus: "When the King came back into the town, he found a good body of horse, which had been persuaded to make a stand;" and after in vain attempting to persuade them to face the enemy, and "staying till very many of the enemy's horse were entered the town, he was persuaded to withdraw himself; and though the King could not get a body of horse to fight, he could have too many to fly with him." [2] This narrative, though constructed with the art of an unscrupulous advocate, is incoherent, and, as its very incoherency proves, is manifestly untrue, except that part of it which states that the King was in his lodging while his troops were fighting.

It was a feat of advocacy more rash than dexterous in

[1] Clarendon's Hist. vol. vi. p. 512: Oxford, 1826.   [2] *Ibid.* vol. vi. pp. 512, 513.

Clarendon to attempt to prove that Charles was a brave man, and his army an army of cowards. He knew, indeed, the importance of what he sought to prove; he knew that mankind will overlook, will bear with, if they will not forgive, many things in a brave man which they will visit severely upon a coward. But it was particularly hard upon the men who composed the army with which Charles marched from Scotland to Worcester to be treated in this way. For if that army had not had among them some men unusually brave, such a march would never have been attempted; for they well knew, and they had had good cause to know, the formidable qualities of the troops they would have to encounter.

Dr. George Bates, who in the titlepage of his book is called " principal physician to King Charles I. and King Charles II.," and is also said, in the " Preface by a Person of Quality," to have been physician to Oliver Cromwell—an assertion which, as has been shown from the Order Book of the Council of State, is so far true that Dr. Bates was one of three physicians sent by the Council into Scotland to give Cromwell advice for the recovery of his health—states that the King, with a Council of War, viewing the enemies from the high steeple of the cathedral-church, perceived them upon their march towards the town; that all presently arm, and the King himself marches out to the defence of Powick Bridge, and to hinder the enemies passing over the bridge of boats. Without specifying any of the King's exploits at Powick Bridge, or saying why His Majesty left it, Dr. Bates begins his next sentence by suddenly informing us, that " the King was scarcely got back into the town," when everything went wrong in the defence of the bridge. And in the next sentence, by a turn equally sudden and remarkable, he informs us that

" whilst these things were acting "—that is, whilst the
King's forces were losing Powick Bridge, in consequence of
the King's Majesty having " got back into the town,"—" the
King's Majesty, turning towards the east side of the town'
resolves to hazard a battle."[1]   The royal panegyrist and
physician then proceeds to state that the King, with a considerable body of foot but a small number of horse (" for,"
he says, " the Scottish cavalry scarce budged") marched
against the enemy at Perry-wood, " with a most undaunted
and present mind," being followed by the Dukes of
Hamilton and Buckingham, and Sir Alexander Forbes, at
the head of his foot ; that at the first charge he beat the
van, and made himself master of the artillery ; but afterwards, " though with wonderful sagacity he gave orders,
in the heat and confusion of the fight, faced the greatest
dangers with a high and steady mind, not to be matched
by others, and with his own hand did many brave actions,
and gave illustrious proofs of his personal valour even in
the judgment of his enemies ;[2] yet being overpowered by
fresh men, whom Cromwell in great numbers sent in, he
thought it best, that he might reserve himself for better
fortune, to retreat in time, and save himself in the town ;
that he then used all manner of persuasions to encourage
the soldiers to renew the engagement ; till, the danger
growing greater and greater, by St. Martin's Gate he went
out to the horse, commanded by David Leslie, being
almost entire, and directed his course towards Barbon
Bridge, earnestly entreating the horse to take courage and
hasten to the assistance of the foot, who were put to
utmost extremity."[3]

If the other account be true—and Clarendon, if as

[1] Bates, part ii. p. 125.
[2] The falsehood of this has been
shown above.
[3] Bates, part ii. pp. 125, 126.

regardless of the truth, was likely to be at least as well informed as Bates—that Charles, during the obstinate and sanguinary conflict in which the unfortunate Scots were shedding their blood for this phantom King, whom they regarded as the representative of their great Robert Bruce, was " in his lodging eating," and afterwards " refreshing himself" with sleep, and that it was the noise of the flying army, driven pellmell into the town, that broke the royal slumbers, the only part of this romance of Bates which has in it a shadow of truth, is that Charles then joined the cavalry, and " was the foremost in flight."

There is a reason for taking more notice of this book of Bates than its intrinsic value merits : for this mendacious description of the King's heroism at the Battle of Worcester is a sort of measure of the degradation to which the Restoration reduced public opinion and everything else in England. The second part of Bates's book was written after the Restoration, with what object is evident enough from the book itself. It is always the last proof of de- basement in a nation, when the corruption of the Govern- ment awards to men who have not risked their lives in battle or in the public service the honours that only belong to those who have. Rome had fallen upon evil days when Caligula drew up his army on the seashore near Boulogne, under pretence of invading Britain; and, having with great parade disposed his warlike engines, ordered his soldiers to gather the sea-shells, and fill their helmets and the skirts of their clothes, saying " these were the spoils of the ocean, fit to be deposited in the Capitol ;" and then, by letters to Rome, ordered preparations to be made for a triumph that should exceed in magnificence all former triumphs. In like manner had England fallen upon evil days, when a man, who performed the part neither of a great commander nor a good soldier, was held up to public view as having performed the part of both; while the brave but unfortunate men, who shed their blood for a worthless and incapable young man, were held up to un-merited obloquy.

When it is considered that the students at the Scottish Universities were usually very young, of the age of boys rather than of young men, it appears, from the following minute of the Council of State, that the zeal of the Scottish Royalist gentry, in favour of their Stuart Kings, for whom they from first to last shed so much of their blood in vain, led them to take with them in this disastrous expedition some of their sons who were mere boys. For here was a mere boy, a student at the University of St. Andrews, who had accompanied his father, and shared with him the hard-ships of the long march, the perils of Worcester, and after-wards imprisonment:—

" Upon the reading of the petition of Sir Adam Hepburne of Hombee, for himself and his two sons, John Cockbourne of Ormestone, and Thomas Hepburne, student at St. Andrews in Scotland, it is ordered that the said Thomas Hepburne shall have liberty to return into Scotland to follow his studies there, he first taking the engagement; and that Sir Adam Hepburne of Hombee and John Cock-burne [sic] of Ormestone shall have the liberty of the city and the places within the late lines of communication— they entering into bonds, in the sum of £1,000 apiece for themselves, and £500 each two sureties, upon the usual terms."[1]

On the 10th of September the Parliament issued a

---

[1] Order Book of the Council of State, Thursday, March 25, 1652 [Petition of Sir Adam Hepburne of Hombee, for himself and his two sons]. MS. State Paper Office.

proclamation, offering a reward of £1,000 "for the discovery and apprehending of Charles Stuart, and other traitors, his adherents and abettors." A month passed, however, and Charles was still uncaptured. On Monday the 13th of October 1651, the Council of State made the following order, which appears to me to show (what before I considered doubtful) that they really desired to apprehend him: "That letters be written to all the ports, to make strict search of all persons that shall attempt to go out of the land, especially such as are in disguise, to prevent the going out of Charles Stuart, who we are informed is still in England; to let them know that £1,000 is appointed by Act of Parliament for them who shall take him."[1] Cromwell, who did not attend the Council of State after the 2nd till the 11th of October (his name not being in the list of those present at the Council on any of the intervening days), was present on this day, the 13th of October. It may thence be inferred that Cromwell really desired the apprehension of Charles. But it seems to have been better, both for Cromwell and the Council of State, that Charles escaped, than that they should have had either the keeping of him prisoner, or the repetition of the scene of the 30th of January $164\frac{8}{9}$ in front of Whitehall.

After many adventures, which have been variously related, some of which are described in the narrative of a Mr. Whitgreaves,[2] at whose house he was secreted two or three days—a narrative which presents a strong contrast to the fictions of Sir Walter Scott's "Woodstock," and represents Charles in a far better light than the romance does; there

---

[1] Order Book of the Council of State, Monday, October 13, 1651, MS. State Paper Office.

[2] See an extract from a then re-cently printed copy of this MS. in the "Westminister Review," vol. v. pp. 432 -434, and the "Retrospective Review," No. 20.

being, instead of insolent airs and attempts on the honour of his host's daughter, a very respectful condescension towards his host and his family, and a full sense of his forlorn condition on the part of the King—Charles found means to hire a vessel on the coast of Sussex, and landed at Havre-de-Grâce. On the 28th of October, an extract of two letters from Paris was published, licensed by the Clerk of the Parliament, and setting forth: "That on the 19th the Scots' King arrived there, and was met by the Duke of Orleans not far from that city: that his Highness conducted him to the Louvre, whither the late Queen, his mother, repaired presently after from Chaliot, where she had been erecting a nunnery: that the King gave the company a full narrative of all the particulars of what happened at the fight at Worcester, threw out some reproachful words against the Scots, put some scurrilous language on the Presbyterian party in England, and boasted much of his own valour. That he told them how he slipt out of Worcester, and how near he was of being taken there—first in the fort, and after in his chamber: how he disguised himself, and went from county to county, and what shift he made for victuals and lodging; sometimes being driven to beg a piece of bread and meat, and ride with bread in one hand and meat in the other, and sometimes setting a guard about a little cottage, while he rested there until the morning: as also his being in London, and the manner of his passing disguised through several counties in England, till he made his escape."[1]

The Council of State was much occupied for some time with the disposal of the prisoners. The noblemen and the superior officers, such as Lieutenant-General David Leslie,

[1] Parl. Hist. vol. iii. p. 1375.

were committed to the Tower of London—the persons next in rank to Windsor Castle. The Order Book of the Council of State, under date 16th September 1651, contains a list of knights, colonels, &c., committed to Windsor Castle. The following minutes of 29th September relate to the other prisoners of lower rank or of no rank :—

" That it be referred to the Committee for Prisoners to examine whether Chelsey College belongs to the State, or to particular persons : if to the State they are to make use of it; if to particular persons, they are to treat with them, that it may be made use of for the accommodating of some of the Scots prisoners." " That it be referred to the same Committee to make use of the church near the ground [Tothill Fields] where now they are, or of the pesthouse, or of any other place for the lodging of the sick and wounded men of the Scots prisoners ; and the said Committee is to speak with the Martial-General about the providing of straw and other necessaries for the lodging of the Scots prisoners."[1]

It is impossible to say what proportion of the Scots prisoners was shipped to the plantations. A doubt may even be raised, as will be shown presently, whether any of them were so disposed of, although undoubtedly the Council at one time contemplated such a proceeding. It is, however, quite certain that they were not all so disposed of, either after the Battle of Dunbar, or after that of Worcester. There are in the Order Book minutes respecting the employ_ ment of some of those of Dunbar in the coal-mines about Newcastle, and of others in agriculture in England. And with regard to those of Worcester, the Council of State, on the 1st of October 1651, made an order: " That 1,000 of

---

[1] Order Book of the Council of State, Monday, September 29, 1651, MS. State Paper Office.

the Scottish prisoners be delivered to the use of the under-
taker for the draining of the Fens, upon condition that, if
ten men of each hundred do escape from them, they do
then forfeit, for every man escaping above the aforesaid
number, the sum of £10."[1]   And again, on the 9th of October, there is this order: "That so many of the Scottish
prisoners, private soldiers, as are in Tothill Fields, and also
at York, and are sound and fit for labour, be delivered over
for the draining of the Fens."[2]

It appears, from the following minutes, that some of the
English prisoners were kept at St. James's.   On the 16th
of October Colonel Berkstead is ordered to choose twenty
out of the English private soldiers, now prisoners at St.
James's, to be proceeded against by a Council of War or
Court Martial ; the Court Martial to be held on Thursday,
25th of October, in the Court of Star Chamber, at Westminster, by 9 o'clock in the forenoon.[3]   And, from the
following minute, it appears that steps were certainly taken
for transporting to the plantations some of the Scots prisoners. On the 25th of October the Council of State ordered,
"That the Committee for Prisoners do, upon usual security,
give license for the transporting of some Scots prisoners to
the Bermudas."[4]

There are various orders of the Council of State respecting
the treatment of the prisoners. An allowance was crdered
of 2d. per diem to each of the Scots prisoners, "for provision
of victuals," at Chester, and of 2½d. per diem in London.
There are orders on the 16th of September for 112 bags of
biscuits for the Scots prisoners, at 16s. per cwt.; for payment
of the "bakers and cheesemongers, which have furnished
provisions to the Scots prisoners, at £56. 5s. per diem and

[1] Order Book of the Council of
State, October 1, 1651, MS. State
Paper Office.

[2] Ibid. October 9, 1651.
[3] Ibid. October 16, 1651.
[4] Ibid. October 21, 1651.

upwards; and that a warrant be issued to the Master and
Wardens of the Company of Chirurgeons, to appoint some
skilful chirurgeons to dress constantly such of the Scots
prisoners as are wounded."[1]   The humanity of this last
order would be creditable to the Council, were it not for its
lateness—thirteen days after the battle. But there may have
been reasons for this apparent delay which we do not know.

On the same day, the 16th of September, the Lord-General
[Cromwell] is "desired to give order that the Earl of Lauderdale, Sir David Leslie, Lieutenant-General, Lieutenant-General David Middleton, Sir William Fleming, Sir David Cun-
ningham, Lieutenant-Colonel Sir William Hart, Sir William
Douglas, now prisoners at Chester, be brought up in safe
custody, under a sufficient guard, to London."[2]   On the 1st
of October it is ordered, "That Ralph Delavall, of Seaton Delavall, in the county of Northumberland, Esquire, desiring
leave to visit the Earl of Leven,[3] now prisoner in the
Tower, in order to supply him with some necessaries, be
permitted, according to his said desire, to come unto the
Earl of Leven in the Tower."[4]   And on the 3rd of October,
" Upon the motion of the Lord-General [Cromwell], it is
ordered that General Leven [the Earl of Leven] shall have
the liberty of the Tower, and that his servant may come
to him, to do him such service as is necessary to him."[5]
On the 11th of November, the Council of State ordered,
"That the Order of Parliament concerning the Earl of
Leven be issued to the Committee for Irish and Scottish

[1] Order Book of the Council of
State, Tuesday, September 16, 1651,
MS. State Paper Office.
[2] Ibid. same day.
[3] The Earls of Leven and Crawford-
Lindsay, Lord Ogleby, and others,
had been surprised by Monk in Scotland, and sent prisoners to London.
The old Earl of Leven had been left

General in Scotland by the King, and
Crawford-Lindsay Lieutenant-General.
—Lord Leicester's Journal, p. 117;
Ludlow's Memoirs, vol. i. p. 366.
[4] Order Book of the Council of
State, October 1, 1651, MS. State
Paper Office.
[5] Ibid. October 3, 1651.

Affairs, who are to consider of what security is fit to be taken of him for his abode at Mr. Delavall his house in the county of Northumberland, and to report their opinions to the Council."[1]   On the 13th of November 1651, the arrangement for enlarging the old Earl of Leven, the veteran general of Gustavus Adolphus, from the Tower was completed : the Earl of Leven to give his parole, under his hand and seal : Ralph Delavall, of Seaton Delavall in the county of Northumberland, Esquire ; John Delavall, of Peterborough, in the county of Northampton, and John Delavall of &c., recognizance of £20,000 before the Lords Commissioners of the Great Seal : the Earl of Leven to be confined to the said house of Seaton Delavall, or within twelve miles thereof." [2]

On the 7th of October it is ordered, " That the Scots prisoners in the Tower shall have liberty to write into

[1] Order Book of the Council of State, November 11, 1651, MS. State Paper Office.—On the same day there is an order for Colonel Keith, prisoner in Windsor Castle, to have liberty for three months on parole, for the recovery of his health ; the Earl of Rothes and the Earl Mareschal of Scotland to have each a servant allowed to attend upon him in the Tower, provided such servant be kept a prisoner in the Tower also. — *Ibid.* November 10, 1651. " That a letter be written to the Lieutenant of the Tower, to secure the Earl Mareschal of Scotland by himself alone, apart from the rest, and to keep him close prisoner in order to a further examination."—*Ibid.* November 11, 1651.

[2] *Ibid.* November 13, 1651.—Roger North, in his Life of his brother the Lord-Keeper Guilford (vol. i. p. 266, 3rd edition, London, 1819), gives an interesting description of Seaton Delaval :

" From Tynemouth his Lordship, by invitation, went to dine at Seaton Delaval. Sir Ralph Delaval entertained us exceeding well. The chief remarkable there was a little port, which that gentleman, with great contrivance and after many disappointments, made for securing small craft, that carried out his salt and coal ; and he had been encouraged in it by King Charles II., who made him collector and surveyor of his own port, and no officer to intermeddle there. It stands at the mouth of a rill of water, which, running from the hills, had excavated a great hollow in the fall as it ran. Sir Ralph had built, or rather often rebuilt, a pier of stone, that fenced off the surge to the north-east, and, at high-water, gave entrance near a little promontory of the shore ; and at low water, the vessels lay dry upon the rock."

Scotland : the letters to be sent open to the Lieutenant of the Tower, who, if he find they write only concerning their own condition, shall seal the letters and deliver them to such person as they shall appoint to carry them."[1] And on the same day an order is made, " That Lieutenant-General David Leslie, now prisoner in the Tower, shall have liberty to have his servant come to him to attend upon him."[2] And on the 3rd of December 1651, a further order was made, " That liberty be given to the wife of Lieutenant-General David Leslie, with two maidservants, to go in and come out of the Tower as they shall have occasion."[3]

On the 17th of December 1651, the Council of State ordered, " That the Earl of Carnwath shall have the liberty of the Tower, to walk for the preservation of his health," and " That the Lord Crawford-Lindsey [sic] shall have a servant allowed to attend upon him in the Tower ; "[4] and on the 24th of the same December, they ordered, " That Sir David Leslie, Alexander Earl of Kellie, John Lord Bargany [sic], and the Lord Oglebie, shall have the liberty of the Tower."[5]

There is a strange and painful contrast between these indulgences, granted to the Scottish officers of rank, and the harsh treatment of the private soldiers and the officers below the rank of field-officers—a treatment which appears to be exactly the reverse of what justice would seem to require, since the soldiers and the officers below field-officers could not possibly have had any share in the counsels which caused the invasion of England that led to the Battle of Worcester. On the day following that on which

---

[1] Order Book of the Council of State, October 7, 1651, MS. State Paper Office.

[2] Ibid. same day.

[3] Ibid. December 3, 1651.

[4] Ibid. December 17, 1651 .

[5] Ibid. Wednesday, December 24, 1651.

the last order above mentioned was made respecting
David Leslie (namely, on the 4th of December, 1651), an
order was made, that a Committee, composed of upwards of
20 members of the Council of State, and including Sir
Henry Vane and the Lord-General [Cromwell], "or any
three or more of them, shall *have power to dispose to plantations all the prisoners under the degree of field-officer* taken
at Worcester, or in any other place, since the invasion by
the Scots' army, as well those abroad in several garrisons
as those that are brought to London. And that they
report to the Council how they shall so dispose of them.
And that the said Committee do also report to the Council
what they conceive fit to be done with the field-officers
that are prisoners."[1]

According to Vattel, it is lawful to condemn prisoners of
war to slavery only in cases which give a right to kill
them—when they have rendered themselves personally
guilty of some crime deserving of death. The ancients
used to sell their prisoners of war for slaves ; but they
thought they had a right to put them to death. "In
every circumstance," says Vattel, "when I cannot inno-
cently take away my prisoner's life, I have no right to
make him a slave."[2] As the orders for regulating the
proceedings of the Council of State required that "nothing
of any debate or argument shall be entered into the book,
but only the result thereof declared in the vote," we know
not on what ground this harsh measure was adopted.
But it was probably a ground similar to that which induced the Czar Peter to send into Siberia all the prisoners
he took at Pultowa. Charles XII., after the Battle of
Narva, only disarmed his prisoners and set them at liberty.

[1] Order Book of the Council of
State, December 4, 1651, MS.
Paper Office.

[2] Vattel's Law of Nations, b. iii.
ch. vii. § 152.

The English Parliament might think, with the Russian Czar, that generosity is a luxury too expensive to be indulged in by statesmen. "The Swedish hero," says Vattel, "confided too much in his own generosity; the sagacious monarch of Russia united, perhaps, too great a degree of severity with his prudence: but necessity furnishes an apology for severity, or rather throws a veil over it altogether."[1] Such statesmen as Vane and Cromwell might probably have shown that a necessity existed, had their arguments in the Council of State been preserved. But, as they have not been preserved, I will not attempt to conjecture what they might have been. And I will only add, in the words of Vattel—"I shall dwell no longer on the subject: and, indeed, that 'disgrace to humanity is happily banished from Europe."[2]

There is another very important minute, relating to the Scots prisoners, made about a fortnight after that just quoted, which, if it can be considered as comprehending all the prisoners, and not merely those who remained after the disposal of the others to the plantations, would speak strongly in favour of the humane treatment of those prisoners by the English Parliament and Council of State. The following is this order, made on Wednesday, 17th of December, 1651 :—

"That it be referred to the Committee for Prisoners to take into consideration the discharging of the Scots prisoners remaining now in Tothill Fields and about London, which were taken at the Battle of Worcester; and also what allowance is fit to be made of clothing and money, for the enabling of them to return into their own country, the sum of which is to be paid by Mr. Frost out

---

[1] Vattel's Law of Nations, b. iii. ch. viii. § 52.   [2] Ibid. § 152.

of the exigent moneys of the Council, and also what time is fit to be given for their performing of the journey." [1]

There is another order of the same date, " That it be referred to the Committee for Prisoners to consider of the disposing of such of the Scots prisoners as are now at Newcastle, or in any other place of this nation, and report what they think fit to be done therein." [2]

On the same day, the Council of State made the following order with regard to the English prisoners taken at the Battle of Worcester :—

" That it be referred to the Committee for Irish and Scottish Affairs, in pursuance of an Order of Parliament of the 28th of November, to consider of the sending of the English prisoners, now at James House and in the Mews, which were taken at the Battle of Worcester, over into Ireland, there to be disposed of for the advantage of the Commonwealth." [3]

The following minutes show that the former minute for sending home some of the Scots prisoners remaining in Tothill Fields and about London was not meant to include those of the higher rank :—

" That Lieutenant-General Fleetwood, Colonel Blake, Mr. Scot, Mr. Herbert, Sir William Masham, and Mr. Nevill, or any two of them, be appointed a Committee to consider of the disposing of the Scots prisoners now in the Tower, to such other places of restraint, where those that are of most consideration and best able to act anything prejudicial, may be separated one from another, and yet all may have the liberty of the respective prisons to which they shall be committed." [4]

---

[1] Order Book of the Council of State, Wednesday, December 17, 1651, MS. State Paper Office.
[2] *Ibid.* same day.
[3] *Ibid.* same day.
[4] *Ibid.* December 24, 1651.

" That notice be given to the Lieutenant of the Tower, that he is to take care that all those persons of quality of the Scottish nation who have had the liberty of the Tower granted unto them, may (notwithstanding the said liberty given) have keepers appointed to them, to take especial care of them, that they make not their escape."[1]

" That the Lord Viscount Lisle be added to the Committee for Prisoners; and they desired to-take care of such of the Scottish prisoners as are now at the Mews."[2]

" That Major Andrew Carr and Captain James Keyth [sic], now prisoners in Chelsey College, be permitted to go into Scotland for four or five months on their parols, on behalf of the rest of the prisoners in Chelsey College, to fetch them some relief from their friends, for their better accommodation and subsistence during their imprisonment here."[3]

On the same day the Council of State also made the following order : " That the seven inferior servants of the Scotch King, which [sic] are now prisoners in the Fleet, be forthwith discharged, upon their taking the engagement, and giving their own bonds, that they will act nothing prejudicial to the Commonwealth."[4]

On the 1st of July 1652, the Council of State ordered, " That the private soldiers of the Scottish nation who are now prisoners at Durham and Gloucester be released, and permitted to return into their own country."[5]   And on the 30th of the same month the Council ordered, " That the sum of £39 3s., laid out for the clothing of some Scots prisonersbefore they went home, be paid out of the con-

[1] Order Book of the Council of State, December 24, 1651, MS. State Paper Office.
[2] Ibid. same day.
[3] Ibid. same day.
[4] Ibid. same day.
[5] Ibid. Thursday afternoon, July 1, 1652.

tingent moneys of the Council." [1]   And on the 3rd of February and 1st of March, 165½, the Council of State ordered, " That the private soldiers now remaining in the gaol of Shrewsbury, of those that were sent thither after the fight at Worcester, be set at liberty, and have 20 days allowed them to go into their own country, they first taking the engagement." [2]   " That Sir Arthur Haselrig have power to discharge all the Scotch prisoners not Highlanders now at Durham, who are under the degree of a captain, and give them passes to go into Scotland, and take from them an engagement that they will never more bear arms against the Commonwealth of England." [3]

Upon the whole, from the preceding and various other minutes, I should infer that only a small proportion of the Scottish prisoners, taken not only at Worcester but at Dunbar, were sent to the English plantations.

On the 11th of September Mr. Scott, from the Council of State, reported to the House the names of nine persons they thought proper to be made examples of justice, and tried by court-martial:—the Duke of Hamilton ; the Earls of Derby, Lauderdale, and Cleveland ; Sir Timothy Featherstonhaugh, Colonel Massey, Captain Benbow, and the Mayor and Sheriff of Worcester.[4] As already mentioned, the Duke of Hamilton died of his wounds four days after the battle. The Earl of Derby was beheaded at Bolton, in Lancashire, on the 15th of October ; Sir Timothy Featherstonhaugh was beheaded at Chester, on the 22nd of October ; and Captain Benbow was shot at Shrewsbury, on the 15th of the same month.[5] These three

[1] Order Book of the Council of State, Friday, July 30, 1652, MS. State Paper Office.

[2] Ibid. Tuesday, February 3, 165½.

[3] Ibid. Monday, March 1, 165½.

[4] Parl. Hist. vol. iii. p. 1372.

[5] Ibid. pp. 1373, 1374; Lord Leicester's Journal, pp. 119, 120, 122.

appear to have been all who were executed.[1] The Earls of Lauderdale and Cleveland were committed to the Tower, as also was Colonel Massey.

There were other prisoners in the Tower besides Lauderdale, whose lives might have well appeared, to many of their countrymen in after-days, to have been saved from the hard doom of Derby and Benbow by some evil rather than good fate. On the 9th of January 165½, the Council of State ordered, " That Major-General Dalyell [sic], now prisoner in the Tower, be allowed 5s. per week for his subsistence during his imprisonment in the Tower." [2] It may be inferred that this was the same person who, in after-years, figured with Lauderdale and Claverhouse in the inhuman persecution of the unfortunate Covenanters of Scotland. In the slaughter of Bothwell Bridge, in striking a prisoner on the face with the hilt of his dagger till the blood sprang, in the business of the torture-chamber of the Privy Council of Scotland, General Thomas Dalzell took such vengeance as was suited to the nature of the man, or rather the beast, for the terrible defeats he had met with, in other and very different times, from Cromwell's Ironsides.

On the 15th of August, Stirling Castle surrendered to Lieutenant-General Monk. On Monday the 1st of September Monk took Dundee by storm, put 500 or 600 of

[1] I have not been able to ascertain the fate of the Mayor and Sheriff of Worcester, further than that, from the following minute, it would appear that they were not executed at the time the Earl of Derby and the two other unfortunate Royalists suffered death. It may therefore be hoped that the Mayor and Sheriff of Worcester were not condemned to death: "That the Judge Advocate of the Army be sent unto, to deliver unto the Committee for Examinations, such papers as he hath now in his hands relating to the carriage of the late Mayor and Sheriff of Worcester in the business of admitting Charles Stuart and his adherents into the town of Worcester."—*Order Book of the Council of State*, Monday, January 5, 165½, MS. State Paper Office.

[2] *Ibid.* Friday, January 9, 165½.

the garrison to the sword, and, according to Ludlow, "commanded the Governor, with divers others, to be killed in cold blood." [1] Attempts have been made to clear Monk's memory from this atrocity, and to show that he not only did not "command" it, but that "it troubled him very much." [2]

[1] Ludlow's Memoirs, vol. i. p. 366.—Ludlow, as may well be supposed, had no love for Monk, of whom he would be apt to say, "Vendidit hic auro patriam."

[2] Lord Wharncliffe, in one of his notes to his translation of M. Guizot's Life of Monk, gives a statement from the continuation to Baker's Chronicle, that as "one Captain Kelly, of Colonel Morgan's regiment, was carrying the Governor to the General, one Major Butler barbarously shot him dead." Lord Wharncliffe further says, "that this account is confirmed by Sir Philip Warwick in his Memoirs, who adds that "it troubled Monk very much."

CHAPTER XII.

THE news of the victory won by their forces at Worcester reached the Council of State in a few hours. On the day after the battle, the 4th of September, they made an order, "That Colonel Berkstead" [who commanded the guard of the Parliament] "do shoot off the guns of his regiment, and cause a bonfire to be made before Whitehall Gate, in token of joy for the good news of the routing of the Scots' army near Worcester."[1] On the same day they ordered a letter to be written to the Lord Mayor, Major-General Skippon, and the Commissioners of the Militia of London, "to acquaint them with the good tidings of the routing of the enemy about Worcester; to let them know their horse are many of them dispersed; to desire them, therefore, to send out their horse, for the gathering up of such of the enemies as shall come this way."[2] On the 6th of September the Council of State ordered, "That the 500 men of Middlesex marched out to Uxbridge be ordered every man to return to his own home."[3] On the same day (Saturday, the 6th of September), the Council of State also made this order:—"That the dispersing of the militia in the several counties be taken into consideration on Monday morning next, after the disposing of the prisoners."[4]

Accordingly, on Monday the 8th of September, they

[1] Order Book of the Council of State, Thursday, September 4, 1651, MS. State Paper Office.

[2] *Ibid.* same day.

[3] *Ibid.* September 6, 1651.

[4] *Ibid.* same day.

made the following order, to which I beg to direct particular attention, for reasons which I will state presently. It is also important to call attention to the fact that Cromwell, the Lord-General, was not present at the Council on this occasion—indeed, he did not enter London till four days after—and that the meeting consisted of Bradshaw the President, Sir Henry Vane, and nine other members of the Council of State. The following is the order:—" That a letter be written to the several [Commissioners of the] Militias of the Counties in England who have sent forces to the appointed rendezvous upon the occasion of the Scots' army coming into England, to return them thanks, and also to the officers and soldiers, for their great readiness in the public service ; and to let them know that they are to disband their forces, and cause the horses and arms to be delivered unto them who set them out." [1]

Now there is a statement of Ludlow[2]—which has been adopted by even eminent modern writers, as denoting Cromwell's treacherous purpose at this period—that the

---

[1] Order Book of the Council of State, Monday, September 8, 1651, MS. State Paper Office.—And on the following day, the Council of State ordered, " That a letter be written to the Lord-General, to let him know that money hath been ready for his army for some days past, but could not conveniently be sent unto him, in regard of the motion of the forces and dispersing of the regiments into several places, for the greater ease both of them and the people. That the Council hath appointed the Treasurers at War to wait on his Lordship, to consider how the money may be speedily sent to them, that there be not free quarter by any means taken."—Ibid. Tuesday, September 9, 1651. On the same day :

" That Major-General Skippon be desired to dismiss such of the trained band of London as are upon the guards."—Ibid. On the 10th the Council ordered, " That it be referred to the Committee of Scottish and Irish Affairs, to consider how the orders of the House, for the disbanding of the forces lately taken into pay, may be put in execution."—Ibid. September 10, 1651.

[2] Ludlow's Memoirs, vol. i. pp. 365, 366: 2nd edition, London, 1721.—The inference drawn by Ludlow (vol. ii. p. 447), from Cromwell's calling the victory at Worcester a " crowning mercy," is quite unwarranted. Cromwell meant no more than to say that their work was done—finis coronat opus.

very next day after the fight at Worcester, Cromwell dismissed and sent home the militia. This is not only a
misstatement of the fact, but a confusion of ideas in the
mind of Ludlow respecting the very rudiments of government. The power of the militia was that which formed
the main dispute between King Charles and the Parliament; and for a very good reason, because it was the
principal characteristic of the sovereign. There is no
question that, at this particular time, the sovereign in
England was the Parliament, of which the Council of State
was the Executive; and in that capacity, as has been
shown above by the minute extracted from their own
Order Book, the Council of State, on the 8th of September,
five days after the Battle of Worcester, ordered the
militia to be disbanded in the several counties of England,
and their horses and arms to be delivered up.

It is little likely that the character and the designs,
whatever they were, of Cromwell—who wrapped himself
in clouds and darkness, so that not even his most intimate
friends knew with any degree of certainty, though some of
them might suspect, which way his ambition pointed—
should be analysed by a man like Ludlow, who had
in his brain such a jumble as this about the power of
the militia, and the very foundations of government and
sovereign power. The whole of what has been said, too,
about Cromwell's excitement and elation after the Battle
of Worcester, partakes of the same error; an error which
Sir Walter Scott has also fallen into, when in "Woodstock"
he represents Cromwell as admitting the swearing, swag-
gering cavalier Wildrake (a likely sort of confidant for
such a man as Cromwell!) into his views for ejecting the
Parliament, and putting the crown on his own head. The
sort of excited self-assertion attributed by some writers to

Cromwell is quite as much out of keeping with all that we know of the character of the real Cromwell, as the absurd supposition of his admitting cavaliero Wildrake into his inmost thoughts. The haughty exultation ascribed to Cromwell on this occasion belongs to the character of a vain, pompous, ostentatious, shallow person. Whatever vices have been or may be imputed to him, the real Cromwell was, assuredly, neither vain, pompous, ostentatious, nor shallow. Pride, indeed—a very different sort of thing from vanity—the sort of pride which the consciousness of great talents directed by an iron will naturally inspires, the real Cromwell no doubt had. It was a great error in Scott's conception of Cromwell's character, to make him babble out his thoughts to a stranger as he does to Wildrake. Vanity indeed is communicative, as well as ostentatious, and infirm of purpose. Cromwell was not only unostentatious, but, though not cruel, he was inexorable as death, and inscrutable as the grave.

In attempting to analyse the springs of action of such a character as Cromwell's, it is difficult to avoid (and I do not pretend to be able to avoid) some apparent or even real inconsistencies. For certain points, which at times seem to be tolerably clear, again become involved in impenetrable darkness, and what seemed the clue is lost. Moreover, as regards inconsistency, may not there be inconsistency in the actual life of a man? In attempting to portray an actual life, we must not condemn a part of that life which is laudable, because we know the end, which is not so. There is a time when we only see and reverence in Cromwell the Wallace, the Tell, the Washington of his country—a man full of compassion for the oppressed, and indignation against the oppressor—a time when we rejoice in his fortune, and honour his wisdom and valour.

But, of all this, clouds and darkness rest upon the end. And while we honour the valour and rejoice in the fortune of the successful champion of his country's liberties, we need not, in order to make a fancy portrait apparently consistent and complete, but really untrue to nature and fact, drag forward the end, which will come soon enough, when we shall have to pass judgment on deeds, which he who did them may once have believed it impossible for all the temptations of earth and hell to make him do.

Dr. Arnold, in speaking of the almost insurmountable difficulties in comprehending such a character, says : " The genius which conceived the incomprehensible character of Hamlet, would alone be able to describe with intuitive truth the character of Scipio or of Cromwell. In both these great men, the enthusiastic element, which clearly existed in them, did but inspire a resistless energy into their actions, while it no way interfered with the calmest and keenest judgment in the choice of their means."[1] What is said about the "enthusiastic element" may be true enough; but I dissent from the assertion that the genius which conceived the character of Hamlet would be able to describe with truth the character of Cromwell. I think it probable that Shakspeare's Cromwell would not have been much more like the real Cromwell than Scott's Cromwell in " Woodstock."[2] And one ground of my opinion

[1] History of Rome, vol. iii. p. 385.

[2] The mention of Shakspeare's Hamlet tempts me to venture a small criticism on the word in Act V., scene 1, printed " Esil," and which some commentators conjecture should be " Weisel," a river which runs into the Baltic. I think there can be no doubt that Shakspeare wrote " eisel," meaning thereby any bitter draught, as vinegar, in which sense " eisel " is used by Sir T. More. See Johnson's Dictionary— " Eisel:" Shakspeare uses the very same word, in the same sense, in his CXIth Sonnet:—

" Whilst, like a willing patient, I will drink

Potions of eysell, 'gainst my strong infection;—

No bitterness that I will bitter think."

It is evident from this, that whatever

is, that Shakspeare's Julius Cæsar is as unlike the real
Julius Cæsar as it was possible to make him.   There is no
point of Cæsar's character better known than his aversion
to anything like either menace or boasting.   He gave one
remarkable example of this, when he entered Rome with
his army, and the tribune Metellus twice opposed him.
The first time Cæsar said to him, ".If you don't like what
is doing, get out of the way, for war needs not bold words."
When Cæsar, as the keys of the treasury were not found,
sent for smiths and ordered them to break the doors, and
Metellus again opposed him, Cæsar, raising his voice,
threatened to kill him if he did not desist from his opposition. "And this," said he, "young man, you well know is
more painful for me to have said than to do."[1] This is
very different from the brag and bluster about courage
and fear, which form the burthen of what Shakspeare has
put into the mouth of his as much a pseudo-Cæsar as
Scott's is a pseudo-Cromwell.

Most of the writers who have treated this particular
period of English History have assumed that, immediately
after the Battle of Worcester, Cromwell had fully made up
his mind to turn out the Parliament, and concentrate all
their powers of sovereignty in his single person. As one
of the principal evidentiary facts adduced for this assump-
tion—namely, Ludlow's misstatement above mentioned,
that Cromwell dismissed the militia immediately after the
Battle of Worcester—is found not to be a fact at all (the
militia having, as has been shown, been regularly dismissed
by the Council of State, when the work for which they had
been called out was done), I think it can by no means be

---

particular liquid Shakspeare meant to
designate, he meant a draught of
"eisel" to denote, not swallowing a
river, but swallowing a particularly bitter or nauseous draught of medicine.
[1] Plutarch, C. Cæsar, c. 35.

concluded that Cromwell had at this particular time made up his mind to pursue such a course, or even that the idea of such a course had entered into his mind at all.

On the 9th of September, the House ordered lands of inheritance, to the value of £1,000 per annum, to be settled on Lambert; £500 each on Monk and Whalley; £300 on Okey; and £200 on Alured, for their great and eminent services to the Commonwealth. The House also ordered a Bill to be brought in, for settling so much of Scotland as is now under the power of their forces, " under the government of this Commonwealth." On the 11th of September, the House resolved " That lands of inheritance, to the yearly value of £4,000, belonging to the State [in addition to £2,500 per annum formerly granted], be settled upon the Lord-General Cromwell and his heirs, as a mark of favour from the Parliament, for his great and eminent services to the Commonwealth." Apartments were also ordered to be fitted up for Cromwell at Hampton Court. The House likewise ordered £2,000 yearly rent to be settled on Henry Ireton, Esq., Lord-Deputy of Ireland, Cromwell's son-in-law.[1] When the news of this grant was brought over to Ireton, he said, according to Ludlow, that the Parliament ought to pay their debts before they made any such presents; that he had no need of their land, and therefore would not have it.[2]

When Cromwell returned to London, he was met at Acton by the Speaker, the Lord-President Bradshaw, and many members of Parliament and of the Council of State, with the Lord Mayor, Aldermen, and Sheriffs of London.[3] He entered the city in a coach of state, and

[1] Parl. Hist. vol. iii. pp. 1371, 2nd edition, London, 1721. 1372.
[2] Ludlow's Memoirs, vol. i. p. 371 :
[3] Parl. Hist. vol. iii. p. 1371, note.

was received, says a cotemporary journalist, "with all possible acclamations of joy."[1]

On the 16th of September Cromwell appeared in the House; when the Speaker, in the name of the Parliament, made an oration to him, and gave him the thanks of the Parliament for his great services to the Commonwealth.

On the very same day the "Bill for an Equal Representation in Parliament"—that is, the Bill for the election of a New Parliament, in which the people should be fairly represented, and consequently putting an end to the present Parliament, called the Long Parliament, which had first met on the 3rd of November 1640—was ordered to be taken into debate the next morning, and nothing to intervene. Accordingly, on the following day, September 17, this Bill was made the subject of debate almost the whole day. But nothing further is entered in the Journals of the House concerning it, than that it was adjourned to that day se'n-night; and then the report was to be made to the House of it, the first business.   The 24th and 25th of this month of September were almost wholly employed in debating the grand point of a new representative. On the latter of these days, the 25th of September, the question being put, " That a Bill be brought in for settling a time certain for the sitting of this Parliament, and for calling a new one, with such fit rules, qualifications, proportions, and other circumstances, as this Parliament shall think fit, and shall be for the good and safety of this Commonwealth," the House divided, and the Yeas went forth, when the Lord-General

---

[1] Parl. Hist. vol. iii. p. 1371.—The following minute, in the Order Book of the Council of State, has reference to this occasion :—" That 40s. be paid to the coachman of the Earl of Pembroke, and 30s. to the postillion, for their attending upon the Speaker upon the occasion of meeting the Lord-General at his return from the Battle of Worcester."— *Order Book of the Council of State*, Friday, September 26, 1651, MS. State Paper Office.

[Cromwell] and Mr. Scott, the tellers of them, brought in the numbers, 33 ; Sir H. Mildmay and Sir James Harrington, for the Noes, 26 ; on which the Bill was ordered to be brought in, and a Committee appointed for that purpose.[1] The result of this business did not appear till November ; and in the meantime it is necessary to describe some important measures, carried out by the Parliament in the month of October.

I have, in a former chapter, mentioned that the Council of State had received several letters from their ambassadors in Holland, St. John and Strickland, relating repeated affronts offered to them there; and that, in consequence of these affronts, the English ambassadors were recalled, and abruptly took their leave and came home. We shall now see the first of the long chain of disastrous consequences to the Dutch, that flowed from the affronts offered to the English ambassadors in Holland.

In little more than a month after the Battle of Worcester, namely, on the 9th of October 1651, the English Parliament passed the famous Navigation Act; whereby it was enacted that no goods should be imported into England from Asia, Africa, or America, except in English ships, nor from any part of Europe except in ships of the country of which the goods were the growth or manufacture : that no salt-fish, whale-fins, or oil should be imported, but what were caught or made by the people of England ; nor any salt-fish exported, or carried from one port to another in England, but in English vessels.[2]

[1] Parl. Hist. vol. iii. p. 1373.

[2] Scobell, part ii. p. 176.—The most eminent political economists agree as to the policy of the Navigation Laws. I have, in the preceding volume, quoted the words of Adam Smith. I will here quote the words of Mr. John Stuart Mill:—"When the English Navigation Laws were enacted, the Dutch, from their maritime skill and their low rate of profit at home, were able to carry for other nations, England included, at cheaper rates than those nations could carry for themselves, which placed all other countries at a great comparative disadvantage in obtaining experienced

On the 22nd of October, the Council of State ordered, "That it be reported to the Parliament that the Council offer the following to be sent Commissioners into Scotland —Lord Chief Justice St. John, Sir Henry Vane (junior) Major Richard Salwey, Colonel George Fenwick, Major-General Lambert, Major-General Deane, Alderman Robert Tichborne."[1] These Commissioners proceeded to Scotland, to offer to unite and incorporate Scotland into one Commonwealth with England and Ireland, and to call upon the Scots to choose their knights of shires and burgesses of towns, and send them to Westminster. But this being refused by the Presbyterian party, the Parliament of England enacted the union of the two nations, and the abolition of monarchy in Scotland, in spite of their opposition On the 21st of November, 1651, the Council of State made the following minute :—"That Mr. Lokier, Mr. Caryll, Mr. Arthur, and Mr. Falconbridge be ordered to go into Scotland, as preachers with the Commissioners that are now going thither from the Parliament; and that the Commissioners do speak with them about it, and signify their answer to the Council."[2] Under date September 10, 1652, Whitelock says : "The Judges newly made and sent from England went their circuit in Scotland ; " with what effects the following entry in Whitelock's Journal of October 4, 1652, shows :—"Letters that sixty persons,

seamen for their ships of war. The Navigation Laws, by which this deficiency was remedied, and at the same time a blow struck against the maritime power of a nation with which England was then frequently engaged in hostilities, were probably, though economically disadvantageous, politically ex- pedient."—*Principles of Political Economy*, vol. ii. p. 535 : 6th edition, London, 1865.

[1] Order Book of the Council of State, October 22, 1651, MS. State Paper Office.

[2] *Ibid.* Friday, November 21, 1651.

men and women, were accused before the Commissioners for Administration of Justice in Scotland, at the last circuit, for witches; but they found so much malice and so little proof against them, that none were condemned." [1] If tried before their own Judges, most of those poor creatures would have been condemned and burnt alive. Such was one result of the charge of Cromwell's pikemen at Dunbar!

Under date 27th of October 1651, the following minutes appear in the Order Book: "That £50 be paid by Mr. Frost to Mr. White, in consideration of his pains in writing the Treatise of the Life and Reign of the late King."— "That the Lord-General, Lord-Commissioner Whitelock, Lord-Commissioner Lisle, Sir Gilbert Pickering, and Major-General Harrison, or any two or more of them, be appointed a Committee, to consider of some fit person or persons to write the history of these times, and to take the care and oversight thereof; and to consider likewise of a fit encouragement for such person or persons as shall be so employed, and how it may be raised and paid to this use." [2]

The appearance of Cromwell's name on this Committee seems to confirm the remark of Waller the poet, Cromwell's relation, that Cromwell was not so wholly illiterate as was commonly imagined. Indeed, his letters of advice to his son Richard show that he had a just appreciation of the usefulness in particular of historical studies. In one letter he advises him to read history, study the mathematics and geography; and in another letter, he recommends to his particular attention Sir Walter Raleigh's History, as " a body of history which would give him comprehensive views."

[1] Whitelock, p. 545.

[2] Order Book of the Council of

State, October 27, 1651, MS. State Paper Office.

This shows that Cromwell had himself read books that required long and continued study and attention.

Unfortunately for the Council of State, however, this care to have the story of their times written by a friendly pen would seem to have been fruitless; for their story was told mostly by their deadly enemies, so that, after all the toils and perils they had passed, they left behind them an execrated name, and a scorched and blackened memory. As they sat round that council-table on that 27th day of October 1651, and "appointed a Committee to consider of some fit person or persons to write the history of these times," they must have been fully aware that they had done deeds which, whether for good or evil, would be long remembered among mankind : but they could hardly have contemplated the fate that awaited some of them living, and all of them dead—the tortures of the old barbarous law of treason, inflicted on the living, which *they never* inflicted when they inflicted death—the gibbeting of the mortal remains of the dead—and after that the gibbeting of their memories, by writers who, in their scurril jest-books told the Stuart King that the men before whom he had only distinguished himself by being the foremost in flight, and by whom his best and bravest had been scattered and destroyed in so many battles and sieges, were not only villains but cowards !

On the 28th of October an order was made by the Council of State, " That it be referred to the Committee of the Admiralty, to consider of the ordering of the offices of Gunner, Boatswain, and Carpenter, in every of the State's ships, in such manner that the State may not be abused in the passing of their accounts, in which they pretend frequently to greater expenses than have really been made

for the public service."[1] It appears that all the care taken
by Sir Henry Vane and the Committee of the Admiralty
was unable wholly to prevent abuses in the details of the
naval service. Mr. Dixon, in his " Life of Admiral Blake,"
quoting from Blake's letter to the Navy Commissioners
about this time, with enclosures, preserved among the
Deptford MSS., says : " From the extracts of letters written
by various captains of vessels, which he submitted to the consideration of the authorities in London, it is still possible
to gather some idea of the extreme poverty of means with
which Blake had to perform his wondrous exploits. An
example or two will suffice for this purpose : Captain
Pearce, he [Blake] says, writing from Londonderry, on the
27th of August of this year [1651], ' complains that the
fleets on that coast generally stand in great need of victuals,
desires speedy supplies thereof, otherwise must greatly
suffer; goes to half allowance, drinks water; hath but
seven days' provisions, most of it stinks ; butter and cheese
not edible.' "[2]   And yet, so far back as the 21st of
March 164$\frac{8}{9}$, the Council of State had made an order, " That
justice may be done upon such as have furnished stinking
victuals to the fleet."[3]   And the care of the Council of
State is further shown by the following orders : " That
an order be sent to the Commissioners of the Navy, to make
sale of such beef and pork as hath been returned from the
State's ships as too short cut in respect to the allowance
usually given to the mariners to the best advantage to the
State."—" That order be sent to the Commissioners of
the Navy, to give order to the victualler at Portsmouth, in

[1] Order Book of the Council of State,
October 28, 1651, MS. State Paper
Office.

[2] Dixon's Robert Blake, p. 174.

[3] Order Book of the Council of
State, March 21, 164$\frac{8}{9}$, MS. State
Paper Office.

regard to the great scarcity of pork, to allow three pounds of beef in lieu of two pounds of pork."[1]

Another abuse was the custom of paying all the seamen's wages in London, on which Mr. Dixon has published, in his "Life of Blake," a letter written by Blake from Plymouth, on the 28th of August 1651, to the Commissioners of the Navy, which runs thus: "Gentlemen,—There hath been this summer divers mariners pressed in this and other western ports into the State's ships; and in respect their habitations are so far distant from London, many of them have, upon the going in of the ships they served in, been discharged here; and one Mr. Edward Pattison of this town, out of charity, hath paid them their tickets, they being poor people, and not able to look after it alone. This man acquaints me that, for some tickets, notwithstanding he hath been without his money a good while, he is in danger to lose it through delay. I know not what the reason is, but I believe what he did was merely to relieve and ease the poor men. I therefore make it my desire to you, that you will give orders for the payment of such tickets as he hath or shall present unto you, they agreeing, both in entries and discharges, with the muster-books, and thereby Mr. Pattison not put to unnecessary attendance. Therein you will not only oblige him, but also your affectionate friend, ROBERT BLAKE."[2]

Such things as this enable us to see the reason why, when Blake died, the seamen lamented his loss as that of a father; even as, when Turenne fell, the French soldiers cried, "Our father is dead!" If the Council of State and their Admiral (Blake) had been immortal,

---

[1] Order Book of the Council of State, March 23, 164⅘, MS. State Pape · Office.   [2] Dixon's Robert Blake, p. 175, from the Deptford MSS.

it would not have been possible for any satirist to give such a picture of the British Navy 90 years after this time as Smollett has done; to describe such captains as Oakham and Whiffle, and such midshipmen as Crampley; nor, in regard to this very matter of tickets, to say—"I got leave to go on shore next day with the gunner, who recommended me to a Jew, that bought my ticket at the rate of 40 per cent. discount!" It may be certainly inferred, from the terms which Blake uses, "paid them their tickets *out of charity,*" that his seamen were not robbed of nearly half their hard-earned money, under the name of discount.

On the 26th of October "a letter came from General Blake, that all the Isle of Jersey was reduced by the Parliament's forces, under him and Colonel Heynes, except the castles of Elizabeth (to which Sir George Carteret was retired) and Mont Orgueil, the latter of which was soon after taken."[1] On the 15th of December, "Elizabeth Castle was surrendered by Sir George Carteret, Governor thereof, to Colonel James Neave, commander of the Parliament's forces in the said island, upon composition, the articles whereof were very favourable."[2]

On the 31st of October, Castle Rughen and Peele Castle were delivered up, on articles, to the Parliament's forces by the Countess of Derby. "And so the whole of the Isle of Man was reduced to the power of the Parliament, the said Countess having only leave with herself and children to go into England, and make addresses to the Parliament; and hopes to go into France or Holland."[3]

We must now return to the vital question of the time of the continuance of the Parliament.

[1] Perfect Diurnal, from November 3 to 10, quoted in Lord Leicester's Journal, p. 125.

[2] General Proceedings, from December 24 to January 1, quoted in Lord Leicester's Journal, p. 128.

[3] Politicus, from November 6 to 17, quoted in Lord Leicester's Journal, p. 125.

Since, after the Battle of Worcester, all the Royalist party, as Clarendon remarks, lay prostrate, the war which the Parliament had upon their hands may be fairly considered as ended; and the plea afterwards set up by some of them, that they "stayed to end the Dutch war, and that they never bid fairer for being masters of the whole world,"[1] is a strange plea indeed, and forms one of the strongest grounds of justification for Cromwell's expulsion of them. In the first place, it is quite evident that this plea was totally inapplicable to the year 1651. The Dutch war might, indeed, be then looming in the distance; but it did not break out till May 1652, and the plea of staying to be "masters of the whole world" is equivalent to staying for an unlimited time. And yet the man who made use of these pleas was, I believe, besides being a man of great eloquence and great administrative talent, as honest and as brave a man as ever lived, and as ever died for what he considered justice and truth.

There is another curious plea put forward by Henry Marten, in the course of a debate during the time of the Dutch war. He told the House, "That he thought they might find the best advice from the Scripture what they were to do in this particular: that when Moses was found upon the river, and brought to Pharaoh's daughter, she took care that the mother might be found out, to whose care he might be committed to be nursed —which succeeded very happily. Their Commonwealth was yet an infant, of a weak growth, and a very tender constitution; and therefore his opinion was, that nobody could be so fit to nurse it, as the mother who brought it forth; and that they should not think of putting it under any other hands, until it had obtained more years

[1] Scot's Speeches, in Richard Cromwell's first Parliament, reported in Burton's Diary.

and vigour. That they had another infant too under their hands, the war with Holland, which had thrived wonderfully under their conduct; but he much doubted that it would be quickly strangled, if it were taken out of their care, who had hitherto governed it."[1] This, as far as it can be called an argument, must depend on the exactness of the analogy between a young child and a young Commonwealth, and is open to the objections applicable to arguments drawn from metaphors. The latter part of it, however, relating to the Dutch war, is not without force; for though, after Cromwell expelled the Parliament, the Dutch war was brought to a successful issue on the part of the English, the peace made with Holland by Cromwell was neither so honourable nor so advantageous as it would have been if the Long Parliament had made it. Cromwell, Scot says in one of his speeches, "was never so successful as when he was a servant to the Commonwealth. What a dishonourable peace he made, and what an unprofitable and dangerous war!"[2]

More than two years after the Parliament had neglected Ireton's plan for a New Parliament, called the "Agreement of the People," and prosecuted John Lilburne for his, we find that Cromwell himself had taken up the matter almost immediately after the Battle of Worcester—in fact, on the very first day he took his seat, the 16th of September, as we have seen. We have also seen that, on the 25th of September, the House voted upon a division (Cromwell and Scot being tellers for the majority), that a Bill should be brought in, for fixing a certain time for putting an end to the present Parliament, and calling another. A Committee was appointed, in which were

[1] Clarendon, vol. vi. pp. 4, 5.
[2] Meaning the peace with Holland and the war with Spain.

included St. John, Whitelock, Vane, and Cromwell. A Bill was brought in and read a first time, and two days after a second time. It was then committed to a Committee of the whole House. The result appears from the following entry in the Journals :—

"*Friday, the 14th of November*, 1651.—The question being propounded, That it is now a convenient time to declare a certain time for the continuance of this Parliament, beyond which it shall not sit: and the question being put, That this question be now put,

The House was divided :

The Noes went forth.

" Lord-General [Cromwell],	⎰ Tellers for the Yeas ⎱	50
" Lord Chief Justice,	⎱ With the Yeas ⎰	
" Colonel Morley,	⎰ Tellers for the Noes ⎱	46
" Mr. Bond,	⎱ With the Noes ⎰	
		96

" On the main question :

" The Yeas went forth.

" Lord-General,	⎰ Tellers for the Yeas ⎱	49
" Lord Chief Justice,	⎱ With the Yeas ⎰	
" Colonel Morley,	⎰ Tellers for the Noe ⎱	47
" Mr. Bond,	⎱ With the Noes ⎰	
		96

"*Resolved*, That this business be resumed again on Tuesday next."[1]

"*Tuesday, the 18th of November*, 1651.—*Resolved*, That the time for the continuance of this Parliament, beyond which they resolve not to sit, shall be the Third day of November, One thousand six hundred and fifty-four."[2] " So

---

[1] Commons' Journals, Friday, November 14, 1651.

[2] *Ibid.* Tuesday, November 18, 1651.

they have three years yet," writes Lord Leicester in his Journal.[1]

Thus, as this Parliament met on the 3rd of November 1640, its duration, to the 3rd of November 1654, would be 14 years; or, according to a later resolution of the House, appointing the 3rd of November 1653, instead of the 3rd of November 1654, before fixed on, its duration would be 13 years.

The Parliament thought fit to proceed to the election of a Council of State for the fourth time, for the fourth year of the new Government, in November instead of in February; and on Monday the 24th of November 1651, in accordance with the plan they had pursued the preceding year, they chose 21 of the Council for the past year, and 20 who were not members the preceding year. Among these new members was Robert Blake.[2] Lord Leicester says, in his Journal, under date Monday, November 24, 1651: "And it was thought strange that Sir Henry Mildmay and Colonel Harrison, who were so active and painful the last year, should now be of the 20 which were of the Council and now left out."[3] I transcribe from the Journals of the House the following names, as having the greatest and least number of votes or subscriptions, as it is called in the Journals:—

Lord-General [Cromwell] . . .	118
Lord-Commissioner Whitelock . .	113
Lord Chief Justice St. John . . .	108
Sir Henry Vane (jun.)	104
John Gurdon, Esq.	103

---

[1] Journal of the Earl of Leicester, p. 126.

[2] Commons' Journals, Monday, No-vember 24, 1651.

[3] Journal of the Earl of Leicester, p. 126.

Lieutenant-General Fleetwood . .	102
Lord Chief Justice Rolle . . .	95
Lord-Commissioner Lisle . . .	91
Serjeant Bradshaw	89
Sir Arthur Haselrig	89
Dennis Bond, Esq.	88
Thomas Scott, Esq.	86
Colonel Purefoy	82
Colonel Wauton	78
&c. &c. &c.	
Robert Blake, Esq.	42
Earl of Pembroke	42
Henry Marten, Esq. (the last and lowest of this year)	41[1]

On the 26th of November it was resolved by the Parliament, that henceforth no Chairman of any Committee shall continue longer in the chair than the space of one month, and that this vote shall extend likewise to the Presidentship of the Council of State. "It was said," writes Lord Leicester in his Journal, under date November 26, 1651, "that Serjeant Bradshaw, who had been President of the Council from their beginning,[2] was much troubled at this vote, by which he lost his Lordship, and came to be plain Serjeant Bradshaw; and that he endeavoured to bring the matter again into debate into the House, upon the point of what was meant by a month: but this for the present was stopped at the Council, and Serjeant Bradshaw was

---

[1] Commons' Journals, Monday, November 24, 1651.

[2] This is not strictly accurate. For the first three weeks of their existence, or rather more—namely, from February 17 to March 10, 164⅞—the Council of State appointed a President at each meeting. But on March 10 they made an order, "That Mr. Serjeant Bradshaw shall be the President of this Council." (See Vol. I. p. 38.)

desired to take the chair, and his time limited to that day month, from Monday the 1st of December."[1]

At this time two events happened, both of them very unfavourable to the Parliament. The first of these was the death of Ireton, who died of the plague at Limerick, on the 26th of November 1651, at the age of 41.[2] The other event was the Parliament drawing on themselves the bitter hostility of Lambert, who was appointed by them Ireton's successor in Ireland; but soon after, thinking himself unworthily treated by them, threw up the appointment.

Henry Ireton, whose career was thus prematurely cut short, and who, had he lived, must have been one of the most powerful opponents or supporters of the Government of Cromwell, belonged to that class of ancient gentry whose names had been unsullied by the honours of the Stuarts. He was born in 1610, and was the eldest son of German Ireton of Attenton, Esq., in the county of Nottingham. His family was related to that of Colonel Hutchinson, also a Nottinghamshire family, and through them to the Byrons of Newstead; but how long they had possessed estates there I do not undertake to say, nor whether, like the Hampdens and others, they professed to go beyond the Conquest.

It was much the fashion at that time to trace descents, either from those who had come in with William or (as Christopher Sly puts it) with "Richard Conqueror," or had been "there when the Conqueror came." No doubt the pedigree of all families extends, in some way or other,

---

[1] Journal of the Earl of Leicester, p. 127.

[2] Ludlow's Memoirs, vol. i. p. 382: 2nd edition, London, 1721.—Lord Leicester, in his Journal (p. 127, in Sydney Papers by Blencowe), says

Ireton died of a fever; but Ludlow (vol. i. p. 383), who was with him till within two days of his death, states that his condition, "a burning fever, rendered him more liable to the contagion."

beyond the Conquest, the pedigree of the Slys no less than the pedigree of the De Veres. But the way is the question. Mrs. Hutchinson—who, with many noble qualities, was not exempt from human infirmities—traces her descent, by her mother's side, from those who came in with the Conqueror, and by her father's side from those who were "there when the Conqueror came;" and says of the Mayor of Nottingham and his wife—"He was a very honest bold man, but had no more than a burgher's discretion; he was yet very well assisted by his wife, a woman of great zeal and courage, and with more understanding than women of her rank usually have:" overlooking the fact that there lived at that time an Englishman, named Thomas Hobbes, to whom Mrs. Hutchinson would hardly have allowed more than a burgher's pedigree,[1] but who possessed an understanding considerably more powerful than all the understandings of all the Apsleys, of all the St. Johns, and of all the Hutchinsons put together.

Besides, these sweeping assertions respecting pedigree—assertions assuming an uninterrupted male descent for 600 years—are, *primâ facie*, always improbable, and, though within the limits of the possible, extremely difficult to prove strictly. It is easy to assert of an obscure family, as Mrs. Hutchinson and Mr. Hyde have asserted, that they had possessed an estate, which "had continued in their family, and descended from father to son, from before the Conquest." But it is not so easy to produce the evidence necessary to satisfy a competent tribunal of the absolute truth of such assertions. The

---

[1] Hobbes's father, vicar of Charlton and Westport near Malmesbury, had an elder brother, Francis, Alderman of Malmesbury, which is the title of the chief magistrate there, " by profession a glover, which is a great trade there, and in times past much greater."—*Life of Mr. Thomas Hobbes of Malmesbury*, in *Aubrey's Lives*, vol. ii. p. 506: London, 1813.

best test of this is to take a given number of families, respecting which, from their conspicuous position, a satisfactory body of evidence is not only known to exist, but is
open to public inspection. Such a given number of families is furnished by the Peerage of England, from the Norman Conquest to the present time. Now, in all that considerable number of families, there is, I believe, but one, of
which the name as well as the lands and honours descended,
through successive generations, from male heir to male
heir, from the 11th to the 17th century. This family is that
of the De Veres, Earls of Oxford. There are one or two
others (for example, the Percys and the Berkeleys) that
in name existed as long; but their lands and honours had,
in the course of time, passed by a female into another
family, which had assumed their name. It will be found,
on a close examination, that in a large proportion of the
families referred to, the line has ended in a daughter or
daughters, through whom their estates have passed into
other families, and have not reverted to the sons of younger
branches of such families. The result is well expressed in
the words of Lord Chief Justice Crew, in his eloquent exor-
dium in delivering the opinion of the Judges on the
case referred to them by the House of Lords in the time of
Charles I., respecting the right to the Earldom of Oxford :
" And yet Time hath his revolutions; there must be a period
and an end to all temporal things, *finis rerum* : an end of
names and dignities, and whatsoever is terrene ; and why
not of De Vere ? For where is Bohun ? Where is Mow-
bray ? Where is Mortimer ? Nay—which is more and
most of all—where is Plantagenet ? They are entombed
in the urns and sepulchres of mortality ? " [1]

[1] 3 Cru. Dig., p. 170.

There was a certain family, by name Burun, which held certain lordships in the county of Nottingham, in the reigns of William II., of Stephen, and of Henry II. The last of these was Roger de Burun, whose barony was given by King John to William de Briwere. After an interval of more than 300 years, Henry VIII. gave Newstead Abbey, in the same county, to a family of the name of Byron, which family is described as " descended from the above family of Burun." Lord Byron, the poet, loudly boasted of his Norman descent, and of the power and greatness of his Norman ancestors, the Buruns. But, besides the change in the vowels of the name, there would need a long and strong chain of proof to bridge over that chasm of 300 years, between Henry II. and Henry VIII. It is also notorious that Henry VIII., like other despots, granted his favours to new men and new women ; for he gave the whole revenue of a religious house, of considerable value, to a woman, as a reward for making a pudding which happened to gratify his palate.[1] The descendant of this fortunate woman-cook, when boasting of his " father's hall—a vast and venerable pile," so old that it would have fallen had not " strength been pillared in each massive aisle"—would be apt to keep the "pudding " in the background. Lord Byron, perhaps, meant emphatically to disclaim descent from the lady above referred to, when he said, on selling Newstead Abbey: " I have parted with an estate which has been in my family for nearly 300 years, and was never disgraced by being in possession of a lawyer, a churchman, or a woman during that period."[2] According to Fuller, " not only all the cooks, but the meanest turnbroach, in the King's kitchen, did lick his fingers."

[1] Fuller's Church History, p. 337.
[2] Moore's Life of Byron vol. i. p. 479.

Socrates, in the " Gorgias " of Plato, divides adulation into several branches, of which, he says, Rhetoric is one, and Cookery another.   The cases above mentioned are apt examples of the way in which the latter branch of adulation performs its work, and attains its object.   It might be an enquiry neither altogether uninteresting nor unimportant, to investigate the proportions in which Cookery and Rhetoric have contributed to the formation of " noble families." But, by whatever branch of adulation an abbey was obtained from Henry VIII., there could hardly be a more strange ethical phenomenon, than that a man should. boast, and be not merely tolerated but admired for boasting, that he inherited an abbey which had been given to his ancestor by Henry VIII.   It might be a just ground of pride to be the inheritor of a " Castle Dangerous."   It might even be matter of satisfaction to be descended from those who had founded an abbey or a priory; such foundation being a proof of ancient power and wealth, and of a zeal sincere, if blind and misdirected, for the glory of God and the well-being of man.   But public morality must have reached a strange state of confusion, when the possession of property which has the mark on it of public robbery[1]—performed too, without personal risk, on women, and on unarmed, unwarlike men—should be esteemed an honourable distinction.   Poets may challenge our sympathy for bold cow-stealers and bold buccaneers.   Hardihood and courage, even when employed in a bad cause, are still hardihood and courage.   But a man has no more cause to boast of the possession of the most picturesque or richest

---

[1] This term belongs to the transaction, because this property was appropriated in direct violation of the King's promise, solemnly declared in Parliament, that none of it for ever, in time to come, should be converted to private use: but that it should be used for the necessary expenses of government; *and the subject never afterwards charged either with taxes or loans.*—See Coke, 4 Inst. 43, 44.

abbey in England, than of that of Crossraguel in Ayrshire, obtained by roasting a man alive ; or than of any trinkets he may have inherited from his ancestors the beadles, who, in the performance of their duty, hauled Hostess Quickly and Mistress Doll Tearsheet to what were termed by Ancient Pistol "base durance and contagious prison," and who, by somewhat overstepping the exact limits of their function, may have obtained the said trinkets from the persons of those ladies.   The analogy seems nearly complete.   In both cases some antiquity of family is proved. And if the office of beadle *temp*. Henry V. should be considered as not quite equal in dignity to that of lackey *temp*. Henry VIII., the greater antiquity of the beadle descent may, perhaps, make up the difference.

In 1626 Henry Ireton went to Oxford, as a gentleman-commoner of Trinity College, and in 1629 he took his degree of Bachelor of Arts.   Lord Macaulay, in his essay on Lord Bacon, mentions it as a remarkable fact, that the statesmen of Queen Elizabeth were all members of the University of Cambridge.   He adds that Cambridge had the honour of educating those celebrated Protestant bishops whom Oxford had the honour of burning ; and at Cambridge were formed the minds of all those statesmen, to whom chiefly is to be attributed the secure establishment of the Reformed religion in the North of Europe. But of the men most distinguished on the side of the Parliament in the great struggle of the 17th century, Oxford produced as many as Cambridge ; for while Cromwell, Fairfax, Milton, Hutchinson, and Marvell were Cambridge men, Hampden, Pym, Vane, Blake, and Ireton were Oxford men.   Of the men most distinguished on the side of the King, Cambridge produced nearly as many as Oxford ; for while Laud and Hyde were Oxford men, Strafford and

Falkland were Cambridge men. Hobbes also was an Oxford man, but Oxford repudiated him ; and if she could not burn him, as she had burned the Protestant bishops a century before, she burned his works. For on the 21st of July, 1683, the "Leviathan," at the same time with a book "Of Purgatory," had the honour to be condemned by the Convocation to be publicly burned in the school-court or quadrangle."[1]

But though the men educated at the two great English Universities do not afford any indication of the spirit of those Universities, the order of the Council of State, mentioned in the preceding volume, that a letter be written to Dr. Hill, Master of Trinity College, Cambridge, respecting the students of that society willing to go to sea in the summer's fleet,[2] shows that the Parliament considered that they had friends among the Cambridge students. I may add here, that no argument in favour of public schools can be drawn from the men of that time ; neither Hampden, nor Clarendon, nor Fairfax, nor Cromwell, nor Blake, having been educated at a public school. But of the public schools, Westminster would appear to have been then particularly conspicuous; and this was before the time of Busby, who was appointed head-master in 1640. Anthony Wood, speaking of Vane's early life, says he "was bred at Westminster School, with Sir Arthur Haselrig, Thomas Scot the regicide, and other notorious antimonarchists."[3]

From Oxford, Ireton removed to the Middle Temple, where, as appears by the Society's books, he entered as a student on the 24th of November 1629 ; but he was never called to the bar. I have already mentioned the important

---

[1] Wood's Ath. Oxon., art. "Thomas Hobbes."

[2] Vol. I. p. 59.

[3] *Ibid.* art. "Vane."

part which the gentlemen of the Inns of Court took in the war between the King and the Parliament. I would add here, that besides Ireton, Lambert, Ludlow, and Michael Jones, the colonels of some of the most distinguished of the Ironside regiments had been members of the Inns of Court, as appears from the following passage of Ludlow's Memoirs, which may be found to possess some interest, as giving an account of the origin of a corps of gentlemen forming a life-guard for the General of the Parliament, many of whom became afterwards distinguished officers :—

"Soon after my engagement in this cause," says Ludlow, "I met with Mr. Richard Fiennes, son to the Lord Say, and Mr. Charles Fleetwood,[1] son to Sir Miles Fleetwood, then a Member of the House of Commons ; with whom consulting, it was resolved by us to assemble as many young gentlemen of the Inns of Court (of which we then were), and others, as should be found disposed to this service, in order to be instructed together in the use of arms, to render ourselves fit and capable of acting, in case there should be occasion to make use of us. To this end we procured a person experienced in military affairs, to instruct us in the use of arms ; and for some time we frequently met to exercise at the Artillery Ground in London. And being informed that the Parliament had resolved to raise a life-guard for the Earl of Essex, to consist of a hundred gentlemen, under the command of Sir Philip Stapleton, a Member of Parliament, most of our company entered themselves

---

[1] It may be mentioned, as an instance of the inaccuracy of Noble (*Memoirs of the House of Cromwell*), that he describes Charles Fleetwood as having risen from the rank of a trooper in the Earl of Essex's forces; whereas, as appears from what Ludlow here says, he was only one of a number of young gentlemen of the Inns of Court, who volunteered to form the Earl of Essex's life-guard, which was to consist of a hundred gentlemen.

therein, and made up the greatest part of the said guard ; amongst whom were Mr. Richard Fiennes, Mr. Charles Fleetwood (afterwards Lieutenant-General), Major-General Harrison,[1] Colonel Nathaniel Rich, Colonel Thomlinson, Colonel Twisleton " [who, as we have seen, as well as Fleetwood, commanded a regiment of horse at Dunbar[2]], "Colonel Boswell, Major Whitby, and myself, with divers others."[3]

Ludlow was ten years younger than Ireton, who, after having devoted some time and attention to the study of the law, left the Inns of Court long before Ludlow came there, and went to reside on his family estate in Nottinghamshire, where he was the neighbour as well as friend of his kinsman Colonel Hutchinson, and, according to Mrs Hutchinson, " a very grave, serious, religious person." When the Civil War broke out, Ireton was one of the very few gentlemen of Nottinghamshire (Sir Thomas Hutchinson and his son, the Colonel, being others) who undertook each to raise a troop of horse for the Parliament. Almost all the nobility and gentry of that county—including the Lord Chaworth and Sir John Byron of Newstead (afterwards Lord Byron), and all his brothers—were, says Mrs. Hutchinson, "passionately the King's."[4] Ireton was major of a Nottinghamshire regiment of horse, of which Thornhagh was colonel, which joined Colonel Oliver Cromwell's regiment of horse before the skirmish near Gainsborough, when the King's troops were routed, and their commander, Sir Charles Cavendish, was killed. After this, Mrs. Hutchinson says, " Major

[1] This appears to contradict completely the Royalist stories of Harrison's low origin; since he here is enrolled first in a company of gentlemen of the Inns of Court, and then in the General's Life-guard, consisting of a hundred gentlemen. Ludlow was himself the son of Sir Henry Ludlow, Member for Wiltshire in the Long Parliament; and his honesty and veracity have never been impeached.

[2] See Vol. I. p. 365 of this History.

[3] Ludlow's Memoirs, vol. i. pp. 43, 44 : 2nd edition, London, 1721.

[4] Memoirs of Colonel Hutchinson, p. 117 : Bohn's edition, London, 1854.

Ireton quite left Colonel Thornhagh's regiment, and began an inseparable league with Colonel Cromwell, whose son-in-law he afterwards was." [1]

Under the " New Model ' of the army, Ireton accepted the appointment of captain in the regiment of horse commanded by Algernon Sydney, who was at least ten years younger than himself; but he soon rose to be a colonel of horse, and, at Cromwell's express request, was nominated Commissary-General of the Horse, being the next officer in authority under Cromwell, who was Lieutenant-General of the Horse.   Ireton also, by Cromwell's express desire, commanded the left wing of the Parliamentary army at Naseby.   Here fortune went against him, for his wing was defeated by Prince Rupert, and he himself wounded and taken prisoner ; though, when Fairfax and Cromwell had gained the battle, he made his escape from his captors. Some modern writers have asserted that Ireton's military knowledge was equal, if not superior, to Cromwell's.   Whatever his military knowledge might be, he certainly was not anything like so fortunate a soldier, not only as Cromwell, but as Lambert.   For here, when Ireton had a splendid opportunity, fortune, which is everything in war, went against him ; while fortune never went against Cromwell, and, as has been shown in the preceding volume, the victory at Dunbar was due very much to Lambert, to whom Cromwell gave the command of the army that morning ; but, much or little, it was more due to Lambert than the victory at Naseby was to Ireton.   In fact, Lambert showed at Dunbar something of that rare quality, military genius, which Ireton, though he may have possessed it, never, as far as I know, had any opportunity of showing.

[1] Memoirs of Colonel Hutchinson, p. 161 : Bohn's edition, London, 1854.

I am not making these remarks for the purpose, in the least, of running down Ireton; but I wish to obtain, as far as I can, a correct estimate of Ireton's abilities, with a view to the elucidation of the question of his influence upon the mind of Cromwell.

Whitelock's criticism of Ireton's " Agreement of the People " was probably influenced by the clause excluding practising lawyers from Parliament. " The frame of this ' Agreement of the People,' " says Whitelock, " was thought to be, for the most part, made by Commissary-General Ireton, a man full of invention and industry, who had a little knowledge of the law, which led him into the more errors." [1] But when the fear lest Ireton should bring about those reforms which the lawyers were averse to was removed by his death, Whitelock speaks of him without disparagement, for he says : " This gentleman was a person very active, industrious, and stiff in his ways and purposes ; he was of good abilities for council as well as action, made much use of his pen, and was very forward to reform the proceedings in law, wherein his having been bred a lawyer was a great help to him. He was stout in the field, and wary and prudent in councils ; exceedingly forward as to the business of a Commonwealth. Cromwell had a great opinion of him, and no man could prevail so much, nor order him so far, as Ireton could." [2] In regard to what is said above respecting Ireton's making much use of his pen, the numerous papers drawn up by Ireton are written in a clear, terse, and masculine style, and display a skilful command of language, as well as great knowledge and sagacity.

---

[1] Whitelock's Memorials, p. 356.   [2] *Ibid.* p. 516.

The " Representation from His Excellency Sir Thomas Fairfax and the Army under his command, humbly tendered to the Parliament, concerning the just and fundamental rights and liberties of themselves and the kingdom, with some humble proposals and desires in order thereunto, and for settling the peace of the kingdom,"[1] was chiefly the production of Ireton; and shows that, as early as June 1647, those who led the opinions of the army desired, on grounds which are very clearly stated, " That some determinate period of time may be set for the continuance of this and future Parliaments, beyond which none shall continue, and upon which new writs may of course issue out, and new elections successively take place, according to the intent of the Bill for Triennial Parliaments. And herein we would not be misunderstood to desire a present or sudden dissolution of this Parliament; but only, as is expressed before, that some certain period may be set for the determining of it, so that it may not remain, as now, continuable for ever, or during the pleasure of the present members. And we should desire that the period to be now set for ending this Parliament may be such as may give sufficient time for provision of what is wanting, and necessary to be passed in point of just reformation, and for further securing the rights and liberties, and settling the peace of the kingdom.'[2]

Now the grounds on which this is put are so clearly stated, that the fact of Cromwell's being a party to

---

[1] Printed at Cambridge, by Roger Daniel, printer to the University, with the following fiat: " St. Albans, June 14, 1647.—By the appointment of his Excellency Sir Tho. Fairfax, with the Officers and Soldiery under his command : J. Rushworth, Secretary."— *Parl. Hist.* vol. iii. pp. 615–625.

[2] *Ibid.* p. 622.

them becomes a most important element in the solution
of that complicated problem, the character of Cromwell.
The grounds are these : " We are so far from designing
or complying to have any absolute arbitrary power fixed
or settled, for continuance, in any persons whatsoever,
as that, if we might be sure to obtain it, *we cannot wish
to have it so in the persons of any whom we might best
confide in, or who should appear most of our own opinions
or principles, or whom we might have most personal assurance of, or interest in ;* but we do and shall much rather
wish that the authority of this kingdom, in *a Parliament
rightly constituted, free, equally, and successively chosen,
according to its original intention, may ever stand and
have its course ;* and therefore we shall apply our desires
chiefly to such things, as (by having Parliaments settled
in such a right constitution) may give more hopes of
justice and righteousness to flow down equally to all in
that its antient channel, without any overtures tending
either to overthrow that foundation either of order or
government in this kingdom, or to ingross that power
for perpetuity into the hands of any *particular person
or party whatsoever.*"
The paper then meets the objection, that the change
of the present Parliament may prove for the worse, as
to the persons elected, with this argument—that the
supreme power, or sovereignty, being " unlimited, *unless
in point of time,* is most unfit and dangerous, as to the
people's interest, to be fixed in the persons of the same
men, during life or their own pleasures ; " but that a
change or new election is required, in order " that the
people may have an equal hope or possibility, if they
have made an ill choice at one time, to mend it in
another ; *and the members themselves may be in a capacity*

to taste of subjection as well as rule, and may be so inclined to consider of other men's cases, as what may come to be their own."

The paper then declares that in England, " by many positive laws and antient constant custom, the people have a right to new and successive elections unto that great and supreme trust, at certain periods of time; which is so essential and fundaméntal to their freedom, as it cannot or ought not to be denied them, and *without which the House of Commons is of very little concernment to the interest of the commons of England:* yet in this we would not be misunderstood to blame those worthies of both Houses whose zeal to vindicate the liberties of this nation did procure that Act for the continuance of this Parliament, whereby it was secured from being dissolved at the King's pleasure, as former Parliaments have been, and reduced to such a certainty as might enable them the better to assist and vindicate the liberties of this nation (immediately before so highly invaded, and then also so much endangered); and this we take to be the principal ends and grounds for which, in that exigency of time and affairs, it was procured, and to which we acknowledge it hath happily been made use of; but we cannot think it was by those worthies intended, or ought to be made use of, *to the perpetuating of that supreme trust and power in the persons of any, during their own pleasures, or to the debarring of the people from their· right of elections totally, now when those dangers or exigencies were past, and the affairs and safety of the Commonwealth would admit of such a change."*[1]

The testimony of Whitelock as to the authorship of

[1] Parl. Hist. vol. iii. pp. 620–622.

this paper is very important. " In these declarations and transactions of the army," says Whitelock, under date June 16, 1647, "Colonel Ireton was chiefly employed, or took upon him the business of the pen; and having been bred in the Middle Temple, and learned some grounds of the laws of England, and being of working and laborious brain and fancy, he set himself much upon these businesses, and *therein was encouraged and assisted by Lieutenant-General Cromwell*, his father-in-law,[1] and by Colonel Lambert, who had likewise studied in the Inns of Court, and was of a subtle and working brain." [2]

We have in these two extracts, taken together, some exceedingly important evidence bearing on the characters of Ireton, of Cromwell, of Lambert, and of that portion of the members of the Rump who pertinaciously resisted the dissolution of that remnant of the Long Parliament.

The first things that must suggest themselves to the reader of the preceding extracts from the " Representation " of the army of the Parliament are, the clearness and masculine force of the language, and the soundness of the constitutional knowledge, the more remarkable as coming from a body of soldiers—soldiers who formed a strange contrast to the cavalier Wildrakes who were their cotemporaries, and a still stranger contrast to the Ensign Northertons who were their successors. And yet, the very same state of things which produced the illiterate

---

[1] Exactly one year before this time, Ireton was married to the eldest daughter of Cromwell; as appears from the following extract from the Register of Marriages in the parish of Holton, near Oxford: "Henry Ireton, Commissary-General to Sir Thomas Fairfax, and Bridget, * * * * daughter to Oliver Cromwell, Lieutenant-General of the Horse to the said Sir Thomas Fairfax, were married by Mr. Dell, in the Lady Whorwood her house in Holton, June 15, 1646."

[2] Whitelock's Memorials, June 16, 1647.

brutality of such military men as Ensign Northerton, and the captain in Hamilton's Bawn—who announced his opinion to be that

> Your Noveds, and Bluturks, and Omurs, and stuff,
> By G— they don't signify this pinch of snuff!

—produced a certain officer, by name John Churchill, nearly as illiterate as they; who, even late in life, owned that for his knowledge of English History he was chiefly indebted to Shakspeare; but who, nevertheless, performed military achievements which proved him to be a man of the greatest genius, for they furnished examples of the successful exertion of some of the highest of man's reasoning and inventive faculties. Men have sat on thrones, on woolsacks, in professors' chairs; men have shone in pulpits, in senates, in courts of justice, in popular assemblies; men have been commanders of armies, leaders of political parties, shrewd and energetic organisers of great popular movements; nay more, men have for a time been oracles, dictators in philosophy and letters, without possessing any extraordinary portion of what is highest in human intellect. But to win great and decisive battles, in the face of such disadvantages and difficulties as were met and overcome by Cromwell and Marlborough, and to make a proper use of those battles when won, implies the possession, in a preeminent degree, of some of the higher faculties that distinguish man as man. And yet neither Cromwell nor Marlborough could have written the passages I have quoted from the "Representation" of the army of the Parliament; while he who wrote it, though an able and well-educated man, and a good soldier, probably could not have won the battles won by Cromwell and by Marlborough.

How then is the extraordinary influence which, by the

concurrent testimony of many witnesses, Ireton possessed over the mind of Cromwell to be accounted for? I think it may, without injustice to either of them, be accounted for by the sincere respect entertained by Cromwell for Ireton's historical and legal knowledge, so much greater than his own, as well as for his capacity, honesty, and singleness of purpose. The mode of accounting for this influence adopted by Clarendon and others, that Ireton prevailed over Cromwell by his obstinacy, is childish. It is only weak people who are vanquished by the mere obstinacy of others. A strong, brave, clearsighted man like Cromwell would treat what is commonly understood by obstinacy with very little ceremony; but he would treat with respect opinions formed deliberately and conscientiously, and supported by sound knowledge and clear and cogent arguments.

Another thing that distinctly appears, from several passages in the extract given above from the paper which, though penned by Ireton, was penned, as Whitelock expressly declares, with Cromwell's encouragement and assistance, is that Cromwell was at that time decidedly averse to the perpetuating of the supreme power in any man or body of men during their own pleasure; that therefore Cromwell's seizing upon that supreme power by force, and treating it so far as his own private property as to assume that he had a right to leave it, whether as an inheritance, or a gift by will,[1] was a direct contradiction of his own

---

[1] It is commonly stated, on the authority of Secretary Thurloe—who, in his letter to Henry Cromwell, announcing the death of his father, the Protector, says, "His Highness was pleased before his death to declare my lord Richard successor,"—that Cromwell appointed his eldest surviving son Richard his successor. But in a preceding letter of August 25, to Henry Cromwell, Thurloe says: "He did by himself declare a successor, in a paper, before he was installed by the Parliament, and sealed it up in the form of a letter, directing it to me, but kept both the name of the person and the

opinions, in this writing deliberately and solemnly expressed. These observations apply to Lambert equally as to Cromwell. In fact, the whole of Lambert's subsequent career shows him to have been a man devoid of principle, and, except as a mere soldier, devoid of talent for action. Cromwell and Lambert were thus both, to a certain extent, in the power of Ireton, who—having been assisted by them in those papers, which so clearly set forth the grounds of constitutional government, and being known to both of them as a man not to be turned aside from what he deemed the path of his duty either by interest or fear—formed an obstacle, which, if not insurmountable, was at least formidable, to any attempt on the part of either to concentrate the supreme power in his own person. Besides, Cromwell, who was a man in whom the family affections appear to have been strong, liked as well as esteemed Ireton, and took a warm interest in his wellbeing and advancement. Mrs. Hutchinson tells a story which is illustrative of this. She says that Cromwell used his utmost endeavours to persuade Colonel Saunders into the sale of a place of his

paper to himself. After he fell sick at Hampton Court, he sent Mr. John Barrington to London for it, telling him it lay upon his study-table at Whitehall; but it was not to be found there, nor elsewhere, though it hath been very narrowly looked for." This account appears to me to confirm the statement made by the Rev. Thomas Morrice, chaplain of Roger Boyle, Lord Broghill, and first Earl of Orrery. This statement is :—" Cromwell had made Fleetwood his heir; but one of his daughters, knowing where his will was, took it and burnt it, before Fleetwood could come at it. When Cromwell was asked who should succeed him, he made no reply; but said, in such a drawer of a cabinet in his closet they should find his will. But his daughter had disposed of it elsewhere, and so they never came to the sight of it."—*Memoirs of Roger Earl of Orrery*, prefixed to *Orrery's State Letters*, vol. i. pp. 53, 54: Dublin, 1743. Though many of Mr. Morrice's statements are of little value, even when made on the authority of the Earl of Orrery, who had a case to make out for himself, there can be no doubt that Lord Orrery had the means of being better informed than most persons, in regard to some matters relating to Cromwell and his family; and his version of the matter above mentioned may very possibly be the true account.

called Ireton, "which Cromwell earnestly desired to buy for Major-General Ireton, who had married his daughter."[1]

These facts furnish, of themselves, a sufficient answer to those modern writers, who treat with contempt the notion of Cromwell's being influenced by Ireton in this matter. But the case is yet stronger: for it is to be remembered that Ireton was at the head of a powerful army in Ireland, and that Ludlow,[2] his second in command, was both an able and hardy soldier, and as firmly opposed as Ireton to the domination of Cromwell, or of anybody else. It is true that, if the matter came to the arbitrament of the sword—as a somewhat similar question had come, some 1,700 years before, also between a father-in-law and a son-in-law, at the Battle of Pharsalia—Ireton and Ludlow would have had to fight two men, Cromwell and Lambert, who were probably greater soldiers than they. Yet, in the great game of war, it is impossible for any human foresight to foretell the issue. And though Cæsar thoroughly defeated Pompey at Pharsalia, it was the opinion of General Sir William Napier, and of a greater authority, Napoleon Bonaparte, that at Dyrrachium, only a short time before the Battle of Pharsalia, Pompey had quite outgeneralled Cæsar. When all these things are borne in mind, it will appear that it is a very shallow view of the question to treat with contempt the notion of Cromwell's being influenced by Ireton. Cromwell knew his situation a little better than these modern writers, and would have regarded this mode of explaining him and his schemes as something even below contempt. I therefore consider it beyond a doubt, that Ireton was a check, and a very powerful check,

---

[1] Memoirs of Colonel Hutchinson, p. 324: Bohn's edition, London, 1854.
[2] Ludlow, as well as Ireton, owed his appointment in Ireland to Cromwell. See Ludlow's Memoirs, vol. i. pp. 321, 322: 2nd edition, London, 1721.

upon Cromwell's restless ambition, and lust of domination and self-aggrandisement. But by Ireton's death Cromwell was at liberty to pursue the instincts of his nature, in which the most profound human calculation was combined with the fierce, quick, restless, ravenous instincts of a beast of prey. " Kean's Richard the Third," says a writer who had had an opportunity of observing Napoleon Bonaparte, " reminded me constantly of Bonaparte—that restless quickness, that Catiline inquietude, that fearful somewhat, resembling the impatience of a lion in his cage."

The other event, unfavourable to the Parliament, which I have mentioned as happening about this time, was connected with the appointment of a successor to Ireton in Ireland. On Wednesday, the 21st of January 165½, the Council of State ordered, " That it be humbly offered to the Parliament as the opinion of this Council, that Major-General Lambert may be appointed Commander of the military forces in Ireland, under the Lord-Lieutenant of Ireland, if the Parliament shall so think fit ; and the Lord President of the Council is desired to offer this to the Parliament accordingly." [1] On Friday the 31st of January, the Council ordered, " That a letter be prepared, in pursuance of an Order of Parliament of this day, to be sent to Major-General Lambert ; to inclose the vote of Parliament unto him, and to desire him to repair hither in pursuance of the said vote." [2]

There is so much difference between the account of this business given in the Memoirs of Ludlow, and the account of it given in the Memoirs of Mrs. Hutchinson, that probably either Lambert or his wife—who was, says Mrs.

---

[1] Order Book of the Council of   MS. State Paper Office.
State, Wednesday, January 21, 165½,   [2] Ibid. Friday, January 31, 165½.

Hutchinson, " as proud as her husband "—had given some offence to that austere and haughty matron. And as we know little of Lambert's pedigree, a matter of immense weight with Mrs. Hutchinson, further than that he " is said to have been born of a good family, and to have been educated for the bar," Mrs. Hutchinson probably considered it a piece of high presumption for a man, whom she might consider as only, at best, belonging to the " underling gentry,"[1] to aspire to the high place of Deputy of Ireland, while her husband, Colonel Hutchinson, was never thought of for such a post. Be that as it may, Mrs. Hutchinson tells a rather long story, in which Lambert's " pride " and " heart full of spite, malice, and revenge," are made to bear a very prominent part. But though Mrs. Hutchinson's story is somewhat long, it fails to state the facts correctly, and therefore need not be repeated. Two sentences of it, however, as characteristic of Cromwell's desire of missing no opportunity of advancing himself and his family, I quote :—

" There went a story that, as my Lady Ireton was walking in St. James's Park, the Lady Lambert, as proud as her husband, came by where she was ; and as the present princess always hath precedency of the relict of the dead prince, so she put my Lady Ireton below ; who, notwithstanding her piety and humility, was a little grieved at the affront. Colonel Fleetwood " [he was then Lieutenant-General Fleetwood] " being then present, in mourning for his wife, who died at the same time her lord did, took occasion to introduce himself, and was immediately accepted by the lady and her father, who designed thus to restore his daughter to the honour she had

[1] A phrase of Mrs. Hutchinson. See Memoirs of Colonel Hutchinson, p. 130 : Bohn's edition, London, 1854.

fallen from."[1]   It is observable that, whatever truth or falsehood there may be in this story, which Mrs. Hutchinson gives as she heard it, she mentions "piety and humility " as virtues really belonging to the widow of Ireton. And she is consistent in her account of Cromwell's children. She says afterwards : " His [Cromwell's] wife and children were setting up for principality, which suited no better with any of them than scarlet on the ape.   His daughter Fleetwood " [the lady mentioned above as Ireton's widow] " was humbled and not exalted with these things ; but the rest were insolent fools."   She afterwards says : " Richard was a peasant in his nature, yet gentle and virtuous—a meek, temperate, and quiet man, but became not greatness."[2]

Mrs. Hutchinson's testimony on some of these points is very valuable, inasmuch as she, with a woman's instinct, has observed and recorded certain shades of character, which writers like Ludlow, whose attention was wholly directed to political and military matters, did not notice, or did not think worth recording.   Her remark that Cromwell's children, with the exception of his daughter Bridget and his son Richard (his eldest son Oliver, who was killed when young, must also be excepted), " were insolent fools," confirms the stories told about his youngest daughter, Frances, who appears to have belonged strictly to that class of women, in whom two ruling passions predominate—

The love of pleasure, and the love of sway.[3]

Her love of pleasure was manifested in carrying on a

---

[1] Mrs. Hutchinson's Memoirs of Colonel Hutchinson, pp. 360, 361: Bohn's edition, London, 1854.

[2] *Ibid*. pp. 370, 376.—His eldest son, Oliver, who was killed when very young in a skirmish before the Battle of Marston Moor, would appear, from his father's estimate of him, to have been a youth of promise.

[3] The idea of Pope, that, while men engage in the career of ambition partly from the love of its very trials and

flirtation with Jerry White, one of her father's chaplains, who was discovered by Cromwell "in the lady's chamber, on his knees, kissing the lady's hand." When Cromwell, in a fury, asked "what was the meaning of that posture before his daughter Frank," Jerry, with wonderful presence of mind, said, "May it please your Highness, I have a long time courted that young gentlewoman there, my lady's woman, and cannot prevail; I was therefore humbly praying her ladyship to intercede for me." The result is so characteristic of Cromwell that the story may be true, though Oldmixon, who tells it, is no great authority: yet he says, "I knew them both, and heard this story told when Mrs. White was present, who did not contradict it, but owned there was something in it." The Protector (the story says), turning to the young woman, cried, "What's the meaning of this, hussy? Why do you refuse the honour Mr. White would do you? He is my friend, and I expect you should treat him as such." The young woman, with a very low curtsey, replied, "If Mr. White intends me that honour, I shall not be against him." "Say'st thou so, my lass?" cried Cromwell. "Call Goodwyn; this business shall be done presently, before I go out of the room." Goodwyn came: Jerry and "my lady's woman" were married in presence of the Protector, who gave her £500 for her portion; and that, with the money she had saved before, made Mr. White easy in his circumstances; "except in one thing," adds the narrator, "which was, that he

perils, and are then glad to escape from it to the quiet and repose of obscurity,

—"every lady would be queen for life," from the mere love of domineering, agrees somewhat with the distinction of Plato in applying the word ἡγεμονικὸς to Zeus, and βασιλικὸς to Juno.— See Ast's note to Plato's *Phædrus*, p. 110:—"'Ἡγεμονικὸν est sensu quem Stoici posthac nobilitârunt, idea regens, quæ principatum omnium rerum tenet, contra βασιλικὸν, id quod potestatem suam regiam manifestat, imperio exercendo; ut dominationis cujusdam significatio in hac voce insit. Imperiosa enim Juno est."--*Ast.*

never loved his wife, nor she him, though they lived together near fifty years afterwards."

The love of sway of this daughter of Cromwell was manifested in the eagerness she displayed to become the wife of Charles II. Lord Broghill, afterwards Earl of Orrery—who, while living with Cromwell, carried on a secret correspondence with some persons about the King—had discovered that Charles was favourable to a design "of making a match betwixt His Majesty and one of Cromwell's daughters, the Lady Frances." But Lord Broghill failed in all his attempts to obtain Cromwell's consent to it. "Upon this my Lord withdrew, and meeting Cromwell's wife and daughter, they enquired how he had succeeded; of which having given them an account, he added, they must try their interest in him; but none could prevail."[1] If "the Lady Frances" had accomplished her wish of becoming the wife of Charles Stuart, she would, most probably, have become acquainted with a somewhat disagreeable illustration of the vanity of human wishes.

While, in pursuance of the Order of Parliament above mentioned, Major-General Lambert was making great preparations to go over to Ireland, in the quality of Deputy to General Cromwell, the commission of the latter, as Lord-Lieutenant of Ireland, expired. Thereupon the Parliament took that affair into consideration; and many of the members affirmed that the title and office of Lieutenant of Ireland was more suitable to a monarchy than to a "free commonwealth." Nevertheless, the question was likely to have been carried for the

---

[1] Memoirs of Roger, Earl of Orrery, by the Rev. Mr. Thomas Morrice, his Lordship's chaplain (pp. 40–43), prefixed to "a Collection of the State Letters of the Right Honourable Roger Boyle, the first Earl of Orrery, Lord President of Munster in Ireland:" 2 vols., Dublin, 1743.—Burnet also states that he had the story from Lord Broghill's own lips.

renewing of Cromwell's commission under the same title. But Cromwell, says Ludlow, " having at that time another part to act, stood up, and declared his satisfaction with what had been said against constituting a Lieutenant in Ireland, desiring that they would not continue him with that character. Upon which, the question being put, the Parliament, willing to believe him in earnest, ordered it according to his motion. He further moved that, though they had not thought fit to continue a Lieutenant of Ireland, they would be pleased, in consideration of the worthy person whom they had formerly approved to go over with the title of Deputy, to continue that character to him. But the Parliament, having suppressed the title and office of a Lieutenant in Ireland, thought it altogether improper to constitute a Deputy, who was no more than the substitute of a Lieutenant; and therefore refused to consent to   . that proposal, ordering that he should be inserted one of the Commissioners for Civil Affairs, and constituted Commander-in-Chief of the Forces in Ireland. In the management of this affair, Mr. Weaver, who was one of the Commissioners of Ireland, but then at London and sitting in Parliament, was very active, to the great discontent of General Cromwell, who endeavoured to persuade the Parliament that the army in Ireland would not be satisfied, unless their Commander-in-Chief came over qualified as Deputy. Mr. Weaver assured them that, upon his knowledge, all the sober people of Ireland, and the whole army there except a few factious persons, were not only well satisfied with the present Government, both civil and military, of that nation, but also with the governors who managed the same; and therefore moved that they would make no alteration in either, and renew their commissions for a longer time. This discourse of Mr. Weaver, tending to persuade the Parliament to continue me in the military command" [the command-in-chief, which he had held since the death of Ireton, his own command being that of Lieutenant-General of the Horse], "increased the jealousy which General Cromwell had conceived of me, that I might prove an obstruction to the design he was carrying on to advance himself by the ruin of the Commonwealth. And therefore, since Major-General Lambert refused to go over with any character less than that of Deputy, he resolved, by any means, to place Lieutenant-General Fleetwood at the head of affairs in Ireland. By which conduct he procured two great advantages to himself, thereby putting the army in Ireland into the hands of a person secured to his interest by the marriage of his daughter; and, drawing Major-General Lambert into an enmity towards the Parliament, prepared the latter to join with him in opposition to them, when he should find it convenient to put his design in execution."[1]

By the proceeding above described, Cromwell secured the assistance of the ablest officer in the army, whom he, according to some accounts, further bound to his interest by " deluding him with hopes and promises of succession " to his place and power on his [Cromwell's] death; though Lambert—who, though an able soldier, was a weak politician—discovered somewhat late that Cromwell " intended to confirm the Government in his own family."[2] Sir Walter Scott, in " Woodstock," has well expressed the opinion entertained of Lambert by the army : " If Lambert had been here," said Pearson boldly, " there had been less speaking and more action." " Lambert ! What of Lambert? "

[1] Ludlow's Memoirs, vol. i. pp. 412-415: 2nd edition, London, 1721.

[2] Mrs. Hutchinson's Memoirs of Colonel Hutchinson, p. 372 : Bohn's edition, London, 1854.

said Cromwell, sharply. "Only," said Pearson, "that I long since hesitated whether I should follow your Excellency or him; and I begin to be uncertain whether I have made the best choice—that's all." "Lambert!" exclaimed Cromwell, impatiently, yet softening his voice, lest he should be overheard descanting on the character of his rival,—"What is Lambert?—a tulip-fancying fellow, whom nature intended for a Dutch gardener at Delft or Rotterdam!"

The horticultural tastes of Lambert are noticed by Mrs. Hutchinson, who never misses an opportunity of having a fling at him. "Lambert," she says, "was turned out of all his places by Cromwell" [when he showed his indignation on finding how he had been swindled], "and returned again to plot new vengeance at his house at Wimbledon, where he fell to dress his flowers in his garden, and work at the needle with his wife and his maids."[1] Cromwell, having thus secured Lambert, then set himself to obtain the concurrence of Major-General Harrison, who, as well as Lambert, had a great interest in the army. This he did by working upon Harrison's fanatical delusions, telling him that the course he was pursuing was the only course for securing the speedy advent of the reign of the saints.[2]

We are now in a position to see the extraordinary significance of those proceedings of Cromwell which immediately followed Ireton's death.

[1] Mrs. Hutchinson's Memoirs of Colonel Hutchinson, p. 372, Bohn's edition.—The editor of Mrs. Hutchinson's Memoirs, in a note to this passage, says that, from a Life of Lambert which had been put into his hands, it appears that Lambert enjoyed a good reputation among his countrymen in the North of England; that his horticulture is much spoken of, and that he is said to have *painted* flowers, not to have *embroidered* them.

[2] Mrs. Hutchinson's Memoirs of Colonel Hutchinson, p. 262, Bohn's edition; Ludlow's Memoirs, vol. ii. pp. 563–566: 2nd edition, London, 1721.

About a week after the execution of King Charles, it had been settled, Cromwell being one of the consenting parties to that settlement, that the "office of a King in this nation was unnecessary, burthensome, and dangerous," and the abolition of that office was voted accordingly.[1]   It appears, however, that between February 1649 and December 1651, Oliver Cromwell saw reason to change his opinions on this important point.   For on the 10th of December 1651—and, what is very remarkable, only two days after he received the news of Ireton's death, which reached London on the 8th of December—"Cromwell," says Whitelock, "desired a meeting with divers Members of Parliament, and some chief officers of the army, at the Speaker's house; and, a great many being there, he proposed to them, that now, the old King being dead, and his son being defeated, he held it necessary to come to a settlement of the nation.   And in order thereunto, he had requested this meeting, that they together might consider and advise what was fit to be done, and to be presented to the Parliament."

"He held it necessary to come to a settlement of the nation."   Why?   He and his brethren of the Rump had already fully settled the nation, two years before, in the way of what they called "a free Commonwealth."   Why seek to reopen the question of settling the nation? was a question that, if any of the abler men had been present—Blake, or Vane, or Ireton, who could never ask question more—would naturally have been asked.   But it is a most significant feature of the business that this meeting was called within fourteen days after Ireton's death, and just two days after the news of that event had reached London; and that none

---

[1] Commons' Journals, February 7, 164⅞.

of the statesmen of the Council of State were present at it, as appears by the names of those who spoke, given by Whitelock.

On the proposition, thus propounded by Cromwell, a discussion took place; and it is remarkable that the point of importance in this discussion is a totally distinct one from that which formed the subject of the division of the House on the 18th of November, just twenty-two days before. The point is raised thus:—

Whitelock.—"I should humbly offer, in the first place, whether it be not requisite to be understood in what way this settlement is desired—whether of an absolute republic, or with any mixture of monarchy?"

Cromwell.—"My Lord-Commissioner Whitelock hath put us upon the right point; and, indeed, it is my meaning that we should consider whether a republic, or a mixed monarchical government, will be best to be settled; and if anything monarchical, then in whom that power shall be placed?"

Whitelock—"There may be a day given for the King's eldest son, or for the Duke of York, his brother, to come in to the Parliament; and, upon such terms as shall be thought fit and agreeable both to our civil and spiritual liberties, a settlement may be made with them."

Cromwell.—"That will be a business of more than ordinary difficulty; but really, I think, if it may be done with safety, and preservation of our rights, both as Englishmen and as Christians, that a settlement of somewhat with monarchical power in it would be very effectual."

"Generally," adds Whitelock, "the soldiers were against anything of monarchy; the lawyers were generally for a mixed monarchical government, and many were for the Duke of Gloucester to be made King. But Cromwell still put off *that* debate, and came off to some other point; and in conclusion, after a long debate, the company parted without coming to any result at all; only Cromwell discovered, by this meeting, the inclinations of the persons that spake, for which he fished, and made use of what he then discovered."[1]

Now, it is certainly a strange proceeding that, not two years after the Government had been settled as what they called "an absolute republic without any mixture of monarchy," one of those who had been a party to that settlement, and who in his individual character was certainly not a limb of the sovereign power in England, which sovereign power was then the Parliament, should take upon him to call a meeting for the express purpose of considering the expediency of changing the Government. Was not this proceeding, in itself, an act of high treason against the State? It was open to Cromwell to have propounded his question in the Parliament: but to propound it at a private meeting—for such this was, though held at the Speaker's house—was, to say the least, a most questionable proceeding. In fact, what Vane said on a subsequent occasion seems quite applicable to this proceeding—"This is not honest! Yea, it is against morality and common honesty!"

There are certain important considerations, connected with this matter, which a man so clearsighted and sagacious as Cromwell could hardly have overlooked, had not his mind been, as it were, fascinated by the idea which had taken possession of it—the idea of transferring the kingship of England, Scotland, and Ireland from the family of Stuart to the family of Cromwell. Coleridge, in the course of his admirable analysis of the character of Pitt, says:

---

[1] Whitelock's Memorials, p. 516.

" The influencer of his country and of his species was a young man, the creature of another's predetermination, sheltered and weather-fended from all the elements of experience; a young man whose feet had never wandered, whose eye had never turned to the right or to the left, whose whole track had been as curveless as the motion of a fascinated reptile." Great as was the difference, in other respects, between the characters and the careers of Pitt and Cromwell, in this one momentous particular the fate of the veteran statesman-soldier—the man who had fought his way to power, in a long series of battles, won by daring that never failed in the hour of trial, and by sagacity that was never at fault—resembled that of the man who, by an education which, according to Coleridge, though it destroys genius will often foster talent, acquired a premature and unnatural dexterity in the combination of words—a dexterity diverting his attention from things, from present objects, obscuring his impressions, and deadening his genuine feelings—and who persuaded himself and the nation, that extemporaneous arrangement of sentences was eloquence, and that eloquence implied wisdom. Thus, by becoming the slave of one tyrant idea, the man whose life had been so stormy, so diversified, so full of experience, died, as it were, to his former self; so that the experience of all that stormy and eventful past was lost to him, and he became like a man " to whom the light of nature had penetrated only through glasses and covers; who had had the sun without the breeze; whom no storm had shaken; on whom no rain had pattered; on whom the dews of Heaven had not fallen;—whose whole track had been as curveless as the motion of a fascinated reptile."

How otherwise could a man like Cromwell have overlooked the consequences of such actions as he now meditated? The army and navy had sworn to the terms of the Covenant, which bound them equally to the King and to the Parliament. If therefore the Parliament, to which they had pledged obedience, should be destroyed, there still remained the royal party to that engagement, which party would then have no rival claimant on their duty; for Cromwell was neither of the two parties specified in it. The state of the controversy would thereby be totally changed, as Whitelock very fairly told Cromwell; though without effect, as might be expected, on a man who was infatuated—whose mind was, as I have said, fascinated—by one idea, which had obtained uncontrollable dominion over him.

On Monday the 1st of December 1651 the members of the Council of State present were the following. I transcribe the list in the form and order given in the Order Book:—

Mr. Sergeant Bradshaw
Sir Peter Wentworth
Colonel Stapeley
Mr. Masham
Colonel Downes
General Blake
Sir Henry Vane
Mr. Scott
Colonel Morley
Mr. Holland
Earl of Pembroke
Lord Viscount Lisle
Mr. Martyn
Mr. Challoner
Mr. Bond

Sir Gilbert Pickering
Mr. Carew
Mr. Burrell
Mr. Herbert
Mr. Salwey
Mr. Hay
Mr. Gurdon
Colonel Wauton
Colonel Purefoy
Mr. Nevill
Mr. Dixwell
Sir William Masham
Sir William Constable
Lord-General Cromwell
(In all twenty-nine.)

The following were their first proceedings :—

" That there shall be now chosen a President of the Council."

" That a President shall now be chosen, to continue until this day month."

" That Mr. Sergeant[1] Bradshaw be President of the Council for the time expressed in the former vote"—*i. e.,* " until this day month."

" That Mr. Scott do acquaint Colonel Blake[2] with the intelligence which he hath received, concerning the sending of some ammunition from Holland to the rebels in Ireland, to the end he may appoint some ships to prevent it, if possibly they can."

" *Memorandum.*—All the members of the Council who were here present this day did take the oath of secrecy."[3]

On the following day, the 2nd of December 1651, the number present was twenty-eight. The business on that day consisted chiefly of the appointment of the various Committees, and settling the " Orders for regulating the Council, made 2nd December 1651," some of which were the same as those before given. Those which were new I will give in a subsequent page.

On Thursday, the 4th of December, the Committee for carrying on the Affairs of the Admiralty was appointed. As this Committee may be considered the governing body which laid the foundation of the naval power of England, so great was the importance of the actions of the English

---

[1] This word is written sometimes with a *g*, sometimes with a *j*.

[2] It will be observed that Blake is sometimes styled " Colonel," sometimes " General; " his rank in the army being only " Colonel," although he was " General-at-sea."

[3] Order Book of the Council of State, Monday, December 1, 1651, MS. State Paper Office.

navy during the ensuing year, I will transcribe the minute of the Order of the Council of State appointing the Committee, and containing the names of the members composing it:—

"That Sir Henry Vane, Mr. Chaloner, Mr. Bond, Lord-Commissioner Whitlocke, Lord-Commissioner Lisle, Colonel Wauton, Colonel Purefoy, Lord-General [Cromwell], Colonel Blake, Colonel Martin, Mr. Nevill, Colonel Morley, Mr. Masham, Mr. Burrell, and Colonel Stapley, or any three or more of them, be a Committee for carrying on the Affairs of the Admiralty, according to the powers formerly given to that Committee." [1]

The following names are added in the margin of the Order Book: "Sir William Masham, added 17th August; Sir Peter Wentworth, Mr. Scott, added 19th August."

On the following day (Friday, the 5th of December, 1651), the Council of State made the following order, which I transcribe, as an example of their unremitting vigilance in the performance of their duties, and their attention to minute details:—

"That three small vessels, not exceeding 120 tons each vessel, be built to ply among the sands and the flats, for the securing those parts from pirates and sea-rovers, which do much infest and annoy the merchant-ships there trading." [2]

On Thursday the 11th of March 165½, the Council of State ordered, "That Mr. Weckerlyn be appointed Secretary Assistant for the business of Foreign Affairs, and shall have the sum of £200 per annum allowed unto him." [3]

There are various minutes expressive of the Council of

---

[1] Order Book of the Council of State, Tuesday, December 4, 1651, MS. State Paper Office.

[2] *Ibid.* December 5, 1651.

[3] *Ibid.* Thursday, March 11, 165½.

State's sense of the services of Milton, to whom an assistant was here appointed, though the designation is usually
" Secretary for Foreign Languages," not (as in the minute
given above) " for the business of Foreign Affairs." Thus,
on the 18th of June 1651, the Council made the following
minute :—" The Council, taking notice of the many good
services performed by Mr. John Mylton [*sic*], their Secretary
for Foreign Languages to this State and Commonwealth,
particularly of his Book in vindication of the Parliament
and people of England against the calumnies and inven-
tions of Salmasius, have thought fit to declare their re-
sentment [sense] and good acceptance of the same; and
that the thanks of the Council be returned to Mr. Mylton,
and their sense represented in that behalf."[1]

In the beginning of the year 1652, John Lilburne again
makes his appearance for a moment. Lilburne having
joined in a petition with Josiah Prymate to the House,
against Sir Arthur Haselrig—complaining of Haselrig's
great oppression and tyranny, in seizing on certain col-
lieries in the county of Durham, and overawing and
directing the Commissioners to whom he had applied for
relief—the said petition was, on the 16th of January 165½,
voted false, malicious, and scandalous, and ordered to be
burnt by the common hangman. Prymate and Lilburne
were fined each £3,000, for the use of the Commonwealth;
£2,000 to Sir A. Haselrig, for damages; and £500 apiece
to the Commissioners before whom the cause had been
heard. Prymate was also committed to the Fleet till payment should be made; and Lilburne was ordered to be
banished out of England, Scotland, Ireland, and the territories thereto belonging, and to suffer death in case of his

[1] Order Book of the Council of State, June 18, 1651, MS. State Paper
Office.

return.[1]   The Parliament had thus got rid of their formidable enemy Lilburne for the present, or, as they perhaps
thought, for ever.   But in that point they found themselves
mistaken.   For the unconquerable Lilburne returned, in
defiance of their penalty of death, was again tried, and
again acquitted.   But, notwithstanding his acquittal, he
was sent a prisoner by Cromwell to Elizabeth Castle, in
the Isle of Jersey ; from which, being far gone in a con-
sumption, he was finally liberated, but only to die.   He
died in August 1657, at the age of 39—a memorable example of integrity, ability, and courage, which, from the want
of certain other qualities, may almost appear to have been
bestowed in vain.

In March 1652 the Island of Barbadoes, which had
adhered to the royal cause, and had also protested
against and determined to resist the Navigation Act,
was reduced to the obedience of the Parliament by Sir
George Ayscue.   The fleet under Sir George Ayscue,
appointed for this purpose, was for a short time diverted
from its original destination, and ordered to make a
part of the force under Blake for the reduction of the
Scilly Islands.   The words of the Order Book of the
Council of State thus set forth the proceeding :—

"That it be reported to the Parliament, that this
Council, in pursuance of the Act of Parliament for the
reducing of the Barbadoes, did cause to be prepared a fleet
of ships for that service, consisting of seven sail, under
the command of Sir George Ayscue."

"That when the fleet aforesaid was ready to set sail,
in prosecution of the said voyage, there being an opportunity offered for the reduction of Scillies, the Council

---

[1] Parl. Hist. vol. iii. p. 1377.

thought fit to make use of that fleet for the said service
at Scillies. And were instrumental for effecting the
same."

" That there are aboard the said fleet many persons
that were banished thence, and who had suffered much
for their fidelity and good affection to this Commonwealth,
who expect their passage thither in the said fleet."[1]

The character which Clarendon has given of this Sir
George Ayscue (or Ascue, as he writes it) may be taken
as an example of that writer's manner of drawing characters. "Ascue," he says, "was a gentleman, but had
kept ill company too long, which had blunted his understanding, if it had been ever sharp; he was of few words,
yet spake to the purpose, and to be easily understood."[2]
Observe the contradiction here. Lord Clarendon doubts
if Ayscue's understanding had been ever sharp; yet he
describes him as a man of few words, who spoke
to the purpose. And he was, on the whole, a very successful commander. The inference then is, that he was
a very able man, whose understanding was not blunted
by the "ill company" he kept; as if the company of
Blake, and Vane, and Cromwell would have been more
likely to blunt a man's understanding than the company
of King Charles, James Duke of York, and Prince
Rupert!—which were surely a strange conclusion.

[1] Order Book of the Council of State, June 12, 1651, MS. State Paper
Office.

[2] Continuation, vol. ii. p. 354, 8vo. Oxford.

CHAPTER XIII.

It has been shown, in . a preceding chapter,[1] that the Council of State of the Commonwealth of England, in their selection of Oliver St. John as their Ambassador Extraordinary to the United Provinces, were as much aware of the importance of that part of their duty which was (to use the words of Blake) "to keep foreigners from fooling us," as they showed themselves awake, in the selection of Blake as their Admiral, to that other and still more important branch of their duty, which was "to keep foreigners from thrashing us." The consummate falsehood of the Italian and Spanish politicians of the 16th century was by no means extinct in the 17th century. The power of that Spanish monarchy, indeed, which had formed the design of becoming master of the whole world, by the systematic use of disciplined brigands, colossal falsehoods, and sacerdotal cruelty, had fallen, as it would seem, to rise no more. A part of its power, and a part also of its ambition, had passed to those tenants of the Netherland swamps, who had fought so long and so bravely against its tyranny, and now formed the Dutch Republic. Some sixty years before, when Elizabeth Tudor was Queen of England, and was engaged in a war against the Spanish tyrant, "English soldiers and negotiators"—to borrow the apt words of a modern historian, whose laborious researches have laid open many mysteries of iniquity—"went naked into a

[1] Chapter IX.

contest with enemies armed in a panoply of lies."[1] I do not believe that the 17th century differed much from the 16th, generally, as regards the matter of falsehood. A considerable resemblance might, indeed, probably be shown to exist between the character of Louis XIV. of France and that of Philip II. of Spain. But during those years of the 17th century in which England was under that Government called the Commonwealth, neither Dutchman, nor Frenchman, nor Spaniard, nor Italian could gain any advantage, either in diplomacy or war, against those statesmen, so skilful

> to unfold,
> The drift of hollow States, hard to be spell'd,
> Then to advise how war may best upheld
> Move by her two main nerves, iron and gold.[2]

The statesmen who composed the English Council of State were men far too clearsighted to be deceived by the expedient resorted to by the Dutch, of sending over to England ambassadors-extraordinary under the pretence of treating about peace. The Dutch writers themselves admit that this measure of sending ambassadors-extraordinary was but an expedient to gain time, in order to make better preparation for war. " But," says the author of the " Life of Cornelius Van Tromp," son of the great Dutch Admiral, Martin Harpertz Tromp, " in regard the late long war they had had with Spain, had not yet given them time enough to recover their

---

[1] Motley's History of the United Netherlands, vol. ii. p. 356.

[2] Milton's Sonnet to Sir Henry Vane.—The writer of " The Life and Death of Sir Henry Vane, Kt." (printed in the year 1662, small 4to), who was a personal friend of Sir Henry Vane, at p. 93 of his work, mentions this sonnet as having been sent to Vane, " July 3, 1652." And the words he uses are curious, as showing that Milton was at that time really a "mute inglorious Milton." He speaks of the sonnet as " a paper of verses, composed by a learned gentleman, and sent him, July 3, 1652."

strength, they chose rather to temporise awhile with
England, than to embroil themselves hastily in a new
war. They, therefore, employed all sorts of means imaginable to divert that storm, by hastening to send ambassadors into England. Accordingly, Heers *Cats*, *Schaap*,
and *Vanderperre* were despatched to London in that
quality, who were received there with great honours,
but yet in such a manner as gave no promise of a happy
issue of their negotiation."[1]

The admission on the part of the Dutch, that " their
ambassadors were received with great honours, but yet
in such a manner as gave no promise of a happy issue
of their negotiation," proves that, in the punctilious
courtesy with which the English Council of State treated
the Dutch Ambassadors, there was no thought of imitating
the Spanish falsehood of Philip II. of Spain, or the Italian
falsehood of his general, Alexander Farnese. Not that
such an imitation was by any means impossible for men
born in England's " cold and cloudy clime," as the feats of
two individuals, by name George Monk and Oliver Cromwell, fully proved. These two men—like those members
of Charles II.'s Pension Parliament, who, according to
Andrew Marvell, " never lied more than when they professed to speak the sincerity of their hearts"[2]—while
wearing the demeanour of plain blunt soldiers, could,
and habitually did, use as much dissimulation as the
greatest Italian or Spanish masters of the art.

Both Cromwell and Monk have had unqualified admirers; and we need not wonder if they had, since
tyranny, maintained by ability and courage, has never

[1] The Life of Cornelius Van Tromp,
p. 12: London, 1697.
[2] " A Seasonable Argument to persuade all the Grand Juries in England
to petition for a New Parliament."—
Marvell's Works, vol. ii. p. 555: 4to,
London, 1776.

wanted panegyrists; and the writers who applaud strong
energetic tyrants may, like the Greek sophist who wrote a
panegyric on Busiris, indulge the ambition of soaring
above vulgar prejudices. But, after all, truth is truth,
and honour is honour; and it will not be ten thousand
treacherous tyrants, nor ten million apologists of their
crimes, who will be able to make falsehood pass for truth,
villany and baseness for integrity and honour. Monk,
indeed, has no pretensions to the dignity of the great
gamesters who play for empire with loaded dice. He
can soar no higher than the sale of a nation for a dukedom
and a large sum of money; and the honour of having
inscribed on his monument, "*Vendidit hic auro patriam.*"
It would be a waste of time to argue with such a man's
panegyrists—as much as to argue the question of selling
one's country, with that profound and unprejudiced politician, who, when charged with selling his country, replied
by thanking God that he had a country to sell !

The English Parliament having, as we have seen, soon
after the Battle of Worcester, passed an Act known as the
Navigation Act,[1] forbidding the importation of merchandise in other than English ships, the Dutch—who, as being
at that time the great carriers of Europe, saw that they
would be thereby losers to a great amount—resolved to
send ambassadors to the English Parliament, to endeavour

---

[1] It may be mentioned, as one example, amid innumerable others, of the
ignorance generally prevalent respecting this period of English History, that
the Navigation Act is cited by modern
writers, generally well informed, as
having been passed under the Government of the Protector Cromwell. The
writer of the " Life of Cornelius Van
Tromp" (London, 1697)—which work,
though that is not stated either in the
preface or on the titlepage, appears to
be a loose translation of the Dutch
"Leven Van Tromp," cited by Mr.
Granville Penn (vol. i. p. 499)—speaks
of the Government of England as if it
had passed at once from the tyranny of
the Stuarts to that of the Protector
Cromwell.— *Life of Cornelius Van
Tromp*, p. 11.

to obtain their former advantages, and to desire that alliance with the English Commonwealth which, before the Battle of Worcester, they had haughtily refused. Their object in sending these ambassadors was, however, chiefly to gain time to complete their preparations for war, and, according to a cotemporary writer, "partly also to inform themselves what naval forces the English had ready, and how the people here were contented with the Government."[1] The proceedings of the Council of State contain some indications ominous of what was to follow. The Dutch Ambassadors were, however, received with punctilious courtesy.[2]

On the 16th of December 1651 the Council of State made an order, "That Sir Oliver Fleming, Master of the Ceremonies, do repair unto Gravesend, to the Lords Ambassadors from the high and mighty Lords the States-General of the United Provinces, and bring them up to-morrow to Sir Abraham Williams's house. And he is to give notice of their coming to the Members of the Council who are appointed to meet them, that they may accordingly do it."[3]

On Tuesday the 30th of December 1651, the Council of State ordered, "That audience shall be given to the Lords Ambassadors from the States-General of the United

---

[1] Hobbes's Behemoth, p. 286 : London, 1682.

[2] This account is confirmed by the Dutch author of the "Life of Cornelius Van Tromp," p. 12, in a passage which I will quote presently.

[3] Order Book of the Council of State, Tuesday, December 16, 1651. MS. State Paper Office.—On January 8, 165½, there is an order—"That the sum of £235 8s. 9d., due unto Mr. Starkey upon accompt, for the entertaining of the Lords Ambassadors from the United Provinces, be paid unto him by Mr. Frost." On the same day, the Council order £20 to be paid for Mr. Starkey for his own pains. There are also other payments for "carriage and portage of goods, and for attendance, &c. on the said Dutch ambassadors."—Ibid. January 8, 165¼.

Provinces upon Thursday next in the afternoon, and Sir
Oliver Fleming is to give them notice hereof."[1]

On the 1st of January 165$\frac{0}{1}$, the Parliament had agreed
to certain Resolutions as to the manner of giving audience
to ambassadors, agents, and other public ministers from
foreign States. The first of these Resolutions was : "That
Ambassadors, ordinary and extraordinary, sent from Com-
monwealths, Kings, Princes, and States, be admitted to
public audience in Parliament, so often as the Parliament
shall think fit." The second Resolution was : " That all
other public ministers, under the quality of ambassadors,
have audience by a Committee of Parliament, sent out of
the Parliament for that purpose, who are to return and
tender their report before the House rise." The third Resolution was, " That the day and hour be appointed by
Parliament." But, as appears by the Order of the Council
of State last given, the Parliament sometimes left the
appointment of the day and hour to the Council of State.
The fourth Resolution was, " That the late House of Lords
be the place for the Committees of Parliament to give
audience in, and to be fitted up for that purpose." The
fifth Resolution was : " That it be referred to the Council
of State to take especial care to provide convenient hang-
ings for this house ; and that the suit containing the story
of 1588" [the Spanish Armada] "be reserved for the service
of the State, and hung up in the late House of Lords."[2]

In accordance with the Order of the Council of State,
given above, on Thursday the 1st of January 165$\frac{1}{2}$, the Ambassadors from the States-General of the United Provinces
arrived in Palace Yard, and were ushered into the presence
of that Assembly, which now held the place that, when their

[1] Order Book of the Council of   Paper Office.
State, December 3, 1651, MS. State   [2] Parl. Hist. vol. iii. pp. 1360, 1361.

countrymen came to England in 1585, had been filled by Elizabeth Tudor,

> Girt with many a baron bold,
> And gorgeous dames and statesmen old.

On the 24th of December 1650, the Council of State had ordered, on the occasion of audience being given to the Ambassador from Spain, that there should be " a guard of the horse that are in town, mounted in their defensive arms ; and that such part of them as shall be thought fit stand in a body at the Broad Place at Whitehall."[1] It may be doubted whether the Spanish or the Dutch Ambassadors had ever seen such cavalry as those cuirassiers of the Parliament of England.

Those Dutch Ambassadors could hardly be ignorant or unmindful of the great change that had taken place between 1585 and 1651. Two years before, an engraving had been published at Amsterdam of the Execution of Charles I. ; and the ambassadors, in their way to this audience, might have had to take note, not only of that formidable body of cavalry, equally remarkable for the stalwart and veteran appearance of the men, and for the excellence of their arms and horses ; but of the old Hall, where three years before sat "the stern tribunal to whose bar had been led, through lowering ranks of pikemen, the captive heir of a hundred kings ; and of the stately pilasters before which the great execution had been so fearlessly done, in the face of heaven and earth."[2]

If we could form to ourselves a tolerably correct picture, first of the reception of the Dutch ambassadors or commissioners by Queen Elizabeth, and then of that of these

[1] Order Book of the Council of State, December 24, 1650, MS. State Paper Office.

[2] Lord Macaulay's Essay on "Sir William Temple."

ambassadors by the Parliament of the Commonwealth, the
contrast between the two pictures would tell us more of
the real history of the life of a nation than volumes of
ordinary history can tell.   In the lines quoted above from
Gray's Bard, the "Great Queen," as it is the fashion to
call her, is described as "girt with many a baron bold."
Alas! I fear it would be more correct to say, "Begirt with
many a gallant slave!"   "Baron bold!"   There was, indeed, a time for such a word; but it was not the time of
the Tudors.

"By the Everlasting God, Sir Earl, you shall go or
hang!" said the first Edward Plantagenet, King of England,
to Roger Bigod, Earl of Norfolk and Earl Marshal of
England.   "By the Everlasting God, Sir King," replied
the bold baron, "I will neither go nor hang!" And he did
neither go nor hang.   Why?   Because he could bring
into the field a force of Norman lances as invincible as the
pikemen of the Parliamentary army of the 17th century.
But between the time of Edward I. and that of Queen
Elizabeth great changes had taken place ; and words less
bold, less rebellious, than those of Roger Bigod cost the
Earl of Essex his head.   For, any of the nobility who re-
tained the smallest portion of the spirit of the Anglo-
Norman barons, had not the consolation of dying on the
battlefield, like Hotspur and De Montfort, but became the
easy prey of the servile subtlety of the crown lawyers.
The royal power, whether it really was so or not, at least
seemed absolute.   Thus, when the Dutch Commissioners
were admitted to an audience by Elizabeth in 1585, as she
passed through the antechamber to the hall of audience,
wherever she turned her glance, all prostrated themselves
on the ground, like Asiatic slaves before their tyrant.[1]

---

[2] It would appear that the whole House of Commons remained either

The Queen's counsellors too, even the best of them—the Secretary Walsingham and the Lord High Treasurer Burghley—in the presence of that imperious lady, who bore on her head a small gold crown as the symbol of her office, notwithstanding their robes of state, had much the look of being merely, what indeed the word "minister" implies, the upper domestic servants of the lady blazing with diamonds, and wearing the gold crown, on whose brow the angry spot did often glow, making those ministers "look like a chidden train."

The very portraits of the most eminent men who served or were formed under the Tudors are sufficiently marked with the "form and pressure" of the time. Who ever gazed upon the portraits of Burghley, of Coke, and of Bacon, without being struck by the contrast between the broad, lofty, statesmanlike brow, and the pinched, cunning, mean expression of the other features; an expression indicative of the circumstances in which they were placed—circumstances which, if favourable to the intellectual development, were unfavourable to the moral development of man? For theirs was an age of duplicity and hypocrisy the most shameless; of crouching servility to those above, of hard cowardly insolence to those beneath.

Great is the contrast presented to us when we turn to the portraits of the men whom these Dutch ambassadors of 1652 beheld when they were ushered into the presence of that assembly, some of the members of

in a prostrate or a kneeling posture, while Her Majesty made them a speech, unless she were graciously pleased to order them to rise. Thus in her speech to her last Parliament, on November 30, 1601, after speaking for some time, Her Majesty was pleased to say, "Mr. Speaker, I would wish you and the rest to stand up, for I fear I shall yet trouble you with longer speech."—*King's Pamphlets*, Brit. Mus., vol. iv., small 4to, Article 15.

which, if they did not wear a crown of gold, bore on
their aspects the image of manhood and the stamp of
empire. A deep change had evidently come over men's
souls, as well as their fortunes. There was the sombre
stern face of St. John, which they had seen not long before
in their own country, lowering somewhat ominously upon
them. There was the bluff bold visage of Bradshaw.
There was the statesmanlike brow of Sir Henry Vane, sur-
mounting features singularly expressive at once of profound sagacity and wild enthusiasm. But, above all, there
were two men whose eyes, very unlike those of the courtiers
who surrounded the throne of Elizabeth, looked as if they
had never beheld a master, or a mistress who, like Elizabeth speaking of Leicester, could have ventured to designate them "creatures of our own." They were both of
them men whose faces, once seen, could never be forgotten,
for they were faces bearing that combination of courage
and intellect which is the true stamp of empire. One of
these men was Oliver Cromwell; the other was Robert
Blake.

The House being informed by their Sergeant, that the
Lords Ambassadors from the States-General of the United
Provinces attended to present themselves to the Parliament, the Sergeant with his mace went to conduct them
into the house. As soon as the Lords Ambassadors entered,
they uncovered themselves, and the Speaker and all the
members stood up uncovered. When the Ambassadors
had come as far as the bar, the Master of the Ceremonies
and the Sergeant attended them, the one on the right hand
and the other on the left, until they came to the chairs
appointed for that purpose, which were placed upon a
Turkey carpet, with cushions in them, and footstools before
them. The Ambassadors then presented their Letters

Credential, which being delivered by the Master of the Ceremonies to the Speaker, one of the Ambassadors stated the substance of the embassy. He likewise delivered a copy, in English, of what he had before expressed by word of mouth. The Speaker having informed the Ambassadors, by the Master of the Ceremonies, that he would acquaint the Parliament with the purport of their embassy, their Excellencies, attended in the same manner as before, withdrew.

On Thursday the 8th of January 165½ the Council of State made the following orders:—

"That Mr. Martin and Colonel Blake be added to the Committee for Foreign Affairs."

"That the Committee for Foreign Affairs, or any five of them, be appointed a Committee to treat with the Lords Ambassadors Extraordinary from the States-General of the United Provinces; and that the Lord-Commissioner Lisle and Lord Bradshaw do take the special care of that business; and that they do give order for all papers to be ready that may be necessary for the transaction of that work."[1]

On Wednesday the 14th of January 165½ the Council of State made the following orders:—

"That all treaties with foreign States and Princes be managed by papers. And that of all such papers as shall be given in on the part of the Commonwealth, there be one, which is to be the authentic one, signed in English, the other a translate [sic] of it in Latin."

"That it be declared that nothing be taken as part of the treaty but what is delivered on paper and signed."

"That the place for the treaty be in Whitehall."

"That the five persons of the Committee who shall

---

[1] Order Book of the Council of State, Thursday, January 8, 165½, MS. State Paper Office.

manage this treaty with the Dutch, according to the Order
of the Council, be the Lord-President Whitelock, Lord
Bradshaw, Lord-Commissioner Lisle, Mr. Bond, and Mr.
Scott."[1] In the margin, " Lord Viscount Lisle, added 16th
January ; Colonel Martin, Earl of Pembroke, Mr. Neville,
Sir Henry Vane, Sir William Masham, added 2nd April ; "
" Lord Chief Justice St. John, Mr. Love, added," the mar-
ginal note does not say when.

The following minute further shows their mode of proceeding : " That the paper now read, to be sent to the
Dutch Ambassadors, be approved of, translated into Latin,
and sent to the said Ambassadors ; *the English paper to be
signed, and the Latin to go as a copy.*"[2]

The next Order of the Council of State, with reference
to the Dutch business, made on Monday the 2nd of February 165½, has a very ominous aspect. It was made on
the same day as an order respecting the Paper Office ; and
probably the importance of the safe keeping of such papers
as those which are the subject of the following order suggested the other order :—

" That all papers which concern the business of
Amboyna be got together, and brought into the Council
on Wednesday next in the afternoon, to be taken into consideration by the Council."[3]

[1] Order Book of the Council of State, Wednesday, January 14, 165½, MS. State Paper Office. "That forasmuch as it is not thought fit that the Lord-President Whitelock should act during the time of his Presidency, that there should be a sixth person added, and that Colonel Purefoy be that person."—*Ibid.* same day.

[2] *Ibid.* Friday, February 20, 165½.—About six weeks before, they had passed an order, "That Mr. Milton be continued secretarie for foreign languages to the Council for the year to come."—*Ibid.* Monday, December 29, 1651. "Mr. Milton's" office was assuredly no sinecure. The minutes show that a very great number of papers was sent from the Council of State to the Dutch Ambassadors, all of which had to be translated into Latin by "Mr. Milton."

[3] *Ibid.* Monday, February 2, 165½.

Again, on Thursday the 5th of February, there is the following order respecting the ominous business of Amboyna:—

" That the business concerning Amboyna, and also the debate of what shall be insisted upon by the Council in the treaty with the Dutch, be taken up on Wednesday next in the afternoon."[1]

The " business of Amboyna," here referred to, and generally known in English History as " the Amboyna Massacre," may serve well to mark the difference between the Government of James I. and the Government which now managed the affairs of England. The English, under a Government which was at once bad and cowardly, had long complained of oppression on the part of the Dutch in their East India trade. At last an event occurred which made a deep and lasting impression on the minds of Englishmen. In February 1623, Captain Towerson and nine Englishmen, nine Japanese, and one Portuguese sailor, were seized at Amboyna, under the accusation of a conspiracy to surprise the garrison, and to expel the Dutch; and having been tried and subjected to the torture—which, under the civil law, was a regular part of a judicial enquiry, and a common method of extorting evidence from alleged criminals in all the kingdoms of Continental Europe, and Holland among the rest—were pronounced guilty and executed.[2] " The accusation," says the historian of British India, " was treated by the English as a mere pretext to cover a plan for their extermination. But the facts of an event, which roused extreme

[1] Order Book of the Council of State, Thursday, February 5, 165½, MS. State Paper Office.
[2] East India Papers in the State Paper Office ; Bruce's Annals of the East India Company, vol. i. p. 256 ; Mill's History of British India, vol. i. pp. 46–50 : 3rd edition, London, 1826.

indignation in England, have never been exactly ascertained."[1]

Be that as it may, we may safely pronounce that it was an event which could not have occurred, except at a time when all the world knew that England was under the government of a profligate coward, who from his childhood to his latest hour had never felt one throb of generous feeling or of manly indignation; and who reserved all his favour for miscreants such as Somerset and Buckingham, and all his indignation for those who, like the Ruthvens, refused to become the victims and accomplices of his own monstrous vices and crimes. It followed, as a matter of course, that the application made to this King, to obtain signal reparation from the Dutch Government for so great a national insult and outrage, was totally fruitless. What cared the Whitehall Solomon for the tortures and the death of nine or ten Englishmen, who in his estimation were but gutterbloods, not having in their veins one drop of the blood of Stuart? But since that dark and evil time a change had come over the English Council Board, at which one Robert Blake now sat, instead of George Villiers Duke of Buckingham, as representative of the Admiralty and of the naval honour of England among the nations of the earth.

On Tuesday the 10th of February 165$\frac{1}{2}$, the Council of State made the following order :—

" That the Commissioners of this Council, appointed to treat with the Lords Ambassadors from the high and mighty Lords the States-General of the United Provinces, do meet with their said Lordships to-morrow morning, being Wednesday, at the hour of 9, at the usual place in Whitehall. And Sir Oliver Fleming, Master of the Ceremonies, is to have notice hereof, that he may attend

[1] Mill's History of British India, vol. i. p. 46 : 3rd edition, London, 1826.

upon the said Lords Ambassadors to the place appointed accordingly."[1]

On Thursday the 12th of February the Council made the following order :—

" That Wednesday next be appointed for the Committee for Foreign Affairs to bring into the Council a paper of demands to be made to the Dutch Ambassadors by the Council on the behalf of this Commonwealth."[2]

And on the 25th of February the Council of State made the following ominous orders, at a meeting at which Blake was present, but neither Cromwell nor Vane :—

" That the paper now read, of demands to be made to the Dutch Ambassadors, be translated."

"That the English copy of the said demands be signed by the Lord President."

"That it be referred to the Committee for Foreign Affairs to prepare and bring in on Friday next *a demand to be made concerning affronts done to this Commonwealth, now debated at the Council.*"[3]

At this time the Council of State had work enough on their hands ;[4] for while they presented this undaunted front to the Dutch Republic, they showed an aspect equally stern and inflexible to the King of Spain. About a year before an ambassador from the King of Spain had arrived in London, and had been admitted to an audience by the Parliament ; to which he had been conducted through streets lined with that Ironside cavalry—a strong body

---

[1] Order Book of the Council of State, Tuesday, February 10, 165½, MS. State Paper Office.

[2] *Ibid.* Thursday, February 12, 165½.

[3] *Ibid.* Wednesday, February 25, 165½.

[4] This is manifested in the following minute :—" That the Lord-Commissioner Whitelock be desired, in respect of the *many weighty affairs now in hand*, to attend the public service at the Council, notwithstanding his other employment."—*Order Book of the Council of State*, Thursday, February 26, 165½, MS. State Paper Office.

of them being drawn up " at the Broad Place at Whitehall"[1] —whose unequalled military qualities threw into the shade the best troops of his master's ancestor Philip II.—even " the famous Terzio of Naples, the most splendid regiment ever known in the history of war." [2] The Council of State on that occasion ordered " a guard of the horse that are in town, mounted in their defensive arms, and that such part of them as shall be thought fit, stand in a body at the Broad Place at Whitehall—Major-General Harrison to see the order put in execution." [3] The Council were willing that the Spanish ambassador should see some of that magnificent cavalry, to whom might have been fitly applied the term employed to describe the invincibility of that Republican horse regiment called " the Brazen Wall " from its never having been broken.

At that audience he had declared the substance of his embassy to be to express the King of Spain's great desire of establishing a peace and good correspondence with the Commonwealth of England.[4] There was a condition precedent, however, on which the Parliament insisted, but which the King of Spain appeared either unable or unwilling to fulfil. For, more than a year after the Ambassadors' audience, we find the following minutes, which show the high and determined tone taken by the Council of State :—

" That it be referred to Mr. Martin and Mr. Nevill to draw up answer to the first paper of the Spanish Ambassador concerning the murder of Mr. Ascham, and present the same to the Council."[5]

[1] Order Book of the Council of State, December 24, 1650, MS. State Paper Office.

[2] Motley's History of the United Netherlands, vol. ii. p. 456.

[3] Order Book of the Council of State, December 24, 1650, MS. State Paper Office.

[4] Parl. Hist. vol. iii. p. 1359.

[5] Order Book of the Council of State, Thursday, January 8, 165½, MS. State Paper Office.

"That Sir Oliver Fleming, Master of the Ceremonies, do carry to the Spanish Ambassador a copy of the Order of Parliament, whereby it is referred to the Council to demand a sight of the powers of the said Ambassador of the King of Spain, and report the same to the Parliament." [1]

"That the paper that was given to the Spanish Ambassador, to *insist upon justice to be done upon the murtherers of Mr. Ascham,* be reported to the Parliament. And the Lord-Commissioner Whitelock is desired to make the report." [2]

And again, on the 10th of November, 1652, the Council directed a paper to be delivered to the Spanish Ambassador, "wherein it is to be insisted that satisfaction be given concerning the murther of Mr. Ascham in Spain, by doing justice upon the murtherers of him." [3]

It has been remarked by Lord Macaulay, that the reigns of princes, such as Augustus and Philip II. of Spain, who have established absolute monarchy on the ruins of popular forms of government, often shine in history with a peculiar lustre; and that the valour, the intelligence, and the energy, which a good Constitution has generated, being directed by one despotic chief, seem, at least during the first years of tyranny, able to conquer all the world. But there is another process, directly the reverse of this, which seems to inspire an all but resistless energy into a nation. This process is exemplified in the case of a nation that has been long oppressed, and has at last, by a fierce and desperate struggle, shaken off its oppressors, and recovered that liberty which it had not known for ages. The French

[1] Order Book of the Council of State, Thursday, January 8, 165½, MS. State Paper Office.

[2] *Ibid.* Tuesday, February 17, 165½.
[3] *Ibid.* Wednesday, November 10, 1652.

Revolution affords one memorable example. Another is afforded by the rise and progress of the Dutch Republic. The Dutch, after a long and desperate struggle, having succeeded in shaking off the grinding oppression of Spain, sprang up with marvellous rapidity into the greatest naval Power, not only at that time in the world, but the greatest that the world down to that time had ever seen. The Dutch enterprise, energy, and valour seemed to promise an indefinite expansion to their colonial empire, which already, in half a century of liberty, had grown to be only inferior in extent to that of Spain. And while their fleets of war were the most powerful in the world, and their admirals the best the world had ever seen, their merchant-ships were the great carriers of the world, not only carrying on the interchange of commodities between all parts of Europe, but bringing to Europe the products of the most distant parts of the globe, from the fish of Newfoundland to the spices and silks of India.[1] In estimating the value, or at least the magnitude, of a victory, the genius of the commanders of the vanquished fleets or armies is an essential element in the question. One of the greatest generals of any time commanded the French at Waterloo. But surely the French admirals who were defeated at the Nile and Trafalgar cannot for a moment be compared to Tromp and Ruyter, whose

[1] The Journal kept by Admiral Sir William Penn, when cruising in search of Prince Rupert, published by his great-grandson, Mr. Granville Penn, in his "Memorials of Sir William Penn," furnishes abundant evidence of the great amount of the Dutch merchant-shipping. I give the following extract as curious in the matter of the flag: "October 26 (1651), *Sabbath day*.—Presently after noon here (New Gibraltar Road) arrived thirteen sail of Hollanders, all from Malaga, bound (as they say) home under the convoy of young Tromp, who came in with his flag in the maintop, which I said nothing to, being in the King of Spain his port."— *Memorials of Sir William Penn*, vol. i. pp. 378, 379.

conqueror's bones lie in an ignominious pit somewhere near the bottom of the street at the top of which towers Nelson's column of victory.

At the commencement of this great struggle, the advantages appeared to be on the side of the Dutch. The whole of the herring and cod-fisheries, together with the commerce of almost all the world, had rendered the Dutch the most powerful nation at sea that the world at that time had ever seen; for they were probably a greater naval power than the Spaniards when they fitted out the Great Armada. They had also greater admirals than the Spaniards ever had—greater, indeed, than at that time had ever appeared in the world. The number of their trading and fishing vessels probably exceeded that of all the other European nations put together.

The Dutch also were naturally elated by their successes against the Spaniards, who before them had been the greatest naval power in the world; and they had a very great number of well-trained seamen. The vast confluence of seafaring men from all the Northern nations of Europe, drawn by the fame of their commerce, furnished them, without pressing, with such numbers of able seamen, that to wage war with them was—particularly when it is considered that the Kings of Europe more favoured the Dutch than the English—to wage war against a great part of Europe. In fact, in the course of this war, their High Mightinesses (as the title of the Dutch Republic ran) had the audacity to issue a proclamation, like Napoleon's Berlin Decree, against English manufactures, and interdicted all correspondence and communication with the British Islands, taking upon themselves to place those islands in a state of naval blockade. Besides the great number of ships of war which they possessed at the beginning of

the war, such were the riches of the United Provinces at
that time, when Amsterdam and Rotterdam were the great
exchanges of Europe, that even during this war, which
was finished in less than two years, they built sixty ships
of uncommon size and force. The Dutch ships were built
flatter-bottomed, and therefore drew less water, than the
English, and were thus more capable of sailing among
the shallows, where they often found a secure retreat
when chased by the enemy. The English ships being
built of tougher wood, and with sharper keels, were less
subject to splinters, and fitter to dispute the weather-
gauge, " which," says an old writer, " they seldom failed
to gain, though not always to their advantage." [1]

While for the last fifty years the Dutch had been thus
rising into the greatest naval Power that the world down
to that time had ever seen, the English, under the mis-
government of the Stuarts, had been sinking into a condition of decrepitude such as England had not known
for a thousand years ; and it was only since the death of
Charles I., in January 1649, that the able and energetic men
who then took upon themselves the English Government
had full leisure and opportunity to turn their attention
to naval affairs. The success which had attended their
armies, and the promise afforded by the first exploits of
their navy, when they had placed Blake in command of it,
afforded them good grounds for believing that, by due
attention to the administrative details of their naval affairs,
they might now be able to assume a very different tone

[1] Columna Rostrata, or a Critical History of the English Sea Affairs; wherein all the remarkable actions of the English nation at sea are de-scribed, and the most considerable events (especially in the account of the three Dutch wars) are proved, either from original pieces, or from the testimonies of the best foreign historians. By Samuel Calliber: London, 1727, p. 93, 1 vol. 8vo.

towards the pretensions of the Dutch from that of the Governments that had preceded them.

I have shown, in the preceding volume,[1] the peculiar advantages arising from the composition of the Council of State. I have shown that the chances of having the Government administered with ability and vigour were much greater when the power was placed, as in the case of the English Council of State, in a really deliberative Council, in which the President had no more weight than any other member, and which consisted of such a number (the number actually present sometimes amounted to nearly forty)[2] as would give a good chance of their being some men amongst them of ability for government, whose arguments and opinions would determine the deliberations of the whole body, than when the power is placed in what is called a Cabinet Council, consisting of a small number; and of that small number many are mere cyphers, and domineered over by a man called the Prime Minister, who may be a man who owes his position to qualities very different from the qualities of a great statesman. It is important to adduce proofs that the conclusions of this Council of State were adopted after the most careful deliberation, and the most ample discussion. The orders made by the Council for regulating their proceedings furnish ample proof of this. One of their orders is, " That whenever any matter or business is propounded and in debate, no man shall interrupt it by offering any new business till that shall be finished, unless such as cannot

[1] Vol. I. p. 119.

[2] Thus on February 27, 165 9/4, the number present was 38. The day before an order had been made, "That a summons be sent to all the members of this Council who are about the town to come to the Council to-morrow in the afternoon."—*Order Book of the Council of State*, February 26 and 27, 165 9/4, MS. State Paper Office.

bear delay." [1]   Another is, "That while any business is in
debate, no members of the Council shall entertain any
private discourse one with another, at the Board, but
attend the matter in debate, that they may give their
counsel and opinion in it as they shall judge fit for the
Commonwealth; and in case any shall so discourse or
speak to one another, the President for the time shall put
them in mind of their breach of order.   And the persons
speaking to the business shall forbear to speak till those
private discourses cease and all the members attend." [2]

It will be observed what careful precautions are taken,—
particularly in that order given before, and requiring that
every matter propounded shall not only be seconded, but
thirded,[3]—against a great nation's being driven into measures that might involve consequences of the most tremendous nature by the will or the passions of any one man.   If
England had possessed such a Government as this Council
of State in 1853, it is not too much to say that she could not
have been driven or "drifted," as she was, into the Crimean
war.   Mr. Kinglake says, in his " History of the Invasion
of the Crimea," that "upon the papers as they stand, it
seems clear that, by remaining upon the ground occupied
by the four Powers, England would have obtained the de-
liverance of the Principalities without resorting to war ; " [4]
but that she was driven into a war, which cost her a hundred million sterling, by the passions and the interests of
one man in France and another man in England,[5] who
domineered over the feebler members of the Council called
the English Cabinet, somewhat in the way Carteret had

---

[1] Order Book of the Council of
State, December 2, 1651, MS. State
Paper Office.

[2] *Ibid.* same day.—These orders
were not given before. See the other

orders, ante, p. 78 of this volume.

[3] Ante, p. 78.

[4] Kinglake's Invasion of the
Crimea, vol. i. p. 455.

[5] *Ibid.* pp. 446, 447.

done about a century before; for that man may perhaps be said to have borne, in some respects, a certain resemblance to Carteret, whose head was always full of Continental politics, of schemes for humbling the House of Bourbon; and who, says Macaulay, "encountered the opposition of his colleagues, not with the fierce haughtiness of the first Pitt, or the cold unbending arrogance of the second, but with a gay vehemence, a good-humoured imperiousness, that bore everything down before it."

It is melancholy to think how small an advance man has yet made in the art of government when he can be driven to have his blood shed and his pockets picked with impunity by such means as these. Who can wonder at the success of great conquerors like Cæsar and Cromwell in imposing their yoke upon the necks of mankind, when he sees such things done by men without the splendour of their genius or the magic of their great achievements? Nevertheless the will of one man, even of the most powerful despot on the earth, like a Russian Emperor Nicholas, or of the most able despot, like an Oliver Cromwell or a Napoleon Bonaparte, has proved itself but a blind guide compared to a resolution struck out from the grave debate and conflicting arguments of the band of masculine and powerful intellects composing the Council of State of the Commonwealth of England.

In order to obtain all the instruction from the proceedings of this Council of State which they are calculated to give to after-ages, it is important to attempt to discover whether their anxious care to ensure every safeguard against any important resolution's not receiving the due attention would extend to such a case as that of most of the members of the Council being *asleep* when any important business was propounded to them. The order which

I have transcribed above, that " in case any of the members shall speak to one another, the President for the time shall put them in mind of the breach of order, and the persons speaking to the business shall forbear to speak till those private discourses cease, and *all the members attend*," particularly the last four words of it, appears to meet even such a case as this. And the other two orders, " That whatever is propounded, *seconded*, and *thirded* be put to the question if none of the members speak against it; and when a business is resolved by the question, the secretary shall enter the vote into the book," appear likely to render it almost impossible that any business of importance should pass the Council while " all the members of the Council except a small minority were overcome with sleep,"[1] or were even " careless and torpid." [2] How otherwise, indeed, can it have happened that this Council of State so seldom made a false step; that, except in the case of their trial of John Lilburne, in their administration of domestic affairs, as well as in their wars, and the management of their fleets and armies, they displayed such undeviating good sense and sagacity, and attained such signal success ?

History may indeed be pronounced to be nothing better than an old almanack, if such lessons as are given to mankind by the construction, the regulation, and the mode of action, of this great English Council of State of the 17th century have been given in vain.

On the 4th of March, in pursuance of an order of Parliament of the 25th of February, the Council of State granted a commission to Robert Blake to command the fleet for nine months, in the following terms :—

" By virtue of the power to this Council committed by the present Parliament, we do hereby commissionate you

---

[1] Kinglake's Invasion of the Crimea, vol. ii. p. 94.   [2] *Ibid.*

to hold and execute the place of Admiral and General of
the said fleet or fleets, and you are hereby authorised and
required, &c. &c.   .   .   .   And this power to continue for
the space of nine months.   Given under the seal of the
Council the fourth day of March 1651 [165½].

"Signed, &c.

"PHILIP LISLE, President."[1]

On the 15th of March, the Victuallers of the Navy were
ordered " to make provisions for 2,500 men more than the
7,500 already declared for; and the provision was to be
made at London and Chatham."[2]

The Order Book contains a great number of orders
during this month of March relating to the details of the
navy—orders which manifest the unremitting vigilance of
the Council of State at this important crisis. Letters are
ordered to be written to all parts of Britain, respecting the
providing of iron ordnance for the defence of Portsmouth,
the Isle of Wight, and other places exposed to attack by
sea ; " to take speedy care to send all the serviceable and
unserviceable brass ordnance to the Tower of London ; "[3]
for the march of companies of foot, and troops of horse, to
the parts where they are required ;[4] for the transmission of
stores of powder, and great and small shot and " match
proportionable ; " " for such repairs and erecting such
forts as shall be found necessary—the soldiers to be put to
work on this—and also the country people to be called in
and set to work,[5] Lieutenant-Colonel Roseworme to be

---

[1] Order Book of the Council of
State, Thursday, March 4, 165½, MS.
State Paper Office.— Philip, Lord
Viscount Lisle, eldest son of the Earl
of Leicester, who was Lord President
of the Council of State for this month,
always signs his name thus. The Lord
Commissioner Lisle, who was Lord
President for the month following,
signs his name thus—" John Lisle,
President."

[2] Ibid. Monday, March 15, 165½.
[3] Ibid. Wednesday, March 10, 165½.
[4] Ibid. same day.
[5] Ibid. same day.

immediately sent down as Engineer to view the places
which are defective ; [1] for the sending up to London "all
the loose iron guns that lie along the coast of Scotland in
places of no security ; and all the loose iron ordnance that
are to be spared upon all the coast of Scotland ; for 500
carriages for guns to supply emergencies." [2]

The Council's mode of proceeding is further shown by
the following orders ; which, in regard to the care to ascertain the fitness of those ships which had been already so
long at sea " to be continued out two or three months
longer," exhibit a striking contrast to the neglect of such
a precaution in the case of Blake's fleet, when Cromwell
had superseded the Council of State, and was more intent
upon the intrigues for his own further aggrandisement
than upon the welfare of the great admiral and his seamen, and the efficient condition of his fleet :—

" That it be referred to the Committee of the Admiralty
to prepare an account, to be given to the Council, of what
ships are already appointed for this summer's guard, and
the several stations to which they are appointed, and the
time when they will be ready; and likewise to take into
consideration what ships more may be necessary to be set
forth, and what other officers for the commanding of the
fleet may be thought fit to be made choice of; and also
what general instructions are to be given to the commanders of the fleet for the direction of them in their employments ; and to report their opinions to the Council upon
the several matters referred to with all possible speed ;
and they are to send for the Commissioners of the Trinity
House, or any other persons whom they shall think fit, to

[1] Order Book of the Council of   MS. State Paper Office.
State, Wednesday, March 10, 165½.   [2] *Ibid*. March 15, 165½.

advise with from time to time upon any of those matters." [1]

"*That all the members of the Council be added, for the matters above referred, to the Committee of the Admiralty ; and that they do sit every afternoon in the Council Chamber at 2 of the clock.*" [2]

"That the Council do proceed to the nomination of a Vice-Admiral and Rear-Admiral of the fleet to be for this summer's service." [3]

"That a letter be written to General Blake, to cause a survey to be made of the four ships now with Captain Penn, which are coming in—viz. the Fairfax, Centurion, Adventure, and Assurance—of their fitness to be continued out two or three months longer, if there be occasion, and to certify the same to the Council." [4]

About this time Walter Frost died, and was succeeded as secretary to the Council of State by John Thurloe, who was to have " after the rate of £600 per annum." [5] " Walter Frost, the son of Walter Frost, the elder, was continued in his place of assistant secretary to the Council of State."

It will be perceived that this was rather less than Walter Frost had had, his salary having been forty shillings per diem. [6] But as Thurloe was to have lodgings in Whitehall, that would fully make up the difference; that is, provided Frost had not lodgings rent-free, a fact which I have not ascertained. However, on the 1st of December following, the Council of State ordered " That Mr. Thurloe have after the allowance of £800 for the year to come, for and in con-

---

[1] Order Book of the Council of State, Tuesday, March 23, 165½. MS. State Paper Office.

[2] *Ibid.* same day.

[3] *Ibid.* Wednesday, March 24, 165½.

[4] *Ibid.* same day.

[5] *Ibid.* Thursday, April 1, 1652.

[6] See Vol. I. p. 117 of his History.

sideration of his attending as Clerk to the Council and the Committee for Foreign Affairs." [1]

" That convenient lodgings be provided for Mr. Thurloe in Whitehall, for the better enabling him to execute his place." [2]

" That it be declared to Mr. Thurloe as the pleasure of this Council, that no fees are to be demanded or taken of any persons for any orders or despatches of the Council." [3]

On the 2nd of April it was ordered, " that Sir Henry Vane and Sir William Masham be added to the committee which meets with the Dutch ambassadors ; " and also " that Sir H. Vane and Mr. Neville be added to the Committee for French Affairs." [4]

The Council of State saw that it was now time to put an end to the solemn farce of the negotiation which the Dutch carried on. On Monday, the 5th of April, it is ordered " That in the conference with the Dutch ambassadors *it be insisted upon* that an answer be given by the said ambassadors to the paper of demands." [5] The demands, moreover, went on increasing in number, and that grim subject of Amboyna was never lost sight of. Thus on Monday, the 12th of April, the Council of State ordered, " That the several petitions this day brought into the Council concerning the sufferers at Amboyna, and other depredations done upon the English in the East Indies by the Dutch, be referred to the Committee for Foreign Affairs, who are to take the same into consideration, and thereupon prepare a paper of *further demands* to be made of the Dutch ambassadors, if there shall be occasion, and to bring the same into the Council." [6] On the same day also an order was made " to press an answer to the paper of demands,

[1] Order Book of the Council of State, December 1, 1652, MS. State Paper Office.

[2] *Ibid.* Thursday, April 1, 1652.

[3] *Ibid.* same day.

[4] *Ibid.* Friday, April 2, 1652.

[5] *Ibid.* Monday, April 5, 1652.

[6] *Ibid.* Monday, April 12, 1652.

and the 36 articles." [1]   And on Thursday, the 15th of
April, it is referred to the Committee for Foreign Affairs to
consider of what *further* proposals and *demands* are fit to
be prepared to be given to the Dutch ambassadors.[2]   And
again on the following Thursday, the 22nd of April, the
Council ordered, " That it be referred to the Committee for
Foreign Affairs to prepare a paper in answer to the Dutch
ambassadors' paper this day read to the Council; in which
paper it is to be insisted upon that answer be given by the
said ambassadors to the paper of demands formerly given
unto them from the Council; and to certify the mis-
takes which were contained in their paper this day read;
and further to signify unto them that the Council will appoint a conference to be had with them upon the 36
articles, to the end there may be no delay on their part in
the carrying on of the Treaty." [3]   A fortnight after,
namely on Thursday, the 6th of May, there occurs the following minute, which affords corroboration to the evidence
already given that the negotiation was likely to terminate
not in peace but in war :—" That the petition of divers
sea-commanders, mariners, and orphans, suffering in the
East Indies by the Dutch, be referred to the consideration
of the Committee for Foreign Affairs." [4]

It will be needless to give any further attention to the
negotiation with the Dutch ambassadors ; while they were
still going on, an event occurred, on the 19th of May 1652,
in the English Channel off Dover, which, says the author of
the " Columna Rostrata," " was the prologue to the tragedy
that was afterwards acted by the mightiest enemies that
ever sailed upon the sea."

On that 19th of May, the Council of State, who had on
the 15th of April ordered men not to be pressed off ships

[1] Order Book of the Council of
State, Monday, April 12, 1652, MS.
State Paper Office.

[2] *Ibid.* Thursday, April 15, 1652.
[3] *Ibid.* Thursday, April 22, 1652.
[4] *Ibid.* Thursday, May 6, 1652.

outward bound, made the following order as to pressing:
" That warrants be immediately issued out to the several
captains of ships yet in the river that they forthwith
hasten into the Downs, with power to press men out of
any merchants' ships as well *outward bound as inward,* so
that they take but a fourth part of the men in each ship;
and none of the officers in such ship are to be meddled
with upon this occasion."[1] This order had not been made
without the careful deliberation that marked all their proceedings. In the afternoon meeting of the Council on the
preceding day an order had been made, " That it be referred to the Committee of the Admiralty to consider how
men may be furnished to the State's ships, notwithstanding
the prohibition of taking men off merchants' ships which
are outward bound." [2]

" That Sir Henry Vane be President of the Council
until this day month." [3]

On Wednesday, the 19th of May, the Council of State
ordered :—

" That Captain Penn shall be Vice-Admiral, and that
Captain Bourne shall be Rear-Admiral, for the summer's
service." [4]

" That it be recommended to the Lord-General Cromwell
to give order to such foot officers in Kent as are with their
forces near the shore, that they be in such a posture that,
if order come from the General of the Fleet or Vice-Admiral
to that purpose, they may be ready to go on board and
observe such orders as they shall receive from the said
General or Vice-Admiral. And also that such other foot
as are farther off the coast may be drawn nearer in order
to the aforesaid service." [5]

[1] Order Book of the Council of
State, Wednesday morning, May 19,
1652, MS. State Paper Office.
[2] *Ibid.* Tuesday afternoon, May 18,
1652.
[3] *Ibid.* Monday, May 17, 1652.
[4] *Ibid.* Wednesday, May 19, 1652.
[5] *Ibid.* same day.

CHAPTER XIV.

THERE is no part of the history of that English Government, called the Commonwealth, which has been so unfairly dealt with as its naval administration. It would seem as if the memory of it had been cast with the body of Blake into that pit in Westminster Abbey yard; and as if those who were not ashamed to do such a deed thought that they might appropriate to themselves all the honour due to the wisdom and valour of the great Admiral to whose mortal remains they had done so mean and cowardly an insult.

But though the dust of Blake, to whom no writer, to borrow the words of Samuel Johnson, " has dared to deny the praise of intrepidity, honesty, contempt of wealth, and love of his country," sleeps not within the venerable precincts of Westminster Abbey; and though the country he served so well has given him no monument with effigy graven by a cunning hand; though it has refused him even a tomb, as if it made itself a party to the "mean revenge" which insulted his body, by dragging it from the place where it had been entombed, as Johnson says, " with all the funeral solemnity due to the remains of a man so famed for his bravery, and so spotless in his integrity;" yet it may be said of Blake, when his deeds and his claims to honourable remembrance are compared with those of the many great men entombed within that renowned cemetery —" præfulgebat, eo ipso quod effigies ejus non visebatur."

So likewise the attempts of the men of the Restoration, to consign to eternal oblivion the great naval achievements of the Commonwealth, will but recoil upon themselves. For they will force us to ask why so many writers have passed over, as a total blank, this by far the most important period in England's naval annals; and what are the claims of those to whom has been given the credit of all the great naval achievements of the admirals of the Commonwealth?

Let the reader first look on the picture of the Council of State of the Commonwealth given in the preceding pages: that Council in which "the persons speaking to the business in debate shall forbear to speak till those private discourses cease, and all the members attend." [1]   And then let him look on this picture of the Cabinet Council of Charles II. "Lord!" says Pepys, "how they [the Council] meet!—never sit down—one comes—another goes—then comes another; one complaining that nothing is done, another swearing that he hath been here these two hours, and nobody come;" or the King playing with his dog all the while, and not minding the business, or saying something "mighty weak;" or the Duke of Buckingham, for the amusement of His Majesty, making mouths at the Chancellor—or "my Lord Chancellor or my Lord General sleeping and snoring" the greater part of the time at the Council table. Such being the Council, what were the men employed by them? "The more of the cavaliers are put in, the less of discipline hath followed in the fleet; and, whenever there comes occasion, it must be the old ones that must do any good. . . . In the sea-service it is impossible to do anything without them, there not being more than three men of the whole King's side, that

---

[1] Order Book of the Council of State, December 2, 1651, MS. State Paper Office.

are fit to command [ships] almost."[1] Soon after the above comes a passage in Pepys, on a subject on which the Restoration might be greater than the Commonwealth— namely, the matter of new periwigs, gold buttons, and "silk tops for my legs, being resolved," says Pepys, "henceforth to go like myself."[2]

The year 1652 was, in truth, the great naval epoch from which the naval history of England dates its origin. Nevertheless, while some writers have given to Cromwell all the credit of all that was then done, other writers have passed over this momentous period as a total blank; and have given all the honour that belonged to those great statesmen and their great Admiral, to that reign, never to be remembered by Englishmen without indignation and shame, when a King of England, while crowds of unpaid and starving seamen swarmed in the streets of the seaports, and clamorously beset the gate of the Navy Office in London, could still spare money from his harlots, not to pay the starving seamen, to whom it belonged, but to corrupt the members of the House of Commons; to that reign when the English people saw a Dutch fleet sail up the Medway, and burn their ships in their very harbours, and when the Dutch cannon startled the effeminate tyrant in his palace. Those Englishmen whose nature had not been thoroughly corrupted by debauchery and falsehood[3] might, in that dark and evil time, reflect with bitterness of spirit on the contrast between that Council of State, whose fleets and armies had made England famous and terrible over the world, and that Cabinet Council of Charles II. whose proceedings resembled those of a pack of mischievous baboons.

---

[1] Pepys's Diary, June 2 and 24, 1663.

[2] Ibid. October 30, 1663.

[3] "The year Sixty [1660], the grand epoch of falsehood as well as debauchery."—South.

While some writers have passed over entirely this
period of our naval annals, Clerk, in the Introduction to
his "Naval Tactics," and Charnock, in the Preface to his
"Marine Architecture," have given altogether erroneous
accounts of the great sea-fights of 1652-3.   They have
stated, having no accurate records of the operations to
guide them, that in those sea-fights of 1652-3, the English
did not fight in line, but " promiscuously, and all out of
order."   Whereas we have the distinct and express testimony of Admiral Sir William Penn, that the English fought
in line whenever they beat the Dutch.[1]   And not only was
the principle of fighting in line, but also that of breaking the
line, known and acted upon in that famous Dutch war of
1652-3.   It appears, from the authorities cited below,[2] that
so far from the English fleet engaging in line for the first
time in June 1665, and breaking through the enemy's fleet
for the first time in April 1782, the English fleet performed
both those operations in June 1653.   Indeed, it is ridiculous
to suppose that a man of such intelligence as Blake should
have failed to perceive what Lord Rodney has so well
described in his note, printed in the third edition of Mr.
Clerk's book ; Mr. Clerk's friends having erroneously
claimed for him the idea of breaking the enemy's line as a
new discovery.   " It is well known," says Lord Rodney,

[1] Pepys's Diary, July 4, 1666;
Granville Penn, vol. i. p. 401.

[2] See Sir Joseph Jordan's "Journal
on the Vanguard, 1653," copied from
the original MS. of Vice-Admiral (afterwards Sir Joseph) Jordan, found
among the papers of Sir William Penn,
and printed in Granville Penn's "Memorials of Sir William Penn " (vol. i.
pp. 522-540).   Sir Joseph Jordan's
Journal states that on June 2, 1653,
the blue or rear-admiral's squadron
first came into action, then the general's
or wd, and then the Vice-admiral's or

white.   This shows that the fleet
was regularly formed in line, or (as in
this case) in column.   Ludlow says,
" Lawson, who commanded the blue
squadron, charged through the Dutch
fleet with forty ships."—Memoirs, vol.
ii. p. 466 : 2nd edition, London, 1721.
Again, in Monk's report of the action
of July 31, 1653, he says : "The Resolution, with the Worcester frigate, led
the English fleet in a desperate and
gallant charge through the whole Dutch
fleet."

" that attempting to bring to action the enemy, ship to
ship, is contrary to common sense, and a proof that that
admiral is not an officer, whose duty it is to take every advantage of an enemy, and to bring, if possible, the whole
fleet under his command to attack half or part of the
enemy, by which he will be sure of defeating the enemy,
and taking the part attacked ; and likewise defeating the
other part by detail,[1] unless they make a timely retreat.
During all the commands Lord Rodney has been entrusted
with, he made it a rule to bring his whole force against
part of the enemy's, and never was so absurd as to bring
ship against ship when the enemy gave him an opportunity
of acting otherwise." [2]

[1] Mr. Granville Penn (vol. ii. p. 358) by way of still further proof that the idea of dividing an enemy's line and defeating the divided parts does not owe its origin to Mr. Clerk, but was familiar long before, quotes these words : " Le duc pouvait aisément sé-parer une partie de la flotte de l'autre et la battre séparément."—Basnage, *Annales des Provinces Unies*, tom. i. p. 741: published in 1726.

[2] I quote this note of Lord Rodney, which explains the whole subject both of outflanking and of breaking the line with admirable clearness and brevity, from Mr. Granville Penn's "Memorials of Admiral Sir William Penn," vol. ii. p. 354: London, 1833. " Here Lord Rodney," observes Mr. Granville Penn, " has placed the manœuvre upon its true ground of sound common sense acting in a mind moulded to practical seamanship. What has given so disproportioned a character of sagacity to this operation has been the manner in which it was presented to the world by Clerk, who, profess-ing himself to be no seaman, nor ever to have been at sea, but fond of scientifically contemplating naval evo-lutions in the abstract, was forcibly struck with the ingenuity and sound-ness of the idea which had suggested itself to his mind in his closet, and proclaimed it in a tone of exultation, from which he would have abstained had he been a seaman—a proceeding not uncommon with persons of inge-nuity, who hit upon a point in a science foreign to their vocation, and who are induced to think that they have struck out something quite new, because they are not aware that others have already thought of it. * * * * That it was original in Clerk is reasonably to be inferred, because he had no ex-ample to guide or instruct him; but that Sir Charles Douglas (Rodney's flag-captain), or Lord Rodney, de-rived the idea from Clerk, cannot with any reason be insisted on, now that we have discovered that commanders placed in similar circumstances with those distinguished officers, conceived and used the idea more than a century before Clerk appeared." This last

I have not the least doubt that Blake acted on this principle throughout his career. To do so only required that amount of sagacity and courage which Blake possessed, and which in their highest degree may be called genius. It may be almost superfluous to add, that the above-mentioned operation in naval affairs is equivalent to what is called the " flank movement " in military affairs. One of the best examples of the operation and effect of this flank movement in naval affairs, of which what is called " breaking the enemy's line " is only one form, is Nelson's mode of attacking the French fleet at the Battle of the Nile, by placing a part of the French fleet between two parts of his own fleet, and thus defeating the enemy's whole fleet. At the Battle of Trafalgar Nelson's fleet accomplished the same object by breaking through the enemy's fleet in two places.

Though the real cause of the war on the part of the Dutch was, to use the words of Hobbes, " their greediness to engross all traffic,"[1] yet, as this was an argument which they could not very well put forward, they chose to begin the war by refusing to strike the flag, or acknowledge the English dominion of the seas. The Dutch showed good policy in making the question of the flag the pretext for the war; since this pretext had the colour of resisting a tyranny which all the great maritime nations were equally with them concerned to oppose.

statement is made to meet the following observation, which naturally suggested itself, and which Mr. Granville Penn quotes in a note : "The only wonder," says the Quarterly Review (No. 83 p. 60), " is that so simple an operation should not have been discovered, and practised generally, a century before either Rodney or Clerk was born. It is only acting by sea what Bonaparte did by land, wherever he could put it in practice." And, it may be added, what Epaminondas did by land, more than 2,000 years before Bonaparte was born. Steam and gunpowder may change the aspect of war; but, under all changes made by steam and gunpowder, the intellectual supremacy of the commander will always determine the fate of battles.

[1] Hobbes's Behemoth, p. 287, London, 1682; and see *ante*, p. 116.

Sir William Temple carries back the claim of England to the dominion of the seas surrounding Great Britain as far as the year 960.[1] What was implied by this dominion of the seas, as regarded the honour of the flag, is explained by the 13th article of the Treaty of Westminster (5th April, 1654), which article is this : "That the ships and vessels of the said United Provinces, as well those of war as others, which shall meet any of the men-of-war of this Commonwealth· in the British seas, shall strike their flag and lower the topsail, in such manner as the same hath ever been observed, at any times heretofore, under any other form of government."[2] Whether or not this claim on the part of England was as old as the year 960, there is no doubt that it was old, and had given rise to much controversy.

In 1635 had been published the celebrated treatise of Selden, entitled " Mare Clausum," which maintains the right of England to exclude the fishermen of Holland from seas which England asserted to be her own, in answer to the treatise of Grotius, entitled " Mare Liberum," which denied the right. But the concession to England of the honour of the flag by the States of Holland, in the treaty above cited, and concluded at Westminster on the 5th of April 1654, was the first formal concession of that honour by any foreign Power.[3] It may be mentioned, as an example

---

[1] Sir W. Temple's Introduction to the History of England : Works, vol. iii. p. 103, 8vo. Granville Penn, vol. i. p. 397.

[2] Granville Penn, vol. i. p. 577, Appendix G.

[3] The inconveniences arising from the honour of the flag appear from the following letter from the Protector, Richard Cromwell, to General Montague :—" My Lord, by your instructions you are to demand the flag of such foreign ships as you shall rencounter in the British seas, upon which some doubt hath been how far the British seas extend. But not being willing to determine that in our instructions, we rather put, in general terms, the British seas only. We judge there is no question of all the

of the manner in which this most important period of
English History has been treated by writers even of note,
that Sir William Temple, in his "Review of the Origin,
the Elevation, and the Fall of the Naval Power of Holland,"
passes over in perfect silence the whole of this first Dutch
war, together with all the naval events and achievements of the Commonwealth; and puts forward the victory
obtained under the Duke of York, in 1665, in the second
Dutch war (which he calls the first), as the blow that first
brought down the Dutch Republic.

While the Dutch, through their ambassadors extraordinary, whom they had sent to London, professed to treat
of peace, they fitted out a fleet of forty sail of men-of-war,
and placed it under the command of their Admiral, Tromp,
with instructions to this effect. Tromp having desired
the States to give him directions how he should behave
towards the English concerning the honour of the flag, the
States asked him how he had behaved on that point in the
time of King Charles. Tromp replied, that when any
English vessels happened to meet them towards Calais or
near the coast of England, *especially if the English were
strongest,* the Hollanders used to salute them with some
discharge of their cannon, and by lowering their flag.
Thereupon the States left the matter to his discretion;
ordering him to do nothing to the disadvantage of the
nation, or prejudicial to the glory of the State; and that
he should defend their vessels against any that should
attack them.[1]

Martin Harpertz (Herbert) Tromp was, like his great

sea on this side of the Shagenriffe, (*Skageriff, north point of Jutland*); on the other side you have need be tender, and to avoid all disputes of this nature, if it be possible, because war and peace depend on it.—Your loving friend, &c." Whitehall, March 18, 165⅔.—*Thurloe*, vol. vii. p. 633.

[1] The Life of Cornelius Van Tromp, p. 13, London, 1697.

opponent Robert Blake, a man who had risen to command solely by his own personal merits. Yet there was a strange difference between the two great admirals as regarded their early education. While the education of Blake had been, as we have seen, that of a scholar and an English gentleman, the education of Tromp had been from his early boyhood that of a plain rough seaman—one of that class of men whom the foppery of the Restoration denominated *tarpaulins*. Yet, different as was the early education of the two great admirals, they had many qualities in common, and may indeed be said to have been kindred spirits. There is a certain likeness even in the fearless, good-humoured, and open expression of their bold bluff square faces ;[1] though Blake's features, with the short curved upper lip, and finely-chiselled nose, mouth, and chin, are much handsomer than Tromp's. They resembled each other too in the homeliness of their manners, and their kindness to their sailors. Tromp was unlike Blake in this, that he accepted knighthood and armorial bearings from kings—namely, from Charles I. of England and Louis XIII. of France ;[2] but he is said to have declined every offer to raise him into the ranks of the nobility.

Tromp was born at the Brill in 1597, and was but nine years old when he first went to sea with his father, Harpertz Martin Tromp, who commanded a ship in the fleet of Admiral Heemskerk in 1607. Young Tromp was thus present at the battle fought near Gibraltar, on the 25th of April of that year, between the Dutch and Spanish fleets, where the former gained a victory and lost their admiral.

---

[1] See the very characteristic portrait of Tromp in Granville Penn, vol. i. p. 407 ; and the portrait of Blake in Dixon's "Robert Blake."

[2] Granville Penn, vol. i. p. 407, note 3.

Some time after, Tromp's father, while cruising off the
coast of Guinea, was killed in an engagement with an
English privateer, and his ship captured.   For about two
years and a half young Tromp, it is said, was constrained
to serve the captain of the English privateer as his cabin-
boy.   After this he made several voyages on board
merchant-ships.   In 1622 he was made a lieutenant;
and two years after Prince Maurice made him captain of a
small frigate.

In 1629 the celebrated Admiral Piet Hein hoisted his
flag in the ship commanded by Tromp, and went to cruise
against the Spaniards off the coast of Flanders.   On the
20th of August the Admiral fell by the side of Tromp, in
an engagement in which three Spanish ships were taken.
His testimony as to Tromp was that he had known many
brave captains, but that Tromp exceeded them all in the
qualities necessary in an admiral.   About this time Tromp
quitted the service in disgust, in consequence of considering
himself illused by the Dutch Government.   In 1637 Tromp
received a commission to command the fleet as Lieutenant-
Admiral.   With this fleet he, in 1637 and 1638, took so
many ships from the Spaniards, that the States presented
him with a gold chain, and the King of France gave him
the Order of St. Michael.   In April 1639 Tromp again set
sail, to cruise against the Spaniards off the coasts of France
and England; and on the 21st of October he attacked a large
Spanish and Portuguese fleet at the back of the Goodwins,
and defeated and dispersed it, taking thirteen richly-laden
galleons.   Tromp, like Blake, was so beloved by his seamen, that both the captains and mariners used to call
him their father, and Tromp used to call them his children.[1]

[1] Life of Cornelius Van Tromp, pp.   Penn, vol. i. p. 407, and Appendix
157-159, London 1697; Granville E.

There appears, however, to have been a certain portion of craft, amounting at times to an unscrupulous use of falsehood, in the character of Tromp, which rendered him more like Monk than Blake. For, by the concurring testimony of all writers of all parties, Blake possessed in an eminent degree the qualities that formed the great charm of Nelson's character—strong good sense, an affectionate heart, a high and fearless spirit; a disposition not merely averse to falsehood or artifice, but in the highest degree frank, open, and truthful; a contempt of money, and a passion for the glory and honour of his country. As it has been said of Nelson, it may be said of Blake, that these qualities formed no small part of his genius; they secured to him the attachment and confidence of those he led, to that degree which made actions possible that might have been otherwise impossible. It may also be said of Blake, as has been said of Nelson, that his understanding was concentrated on that occupation which so late in life became his profession; and that danger, as it always excites when it does not disturb, by stimulating his mind in the moment of action, roused his genius to the highest exertions.

On Tuesday the 18th of May, 1652, while the Dutch Ambassadors were still in London, making long and tedious harangues about the horrors and evils of war and the blessings of peace—quoting, after their fashion, authorities divine and human, from " holy fathers of the Church," who " have said that men ought to have war in abomination," to " the most excellent wines, changed by corruption into the sharpest vinegar, as experience shows us in natural things," and " those sons of the earth, that destroyed one another, as we are told in the story of Cadmus " [1]—Blake,

[1] Life of Cornelius Van Tromp, pp. 29, 30.

with a squadron of fifteen ships, being in Rye Bay, received intelligence from Major Bourne, who was stationed with eight ships near Dover, that Tromp with forty sail was off the South Sandhead.[1] It should be mentioned that a few days before, namely, on the 12th of May, Captain Young, who was sailing to the westward, to take the command of the west guard, fell in with a fleet of Hollanders from Genoa and Leghorn, under the protection of a convoy of three Dutch ships of war. One of the Dutch ships of war, in answer to Captain Young's request that he would strike his flag, sent word that he would not. Upon this the English and Dutch ships exchanged four or five broadsides; and the Dutch captain then took in his flag, and sent word to Captain Young, that "he had orders from the States not to strike, and that if he struck he would lose his head." "But at length," adds Captain Young, "he

---

[1] Blake to the Council of State, May 20, 1652.—I quote this letter of Blake from the copy printed in Mr. Granville Penn's "Memorials of Admiral Sir William Penn." (vol. i. pp. 421, 422). Mr. Granville Penn gives several letters of Blake from the originals, in Blake's handwriting, among Sir W. Penn's Papers. And though he does not specify this letter as printed from Sir W. Penn's papers, it may be inferred that it is so, since it is neither to be found among the MSS. in the State Paper Office, nor in Thurloe's Collection of State Papers, the principal part of which consists of a series of papers discovered in the reign of King William, in a false ceiling in the garrets belonging to Secretary Thurloe's chambers, No. 13, near the chapel in Lincoln's Inn, by a clergyman who had borrowed those chambers during the long vacation of his friend Mr. Thomlinson, the owner of them. This clergyman soon after disposed of the papers to Lord Somers, then Lord Chancellor, who caused them to be bound up in 67 folio volumes. These afterwards descended to Sir Joseph Jekyll, Master of the Rolls; upon whose decease they were purchased by Mr. Fletcher Gyles, bookseller, and published by Mr. Gyles's executors. These papers had, no doubt, been thus secreted by Thurloe at the Restoration—a circumstance which explains the absence from the State Paper Office of most of the papers containing the voluminous correspondence referred to in the minutes of the proceedings of the Council of State. How these original letters of Blake and others came to be among the papers of Admiral Sir William Penn is not explained.

did strike, which makes me conceive he had had enough of it."[1]

Blake was not a man to suffer any honour that had been paid to the royal flag of England to be withheld from the flag of the Commonwealth of England, as long as he was alive and the Admiral of that Commonwealth. Immediately on the receipt of this intelligence, he made all possible speed to ply up towards the Dutch fleet, commanded by Tromp; and in the morning of Wednesday the 19th of May, 1652, he saw them at anchor in and near Dover Road.[2] Thus in the same straits where, 64 years before, Lord Howard and the Duke of Medina-Sidonia had brought their dispute to an arbitrament, two men, albeit plebeians and neither barons nor dukes, of haughtier name than either Howard or Medina-Sidonia, the two great admirals of the 17th century, first came in view of each other.

When Blake came within three leagues of the Dutch, they weighed anchor, " and stood away by a wind to the eastward; we supposing," says Blake, " their intention was to leave us, to avoid the dispute of the flag. About two hours after, they altered their course, and bore directly with us, Van Tromp the headmost; whereupon we lay by and put ourselves into a fighting posture, judging they had a resolution to engage."[3]   Some accounts state that this alteration of Tromp's course was caused by his falling in with a ketch coming from Holland, and bringing important orders.[4]   But Blake makes no mention of this in his letter to the Council of State.

There is so wide a discrepancy between the statements

[1] Captain Young to the Council of State, May 14, 1652.—This letter of Captain Young is also quoted from the copy printed in Mr. Granville Penn's " Memorials of Admiral Sir William Penn," vol. i. pp. 419–421.

[2] Blake to the Council of State, May 20, 1652.

[3] *Ibid.* same date.

[4] Dixon's Robert Blake, p. 191.

made by the two admirals, Blake and Tromp, that it is
impossible to reconcile them, each stating that the other
fired the first broadside.   Englishmen esteem themselves,
I think justly, as standing high for veracity among nations; and I think Blake may be considered as standing
high for veracity among Englishmen.   I also know more
of Blake than I do of Tromp.   Therefore, when these two
witnesses differ, I am inclined to strike the balance in
favour of Blake.   In no part of history does the difficulty
of obtaining the exact truth press so painfully upon the
writer, who is conscientiously dealing with historical evidence in the search of historical truth, as in the narratives of battles.   Did any two men ever fight either a
single combat, or a great pitched battle at the head of two
fleets or armies, and, when it was done, give the same account of it?   If we find it difficult to get at the exact
truth in regard to battles fought within ten or fifteen
years, how greatly must the difficulty be increased when
we go back 200 years, to say nothing of 2,000!

Besides some strong circumstantial evidence, tending to
prove that Tromp fired the first broadside,[1] there is an
admission in the Dutch "Life of Cornelius Van Tromp,"
which is greatly in favour, if not absolutely conclusive, of
the view that Tromp was the aggressor.   It is stated, as a
reason for laying aside Tromp for a time, that his having
not been so fortunate in his last undertakings as was expected was " looked upon *as a judgment upon him, for being
the cause of that great war.*"[2]

I will now allow Blake to tell his story in his own clear,
plain, and simple language, as he told it in his letter to

[1] See particularly Dixon's " Robert   [2] Life of Cornelius Van Tromp,
Blake," pp. 192, 193:—new edition.   p. 72.
pp. 158, 159.

the Council of State, dated "From aboard the *James*, three leagues off the Hyde, the 20th of May, 1652."

Tromp having, as stated, stood away, as if his intention was to avoid, as Blake thought, the dispute of the flag; and having two hours after altered his course, so as to bear directly down upon Blake's fleet, and to come, as Blake asserts, within musket-shot without striking his flag, the legitimate conclusion was that Tromp did this in direct bravado and defiance of the fleet of the English Commonwealth; and, consequently, no other course was left for Blake, in the strict execution of his duty, than that which he pursued, as thus described by himself. It is important to observe that the words "being come within musketshot" mean that Tromp came within musket-shot; for Blake had said, just before, "We lay by, and put ourselves into a fighting posture":—

"Being come within musket-shot, I gave order to fire at his flag, which was done thrice: after the third shot he let fly a broadside at us. Major Bourne, with those ships that came from the Downs, being eight,[1] was then making towards us. We continued fighting till night; then our ship [his own ship, the *James*] being unable to sail, by reason that all our rigging and sails were extremely shattered, our mizenmast shot off, we came, with advice of the captains, to an anchor about three or four leagues off the Ness,[2] to refit our ship, at which we laboured all the night. This morning we espied the Dutch fleet, about four leagues distance from ours, towards the coast of France; and, by advice of a council of war, it was resolved to ply to windward to keep the weather-gage; and we are now ready

---

[1] Tromp, in his letter to the States of the Netherlands, calls the number of Bourne's ships twelve. He admits, however, that the number of ships with Blake was fifteen.—*Life of Cornelius Van Tromp*, p. 17.

[2] Dungeness.

to let fall our anchor this tide. What course the Dutch fleet
steers we do not well know, nor can we tell what harm we
have done them; but we suppose one of them to be sunk,
and another of thirty guns we have taken, with the captains of both: the mainmast of the first being shot by the
board, and much water in the hold, made Captain Lawson's
men to forsake her. We have six men of ours slain, and
nine or ten desperately wounded, and twenty-five more not
without danger; amongst them our master, and one of
his mates, and other officers. We have received about
seventy great shot in our [1] hull and masts, in our sails and
rigging without number, being engaged with the whole
body of the fleet for the space of four hours; being the
mark at which they aimed. We must needs acknowledge
it a great mercy that we had no more harm, and our hope
is the righteous God will continue the same unto us, if
there do arise a war between us; they being the first in
the breach, and seeking an occasion to quarrel, and watching, as it seems, an advantage to brave us upon our coast.

" Your most humble servant,

" ROBERT BLAKE."[2]

It may be mentioned, as a proof of the difficulty of obtaining accurate and thoroughly trustworthy accounts of
the numbers engaged on such occasions, that Algernon
Sydney, who was not only a cotemporary, but a member

---

[1] By " we " and " our " Blake means
his own ship, the *James*—the Admiral's
flag-ship on this occasion.

[2] Blake to the Council of State,
"from aboard the *James*, three leagues
off the Hyde, May 20, 1652." " That
Mr. Thurloe do prepare an extract of
the several letters which have come to
the Council, giving an account of the
fight between the Dutch fleet and the
English fleet in the Downs, as also of
that made by Captain Young off Plymouth; and bring the same to the Committee of Foreign Affairs to-morrow
morning, who are to sit for that purpose."—*Order Book of the Council of
State*, Monday, May 24, 1652, MS.
State Paper Office.

of the Parliament at this very time, says—"When Van Tromp set upon Blake in Folkestone Bay, the Parliament had not above thirteen ships against threescore."[1] Whereas the Parliament had fifteen ships with Blake, which, with the eight brought up by Bourne, made twenty-three against forty, the number of the Dutch, stated in Blake's letter to the Council of State. Also, the English ships were generally larger than the Dutch, carrying more guns and more men. But there is truth in the further remark of Sydney, which only does justice to the obstinate valour of Blake and his seamen, that the Parliament at this time " had not a man that had ever seen any other fight at sea than between a merchant-ship and a pirate, to oppose the best captain in the world, attended with many others in valour and experience not much inferior to him."[2] A nation that could at once produce such an admiral as Blake out of an Oxford student, and such a supply of naval fighting-men out of her merchant-seamen, assuredly may laugh at the menaces of the world in arms against her.

On Thursday the 20th of May, 1652, in the Council of State, an order to make stay of all Dutch ships in all the ports throughout England, Wales, and Scotland, was negatived when put to the vote. But in the afternoon of the following day, an order passed, " That the letters prepared to be sent to the several ports, concerning the stay of what

[1] Discourse concerning Government, chap. ii. sect. 28.

[2] Algernon Sydney, ibid.—Algernon Sydney's father, the Earl of Leicester, has also stated the numbers inaccurately in his Journal: "Wednesday, May 19, 1652.—There was a fight at sea, betwixt Dover and Folkstone, between Van Tromp, Admiral of the Hollanders' fleet, consisting of forty-two men-of-war; and Robert Blake, Admiral of the English fleet, consisting then only of about 14 sail. This was the first fight between the nations, and lasted from 4 o'clock in the evening till after 8, when the Dutch went away with loss of two ships."—Journal of the Earl of Leicester, in Blencowe's Sydney Papers, p. 135: London, 1825.

Dutch ships are in the several ports of this nation, be sent away."[1]

On the 20th of May, the Council of State made the following orders:—

"That the Commissioners of the Navy, some of the Trinity House, and the officers of the Ordnance, be sent unto to come to the Council to-morrow morning, at 7 of the clock."[2]

"That Lieutenant-Colonel Kelsey be despatched down to Dover Castle, and be authorised, if there be occasion, to reinforce himself, and to entertain 200 or 300 soldiers, over and above what he hath in garrison, for a month, which the Council will pay; and he is to give frequent intelligence to the Council of what shall pass in the Downs, between the fleet of the Commonwealth and the Hollanders; and he is likewise to take care that the town of Sandwich may be encouraged to stand up in their own defence, against any attempts which shall be made upon them."[3]

"The Council of State being certified of a fight at sea, occasioned by a fleet of ships of war belonging to the States of the United Provinces against the ships of this Commonwealth, by which action, especially during the time of the treaty begun and continued by the Lords Ambassadors of the said States with the Parliament, when the same could be least suspected or justified; the Council, doubting that many people, being thereby highly incensed, might make attempts of violence upon the said persons of the Lords Ambassadors, or any belonging to them, have thought fit, for the prevention thereof, to order that some troops of horse be appointed to quarter near the house of

[1] Order Book of the Council of State, Thursday, May 20, and Friday afternoon, May 21, 1652, MS. State Paper Office.
[2] Ibid. May 20, 1652.
[3] Ibid. same day.

the said Ambassadors, and to keep strict guard about the same, for their Lordships' preservation and secure residence there." [1] And on the afternoon of the following day, the Council ordered that four files of musketeers of the guards about the town, and also twenty horse, be appointed, under the command of some civil officer, to repair to Chelsea for the guard of the Dutch Ambassadors. [2] But in appointing this guard the Council had no intention of imposing any restraint on the personal liberty of the Dutch Ambassadors, as appears from the following minute :—

"That it be signified to Commissary-General Whalley that, the instruction of the Council in appointing a guard at the house of the Extraordinary Ambassadors of the United Provinces being only for the safety of their persons against injury and violence, that he manage the said guard in such manner that it may appear to be honourable, and no restraint at all upon them or any of their retinue ; but that it be at their liberty, and the liberty of their attendants and servants, and others amongst them, to go and come as their occasion shall require, and leaving it wholly to them, when they go abroad, whether they will have any guard to attend them." [3]

In the afternoon of Friday the 21st of May, the Council ordered :—

"That a letter be written to General Blake, to take notice to him of the receipt of his letter, and to inclose to him the copy of the Order of Parliament, approving of what he relates in his letter ; to let him know the Council will take all possible care for the supplying him with

---

[1] Order Book of the Council of State, May 20, 1652, MS. State Paper Office.

[2] *Ibid.* Friday afternoon, May 21, 1652. "Six hommes font une file."—

Mémoires de Montecuculi, p. 30 ; Paris, 1760.

[3] Order Book of the Council of State, Friday, May 28, 1652, MS. State Paper Office.

victuals and ammunition, and for the hastening out of the rest of the ships now in the river, which are to come to him ; to return him the thanks of the Council for what he hath done." [1]

At the same sitting this order was made: " That the Council do sit to-morrow morning at 8 of the clock, as also on Monday morning, and the members of the Council be sent unto to that purpose ; and that the Council do sit also on Lord's Day in the afternoon, if there shall be occasion, which is left to the judgment of the Lord-General." [2]

On the same day there was issued a great number of warrants to the captains of the State's ships, to make speedy repair to the Downs, or wheresoever they shall be informed General Blake is, and observe the orders he shall give them. Messengers were also despatched to Harwich, Yarmouth, and elsewhere, to carry orders to the State's ships there, and the merchant-ships in the State's service, to make all the speed they could to join General Blake's fleet.

On Saturday the 22nd of May, the Council ordered, " That the members of the Council be sent unto, to come to the Council on Monday morning next, by 9 o'clock, in order to give audience to the Dutch Ambassadors at the Council." [3]

The Council of State met on the following day (Sunday, the 23rd of May 1652), and made the following orders :—

"That a letter be written to the Commissioners of the Navy, and the officers of the Ordnance, to desire them to send to General Blake all the boatswains' and gunners' stores for which he hath written." [4]

---

[1] Order Book of the Council of State, Friday, in the afternoon, May 21, 1652, MS. State Paper Office

[2] *Ibid.* same time.

[3] *Ibid.* Saturday, May 22, 1652.

[4] *Ibid.* Sunday, May 23, 1652.

" That a messenger be despatched, to go down the River of Thames, to take an account of the going out of the ships which are ready, of which he is to have a list; and is to give an account to the Council of what ships are gone, and how far the rest are on the way." [1]

" That the warrant yesterday signed by the Lord President, in the name of the Council, for the impresting of men for the service of the fleet, be approved of as the warrant of the Council." [2]

" That the Committee of the Admiralty do sit to-morrow morning, at 7 of the clock, in the Council Chamber, and confer with the victuallers of the navy, concerning the making of further provisions of victual for the navy; and also with such of the Commissioners of the Navy, and of the Trinity House, as have subscribed the letter to the Council concerning the furnishing out of more ships; to which purpose a summons is to be given unto them, to come to the Committee to-morrow morning." [3]

On the following day (Monday), the Council evinced their opinion of the conduct of the Dutch by the following order :—

" That the Council doth declare, that it is the pleasure of this Council, that none of the members thereof do speak with the Heer Newport, lately come from Holland, or hold any correspondence with him." [4]

On the same day the Council ordered: "That it be humbly represented to the Parliament, that the Council

---

[1] Order Book of the Council of State, Sunday, May 23, 1652, MS. State Paper Office.

[2] *Ibid.* same day.

[3] *Ibid.* same day.

[4] *Ibid.* Monday, May 24, 1652.— Nieuport, who had been sent over " as well to carry some papers to the ambassadors concerning the negotiation, as to tell them several things by word of mouth that were entrusted to him by the States, ran great danger of his life," says the Dutch writer of the "Life of Cornelius Van Tromp," " because he was taken for a spy."—*Life of Cornelius Van Tromp*, p. 32.

finds it necessary, upon consideration of the present state of
affairs, that forty sail of ships more should be taken on,
and have already given order to that purpose. That the
Parliament be humbly moved, thereupon, to take it into
consideration, where money may be had for the paying of
the said ships." [1]

The following, also made the same day, is an instructive minute, as showing how easily the merchant-ships of
that time, being all armed and manned by seamen, who, as
being always ready to defend their ships against pirates,
were to a certain extent fighting seamen, could be converted into ships of war:—

" That a letter be written to the Commissioners of the
Trinity House, to let them know that they are to give
directions to the ten ships bound for the Newfoundland
fishery, to fall down forthwith into the Downs, and there
to remain with the fleet till further orders; and to let them
know that if the State shall have occasion to make use of
them, they will take care that they shall receive reasonable
satisfaction and allowance for the time they shall be employed, and that they shall have Jacks provided for them." [2]

The business of completing the equipment of the merchant-ships for ships of war, is further set forth in the
following "memorandum" of 29th June, 1652:—" Sir
Arthur Haselrig reports from the Committee for the
Ordnance, that all the merchants' ships, which have been
taken on to be an addition to the fleet, are all of them fitted
with guns and gunners' stores." [3]

On the 24th of May, the Council of State also issued an
order and commission to the Vice-Admiral of Essex, and

[1] Order Book of the Council of
State, Monday, May 24, 1652, MS.
State Paper Office.

[2] *Ibid.* same day.
[3] *Ibid.* Tuesday, June 29, 1652.

the like to the Vice-Admirals of Norfolk, Suffolk, Kent, Sussex, and Hants, " to summon before them all the seamen and mariners from fifteen to fifty years of age, and to acquaint them with the State's emergency of service, and the want of seamen, to man a fleet of ships now in preparation in the River of Thames, for the seas; and withal to press for that service so many able seamen as they can possibly get, giving unto each man xii*d*. prest-money, and 1*d*. a mile conduct, from the place where they shall be so impressed, to the place of their appearance at Deptford, in Kent, within two miles of London, where they shall be entered on board the respective ships, by the State's Clerk of the Cheque, &c.;" "and you are to cause a note to be written by the clerks, and delivered to each seaman, specifying his name, age, stature, complexion, where prested, when he shall appear before the Clerk of the Cheque aforesaid, which must be with all expedition." [1]

On Wednesday the 26th of May, " A letter from the Commissioners of the Navy was read, whereby they desire directions as *to the pressing of five ships already laden for merchant voyages* : ordered, that a letter be written to the said Commissioners to *proceed with the pressing the said five ships*, and to give orders for their speedy setting forth." [2]

" That a letter be written to the Commissioners of the Navy, to let them know that the General of the Fleet hath signified his desire to the Council to have a further number of fireships provided for the fleet; and, therefore, that they do look out for six ships fit for fireships, and provide all materials requisite to the fitting of them out, and to certify their proceedings to the Council."[3]

---

[1] Order Book of the Council of State, Monday, May 24, 1652, MS. State Paper Office.

[2] *Ibid.* Wednesday, May 26, 1652.
[3] *Ibid.* same day.

On Thursday the 27th of May, the Council ordered, " That Mr. Bond be desired to acquaint the Parliament with the Dover seamen's *voluntary aud cheerful going aboard the fleet before the engagement;* " and " that a sum of money be provided for repair of Dover Pier." [1]

On Saturday the 29th of May, the Council ordered, " That a letter be written to General Blake, to enclose unto him the letter from the Mayor of Weymouth, giving notice of the coming by of sixty sail of Dutch ships toward the Downs; to desire him to make stay of them, or any other ships belonging to the Dutch, and send them into port, or secure them otherwise as he shall think fit, without embezzlement, or taking anything from them, provided it be not to divert from prosecuting his former instructions." [2]

" That it be referred to the Committee of the Admiralty to consider how the charge of keeping of the Dutch prisoners at Dover may be satisfied, and report their opinions to the Council." [3]

On Monday the 31st of May, the Council ordered, " That a warrant be issued to the victuallers of the fleet, to victual the whole fleet, except Sir George Ayscue's squadron, and the ships that came lately home from the southward, under the command of Captain Penn, till the 1st of October next." [4]

On Tuesday the 1st of June, the Council received a letter from General Blake, concerning his want of men. At this time the Council were in constant communication with Blake. Several letters were written to him every or almost every day, many of them concerning the disposal of the numerous prizes taken by him from the Dutch. Thus, on the 2nd of June, " That a letter be written to General

---

[1] Order Book of the Council of State, Thursday, May 27, 1652, MS. State Paper Office.

[2] *Ibid.* Saturday, May 29, 1652.
[3] *Ibid.* same day.
[4] *Ibid.* Monday, May 31, 1652.

Blake, to take notice of the receipt of his letter of the 1st of June; to let him know he is to send the Dutch ships taken by him into the River of Thames, and to send all the common seamen, if they be not English, into Holland by the first opportunity, and cause the captains and commanders of the said ships to be secured." [1]

By the 14th of June, however, the Council had changed their mind about the disposal of the Dutch common seamen:—"That a letter be written to General Blake, to take notice of the receipt of his letter, and the enclosed list of Dutch ships taken; to desire him to send such ships as are already taken, and such as shall hereafter be taken, into the River of Thames, and to give notice of the sending of them to the Commissioners of the Customs, to whose care the Council have committed the managing of that business, both as to the securing of the ships, as also goods, without embezzlement; to let him know that, notwithstanding the former Order of the Council, whereby he was directed to send home the common seamen, he is now to permit them to remain aboard their ships till further order, provided the ships (notwithstanding their remaining aboard) be secured; to desire him to give directions to all officers of the Customs, when there shall be occasion to put in any Dutch ships, to secure the ships and take a strict account of the goods, and preserve them from embezzlement, and to send them to London with the first opportunity of a safe convoy, to be disposed of by the Commissioners of the Customs." [2]

The effect of these proceedings on the part of the English Commonwealth, carried out with a vigour and

---

[1] Order Book of the Council of State, Wednesday, June 2, 1652, MS. State Paper Office.

[2] *Ibid.* Monday morning, June 14, 1652.

energy of which Europe had seen no example for ages, was such as somewhat to disturb the schemes of the Dutch, who, confident in the strength of their navy and the ability of their admirals, had reckoned on an easy conquest of the navy of the Commonwealth of England. Cotemporary Dutch writers inform us that the Dutch merchants " were almost out of their wits, by reason of the great loss they daily sustained, both of their ships and goods, which became a prey to the English privateers." [1] It is probable that the Dutch were about as sincere in their professions of treating about peace, as Philip II. and Alexander Farnese had been, sixty-four years before, while they were preparing the Spanish Armada. It is probable that the Dutch Government of 1652 were as much determined on the destruction of the English Commonwealth of 1652, as Philip II. was determined on the destruction of the English Monarchy of 1588. But the Dutch of 1652 were destined to discover, somewhat late, that the English Government of 1652 was a far more able and energetic Government than the English Government of 1588; that Blake was an enemy far more formidable than Drake ; and that the English navy of 1652 was a navy able to contest the dominion of the seas with them, the greatest naval Power that, down to that time, had ever appeared in the world.

If, before the fight that has been described between Blake and Tromp, the English Parliament and Council of State gave a cold reception to the pacific professions of the Dutch Ambassadors, still more coldly and unfavourably

[1] Life of Cornelius Van Tromp, p. 37.—Of the losses of the Dutch merchants, some idea may be formed from the fact that six Dutch " Straits-men," taken by Captain Penn, as notified to the Council in his letters, received August 29, are estimated as being "most richly laden (one of them of 30 guns), worth above £200,000."—*Granville Penn*, vol. i. p. 438.

did they receive the further professions of those ambassadors, made after that event. The temper of mind of the Council of State is shown by the following order, made by them on Friday the 4th of June :—

" That a Committee be appointed, to prepare an answer as to the Dutch papers, in pursuance of the Order of Parliament of the 4th of June instant, as well upon the grounds expressed in a paper now read, as the grounds now debated in the Council; and that, by way of aggravation, mention be made in the said answer, that the late act of hostility committed by the Dutch fleet upon the English was *during the treaty*; and that Sir Henry Vane, Lord-President, Lord-Commissioner Lisle, the Lord-General, Lord Bradshaw, Mr. Scott, &c., or any three of them, be a Committee for the purpose."[1]

The answer referred to above, as well as the answer made a week or two later to Adrian Pauw, Pensionary of Holland, sent as another ambassador-extraordinary, particularly insisted upon the point indicated in the above minute of the Council of State : that the Dutch had made, during the negotiation of a treaty, an unexpected attempt upon the English fleet—an attempt " *by surprise,*" which, under the circumstances, amounted to treachery and falsehood, to " *destroy our fleet, which is our barrier and our securest rampart, and by that means to expose this Commonwealth to an invasion.*"[2] The answer further set forth, " that if the attempts made by the Holland fleet, *as much by surprise as it was,* had succeeded according to their hopes, the Commonwealth of England would have been itself plunged into the greatest disasters imaginable, and

---

[1] Order Book of the Council of State, Friday, June 4, 1652, MS. State Paper Office.

[2] Life of Cornelius Van Tromp, p. 37.

that, therefore, it was not reasonable, after they had been *so miraculously preserved*, that they should expose them-selves again to the like disgraces for the future. That they could not suffer themselves to be any longer *amused under the specious pretence of an examen, or by examples not pertinent to their case*, of what other States may have done; but that rather they were resolved to employ those means which necessity and the nature of the fact require to be used; that, besides, they could not consent to the con-clusion of a treaty of alliance, till they had received satisfaction about the point in question." [1]

The Parliament of the Commonwealth of England, as they style themselves, in these answers to the Dutch Ambassadors, also declare that, " after a mature delibera-tion, and examination of the writings which their Excel-lencies the Ambassadors of the United Provinces have put into their hands, although the Parliament were inclined to receive favourably the expressions contained in the aforesaid. writings, tending to represent the late fight between the two fleets as a thing that happened without the knowledge and against the will of their High Mighti-nesses; yet upon due reflection made thereon, it appears *that the resolutions of the States and the conduct of their admirals do noways agree with all those protestations*, especially at a time whilst a treaty of alliance was managing, which they themselves had sought for, and which had been negotiated by their own ambassadors. Besides, what could be the scope of so formidable an arming of 150 ships of war, made by them without any occasion for it, but to wrest from England by force of arms her ancient prerogatives, and the rights she has over the seas; and that, further, they aim at nothing else

[1] Life of Cornelius Van Tromp, pp. 49, 50.

but the destruction of our fleet, which is our barrier and our securest rampart, and by these means to expose this Commonwealth to an invasion, as they intended to do by the late attempt. Upon which the Parliament think themselves indispensably engaged, with the assistance of Heaven, to exact speedy satisfaction for the outrages done to the nation, and to put themselves in such a condition that the like may happen no more for the future." [1]

The words " after they had been so miraculously preserved," are to be particularly noted, in connection with a remark before made in this history, with reference to the conduct of the Government of Queen Elizabeth in its preparations to meet the Spanish Armada, that the Government which has to trust to miracles for its preservation must be a bad Government. It is indeed true, that Tromp's sudden attack upon Blake, with a force the overwhelming superiority of which, commanded by a veteran admiral the most renowned at that time in the world, might well have led to the conclusion, that nothing short of a miracle could have saved the English fleet from destruction and, by consequence, England from invasion, not merely by the Dutch, but by half the despots of Europe—partly for the purpose of the plunder of London and the other wealthy towns, and partly for that of bringing back the Stuarts, with all their oppressions and vices. But the Commonwealth statesmen were not men to trust to the working of miracles for the preservation of their country. They had placed in command of their fleet a man whom they had already often tried and never found wanting. The miracle which at that time saved England·from such a fate, was the fertile and rapid genius and the indomitable courage of Blake.

---

[1] Life of Cornelius Van Tromp, pp. 36, 37.

By a list sent by Blake to the Council of State, it appears that the number of the fleet now with him in the Downs amounted to fifty-five ships or thereabouts.

On Tuesday the 8th of June, the Council ordered, " That the Here of Hempstead [Pauw], having signified to the Council that he is arrived at Gravesend, being sent from the Lords the States-General of the United Provinces in the quality of an Extraordinary Ambassador to the Parliament of the Commonwealth; that the letter of the said Here Hempstead be humbly represented to the Parliament for their direction to his reception, and that my Lord President [Sir Henry Vane was President during that month] do represent the same." [1]

" That all ships belonging to this nation that trade to the Baltic Sea, and are homewards bound, do come to a rendezvous at Elsinore Castle, and not set sail out of the Sound until such time as a convoy from General Blake shall be there ready to receive them; with which they are to sail to their designed port." [2]

" That a letter be written to General Blake, to acquaint him with the increase of the enemy's fleet; to desire him to lose no opportunity to put his instructions in execution; and to enclose to him the Order of Parliament, whereby the Extraordinary Ambassador from the United Provinces is referred to the Council, and *notwithstanding* to desire him *to pursue his instructions.*" [3]

" That a letter be written to General Blake, to desire him to dismiss the ships which are now in the Downs bound for Newfoundland; and to let him know that they are to go together in company, for their better security." [4]

[1] Order Book of the Council of State, 1652. Tuesday, June 8, 1652, MS. State Paper Office.
[2] *Ibid.* Monday afternoon, June 14,
[3] *Ibid.* same time.
[4] *Ibid.* Tuesday, June 15, 1652.

" That a letter be written to Sir George Ayscue, to hasten him with the ships with him into the Downs." [1]

" That the Council do approve of what hath been done by General Blake, in the fitting out to sea of the three Dutch men-of-war." [2]

" That a letter be written to the Commissioners of the Navy, to certify unto them what hath been done by General Blake in the ordering the setting forth of three Dutch men-of-war; to let them know the Council do approve thereof; to desire them to hold correspondence with General Blake, concerning the fitting out of the said ships; and to take care that they may be furnished with men and victuals, which are to be supplied from hence and not from the fleet, as also with all other things necessary for them." [3]

" That a letter be written to the Committee [4] of the Navy, to let them know that the Council finds it necessary for the service of the public that, besides the five ketches already taken up, that five more should be taken on; to desire them, therefore, to order that they may be paid according to contract." [5]

" That a warrant be issued to the officers of the Ordnance, to provide and send down to the fleet a good proportion of hammered iron shot, which may be proportionable to the fleet now in the Downs, to be distributed amongst them by order of the General of the fleet." [6]

On Friday the 25th of June, the Council of State ordered, " That it be referred to the Committee for Law

[1] Order Book of the Council of State, Tuesday, June 15, 1652, MS. State Paper Office.

[2] *Ibid.* Thursday, June 17, 1652.

[3] *Ibid.* same day.

[4] For an explanation of the distinction between the Committee of the Navy and the Commissioners of the Navy, see Vol. I. p. 49, note 1.

[5] Order Book of the Council of State, Thursday, June 17, 1652, MS. State Paper Office.

[6] *Ibid.* same day.

and Examinations to prepare a Declaration, in pursuance
of the Order of Parliament, referring it to the Council to
prepare a Declaration for asserting the right of this nation
to the *sovereignty of the sea* and the fishery, and to bring
it into the Council with all convenient speed; and the
Lord Bradshaw is desired to take care of this business." [1]

" That the Commissioners for treating with the Lord
Pauw, do desire his Excellency to give a speedy and
positive answer to the propositions of the Parliament, to
be delivered unto him by the said Commissioners, at a
conference to be held at 6 of the clock this night." [2]

On the following day the Council ordered, " That Mr.
Frost do pay for the printing of a book printed in justification of the engagement [with the Dutch fleet] out of
the incident moneys belonging to this Council." [3]

" That it be referred to the Committee for Foreign
Affairs, to take order for the printing of the book called
Mare Clausum; and that Mr. Du Guard be commanded
to print the same.' [4]

The Council of State met on the following day, Sunday,
the 27th of June, and ordered: " That, the Lord Pauw
having, by a paper this day delivered into the Council,
desired audience this afternoon, the Commissioners appointed to treat with his Lordship do give him a meeting
at the house of the said Lord Ambassador, to hear what he
hath to offer, and make report thereof to the Council." [5]

The following minute shows the watchful care of the
Council of State over all the public interests, and it also
shows the extensive commerce carried on at that time by
England with all parts of the world :—" That a letter be
written to the Mayor of Plymouth, to let him know that

---

[1] Order Book of the Council of State, Friday, June 25, 1652, MS. State Paper Office.

[2] *Ibid.* same day.

[3] *Ibid.* Saturday, June 26, 1652.

[4] *Ibid.* same day.

[5] *Ibid.* Sunday, June 27, 1652.

the Council is informed that the East India ships, the Barbadoes fleet, and several other ships from Turkey, the Streights [the Straits of Gibraltar], and Spanish coasts, and also some Guinea ships, are expected into the Channel daily; which, being ignorant of the present affairs in reference to the Dutch, may be in danger of being surprised by them, ten Dutch men-of-war being, as the Council is informed, upon those coasts; and, therefore, desire him to give order to the two small vessels that were formerly sent out, to ply up and down off the Land's End, to give notice to any English ships that they meet, to go into the next convenient port, and there to stay until convoys can be appointed for them." [1]

On the same day an order was made, that " by reason of the troubles between this Commonwealth and the Dutch, Danish ships be saved harmless from the penalty of the Navigation Act, in order to import into England Riga hemp from Riga." [2]

On the following day the Council ordered : " That the business of letters of marque and reprisal against the French and Dutch be taken into consideration on Friday next, in the afternoon ; and the members of the Council who are in town are to be sent unto, to come to the Council at that time." [3]

" That it be referred to the Committee who were formerly appointed to consider of the manner of the entertainment to be given to the Dutch Ambassadors at their coming, to consider of what civilities are fit to be shown to them at their departure." [4]

" That orders, passes, and safe-conducts, in pursuance of the Order of Parliament in that behalf, be given to the Lord

---

[1] Order Book of the Council of State, Monday, June 28, 1652, MS. State Paper Office.

[2] Ibid. same day.

[3] Ibid. Tuesday, June 29, 1652.

[4] Ibid. same day.

Pauw and the three Extraordinary Ambassadors, for their safe passage into the Low Countries." [1]

I have, in a note in a former page of this chapter, quoted a statement from a Dutch writer, that when Nieuport arrived in London from Holland, with papers and verbal messages for the Dutch Ambassadors, he ran great danger of his life, because he was taken for a spy. How far those who took him for a spy, and more, how far those who took all the Dutch Ambassadors for spies, were right in so doing, may be partly determined by the following statement, made not by an English but by a Dutch writer :—" On the 11th of July,[2] that is to say, four days after the English fleet set sail for the North Sea, to go and destroy the Dutch fleet of herring busses, and to watch for their ships coming from the Indies, the Dutch Ambassadors departed from London, and on the 13th met with Admiral Tromp, to whom Mr. de Heemsted [Pauw] gave a memorial containing an account of the forces of England. He likewise informed Tromp that Admiral Ayscew was then in the Downs, with a squadron of twenty-one men-of-war, *where he might be easily attacked and beaten.*" [3] Upon this information, Tromp resolved to go and attack Ayscue, with a force more than treble that of Ayscue. But there happening a calm, and after that a contrary wind, it was impossible for him to execute this design. He therefore directed his course northward in search of Blake, with a fleet of seventy-nine ships of war, consisting of a squadron of twenty-one ships, forming the van under Vice-Admiral Evertsz, of the main body of thirty ships under his own

---

[1] Order Book of the Council of State, Tuesday, June 29, 1652, MS. State Paper Office.

[2] The Dutch writer uses the " New Style ; " the minute of the Council of State last given, and dated June 29, was the " Old Style."

[3] Life of Cornelius Van Tromp, p. 60.

immediate command, and of twenty-eight ships, forming the rear under Rear-Admiral Florisz.[1]

By this time Blake, who some days before, with a fleet of sixty sail, had left the Downs, was sailing northward, with a view of intercepting the great Dutch herring-fleet. The anxiety of the Council of State to keep up, as far as possible, an uninterrupted communication with their great Admiral, is strikingly evinced by such minutes as the following, bearing date Wednesday, the 30th of June (O. S.) :—

"That a letter be written to the Mayor of Newcastle, as also to the Bailiffs of Yarmouth, to desire them that, in case none of the State's ships shall be found there upon the receipt of the Council's letters, that they will then *cause a ketch to be hired to carry the messenger of the Council to the fleet.*"[2]

Whitelock's Journal marks the progress of Blake's advance northward :

"*July* 3.—Letters, that General Blake, with a gallant fleet, went northwards, and left Sir George Ascue to command the rest of the fleet in the Downs, who took five Dutch merchantmen, and General Blake took two men-of-war and two merchantmen :—500 soldiers sent on board Sir George Ascue."[3]

"*July* 9.—Letters, that General Blake, with a fleet of sixty sail, passed in sight of Dunbar towards the north, to attend the Holland busses, and sent for the frigates and Parliament's vessels in those parts, who went to him."[4]

"*July* 12.—Letters from Yarmouth, that the Hol-

---

[1] Life of Cornelius Van Tromp, p. 61.
[2] Order Book of the Council of State, Wednesday, June 30, 1652, MS.
[3] Whitelock's Memorials, July 3, 1652: London, folio, 1732.
[4] *Ibid.* July 9, 1652.

State Paper Office.

landers have 180 busses at sea, and sixty men-of-war for their guard; that General Blake was near them. That Van Tromp was seen in the Downs, with about one hundred sail of ships, nearer to Sir George Ascue." [1]

"*July* 17.—Letters, that the fleet could get no farther than Aberdeen by reason of the contrary winds. That General Blake had taken three or four of the Dutch busses and one man-of-war, and sent them up." [2]

"*July* 24.—Letters, that General Blake took one hundred of the Holland busses, and in them 1,500 men; the rest secured themselves in Bressie's Bay [*sic*] in Scotland." [3]

"*July* 27.—That the Holland fleet were still off about Newcastle, about 105 ships. That the Dutch took several English vessels, and made their men serve under them." [4]

"*July* 31.—That no intelligence could come from General Blake, being so far to the northward, and the Dutch fleet between him and home." [5]

On Sunday, the 11th of July, the Council of State ordered :—

"That a letter be written to General Blake, to give him notice of the appearance of the Dutch fleet, being 102 men-of-war and 10 fireships, and are every day in sight of the

[1] Whitelock's Memorials, July 12, 1652.

[2] *Ibid.* July 17, 1652.

[3] *Ibid.* July 24, 1652.—On the toll of every tenth herring being paid, Blake sent the vessels with the men back to Holland, under a charge of fishing there no more without English leave.—*Granville Penn*, vol. i. p. 434, note. "This action," says Ludlow, "was blamed by some, who thought by the help of those ships we might have been enabled to erect a fishery, and thereby have made some reparation to the English nation for the damages which they had sustained from the Dutch; and that by detaining their mariners we might have weakened and destroyed them considerably, they wanting men for the management of their shipping."—*Ludlow's Memoirs*, vol. i. p. 420. But, as Mr. Dixon observes, "The only fault ever advanced by friend or foe against Blake, was an excess of generosity towards his vanquished enemies."—*Dixon's Robert Blake*, p. 204.

[4] Whitelock's Memorials, July 27, 1652.

[5] *Ibid.* July 31, 1652.

fleet of Sir George Ayscue; that they are divided into
three squadrons; that Sir G. Ayscue intends to put his
fleet, being fourteen or sixteen sail, under the protection of
the Castle [Dover] ; that the ships under Captain Harrison
are in Lee Road, stayed for the completing of their men,
that they may the better make their conjunction with Sir
G. Ayscue." [1]

We have seen in the preceding volume [2] that the summer
of 1650, in which the Battle of Dunbar was fought, was a
rainy summer in Scotland.   It would appear that the
summer of 1652 was a hot summer in Scotland, and also in
the Orkney and Shetland Islands and the surrounding seas.
Those who have experienced, when grouse-shooting in
the North of Scotland, the great heat about the middle
of August, in the mountain hollows—heat which I have
heard men say they thought as intense as they had ever
felt in India—and have also seen the tops of the same
mountains covered with snow about the end of August,
will readily recognise the truth of the following passage of
Whitelock, under date July 23, 1652 :—" Of the difficulties
passed by the English forces in the Highlands, the ex-
tremities there both of heat and cold at this time, scorch-
ing of the sun, and yet snow upon the mountains to cool
them; that the inhabitants faced them continually; that
venison is plenty there, though mutton be dear; and the
springs better than sack at Leith." [3]   The great heat in the
North of Scotland in those months of July and August
1652, may partly account for the description given by

---

[1] Order Book of the Council of
State, Sunday, July 11, 1652, MS. State
Paper Office.

[2] Vol. I. pp. 346 and 356.

[2] Whitelock's Memorials, p. 539,
July 23, 1652.—Under the same date

Whitelock adds, "That the horsemen
are apt to ride over the tops of their
houses; that the army had 400 baggage
horses, led by the countrymen, loaden
with bread and cheese, that they guarded their horses from the corn."—*Ibid.*

cotemporary writers of a tempest which, when the fleets of
Blake and Tromp were about to engage on the evening of
the 5th of August, about halfway between the Orkney and
the Shetland Islands, gathered, and burst with the sudden-
ness and fury of a tropical tornado.   The wind, the rain,
and the darkness rendered all manœuvring, almost all
communication by signal between the ships, impossible.

Tromp, as has been related, directed his course northward with a fleet of about eighty sail, according to the
Dutch accounts, of about one hundred sail, according to
the English accounts.   There was now, in addition to the
bitter enmity between the two nations, a feeling of strong
personal hostility raised between Tromp and Blake.   It was
not merely mortifying but exasperating to Tromp, to see
the laurels of a life of successful naval warfare torn from
his brow by a man who but two or three years before had
never set foot on a ship's deck as a commander, or even
as a seaman.   Blake, on the other side, was exasperated
at what he considered dishonourable conduct on the part
of Tromp, in attempting to destroy his fleet by a sudden
surprise, while a treaty was pending between the two nations, and Dutch ambassadors were in London.   It is
stated in the "Life of Cornelius Van Tromp" that, after the
fight near Dover, Tromp wrote a letter to Blake, in which
he entreated Blake to release the two Dutch captains he
had made prisoners, and also to order the restitution of the
Dutch ship taken in that fight.   Blake—not only surprised,
but indignant, that Tromp should presume to write to him,
upon such a subject, after what had passed—made him,
according to the same authority, the following answer:

" Sir,—Nothing ever surprised me more than yours of the
2nd of June last, in that, though you affect with so much
vanity to pass for a man of honour, yet 'tis no way visible

that you maintain that character by any of your actions. The cruel attempt you lately made against the Parliament of England's fleet, whose ruin you had conspired, is an evident proof of this . . . . That act of hostility you have so lately committed is so much the more criminal, since you were pleased to do it in a time when your ambassadors were flattering our Commonwealth with new hopes of peace and union, and pretended to solicit with much earnestness a speedy conclusion of a treaty of mutual alliance and confederation. That is the brave exploit upon which at present you found your glory, and for which you frame an unjust apology, as pretending you did nothing else but defend yourself. But God, in whom we put our greatest hopes, having made your designs serve to your own destruction, we have taken some of your ships, which you now are pleased to redemand with as much confidence as if the action lately committed had been no act of hostility, as it appears in your writings, by your affecting to give it another name. In fine, I thought not fit to give you any other answer but this, that I am persuaded you will find the Parliament of England very ill-satisfied with your conduct; because they cannot but regard with horror the innocent blood of their subjects that has been spilt; and, on the other side, that after all you will find yourself constrained always to give them the marks of an entire submission."[1]

I see no reason to doubt the authenticity of this letter; and, whether authentic or not, it may be taken as a fair exponent of the state of feeling existing at that time between Blake and Tromp, who looked upon each other pretty much with the feelings of two bulldogs who had a quarrel of some standing to fight out.

[1] Life of Cornelius Van Tromp, pp. 25, 26.

Towards evening, on the 5th of August (N. S.), the
Dutch and English fleets came in sight of each other
between Foula and Fair-Isle, the two most detached
of the Shetland group of islands.   Foula is computed
to be twenty miles to the west of the largest of the Shetland Isles, called Mainland of Shetland, and Fair-Isle
to be twenty-five miles south-south-west of the nearest
headland of the Mainland.   Foula is distinguished from
the other islands called the Shetland Isles—the general
appearance of which, as seen from the sea, is an unvarying
line of abrupt coast—by a cluster of five lofty hills, termi-
nating in pointed cones, the highest of which rises to the
height of nearly 1,400 feet.

The two hostile admirals were eagerly preparing for
immediate action, when, as the sun declined, dark masses
of clouds began gradually to spread themselves over the
sky, the sea grew black, distant thunder was heard, and
that ominous sound, well known to mariners (which the
English word *sob* does not so well express as the Scotch
word *sough*) of an approaching tempest, became distinctly
audible. As the sun disappeared, and the twilight deepened,
the sky assumed an aspect of pitchy darkness, very unusual
at that season of the year in that latitude, where the sun
sinks so little below the horizon that a certain degree of
light continues throughout the night.   Every appearance
betokened the near approach of a violent tempest.   At
length it burst.   For the wind, which had long been
shifting about, turned at last suddenly to the north-
north-west, and blew with such fury that, says the writer
of the "Life of Cornelius Van Tromp"—who gives so
minute a description of this terrible tempest, that it seems
probable he was either on board the Dutch fleet at that
time, or received his information direct from some of those

who were—" our sails were all rent and torn in pieces, and the waves rolled through them, and so went and spent themselves against the rocks of Hitland [Shetland?], throwing their foam up to the very heaven. Thus the fleet, being, as it were, buried by the violence of the sea in most horrible abysses, rose out of them only to be tossed up to the very clouds. Here the masts were beaten down into the sea, there the deck was overflown by the prevailing waves ; here the tempest was so much mistress of the ships that they could be no longer governed, and, on another side, appeared all the doleful forerunners of a dismal wreck. And the darkness increasing the danger, and the confused cries of the mariners redoubling the common fear, both together made the saddest and most frightful spectacle that was ever seen." [1]

The storm lasted all night with unabated violence. When the day broke, the effects of the tempest appeared. The Dutch fleet had suffered considerably, some ships being lost and many disabled. But of sixty of Tromp's ships that were missing, forty-two were ascertained to be safe among the Shetland Isles, and also two East India ships supposed to be lost. Blake had suffered less than Tromp. He had been able to keep his fleet together. Tromp discovered him after the storm in the latitude of Scotland, with sixty-two great ships much less damaged than his own; the tempest having driven him to the northward of Shetland, on which side he found more shelter.[2]

On the 10th of August, letters reached the Council of State that General Blake was off at sea near Scarborough; and that forty Dutch ships were near Rye, in Sussex.

---

[1] Life of Cornelius Van Tromp, p. 62.   [2] *Ibid.* p. 63.

There is some confusion in the accounts we have of the relative movements of Tromp and Blake after the storm above described. The writer of the "Life of Cornelius Van Tromp" says that, after the storm, when Tromp, with a fleet of thirty-nine sail, discovered Blake with sixty-two great ships, he offered Blake battle, which the latter declined. This story is not credible to me, though it may be credible to Dutchmen.

On the 14th of August, the Council of State received intelligence from General Blake, that he was safely arrived with his fleet from the northward.[1] And on the 15th of August Whitelock reports, "Letters to the Council of State of General Blake's standing off to the coast of Holland to look after the Dutch fleet, who were gone off from the coast of Sussex."[2] Soon after, Blake returned to the English coast with his prizes, and 900 prisoners.[3]

[1] Whitelock's Memorials, p. 541.— "That a letter be written to General Blake, to let him know what intelligence the Council have received this day concerning the motion of the Dutch fleet westward; and that he make all possible speed with the fleet into the Channel to find out the Dutch fleet." "That a letter be written to the Mayor of Ipswich, to send away two nimble ketches with two despatches to General Blake." — Order Book of the Council of State, Sunday, August 15, 1652, MS. State Paper Office.

[2] Whitelock's Memorials, p. 541.

[3] Hobbes's Behemoth, p. 293; London, 1682.—"That a letter be written to the Commissioners of the Navy, to view the five prizes lately sent in by General Blake, and give an account to the Council how soon they may be fitted out as men-of-war, and at what charge."—Order Book of the Council of State, Monday morning, August 30, 1652, MS. State Paper Office. The following minute, made in the afternoon of the same day, shows the vigilance of the Council of State: "That a letter be written to the Commissioners of the Navy to desire them to give a speedy account to the Council why the ships Swiftsure and the new frigate at Woolwich are in no better forwardness."—Ibid. Monday afternoon, August 30, 1652. About the same time the number of minutes respecting private men-of-war shows that the number of those privateers must have been very great. Thus, on August 26 and 27, 1652, orders were made by the Council, "That warrants be issued to the Judges of the Admiralty to give letters for private men-of-war to Captain Isaac Phillips, commander of the ship Assistant; to

On the 6th of September Whitelock has this entry: "That Van Tromp desired to be excused from going to sea, and that De Witt was appointed by the State to command-in-chief their navy; that they had not half men enough to man their fleet."[1]   The De Witt here mentioned was a Vice-Admiral, Cornelius De Witt, but not, as some writers appear to suppose, Cornelius, the elder of the two celebrated brothers, Cornelius and John De Witt. That Cornelius De Witt, the brother of John De Witt, is said, indeed, to have served several years in the fleet of the United Provinces in his early youth. But his later career was altogether that of a civilian. In 1650 he was elected burgomaster of Dordrecht, his native town, and deputy to the States of Holland and West Friesland; and during his brother John De Witt's administration, he held the office of Inspector of Dykes in the district of Putten. The De Witt here mentioned as appointed to command-in-chief in the place of Martin Tromp is probably the same person who, under the name of Cornelius Van Witt, acted as Vice-Admiral under Tromp in the engagement with the combined fleets of Spain and Portugal in 1639. As Cornelius, the brother of John De Witt, was born in 1623, it is impossible that he should have commanded as Vice-Admiral in the action of 1639; and as he was but 29 years of age in 1652, it is, if not impossible, to the last degree improbable that he should have been appointed commander-in-chief of the Dutch fleet in 1652. The

Lieutenant-Colonel Hazard, to W. Dale, to Colonel Tizon, to Lieutenant-Colonel Yeomans, to John and Edward Mole, merchants."—*Ibid.* August 26 and 27, 1652. The Council of State committed a serious error in granting so many of these letters to private men-of-war. We shall see that Blake, in his letter to the Council of State after the fight with the Dutch fleet, on November 30, 1652, attributes the want of seamen to "the great number of private men-of-war, especially out of the River Thames."

[1] Whitelock's Memorials, p. 543.

commander-in-chief was clearly another Cornelius Van Witt, or Cornelius De Witt, and most probably the same person who acted as Vice-Admiral under Tromp in 1639. The reasons that moved the States to appoint Vice-Admiral De Witt admiral instead of Martin Tromp are stated to have been their hopes that De Witt would perhaps have better luck than Tromp had in his last expedition, and the murmurs of the people, who began to look upon Tromp's late 'ill-success as a judgment upon him for being the cause of that great war;[1] the last circumstance amounting, as I have before observed, to an admission that Tromp was the aggressor in the first fight near Dover.

But besides this De Witt, the States of Holland appointed to the command of a fleet a man of far greater naval name. This was the celebrated Michael Ruyter, afterwards De Ruyter; for in 1659, as a reward for defeating the Swedish fleet, he received from the King of Denmark a title of nobility, with a pension. Michael Ruyter was born at Fleissingen in 1607, went to sea at eleven years as a cabin-boy, and rose successively, through the various grades of service, to the rank of admiral.[2] It is said that Ruyter had resolved to pass the rest of his days in peace and repose, and was prevailed on with some difficulty to accept the command offered to him.[3]

In the course of the month of August there was fought a battle between Ruyter and Sir George Ayscue near Plymouth, wherein, according to the English accounts, Sir George Ayscue had the better; but amid the conflicting

[1] Life of Cornelius Van Tromp, p. 72.
[2] The Dutch raised a splendid monument to De Ruyter at Amsterdam; and Gerard Brandt wrote his life (Amsterdam, 1690), which was translated into French (Amsterdam, 1698).
[3] Life of Cornelius Van Tromp, p. 64.

authorities it is difficult, if not impossible, to state either the exact numbers engaged on each side, or the exact result. " Whatsoever was the matter," says Hobbes, " the Rump, though they rewarded Sir George Ayscue, never more employed him in their service at sea." [1]

There are various minutes in the Order Book of the Council of State about this time, indicating that the Prince of Condé [2] wished to obtain some assistance from the English Parliament in the contest in which he was then engaged with Cardinal Mazarin, who at that time, when Louis XIV. was about fourteen years of age, governed France. Dunkirk was besieged by the Spanish forces under the Archduke Leopold. As France then leaned to the Dutch, the Parliament of England considered it better that Dunkirk should fall into the hands of Spain, and Blake had received instructions accordingly. While cruising in the Channel in the beginning of September, Blake fell in with a French fleet under the Duke of Vendôme, who had just defeated the Spanish Admiral, Count D' Oignon. This French fleet was about to relieve

[1] Hobbes's Behemoth, p. 293.— "That a letter be written to General Blake, to let him know that the engagement of Sir George Ayscue's fleet with the Dutch is over for the present; to desire him that he will, out of the fleet now with him, despatch to Sir George Ayscue six or eight good frigates, whereby he may be enabled by himself to rencounter that fleet, in case he can find it out; to let him know that Tromp's [sic] fleet is in preparation to come forth again; to desire him, therefore, to come back again towards the coast of Holland to attend his coming out, and to let him know that the *Sovereign* and the rest of the ships which are to come out of the River of Thames are to join with his fleet."—*Order Book of the Council of State*, Sunday morning, August 22, 1652, MS. State Paper Office. The Council of State held three meetings on this Sunday, August 22, 1652. The first is headed "Sunday, morning;" the second, "Sunday, 1 o'clock, afternoon;" the third, "Sunday afternoon, at 4 of the clock."

[2] Letters from the Prince of Condé, referred to in a minute of April 1, 1652, and other subsequent minutes.— Order Book of the Council of State, MS. State Paper Office.

Dunkirk, by throwing into that piratical town men, arms, stores, and fresh provisions. Blake, in the *Resolution,* followed by about twenty other ships, attacked the French fleet.[1] There had been no formal declaration of war between France and England; but the privateers of Brest and Dunkirk had long carried on a course of depredations on English merchantmen, and many English ships bore letters of marque and reprisal against the French.[2] "The *Sovereign,* then the largest as well as swiftest vessel in the English navy—carrying 1,100 men and 88 guns, of which 20 were 44-pounders—led the way, and was the first to engage the enemy. Its fire was terrible—the second broadside sinking one of the French frigates, and its key-shot[3] cutting off the mainmasts of five others. As the frigate was going down, Blake bore into action, and, immediately singling out the *Donadieu,* commanded by one of the Knights of Malta, he ran alongside, and boarded her. The rapidity of the attack, and the instantaneous advantages gained, disconcerted the French : some struck their colours—some fled, fiercely pursued by the *Sovereign* and the lighter vessels towards Dunkirk; and in a few hours the whole body of the French squadron, ships of war, fireships, and transports, were either gone down or safely harboured under the guns of Dover Castle. Dunkirk immediately surrendered to the Archduke Leopold."[4]

It is most important to call attention to the policy of the Parliament and Council of State in this matter, as compared with the policy afterwards pursued by Cromwell, when he had destroyed the Parliament and Council of

[1] Dixon's Robert Blake, p. 173, new edition ; London, 1858 ; Hobbes's Behemoth, p. 293.

[2] There are very many orders to this effect in the Order Book of the Council of State.

[3] Chain-shot.

[4] Dixon's Robert Blake, p. 173, new edition, London, 1858.

State.　France was at this time a Power rising into a
condition that was to make her dangerous not only to the
peace but to the liberty of Europe.　Spain, on the contrary,
had long been and was still sinking.　It was, therefore,
the part of sagacious statesmen to throw the weight of the
power of England into that scale where it would be likely
to produce good, and not evil.　The statesmen of the
Parliament of England, of whom Blake may be reckoned
one, consequently sought to weaken France rather than
further to depress and weaken Spain.　Cromwell pursued
an opposite course, and threw the power of England into
the wrong scale; though he discovered his mistake before
he died, and when it was too late to remedy it.　This was
one of the evils which Cromwell's usurpation inflicted
upon England.　We shall have to note many more in the
sequel; and if there appear—

> ——On History's fruitless page
> Ten thousand conquerors for a single sage,

History's page may nevertheless be not altogether fruitless,
if it hold up as a warning to after-ages some of the terrible
calamities which ignoble ambition brings upon mankind.

A very few days after Blake's encounter with the French
fleet under the Duke of Vendôme, the Dutch fleet of sixty
sail, under the command of De Witt and De Ruyter,
appeared off the South Foreland.　The intelligence reached
the Council of State on Saturday, the 11th of September,
1652.　The Council met on the following day, Sunday,
the 12th of September, and proceeded, with their usual
promptitude, energy, and ability, to take the steps which
the emergency called for.　The mode in which the Council of State did its business on such an occasion will
best appear from the following minutes, all made on that
Sunday :—

" That a letter be written to General Blake, to enclose to him the intelligence received from Deal and Dover of a Dutch fleet appearing on the back side of the South Sand Head." [1]

" That the Governor of Dover take care that all the. Dutch and French prizes be secured, lest the Dutch fleet should any way attempt to seize them." [2]

" That a letter be written to the Bailiffs of Yarmouth, to let them know of the intelligence the Council have received of a Dutch fleet appearing on the South Sand Head; to desire them to give order to the masters and commanders of such ships as are or shall come into Yarmouth Roads, to be careful how they put forth to sea, but to stay for some time till they receive further order from the Council; and to desire them to send to Hull, Lynn, Boston, Scarborough, and Newcastle, to the same effect." [3]

On Friday, the 17th of September, the Council of State made the following order :—" That a letter be written to Captain Moulton to take notice of the receipt of his ; to desire him to send out a small boat to take notice of the motions of the Dutch fleet off the Beachie [Beachy Head] ; and to give notice of their being there to as many English merchants as they can meet with, to the end they may avoid them." [4]

About noon on the 28th of September, " we got sight of the Dutch fleet," says Blake, " standing to the westward. Between three and four in the afternoon, they got their fleet together, being sixty sail,[5] and, hauling their

[1] Order Book of the Council of State, Sunday, September 12, 1652, MS. State Paper Office.

[2] Ibid. same day.

[3] Ibid. same day.

[4] Ibid. Friday morning, September 17, 1652.

[5] The Dutch statement is: " The Dutch fleet, commanded by Vice-Admiral De Witt, after the departure of the ten ships that were detached from it, consisted of sixty-four men-of-war, and

foresails upon their masts, made ready to fight." [1]   During
the interval between the fleets' first coming in sight of each
other and the commencement of the action, De Witt, who
commanded the Dutch fleet, left his own ship of forty guns,
and went on board the largest of the India ships of fifty-
six guns, where he " wore the flag, his own ship taking it
in." [2]   Tromp's flag-ship, the *Brederode*, was in the fleet;
but the men in her would not receive De Witt.[3]   This
proceeding may be considered as attributable partly to the
intractable character of the Dutch seamen, partly to their
opinion of the professional superiority of Tromp to De Witt,
and partly to the personal characters of the two commanders; for, says the Dutch writer already quoted,
" Martin Tromp was as much beloved by the seamen
for his mild temper, as De Witt was hated by them
for his cruelty." [4]

It is impossible to make a narrative, which is obscure
from its brevity, clearer by conjectural interpolations.
I therefore give the few words in which Blake describes
the fight: " There were then by me the Vice-Admiral
[Penn,] and some others; but a great part of the fleet was

that of the English, under the conduct
of Admiral Blake, was composed of
sixty-eight. But the English ships
were much better furnished for the
war than the Dutch."—*Life of Cornelius Van Tromp*, p. 77. The writer
adds that De Witt resolved to fight
the English fleet in opposition to De
Ruyter's advice.

[1] Blake to the Council of State,
from aboard the *Resolution*, off the
North Foreland, October 2, 1652; from
a MS. copy of the despatch, among Sir
W. Penn's Papers, published by Mr.
Granville Penn in his Memorials of
Admiral Sir William Penn, London,

1833, vol. i. pp. 450–453.

[2] Blake says, " De Witt and Ruyter
commanded the Dutch fleet, each of
them wearing a flag on the maintop."
—Blake to the Council of State, same
date.

[3] Admiral Sir William Penn to
George Bishop, Esq., Whitehall—*James*,
in Margate Roads, October 2, 1652;
from the original in Sir W. Penn's
handwriting, published in Mr. Granville Penn's Memorials of Admiral Sir
William Penn, vol. i. pp. 446–450.

[4] Life of Cornelius Van Tromp,
p. 83.

astern, by reason of their late weighing in the Downs, which I suppose was occasioned by the late storm we had there. As soon as a considerable part was come up to us, the Dutch then tacking, we bore in right with them, their Admiral in the head. I commanded no guns to be fired till we came very near them; and, by means of their tacking, the greatest part of our fleet came suddenly to be engaged, and the dispute was very hot for a short time, continuing till it was dark night." [1]

The statement that the greatest part of the English fleet came suddenly to be engaged by means of the Dutch fleet's tacking is somewhat explained by the report of Sir W. Penn. "About four," he says, "most of our fleet being come near, our General bore in amongst them. We presently filled to bear after him; but it pleased God to disappoint us, being aground upon a sand, supposed the Kentish-Knock.[2] It was reasonably smooth, and for my part I did not feel her strike;·the master and others said they did; but the man that hove the lead overboard said we had not three fathoms water, by which account it was too true. The *Sovereign* was near musket-shot without us, and struck several times. The goodness of God was eminent to us in this particular, for hereby we were forced to tack our ship to clear ourselves of the sand; and, indeed, it fell out better for doing execution upon the enemy than we could have cast it ourselves; for, as the Dutch fleet cleared themselves of our general, he standing to the northward, and they to the southward, we fell patt to receive them, and so stayed by them till the night caused our separation." [3]

[1] Blake to the Council of State, October 2, 1652.
[2] "A small sand, about S. by W., from the east end of the Long Sand, at the mouth of the Thames."—Note in *Granville Penn*, vol. i. p. 447.
[3] Admiral Sir W. Penn to George Bishop, Esq., October 2, 1652.

The Dutch account of the battle is this :—"De Ruyter had the vanguard, De Witt the main body of the fleet, and De Wilde commanded the rear. And Evertz attended besides with a body of reserve, to be ready to give assistance to those that should have need. The two fleets, piercing one into the other, plied one another hotly with their cannon. De Ruyter and De Witt did wonders, but for all they could do, in a little time they were so roughly handled that they had much ado to turn themselves. De Ruyter had a great many killed and wounded; he had received four shots between wind and water. The main-yard of his ship was overturned to the left side, and his main and mizen sails, as well as his rigging, were all torn to pieces." [1]

Comparing these three accounts, we are led to the conclusion that Blake, on this occasion, *broke the Dutch line*, and, to use the words of Lord Rodney (already quoted in this chapter), "defeated the broken parts by detail." The operation must have appeared to Blake so much a matter of course, and any other proceeding so "contrary to common sense," as Lord Rodney says, that he considered it quite needless and a waste of words to dilate upon it.

That night the two fleets lay in sight of each other; "we," says Blake, "refitting our ships, which were much torn." [2] "All night," writes Penn, "we could see their lights plain, a small distance to leeward of us; which made us believe they wished to engage us the next morning. As the day broke, we saw the Dutch fleet N.E. more than two leagues from us. . . . Now I shall tell you what damage, visibly, we did them in the engagement. One of my squadron, Captain John Mildmay, in the *Nonsuch*,

---

[1] Life of Cornelius Van Tromp, p. 78.
[2] Blake to the Council of State, Octo-

ber 2, 1652 in Granville Penn, vol. i. p. 451.

took a fly-boat of near 500 tons, with thirty pieces of ordnance ; and, presently after, took possession of another frigate of thirty guns, twelve whereof brass, who had all her masts shot by the board, and lay like a wreck in the sea. This he was forced to quit again about midnight, being driven to leeward near the Holland's fleet. He took the Hollanders out of her, and suffered her to sink, she being very leaky. On board the fly-boat he had De Witt's rear-admiral, who quitted his frigate, that had in her two brass guns, but also in the other's condition, without masts. On Tuesday, before we engaged, we told fifty-nine sail, besides small vessels, and the next morning could not tell above fifty-two, two whereof without bolt-sprits. In the morning betimes, we saw one ship without masts in the midst of their fleet, which was presently after sunk." [1]

"The next morning" (29th September), continues Blake, "being little wind and variable, we bore with them as fast as we could, they seeming awhile to stay for us,[2] till after noon, when the wind coming northerly, they made all sail they could, and stood away to the eastward, towards their own coast. We followed them as much as possibly we could, they then having the wind of us. Many shots passed between some of our headmost ships and their stern fleet ; but nothing could engage them. Then, it beginning to grow dark, we tacked to get our fleet together ; and, if we might, get to the weather-gage. And being then half Channel over, it was advised by the captain, master, and

---

[1] Sir W. Penn to George Bishop, Esq., October 2, 1652, in Granville Penn, vol. i. p. 449.

[2] This and the expression used by Penn, as quoted above, would seem to indicate that a change took place in the plans of the Dutch commander. It is stated that the desire of De Witt to risk another engagement was over-ruled in a council of war by De Ruyter and Evertz.—*Life of Cornelius Van Tromp*, p. 79.

mates, the pilot and others, to lie close upon that tack till ten of the clock, that so we might have length enough to spend that night, presuming likewise that they would tack before the morning, which would again have brought us together if the wind had stood; but it pleased God that it proved but little wind that night, which was westerly. The next morning (30th) the wind came at S.W.; and from the topmast-head, we discovered their fleet, and stood away after them; many of our frigates ahead of us, some so far that they saw West Gable. Then, perceiving that they fled from us as fast as they could, and bent their course for Goree, it growing less wind, I sent for the vice and rear-admiral; and also a great part of the captains being then come aboard for a supply of some necessaries, we advised together what was fittest to be done; and, it appearing that the merchant-ships were almost, the most part altogether, out of victuals, and ours not able to supply them, it was resolved that we should return to our coast.

" What harm we have received by loss of men, or otherwise, I cannot yet give your Honours a just account. In our ship we have only three that we know slain, whereof our lieutenant, Captain Purvis, is one ; about twenty hurt; which is a great mercy of God, considering the multitudes of shot flying among us, and our nearness each to other in the fight. We are also bound, with much thankfulness, to acknowledge God's goodness towards us, in affording us such fair weather and smooth water at our engagement; otherwise, many of our great ships might have perished without a stroke from the enemy ; for both this ship [the *Resolution*] and the *James* touched once or twice, and the great ship [*Sovereign*] had three or four rubs upon the Kentish Knock. What loss the enemy hath sustained we know not. Three of their ships were wholly disabled at the first brunt, having lost all their masts; and another, as he was towing off the rear-admiral, was taken by Captain Mildmay; and the second day they were many less in number than the first. The rear-admiral and two other captains are prisoners, who say that they conceive by the striking of De Witt's *antient*, and the putting forth another of a blue colour, that he is slain." [1]

On the 4th of October the Council of State ordered a letter to be written to the Lord Mayor, directing him to prepare reception in the several hospitals and in the Savoy for the wounded in the late engagement between General Blake and the Dutch. They also ordered the Governors of Deal and Sandown Castles to draw into their respective castles the guns placed in works for defence of the fleet commanded by Sir George Ayscue. At the same time thirty frigates were ordered to be built. [2]

The following minute, which I transcribe from a rough draft in Secretary Thurloe's handwriting, affords very important evidence respecting the difference between the

[1] Blake to the Council of State, October 2, 1652, in Granville Penn, vol. i, pp. 451, 452. De Witt was not slain.

[2] Order Book of the Council of State, October 4, 1652, MS. State Paper Office. —The following minute shows the size of some of their frigates: "That Captain Pett be directed to build the frigate which he is now going in hand with 115 foot [sic] by the keel."—*Ibid.* July 2, 1652. It would appear from this that the Parliament were building larger frigates than those formerly built. The *Sovereign*, before mentioned, was much above the average. A correspondent of Strafford, writing in October 1637, thus describes the *Sovereign*: "She is 1,637 tons, the goodliest ship that was ever built in England. The length of her keel is 128 foot, her main breadth 48 foot, her length 232 foot, her height, from the bottom of the keel to the top of her lanthorn, 76 foot. She carries 144 great guns of several sorts, and 11 anchors; one weighing 4,400 lbs."— *Strafford's Letters and Dispatches*, vol. ii. p. 116. This shows that some portion, though not a large portion, of the "ship-money" was applied to the purpose of shipbuilding. This unusually large ship was intended to make a show of the use of the ship-money. It was but a show, for the utter inefficiency of the navy, at the time when Charles I. levied ship-money, is notorious.

Government of the Long Parliament and the Government of the Stuarts : —

"The Council, having considered of a petition of Sir Oliver Fleming, Knight, find that by an Ordinance of Parliament, made the 2nd November, 1643, Sir Oliver Fleming was appointed Master of the Ceremonies. That the Council is informed that the profits and incidents of the said office were in the king's time worth about £1,000 per annum ; but now there is only the antient £200 per annum, payable out of the Exchequer, *gratuities from foreign public ministers and other profits being laid down as dishonourable to the Commonwealth.* That the said sum of £200 per annum is not wages sufficient for the support of the said Sir Oliver Fleming in the quality the said employment doth necessitate him to live in ; the slenderness whereof for the time past having (as is set forth in his petition) reduced him to wants, and constrained him to contract great debts. Upon consideration of all which, it is the opinion of the Council that the case and condition of the said Sir Oliver Fleming be humbly represented to the Parliament, to the end they may be pleased to settle a fit and competent salary upon the said office, that neither the said Sir Oliver Fleming, nor others that shall enjoy it after him, may be under the temptation of doing things dishonourable to the Commonwealth. And in respect he hath served for many years past for so small an allowance as £200 per annum in which time his services have been very many, wherein he hath demeaned himself faithfully to the Commonwealth, and very diligently, having under him no Marshal of the Ceremonies, as formerly—to confer upon him such reward as the Parliament shall think fit ; which may in some measure help him out of his present debt, and remain upon him and his family as a mark of their bounty. And the

Lord-General and Mr. Neville, or either of them, are desired humbly to represent this to the Parliament." [1]

The following minute also presents important evidence of the exemption of the Council of State from all corrupt favouritism, as well as of their conscientious care in their choice of those employed in their service—evidence eminently corroborative of the testimony even of their enemies, that " they were a race of men most indefatigable and industrious in business, *always seeking for men fit for it, and never preferring any for favour, nor by importunity*" [2]—

" That the petition of Andrew Brograve, Christopher Pett, and Mr. Taylor, desiring the place and employment of Mr. Peter Pett [Master-Shipwright, corresponding to Surveyor of the Navy], deceased, be referred to the consideration of the Committee for the Admiralty, who are to inform themselves of the *fitness of the petitioners, or any other persons*, for that employment, and report what they find concerning them to the Council." [3]

I have in a former page noticed some errors of the Council of State in political economy; and I may therefore give here, as the more remarkable, the following minute on the subject of *Free Trade* with France :—

" That it be humbly represented to the Parliament as the opinion of this Council, that it is of great advantage to this State in many respects to have a *free trade and commerce* between this Commonwealth and many ports and places in France ; and therefore that the Parliament be humbly moved to give liberty and licence, by such means and under such restrictions as they shall think fit, for such

[1] Order Book of the Council of State, Thursday, July 15, 1652, MS. State Paper Office.

[2] Roger Coke, Detection of the Court and State of England, vol. ii. p. 30.

[3] Order Book of the Council of State, Monday, August 2, 1652, MS. State Paper Office.

trade and commerce as aforesaid, notwithstanding an Act, intituled An Act prohibiting the importing of any Wines, Wool, or Silk, from the Kingdom of France into the Commonwealth of England or Ireland, or any of the Dominions thereunto belonging." [1]

On the 18th of May, two ambassadors-extraordinary had arrived in London from the King of Denmark.[2] The mode of their reception will be seen by the following minutes of that date :—

"That thirty coaches be provided, to accompany the Danish ambassadors from Tower Hill." [3]

"That the same proportion of diet as to the Dutch— viz., forty dishes for first and second courses, and twenty dishes of fruit and sweetmeats for each meal—be allowed, and a convenient allowance for other tables for their attendants." [4]

"That the ambassadors be entertained nine meals, and that sewers, butlers, and such other officers as shall be requisite be provided; and that £300 be immediately paid to Mr. Bond, to make provisions against their arrival, to be paid out of the Council's contingencies." [5]

"That some members be appointed to dine with them, and sup with them." [6]

"That plate be delivered out for their service." [7]

---

[1] Order Book of the Council of State, Thursday, July 29, 1652, MS. State Paper Office.

[2] *Ibid.* Tuesday morning, May 18, 1652.

[3] *Ibid.* Tuesday afternoon, May 18, 1652.

[4] *Ibid.* same time.

[5] *Ibid.* same time.

[6] *Ibid.* same time.

[7] *Ibid.* same time.

CHAPTER XV

THE two great naval Powers of the world were now at open war with each other. The Dutch Government sought to strengthen themselves by engaging other nations in their quarrel with the English Parliament. They sent ambassadors to Denmark, to Poland, and to other Powers in the North of Europe, to engage them in a league against England. The English Council of State showed that they were fully aware of the importance of this step, by their manner of treating the ambassadors of the King of Denmark. The following minutes furnish very significant evidence on this point :—

"That letters be written to the Lord Grey and Mr. Thomas Chaloner, to desire them to permit the Lords Ambassadors Extraordinary from the King of Denmark to take their pleasure in the parks under their command, and to kill in them what venison they shall think fit."[1]

"That Sir Oliver Fleming, Master of the Ceremonies, do acquaint the Lords Ambassadors Extraordinary from the King of Denmark that the Council have given order to the keepers of Hide [sic] Park, and of Hampton-Court Park, to permit their Excellencies to take their pleasure in those parks as oft as they shall think fit, and in them to kill what venison they please."[2]

There were reasons stronger than those arising from

---

[1] Order Book of the Council of State, Wednesday, July 28, 1652, MS. State Paper Office.

[2] Ibid. same day.

any fear of the naval power of Denmark—which, in truth, was never at any time great, except in the form of pirates or sea-robbers—to induce the sagacious statesmen who then governed England to offer such civilities to the Danish ambassadors.   There was at that very time in the harbour of Copenhagen a fleet of English merchantmen, laden with naval stores, which were urgently needed in the English dockyards, and which the Council of State were most anxious to secure.   But when Frederick III., then King of Denmark, had succeeded to the crown, four years before this time, the kingdom of Denmark had been brought to a very low condition by the wars of the last reign; and it appeared to Frederick III. that the best mode of replenishing his exhausted exchequer was to seize the fleet of English merchantmen laden with naval stores in the harbour of Copenhagen.[1]   By this act of piracy (for such I think it may be fairly considered), this Danish King obtained at once a large supply to his exchequer,

[1] " That the paper concerning the detaining of the English ships at Copenhagen by the King of Denmark, which was now sworn at the Council, be part of the report which is to be made to the Parliament concerning that affair."—*Order Book of the Council of State*, Thursday morning, October 21, 1652, MS. State Paper Office. " That it be referred to the Committee for Foreign Affairs to confer with some from New England, concerning the furnishing from them of the commodities usually had from the Eastlands for the accommodating of the shipping of this nation."—*Ibid*. Monday, November 1, 1652. " That a letter be written to General Blake, to desire him to give orders to all the ships in the service of the Commonwealth, to make stay of all ships and vessels which they shall meet with belonging to the King of Denmark, and to send them into the first convenient port free from all embezzlement, to be there kept till further orders shall be given concerning them, by the Parliament or Council."—*Ibid*. same day.   The following minute also shows the care of the Council to make provision for the great naval war they were now engaged in : " That a letter be written to the wardens of the several forests throughout this nation, to require them to suffer no timber to be felled in their respective forests, upon any pretext whatsoever, without special order from the Parliament or Council of State."—*Ibid*. Friday, October 29, 1652.

and an alliance with Holland.   The alliance with Holland
was probably more useful to him than an alliance with
England would have been; for Holland was much nearer
to him, and therefore more able either to injure or assist.
him.   But if Blake, in requital for the wrong and insult
done to England, had destroyed his fleet and battered
down his capital about his ears, he would not have had
much cause to congratulate himself on the wisdom of his
policy.   And something of that kind Blake would have
probably done had not Cromwell, for his own purposes,
preferred to keep Blake at as great a distance from himself
as he could.

As the naval stores thus seized by the King of Denmark
consisted chiefly of hemp and tar, the Council of State,
with their usual vigilant activity, looked about to supply
the wants of the navy by other means, as appears by the
following minute :—" That it be referred to the Committee
of the Admiralty to confer with a certain person, who pro-
pounds the making of pitch and tar out of the fir-timber
in Scotland " [a proof that Scotland was not then bare of
timber, as Dr. Johnson affirmed it to be a century after
this time] ; " and to report to the Council their opinions
concerning the business, after they have had conference
with him." [1]

As the Dutch lied enormously in their statements respecting their transactions with the English at this time,
and in none more than with regard to the English treatment of the Dutch prisoners, it will be proper, in vindication of the English Government, to give one or two minutes on this point from the Order Book.   A report was
spread abroad in Holland, no doubt for the purpose of

---

[1] Order Book of the Council of State, Friday, July 30, 1652, MS. State
Paper Office.

exasperating the Dutch people against such "supposed barbarity,"[1] that the Dutch prisoners in England were most of them shut up in the then unfinished and uncovered College of Chelsey, between four bare walls, laid upon straw without anything to cover them, exposed to the open sky, and to all the rigours of the season; so that many of them died of their ill-treatment. It was further affirmed that the hard-heartedness of the English went so far as to forbid those of the Dutch nation that lived in London to assist them; so that many of them died of starvation, and others, attempting to escape from such sufferings, were mercilessly shot or put to the sword by the soldiers.[2] In answer to this statement, I will give some minutes of the Council of State respecting the treatment of the Dutch prisoners, reminding the reader that 6d. a day was at that time equivalent to about 2s. a day at present, and that it was the rate of pay the English Parliament allowed to their own soldiers of the infantry regiments :—

"That 6d. per diem be allowed for the keeping of such Dutch prisoners as have been taken and are secured at Falmouth."[3]

"That orders be given to the Commissioners for sale of Dutch prizes, to allow 6d. per diem a man for the maintenance of such Dutchmen as are prisoners in this Commonwealth."[4]

---

[1] The Dutch writers themselves use this guarded expression:

[2] Life of Cornelius Van Tromp, pp. 162, 163: London, 1697.

[3] Order Book of the Council of State, Tuesday, August 24, 1652, MS. State Paper Office.

Ibid. Tuesday, September 7, 1652. "That a letter be written to the Mayor of Dover, to desire him, out of the last £500 assigned to him for the charge of wounded men and prisoners, to pay unto Mr. William Whiting, of Canterbury, the sum of £8 9s. 6d., being for so much disbursed by him at Canterbury for the maintenance of the Dutch." —*Ibid.* Monday, October 18, 1652.

"That the Dutch prisoners at Hull be discharged, and 5s. a man given them to carry them home." [1]

The following minutes respecting the treatment of the French prisoners taken in the engagement with the Duke of Vendôme's fleet afford further evidence of the humane treatment exercised by the Council of State towards their prisoners of war, even while they complained, as the minutes show, that such prisoners were "a very great charge to the Commonwealth" :—

"That order be given to the collectors for prize-goods to allow 6d. per diem a man for the maintenance of such French as are prisoners in this Commonwealth." [2]

"That a letter be written to the Mayor of Dover and Governor of Dover Castle, to let them know that they are to send away into France the Frenchmen which were lately taken prisoners, and landed there, reserving only the masters of the ships taken, and so many of the mariners as may be sufficient to give testimony in the Court of Admiralty, when they shall proceed to the adjudication of the ships, in which they were taken ; to let them know that 6d. per diem is ordered for the maintenance of the private men ; and for the officers they are to take care

[1] Order Book of the Council of State, Friday afternoon, September 17, 1652, MS. State Paper Office.— There was, at least at this time, a discharge of prisoners on both sides, as appears from the following minutes: "That such of the Dutch prisoners as are now at Dover and Canterbury be released, and permitted to repair to their own country."—*Ibid.* Wednesday, October 6, 1652. "That the Mayor of Dover do pay the sum of £20 to the master of the vessel who brought over from Ostend 120 English seamen, who had been taken by the Dutch, and dismissed in order to repair to England."—*Ibid.* same day. "That a letter be written to General Blake, to let him know that he is to discharge the Dutch captains with him, and to permit them to return home, unless he knows that the Dutch detain any Englishmen of that quality prisoners, which, if he do, he is to detain them, or such of them as he shall think fit, for the making of exchange for such of the English of that quality as shall be detained by the Dutch."—*Ibid.* Monday, October 11, 1652.

[2] *Ibid.* Tuesday, September 7, 1652.

that they be civilly treated; and for the charge thereof, the Council will take care to order the payment of it; and they are to be desired *to take care likewise of the sick men.*" [1]

The following minutes show what Blake's energy and success did towards the support of the Government:—

"That a letter be written to the Committee for the Navy, to desire them that such moneys as shall arise upon the sale of Dutch prizes may be reserved towards the paying of seamen." [2]

"That order be given to the Commissioners for sale of Dutch prizes, to pay unto the Treasurer for the Navy such money as they have made by the sale of Dutch prizes, it being for the paying off of the ships in the State's service, as they come in from sea." [3]

"That the Commissioners for Prize-goods do deliver unto the Corporation for the Poor the three busses taken from the Dutch, now in the River of Thames, together with the nets and other fishing utensils which were taken with them, to be employed by the said Corporation." [4]

"That order be given to the Commissioners for Dutch Prize-goods, to give direction to one of their deputies at Plymouth to bring up the chests of gold taken and brought in by Captain Stoakes, and to be very careful in the bringing of them up, that they be not violated and the gold embezzled; and that it be signified unto them that order is given to Major-General Desborowe to appoint a fit guard of horse to come along with the gold; as also that they are to take especial care that a strict search be made after such writings and papers as were found aboard the ships in which the gold was at their taking, that none may be lost which may be of use in the adjudication of

---

[1] Order Book of the Council of State, Wednesday, September 8, 1652, MS. State Paper Office.
[2] *Ibid.* Monday, September 6, 1652.
[3] *Ibid.* Thursday, September 9, 1652.
[4] *Ibid.* same day.

the said ships, which they are in this case, and in all others of this nature, to deliver to Doctor Walker to be made use of by him." [1]

" That a letter be written to Major-General Desborowe, to acquaint him with the taking of the gold chests from Guinea; to desire him to afford a competent guard of horse for the bringing of them up in safety to London." [2]

In their great need of money at this time, the Council entertained some propositions for the discovery of gold nearer home than Guinea :—

" That all the members of the Council, or any three of them, be appointed a Committee, to consider of such propositions as shall be made unto them, for the discovery of mines of gold and silver in any of the territories of this Commonwealth, and to report the same to the Council, with their opinions thereupon." [3]

" That the proposition delivered in to the Council by Mr. Scot, concerning the discovery of gold in Scotland, be referred to the consideration of the Committee for Mines." [4]

The all-pervading vigilance and prompt and energetic action of this Council of State were equal to those of the most energetic single ruler. If such an affair as a seaman's being killed by his captain had occurred under the Government of the Stuarts, it would most probably never have attracted the attention of the Government. It certainly never would, if the captain had been a Prince Rupert, or anyone favoured by him. The Council of State proceeded in a different fashion. One of their captains had killed one of his seamen. The following minutes show what followed :—

" That three of the deputies of the Serjeant-at-Arms do go down to Rye, and take into their custody the late

[1] Order Book of the Council of State, Friday, September 24, 1652, MS. State Paper Office.

[2] Ibid. same day.
[3] Ibid. Monday, September 20, 1652.
[4] Ibid. same day.

captain of the *Merlin* frigate, and bring him up to the Council." [1]

"That a letter be written to the master of the *Merlin* frigate, to desire him to send up three such persons, along with the late captain, as can testify concerning the action of his killing a man aboard the frigate." [2]

"That a warrant be drawn for the committal of Captain Warren to Newgate for murther, in order to be tried for the same." [3]

By the 21st of October, that is, just three weeks later, Captain Warren had been tried, found guilty of murder, and executed, as appears from the following minute, relating to a petition to the Council of State from his widow :—"That the petition of Elenor Warren, widow, be referred to the Committee of the Admiralty, who are to consider what may be done thereupon, and report their opinion thereupon to the Council." [4]

The vigilance of the Council of State is further manifested by the following minute :—"That it be referred to the Committee for Examinations, to examine the complaint made by some prisoners, of great fees exacted from them by certain persons who have solicited their release; and to send for such persons before them, as can give testimony herein, and likewise for such persons as have exacted such fees; and examine and report the state of the whole business to the Council." [5]

And their attention to details is shown by the following order :—

"That the Dutch prize taken by Captain Peacocke, called the *Morning Star*, be now named the *Plover*." [6]

---

[1] Order Book of the Council of State, Friday, September 24, 1652, MS. State Paper Office.

[2] *Ibid.* same day.

[3] *Ibid.* Thursday, September 30, 1652.

[4] *Ibid.* Thursday, October 21, 1652.

[5] *Ibid.* Monday, October 25, 1652.

[6] *Ibid.* Saturday morning, October 30, 1652. At the same meeting, there is made in the Order Book the following memorandum : " Look out General Blake's commission."

" That an extract of the intelligence, now read in the Council, from Holland, be sent unto General Blake." [1]

The following minute, of 12th November, has reference to a resolution of the Council, to send twenty ships at this time to the Mediterranean. The Council here committed a great blunder. By sending off those twenty ships, they so weakened Blake that he was not a match for Tromp, and thus met with the only disaster that befel him in the whole course of his career. The intelligence they had received, respecting the plans of the Dutch, render their proceeding the more inexcusable :—

" That a letter be written to General Blake, to acquaint him with the resolution of the Council, for the sending of twenty ships to the Streights; to give him a list of the names of the ships, to let him know that it is not the intention of the Council to disable him " [of course it was not their intention, but the result was to disable him effectually] " (by the taking of these ships) from waiting upon the service in these parts, which the Council doubt not but will be supplied by the coming out of others appointed for the winter guard. However they thought fit, before they came to any positive resolution concerning this business, to acquaint him therewith, to the end that if he had anything to offer concerning it, it might be taken into consideration." [2]

---

[1] Order Book of the Council of State, Wednesday, November 10, 1652, MS. State Paper Office: "That a letter be written to the Mayor of Dover, to desire him to speak to the master of the pacquet-boat which passeth between that place and Flanders ; that it is the Council's pleasure that he do take aboard him in Flanders all such English seamen as do come thither to pass into England, as well those who have left the service of the Dutch, in obedience to an Act of Parliament, as also those who have been taken prisoners by the Dutch, and have been released, and do and shall repair to Dunquerque for passing into England; and to let him know that he is to relieve each of them as shall want it upon their landing, and place it to account. And further, to signify to him that the master of the pacquet-boat shall have, for every person which he shall so bring over, according to the rate he usually hath of other passengers."—*Ibid.* same day.

[2] *Ibid.* Friday, November 12, 1652.

The sending of a fleet of twenty ships to the Streights, at that particular time, was one blunder of the Council of State; the granting of so great a number of letters of marque to privateers or private men-of-war was another. In regard to the latter, Blake complains in his letter after the fight with Tromp; and it would appear, from the following minute, that he had remonstrated on the subject of the want of men before the fight :—

"That the letter from General Blake, dated the 21st instant, for so much of it as refers to men and victuals, be referred to the consideration of the Committee of the Admiralty." [1]

In November 1652 the House proceeded, for the fifth and last time, to the election of a new Council of State for the ensuing year. The Serjeant-at-Arms was ordered to go out with his mace, and summon all the members in Westminster Hall, and the parts adjacent, to attend the House. The doors were then ordered to be shut, when the number of members present appeared to be 122. The twenty-one members of the Council of State to be continued for the year ensuing were the Lord-General Cromwell, Lord-Commissioner Whitelock, Lord Chief Justice St. John, Lord Chief Justice Rolle, Sir Henry Vane, jun., Sir Arthur Haselrig; Thomas Scott, Herbert Morley, and Dennis Bond, Esquires; Colonel Purefoy, John Bradshaw, Serjeant-at-law, John Gurdon, Esq., Lord-Commissioner Lisle, Colonel Wauton, Sir James Harrington, Sir William Masham, Thomas Chaloner, and Robert Wallop, Esquires; Sir Gilbert Pickering, Sir Peter Wentworth, and Nicholas Love, Esq. The twenty new members now elected were Robert Goodwin, Esq., Alderman Allen, Colonel Thompson, Walter

[1] Order Book of the Council of State, Monday, November 22, 1652, MS. State Paper Office.

Strickland, Esq., Sir Henry Mildmay, Major-General Skip-
pon, Lord Grey, Colonel Sydney (Algernon Sydney), Edmund
Prideaux, Esq. (Attorney-General), Sir John Trevor, Colo-
nel Norton, Thomas Lister, Esq., Colonel Ingoldsby, Sir
John Bourchier, William Earl of Salisbury, William
Cawley, Esq., Sir William Brereton, John Fielder and
William Say, Esquires, and Major-General Harrison.[1]

It will be observed that Blake was not one of the twenty-
one members of the Council of State for the preceding
year who were re-elected. He was not, therefore, for
more than one year a member of the Council of State.
It will also be observed that Algernon Sydney, who had
never before been a member, was one of the twenty new
members who were now elected members of the Council, to
fill up the places of the twenty members of the last year's
Council who now went out. As Blake was at this time
constantly with the fleet, he could not, even if he had been
re-elected, have been present at the deliberations of the
Council.

On Thursday, the 25th of November 1652, the Council of
State ordered, "That the two letters of the 24th instant, from
General Blake to the Council, be humbly presented to the
Parliament; and the Parliament put in mind that General
Blake's commission determines upon the 4th of December
next, to the end they may be pleased to declare their
pleasure touching the same." [2] Blake requested that two
colleagues should be joined with him in the command, as
had been the case in the first year of his naval service.
Accordingly, Colonel Deane (his former colleague) and
General Monk were appointed his colleagues in the

---

[1] Commons' Journals, November,   State, Thursday, November 25, 1652,
1652, Parl. Hist., vol. iii. p 1379.   MS. State Paper Office.
[2] Order Book of the Council of

command of the fleet. Both these officers, being then employed in Scotland, could not for some time take any active part in the naval war.

I at one time thought that, notwithstanding the incessant care of the Council of State, and the large sums paid by them for intelligence, their information was defective about this time in regard to the movements of the Dutch; and that they made a distribution of their fleet for the winter, as if the Dutch preparations for renewing the contest would not be completed till the spring. But a careful examination of their Order Books shows that they were by no means uninformed of the state of the Dutch fleet and the great preparations of the Dutch Government. Evidence of this has already been given. And further, on Thursday, the 25th of November 1652, there is a minute, "That the Lord-General be desired to give order to some foot forces of the army to march to Dover, Sandown, and Deal, to be there in readiness to go aboard the ships of this Commonwealth, when they shall receive orders from the same from General Blake."[1] And on the following day there is a minute, "That so much of the Dutch letters as gives the state of the Dutch fleet be signified to General Blake."[2]

Notwithstanding all these warnings, however, the Council of State had, as we have seen, despatched twenty ships of war to the Mediterranean. Moreover, twenty ships of the English fleet had been sent to Elsinore, under Captain Ball.[3] Penn sailed northward with an equal number of vessels,

---

[1] Order Book of the Council of State, Thursday, November 25, 1652, MS. State Paper Office.

[2] *Ibid.* Friday, November 26, 1652.

[3] "Instructions to Captain Ball upon his repair to the Sound:—1. You are forthwith to go to the Sound, with the squadron of ships ordered for that purpose by the letter you shall herewith receive, and there take into your charge such English ships as are homeward bound from thence, and use your best endeavours to convoy them safely home to their several ports." The 5th instruction is "to observe such orders as you shall receive from the

to convoy a fleet of colliers from Newcastle to London.
Twelve ships were stationed in Plymouth Sound, and fifteen
of the ships that had been most damaged were ordered
into the river for repair.   Towards the end of November
the Council of State began to perceive, when it was too late,
the blunder they had committed in crippling their Channel
fleet.   On Saturday, the 27th of November, the Council
ordered, " That a letter be written to General Blake, to acknowledge the receipt of his of the 26th, and of his intention
to go to sea, wherewithal the Council is satisfied; and that
the Council have written to Portsmouth, for the State's
ships there to repair to him immediately." [1]   And on the
same day they order, " That a letter be written to Mr.
Willoughby at Portsmouth, to hasten out the *Spenker* and
other ships of the State there to General Blake; and to
enclose to him a warrant to all captains of ships, to repair forthwith with their ships to General Blake.' [2]   But
these orders would, manifestly, not be in time to furnish
any effectual reinforcement to Blake by the 29th of November.   Accordingly, on the 29th of November, Blake
rode in the Channel, between Dover and Calais, with a
fleet, consisting of 37 men-of-war and frigates, the fireships, and a few hoys.

After the defeat of De Witt, related in the preceding
chapter, the States of the United Provinces again cast their
eyes upon Martin Tromp, who, as has been before
stated, "was as much beloved by the seamen for his mild
temper, as De Witt was hated by them for his cruelty." [3]

Parliament, the Council of State, or
General Blake."—*Order Book of the
Council of State*, Monday, August 30,
1652, MS. State Paper Office.   However, as has been said, the King of
Denmark seized the fleet of English
merchantmen in the harbour of Copenhagen.

[1] *Ibid.* Saturday, November 27,
1652.

[2] *Ibid.* same day.

[3] Life of Cornelius Van Tromp,
p. 83.

Accordingly, at the beginning of November, the States resolved to give him the command of the fleet they were then
fitting out.   Vice-Admirals Evertz and De Witt, and Rear-
Admiral Floritz, were appointed to command under him.
But De Witt falling sick was put ashore, and De Ruyter
was substituted in his place.[1]   The Dutch accounts say
that this Dutch fleet was composed of 73 men-of-war, besides fireships and other smaller vessels, and tenders.[2]
Blake's own statement is that the Dutch fleet " consisted
of 95 sail, most of them great ships." [3]

On Monday, the 29th[4] of November 1652, the hostile
fleets found themselves in presence of each other, between
Dover and Calais.   Blake called a council of war on board
the *Triumph*, his flag-ship; but it was rather to apprise his
captains of what he had resolved to do, than to ask their
opinion of what ought to be done.   He spoke of the situation of the two nations at that moment, of the superior
force of the enemy, of the distance of his own squadrons;
and ended by declaring his resolution to fight, if it were
necessary, but on no account to fall down the Channel,
leaving the coast towns to be insulted, and perhaps destroyed, by that powerful armament.   The captains, as a
matter of course, when the Admiral was a man of Blake's
commanding character, accepted his decision—though, as
the result proved, they could hardly have all of them accepted it with alacrity—and returned to their several ships.

All that day the two admirals watched each other's
movements, with a view to gain the weather-gage.   Blake's

---

[1] Life of Cornelius Van Tromp, p. 83.
[2] *Ibid.*
[3] Blake's letter to the Council of
State, from aboard the *Triumph*, in the
Downs, December 1, 1652; printed in
Granville Penn's Memorials of Sir
Wm. Penn (vol. i. pp. 458–460), from
the original letter to the Council, with
Blake's signature, among Sir W. Penn's
papers.

[4] This was Old Style, by which the
English then reckoned.   The Dutch,
who reckoned by the " New Style,"
make it December 9.

own account is, that the wind, "which was awhile somewhat variable, after blew strongly at north-west, so that
we could not that day engage. The wind increased at
night, we riding in Dover Road, and the enemy about two
leagues to leeward of us at anchor."[1]   Next morning, the
wind having somewhat abated, the two fleets weighed and
stood away to Dungeness, the English keeping the wind.
"About the pitch of the Nesse,"[2] says Blake, "the headmost of our fleet met and engaged the enemy's fleet, consisting of 95 sail, most of them great ships—three admirals,[3] two vice-admirals, and two rear-admirals.   They
passed many broadsides upon us[4] very near, and yet we had
but six men slain and ten wounded.   About the same time,
the *Victory* was engaged with divers of the enemy, but
was relieved by the *Vanguard* and some others.   The *Garland* sped not so well; but being boarded by two of their
flags and others, and seconded only by Captain Hoxton,
was, after a hot fight board-and-board, carried by them,

---

[1] Blake to the Council of State,
December 1, 1652.—Granville Penn's
Memorials of Sir Wm. Penn, vol. i.
pp. 458–460.

[2] Some writers have supposed that
by "Nesse" here Blake meant the Naze,
a headland in Essex near the border
of Suffolk. The minutes of the Council of State place the matter beyond a
doubt. There is a minute of January
26, 165⅔, relating to the petition of
"Rachel Hoxon, relict of Captain
Hoxon, commander of the ship *Anthony
Bonaventure*, who was slain in the
late fight with the Dutch off Dungey
Nesse."—*Order Book of the Council of State*, Wednesday, January 26
165⅔, MS. State Paper Office. Also
in a minute of January 12, 165⅔,
relating to the trial of Captains
Young and Taylor, "the late fight
with the Dutch" is stated to have been

"off Dunginesse."—*Ibid*. Wednesday,
January 12, 165⅔. The name of the
opposite French headland, "Cap Gris
Nez," has a close resemblance to the
name of the English, if the latter
means "dun nose."

[3] There seems to be some confusion
here. There was Tromp, the admiral;
De Ruyter and Evertz, vice-admirals;
and there were also, probably, two
rear-admirals.

[4] By "us" he means his own ship,
the *Triumph*. "Out of 200 men on
board the *Garland*, at the beginning of
the action, the Captain and 60 officers
and men were killed, and a still greater
number severely wounded. The *Bonaventure* had suffered to an equal
extent."—*Dixon's Robert Blake*, p. 223,
London, 1852: p. 185, new edition,
London, 1858.

and his second with him. It was late before I took notice
of it, whereupon I gave order to bear up to them; but immediately our foretopmast was shot away, our mainstay
being shot off before, and our rigging much torn, so that
we could not work our ship to go to their relief. And by
occasion thereof, and night coming on, we were saved ourselves, who were then left almost alone. As soon as it was
night, we made sail towards Dover Road, and came to
anchor. This morning, the weather growing thick, and
fearing a south wind, we stood away to the Downs, where
(by God's providence) we now are." [1]

Few are the men who can or will acknowledge a defeat.
It may indeed be assumed, as a maxim of strategic science,
that it is one of the duties of a commander to turn a
defeat into a victory, at least in his narrative of it. But
there can be no doubt that the Dutch had on this occasion gained a victory, and were, for the time, masters of
the Channel. The common story that Tromp, after this
affair, carried a broom in his maintop, thereby intimating
that he would sweep the narrow seas of all English
shipping, seems unworthy of the general character of
Tromp, who might have been supposed too great a commander, and too brave a man, to be a braggart. But there
is no occasion on which the manly truthfulness and
genuine modesty of Blake's nature shine forth more con-
spicuously than they do on this. His letter to the Council
of State begins thus: "Right Honourable, I presume
your Honours do long for an account of what hath passed
between us and the Dutch fleet; and I hope you have
hearts prepared to receive evil, as well as good, from the
hands of God." [2]

[1] Blake to the Council of State,
December 1, 1652, in Granville Penn's
Memorials of Sir Wm. Penn, vol. i.
pp. 458, 459.

[2] Ibid. vol. i. p. 458.

After a short account (already cited) of the battle, Blake thus proceeds :—" In this account, I am bound to let your Honours know in general, that there was much baseness of spirit, not among the merchantmen only, but many of the State's ships; and, therefore, I make it my earnest request, that your Honours would be pleased to send down some gentlemen, to take an impartial and strict examination of the deportment of several commanders, that you may know who are to be confided in, and who are not. It will then be time to take into consideration the grounds of some other errors and defects, especially the discouragement and want of seamen.   I shall be bold at present to name one, *not the least*—which is, *the great number of private men-of-war, especially out of the River of Thames.*   And I hope it will not be unreasonable for me, in behalf of myself, to desire your Honours, that you would think of giving me, your unworthy servant, a discharge from this employment, so far too great for me; especially, since your Honours have added two such able gentlemen[1] for the undertaking of that charge: that so I may spend the remainder of my days in private retirement, and in prayers to the Lord for a blessing upon you and the nation. . . . . At the close of this, I received your Honours' of the 30th of November, together with your commission, which I shall endeavour to put in execution with all the power and faithfulness I can, until it shall please your Honours to receive it back again, which I trust will be very speedily; that so I may be freed from that trouble of spirit which lies upon me, arising from the sense of my own insufficiency, and the usual effects thereof—reproach and contempt of men, and disservice of the Commonwealth, which may be the consequent of both.

[1] Deane and Monk.

" Into what capacity or condition soever it shall please the Lord to cast me, I shall labour still to approve myself a faithful patriot, and

" Your Honours' most humble servant,

ROBERT BLAKE.

" *Triumph*, in the Downs, this 1st December, 1652." [1]

On Wednesday, the 1st of December, 1652, the number present in the Council of State was twenty-eight,[2] being eight or ten above the average number. Colonel Sydney (Algernon Sydney) was one of those present. The Lord-General (Cromwell) was not present. The energy and ability with which the Council of State immediately set about repairing the error they had committed, in crippling their Channel fleet, are well worthy of the most careful attention, and are very interesting as well as very instructive. On that day, the 1st of December, 1652, they made an order :—

" That a letter be written to the three frigates at Plymouth, to acquaint them with what is come to the Council, concerning the engagement with the Dutch; to desire them, therefore, to sail towards General Blake, now in the Downs, and to send a ketch before them to the General, to acquaint him with the orders they have received from the Council; and to desire his directions, unless they have already received orders from him in reference to this service." [3]

On the following day, Thursday, 2nd December, the Council of State made the following orders :—

---

[1] Blake to the Council of State, from the original among Sir W. Penn's papers.—Granville Penn's Memorials of Sir W. Penn, vol. i. pp. 458–460.

[2] Order Book of the Council of State, Wednesday, December 1, 1652, MS. State Paper Office.

[3] *Ibid.* same day.

" That a warrant be drawn, to give power to the captains
of the private men-of-war now in the River of Thames (for
the enabling of them, upon the present occasion, to join
with the fleet with General Blake), to imprest [*sic*] seamen
for their respective ships; and that this warrant be continued in force for the space of one month, and no longer;
and the captains of the several ships are to bring in the
numbers of men which they desire." [1]

" That three members of the Council—Colonel Wauton,[2]
Colonel Morley, and Mr. Chaloner—be sent as Commissioners to the fleet with General Blake, to pursue such
measures as the Council shall give unto them." [3] These
Commissioners are empowered to take up money not exceeding £500, to be disposed by them as they shall see
occasion.[4]

" That Mr. Smyth and Major Thompson do repair
aboard the several ships in the State's service now in the
river, and use all possible endeavours for hastening them
out to General Blake." [5]

" That a letter be written to General Blake, to take
notice to him of the receipt of his, giving an account of
the late engagement with the Dutch; to take notice to him

[1] Order Book of the Council of
State, Thursday, December 2, 1652,
MS. State Paper Office.

[2] This name is sometimes spelt
"Walton," and sometimes "Wauton;"
it is on this occasion spelt "Wauton."

[3] Order Book of the Council of State,
Thursday, December 2, 1652, MS.
State Paper Office.—The following are
among the instructions to these Commissioners: "6. You, with the General, are hereby authorised to examine
the deportment of several captains and
commanders, as well of the State's
ships as merchantmen, in the late
fight with the Dutch fleet; and to remove from the command such of the
captains and other commanders as
you, upon examination, shall find not
to have performed their duty in
the said action, and to supply their
places with other fit persons, until the
Council shall take further order.—7.
You are, during your residence there,
to be present at councils of war, and
advise in all things that may emerge
or fall into consideration upon the
place relating to the premises."—*Ibid.*
same day.

[4] *Ibid.* same day.

[5] *Ibid.* same day.

of his good deportment in that action, and to give him thanks for the same; and also to acquaint him that the Council have despatched some Commissioners to him, to visit him from them, and to consult with him concerning the carrying on of the public service." [1]

" That the Lord-General be desired to give order to such foot forces of the army as he shall find necessary, to march down towards Dover and the seaside in those parts, and to be there in readiness for further service." [2]

On the following day, Friday, the 3rd of December, 1652, the Council of State ordered :—

" That warrants be issued to the Vice-Admirals of the adjacent counties, and, where there are no Vice-Admirals, to the Mayors or Bailiffs and other officers of the port towns, to imprest seamen for the service of the Commonwealth." [3]

" That it be referred to the Commissioners of the Navy, to treat with Mr. Marston concerning the setting out of his ships into the public service; and to offer unto him protection for the freeing of his men from being pressed into the State's ships, he undertaking to carry the said ships to the General [Blake] by a certain day, as they can agree, and wind and weather shall serve ; and to remain there for some time, which the said Commissioners are likewise to ascertain with him as they shall be able." [4]

On Saturday the 4th of December they made the following orders :—

" That a letter be written to the commanders of the State's ships of war at Harwich and Yarmouth, to require

---

[1] Order Book of the Council of State, Thursday, December 2, 1652, MS. State Paper Office.

[2] Ibid. same day.

[3] Ibid. Friday, December 3, 1652.

[4] Ibid. same day.—The following minute, made the same day, has reference to Blake's remonstrance respecting the number of private men-of-war: " That all petitions for private men-of-war be read publicly at the Council."—Ibid. same day.

them to make haste to General Blake, now in the Downs,
and to go in consort together; and to take especial care,
in their passage thither, that they be not surprised or
unawares set upon by the enemy." [1]

" That the like letters which were sent to the western
ports last night, for the giving notice to them of what hath
happened between the English and Dutch fleets, be despatched thither again, and the same also to the northern
ports." [2]

" That a warrant be directed to Mr. Willoughby and
Mr. Coytmore, to repair down the River of Thames to all
ships of war, whether the State's or private men-of-war,
and require them from the Council to hasten to General
Blake, now in the Downs, with all possible expedition;
and all Justices of the Peace are required to permit the
said Mr. Willoughby and Mr. Coytmore *to pass upon the
Lord's Day, it being for a special service.*" [3]

" That a letter be written to General Blake, to acquaint
him with what the Council hath done for the giving him
an addition of strength; to let him know that (in regard
the state of affairs is before him, and he hath a perfect
understanding of them), the Council do leave it to him,
upon the place, to do what he may for his own defence and
the service of the Commonwealth." [4]

" That General Monk be sent unto, and desired to be in
readiness, at twenty-four hours' warning, to go to sea, to
take upon him the charge to which he hath been appointed
by the Parliament." [5]

" That the Parliament be humbly moved to give orders

[1] Order Book of the Council of State,
Saturday afternoon, December 4, 1652,
MS. State Paper Office.
[2] *Ibid.* same time.

[3] *Ibid.* same time.
[4] *Ibid.* same time.
[5] *Ibid.* same time.

for the granting of commissions to General Deane and General Monk, as to the exercising that command at sea, to which they have already been appointed by order of Parliament; and the Lord President [of the Council of State] is desired humbly to move the Parliament herein."[1]

"The Lord-General Cromwell acquainting the Council that he had drawn out 500 men out of the guards here, and given them orders to march to Dover and the seacoast thereabouts, and likewise had commanded Colonel Rich's regiment of horse to draw together upon that coast, the Council doth approve thereof; and desire his Lordship to give further orders for speeding away the said 500 men, and also to give orders to another regiment of horse to strengthen the seacoast with."[2]

The indefatigable exertions of the Council of State, to put their fleet into that thoroughly efficient condition which it displayed in the next great fight with the Dutch, in the following February, can only be known completely by a careful perusal of their minutes. But to give these minutes in full would, I fear, appear tedious to the reader. On this, however, the last and greatest occasion they were to have for the exercise of their great administrative genius, some indulgence may, perhaps, be accorded to an attempt to give as many of them as may convey some idea at least of the labours of the most remarkable body of statesmen that ever sat together in Council.

On Sunday the 5th of December, 1652, the Council recommend Harwich to Blake, as a port to refit, instead of Lee

---

[1] Order Book of the Council of State, Saturday afternoon, December 4, 1652, MS. State Paper Office.—At the same time, "The Lord-General is desired to think of some fit person, to be immediately despatched into Scotland, to be Commander-in-Chief there, the Parliament having appointed Major-General Deane, the present Commander-in-Chief, to be one of the Generals of the Fleet."—*Ibid.* same time.

[2] *Ibid.* same time.

Road, but leave the decision to him.   Blake chose to come
into the river, to Lee Road.   On Monday morning the
Council order, "That a letter be written to General Blake,
to take notice to him of his coming into Lee Road; to desire
him that he will forthwith give a particular account to the
Council of the state of the fleet, and be very careful in the
keeping of his men aboard."[1]   On the afternoon of the same
day, the Council ordered, "That letters be sent to desire
those of the western ports to set out some small boats to give
notice to merchant-ships homewards bound of what hath
happened, that they may take care of their own safety." [2]

" That the Council do approve of the Lord President's
opening of letters directed to the Council, and authorise
him to open such as shall come, and thereupon to summon
the Council if he shall see cause." [3]

On the 17th of December the Council of State wrote
to Blake, " to let him know they have received an account
from the Commissioners sent down to him of the state
of the fleet, and of his readiness to give them assistance
in the business for which they were sent; to return him
thanks for his faithful service, and to acquaint him that
all possible endeavours are using for the speedy setting
forth of the fleet to sea." [4]

" Upon consideration had of the qualities and rates of
the several ships which are to be set forth in the fleet for
the next summer, it is ordered that it be declared that all
such merchant-ships as shall be taken on and hired for
that service, shall be vessels carrying twenty-six guns at
the least, and not under." [5]

---

[1] Order Book of the Council of
State, Monday morning, December
6, 1652, MS. State Paper Office.

[2] Ibid. Monday afternoon, December
6, 1652.

[3] Ibid. Wednesday morning, December 8,

[4] Ibid. Friday, December 17, 1652.

[5] Ibid. same day.

"That the captains of such ships as shall be hired for the service of the Commonwealth shall be chosen and placed by the State; and the other officers are likewise to be approved of." [1]

The following minute affords a graphic picture, in a small compass, of the rigour with which the press-warrants were executed, in order to man the State's ships in that great naval war :—

"That a warrant of protection be granted to Thomas Girling, waterman, son of Christopher Girling of Richmond, in the county of Surrey, waterman, to protect him from being imprested into the State's service, in regard that by his labour only his aged father is supported, who is unable now to support himself; and that he, the said Christopher, hath lost two sons already in the service of the Commonwealth." [2]

"That order be given to the Commissioners for Prize-goods, to bring up the prize-silver and cochineal from Plymouth, and to coin the silver in the Tower of London; and to let them know that Major-General Desborowe is written unto, to afford convoy to the bringing of it up." [3]

---

[1] Order Book of the Council of State, Friday, December 17, 1652, MS. State Paper Office.—Sir Wm. Penn, in a letter to the Lord-General Cromwell, dated June 2, 1652, says : "My Lord, it is humbly conceived that the State would be far better served if, as formerly, they placed commanders in all the merchant-ships taken up; for the commanders now employed, being all part-owners of their ships, I do believe will not be so industrious in engaging an enemy as other men ; especially considering that by engagement they not only waste their powder and shot, but are liable to receive damage in their masts, rigging, and hull, and endanger the loss of all, when they may be quiet and receive the same pay."—*Granville Penn's Memorials of Sir Wm. Penn*, vol. i. p. 427, from Milton's Collection.

[2] Order Book of the Council of State, Wednesday, January 5, 165⅔, MS. State Paper Office.

[3] *Ibid.* Friday, January 7, 165⅔.— On the same day an order was made, "That Mr. Isaac Dorislaus be appointed Solicitor in the Court of Admiralty on the behalf of the Commonwealth, and that he have the allowance of £250 per annum for himself, and a clerk in consideration of this employment." At the same time instructions for the directing of him in

The wording of the following minute is curious, and would seem to show that the Council of State had some. doubts as to the precise meaning of the word Commonwealth.   They would have been more accurate, however, if they had left out the word "Republique," to which title the Government of Venice had very small claim, less than their own Government had :—

" That Sir Oliver Fleming do carry the letters from the Parliament directed to the Republique of the Commonwealth of Venice to the Secretary now here from that Commonwealth." [1]

The business of the Council of State extended to transactions with all the Powers of the world.   At this time they had, besides their conferences with the ambassadors of some Powers, correspondence by letters to carry on with many others—with the Great Duke of Tuscany, with " Jacobus Duke of Courland," with the Archduke Leopold.[2] Their mode of dealing with those personages may be seen from the minute respecting a letter from the Duke of Vendôme, complaining of the destruction of his fleet by Blake in September of this year.   This minute is as follows :—

" The Council of State having, in pursuance of the Order of Parliament in that behalf, taken into consideration the Duke of Vendôme's letter, and the matter of fact of taking the ships mentioned therein, do find the state of it to be,— That General Blake, being with the fleet, in the Narrows, about the 5th of September last, part of the fleet, after some hours' chase, did take . . . [blank in orig.] French men-of-war, being the King's own ships, who, as the commander said, were with several other ships going to the relief of Dunkirk."

that employment were signed and delivered to him.

[1] Order Book of the Council of State, Tuesday, January 11, 165⅔, MS. State Paper Office.

[2] Ibid. Thursday, January 6, 165⅔.

Whether any further explanation or satisfaction the Council may have given in their letter I do not know, as, though the "draught of a letter" to the Duke of Vendôme is said in the minute to be "annexed hereunto,"[1] I have not been able to find any such draught. But there is little doubt that the substance of the minute given above formed the substance of the letter.

On the 11th of January 165⅔ letters were ordered to be sent to the Vice-Admirals and Mayors of port towns, for the impresting of seamen in their respective jurisdictions, for the effectual manning of the fleet now to go forth; and the ships at Portsmouth and Plymouth and in the western ports were ordered to cruise up and down in the Channel for the discovery of the enemy.[2]

On the following day a letter, which shows in a striking manner the extent to which the Barbary pirates carried on their depredations, particularly in carrying Englishmen into captivity, was written to "Mr. Longland, to acquaint him that it is the opinion of this Council that, for the furnishing of the English shipping in the Straits with Englishmen, he do, by such vessels as he shall have occasion from time to time to send to the African shore, bring from Algiers some of the English captives; which the Council conceive may now be effected upon the paying for every man who shall be brought away the price of his redemption; which the Council is informed is now set and agreed upon."[3]

[1] Order Book of the Council of State, Tuesday, November 23, 1652, MS. State Paper Office.

[2] *Ibid.* Tuesday, January 11, 165⅔.

[3] *Ibid.* Wednesday, January 12, 165⅔. On the same day the Council made an order, "That Mr. Thurloe do prepare a paper to be brought into the Council, in pursuance of an Order of Parliament, whereby it may be signified to the ambassadors and public ministers now here, sent from foreign states and princes to this Commonwealth, that they are not to permit any of the people of this Commonwealth to resort to the hearing of Masse in their

. I have repeatedly had occasion to call attention to the sensitiveness of the Council of State on the subject of what they termed "libellous and scurrilous books and pamphlets." It is due to the memory of the statesmen who composed that Council to state that their aversion to scurrility extended even to scurrility against their enemies, as will appear from the following minute of 27th of January 165⅔ :—

"That the printed paper this day brought into the Council, containing scurrilous matter against the Dutchmen, be referred to the Committee of the Council appointed for putting in execution the late Act for regulating the press; who are to cause enquiry to be made after the author, printer, and publishers of the said paper, and also search to be made for them, and seizure of such of them as can be found; and to report to the Council what they shall do herein." [1]

An adequate conception cannot be obtained of the labours of the Council of State without mentioning that a vast number of petitions came in almost every day, which necessarily occupied some part of their time. Many of these petitions were from the widows who had lost their husbands in the service of the State. All these petitions received careful attention; even when the Council could do nothing for the petitioners, as in the following case:

houses, it being contrary to the laws of the nation."—*Order Book of the Council of State*, January 12, 165⅔, MS. State Paper Office.

[1] *Ibid.* Thursday, January 27, 165⅔. —Some specimens of the "scurrilous matter" here referred to, matter containing more scurrility than wit, may be seen in the King's Pamphlets, Anno 1652-3, Brit. Mus. The English scurrility had, however, the excuse that it had been provoked by the demeanour of the Dutch, who had made bragging and scurrilous songs of their own success in the war— a success of which they had, in truth, small cause to boast, since they owed it to a superiority of force amounting to three to one.

"Upon the reading of the petition of Susanna Cowling, it is ordered that it be returned in answer to the said petition, that the matter of the petition is not within the cognizance of the Council."[1]   And yet Cromwell charged this Council of State with neglect of their duty and delays of business.

On Wednesday, the 19th of January, it was ordered :—

"That it be signified to the Commissioners for the Navy, that the Council hold it fit that directions be by them given to such as they employ under them as prest-masters, that they do not for the future press out of any vessel trading for coal to Newcastle, any man who is aged above forty-five years, or any boy under the age of sixteen years, to the end that that trade, which is so necessary to this Commonwealth, may be continued, and the ships in the service of this Commonwealth be well and effectually manned."[2]

"That the paper in answer to the ambassadors from the King of Spain and Duke Leopold be humbly reported to the Parliament by Colonel Sydney."[3]

I will give here several other minutes, throwing light on the Parliament's relations with the Great Powers of Europe at that time :—

"That six thousand pounds be allowed unto the Lord Viscount Lisle " [Algernon Sydney's elder brother],

---

[1] Order Book of the Council of State, Tuesday, January 18, 165⅜, MS. State Paper Office.

[2] *Ibid.* Wednesday, January 19, 165⅜.

[3] *Ibid.* same day.—Such minutes prove that Algernon Sydney did not speak without authority when he said, "All the states, kings, and potentates of Europe most respectfully, not to say submissively, sought our friendship."—*Algernon Sydney on Govern-* *ment*, chap. ii. sect. 28.   I may add here another minute, showing the active part taken by Sydney in the business of the Council of State :— "That Colonel Sydney, Mr. Strickland, Colonel Purefoy, Sir H. Mildmay, or any two of them, be desired to go out to treat with the French agent, they being the Commissioners formerly appointed to that business."—*Order Book of the Council of State*, Thursday, February 10, 165⅜, MS. State Paper Office.

"nominated ambassador for Sweden, for his preparations, journey, house-expenses, and all other ordinary necessaries for the space of six months; of which £3,000 be paid unto him in money here, and the other three thousand to be sent over by bills of exchange either to Stockholme, or Hamburgh, as shall appear most convenient; and that £6,000 be set apart for that service by the Council out of the exigents accordingly." [1]

"That Mr. Thurloe do prepare the letter this day passed in the Parliament to be sent to the Archduke, for the signature of Mr. Speaker; and that it be sent by Sir Oliver Fleming to the Lord Ambassador of Spain, in order to be sent to the Archduke Leopold." [2]

---

[1] Order Book of the Council of State, Monday, January 24, 165$\frac{3}{4}$, MS. State Paper Office.—It appears, therefore, that Ludlow was in error when he stated that at this time "The Parliament sent the Lord-Commissioner Whitelock on an extraordinary embassy to the Crown of Sweden." — *Ludlow's Memoirs*, vol. ii. p. 439: 2nd edition, London, 1721. But as it would appear that Lord Viscount Lisle, though nominated, did not go, probably in consequence of the change in the English Government that took place soon after, Ludlow might easily confuse this appointment of Lord Lisle with that of Whitelock by Cromwell in less than a year after. A story told by Whitelock, in his account of his embassy to Sweden, may show that the English Parliament had special reasons for nominating to that appointment a man of the rank of the Lord Viscount Lisle. When Whitelock, after having had the honour of dancing with Christina, the Queen of Sweden, had conducted the Queen to her chair of state, she said to him,

"Par Dieu! these Hollanders are lying fellows." "I wonder," replied Whitelock, "how the Hollanders should come into your mind upon such an occasion as this is, who are not usually thought upon in such solemnities, nor much acquainted with them." "I will tell you all," replied the Queen. "The Hollanders reported to me a great while since, that all the noblesse of England were of the King's party, and none but mechanics of the Parliament's party, and not a gentleman among them. Now I thought to try you, and to shame you if you could not dance; but I see that you are a gentleman, and have been bred a gentleman; and that makes me say the Hollanders are lying fellows, to report that there was not a gentleman of the Parliament's party, when I see by you chiefly, and by many of your company, that you are gentlemen."—*Whitelock's Journal of his Swedish Embassy*, vol. ii. pp. 155, 156, 2 vols. London, 1772.

[1] Order Book of the Council of State, Thursday, January 27, 165$\frac{3}{4}$, MS. State Paper Office.

"That the Commissioners of the Council appointed to meet with the public minister from the King of France do give a meeting unto him to-morrow, in the afternoon, at the usual place in Whitehall. And Sir Oliver Fleming, Master of the Ceremonies, is to give notice hereof unto him, and to bring him to the place of meeting." [1]

"That the members appointed to meet with the public minister from the King of France, or any two of them, be appointed to receive from the agent of the Prince of Condé what he hath to offer." [2]

"That Sir Oliver Fleming, Master of the Ceremonies, do carry to Seigneur Armerigo Salvetti, Resident with this Commonwealth from the Great Duke of Tuscany, the letter written from the Parliament to the Duke of Tuscany ; and he desired to transmit the same to the Duke, his master." [3]

"That the letter now read to the Duke of Venice be approved of and translated into Latin, and sent to the secretary of that Commonwealth now here, in order to be sent by him to Venice. And the Commissioners of the Council appointed to treat with the said secretary are to represent unto him the state of the business contained in the letter, and to press him, on behalf of the merchants concerned, that justice may be done unto them according to the desire of the Council's letter." [4]

"That Mr. Thurloe do send a letter to the Mayor of Gravesend, about sending in men to the fleet, according as hath been sent to other Justices of the Peace to that purpose." [5]

[1] Order Book of the Council of State, Friday, January 27, 1654, MS. State Paper Office.

[2] Ibid. same day.

[3] Ibid. January 14, 1655.

[4] Ibid. Wednesday, February 2, 1655.

[5] Ibid. Friday, January 28, 1655.— In the margin of this minute in the Order Book is this marginal note, in Secretary Thurloe's hand (the minute being in a clerk's hand, though a rough draft written fast) :—" Let a duplicate of the former letter be writt."

The minutes of the next meeting of the Council of
State (held on the following day, Saturday, the 29th of
January 165⅔), are all in Secretary Thurloe's hand—a hand
which persons more accustomed to read manuscript than
Tony Lumpkin might be excused for describing as a very
"cramp piece of penmanship."   At this meeting there
were eighteen members of the Council present.[1]

At this meeting of the Council the following orders were
issued :—

" That Mr. Scott be desired to make extracts of such
of the intelligence now read by him, as is fit for the
knowledge of the Generals of the fleet, and to send it unto
them." [2]

" The Council, upon consideration of the whole business
now before them concerning the fleet, do think fit and
order that all the three Generals go forth to sea with the
fleet upon this present expedition." [3]

" That the Council doth declare and order, that there be
one secretary for the three Generals of the fleet, and that
the Commissioners of the Admiralty do allow him a sufficient salary."[4]

" That Francis Harvey, late secretary to General Blake,
be not employed in the service of the fleet." [5]

" That Captain Benjamin Blake be discharged from his
present command in the fleet, and that he be not employed,
nor go forth in the service."[6]

Campbell, in his Life of Blake, places the supercession of
Benjamin Blake, the General's brother, at the attack on
Santa Cruz, in 1657, on the authority of a work entitled

[1] On Monday, 17th of the same month, there were thirty members present.— *Order Book of the Council of State,* Monday, January 17, 165⅔.
[2] *Ibid.* Saturday, January 29, 165⅔,
MS. State Paper Office.
[3] *Ibid.* same day.
[4] *Ibid.* same day.
[5] *Ibid.* same day.
[6] *Ibid.* same day.

" Lives, English and Foreign." And as Campbell has not noticed this supercession in 1653, it is evident that he has confounded this case of Benjamin Blake, in 1653, with that of General Blake's brother Humphrey at the attack. on Santa Cruz in 1657. Benjamin Blake was in the autumn of the following year (1654) appointed to the command of the *Gloucester*, in the fleet sent under Penn to the West Indies; and there are good reasons for believing that Benjamin Blake was not in his brother's fleet in 1657.[1]

On the 2nd of February 165⅔, the Council of State made the following orders :—

" Upon consideration had of what hath been offered to the Council from the Commissioners for the Admiralty, for the better manning of the fleet now going forth to sea; it is ordered, that 1,200 land-soldiers, besides officers, be sent with all expedition to the fleet; wherein care is to be taken that they be persons fitly qualified for that service, according as it is propounded by the Commissioners of the Admiralty." [2]

" That, for the rendering of the land-soldiers the more serviceable when they shall come on shipboard, it is ordered, that one sergeant and two corporals be appointed to each sixty men; and that each soldier have the pay of eighteen shillings *per mensem,* and his victuals; and the officers to have their victuals, and also their pay as when employed ashore—viz., for a sergeant, eighteen pence *per diem;* and a corporal, twelve pence." [3]

[1] Granville Penn's Memorials of Admiral Sir William Penn, vol. i. pp. 471, 472; London, 1833.

[2] Order Book of the Council of State, Wednesday night, February 2, 165⅔, MS. State Paper Office.—At this meeting there were thirteen members of the Council present, including the Lord-General Cromwell.

[3] *Ibid.* same time.—It may be inferred from this and the following order, that no officers above the rank of sergeants were to accompany the " land-soldiers " aboard ship.

" That the aforesaid officers and soldiers now appointed to go to the fleet are (when they shall come there) to perform, as far as they are able, all service as seamen; and .to be ordered in the like capacity as the rest." [1]

On Friday, the 4th of February 165⅔, the Council made the following orders :—

" That Sir John Bourchier be desired to communicate with the Lord-General the letter from Mr. Rymer of York, informing of great robberies committed by companies of armed men in that county; and to desire his Lordship from this Council to give orders that some forces may be appointed for the suppressing of them." [2]

" That the intelligence this night received, contained in three letters, concerning the state and condition of the Dutch fleet, be sent to the Generals of the fleet." [3]

" That the order made by the Commissioners of the Admiralty, concerning the entertainment of midshipmen on board the several ships for the year ensuing, in such manner as in the said order is expressed, be approved of." [4]

When the following order was made, on Wednesday, the 9th of February, there were twenty-four members present at the Council, including the Lord-General [Cromwell], Sir Henry Vane, and Colonel Sydney [Algernon Sydney] :—

" That the regiment of the Lord-General, out of which 500 men have been taken for the supplying of the fleet, be recruited to the former numbers. And that the Lord-General be desired to give order to his officers for the recruiting of his regiment accordingly." [5]

On Friday, the 11th of February, the following order was made :—

[1] Order Book of the Council of State, Wednesday night, February 2, 165⅔, MS. State Paper Office.

[2] *Ibid.* Friday, February 4, 165⅔.

[3] *Ibid.* same day.

[4] *Ibid.* same day.

[5] *Ibid.* Wednesday, February 9, 165⅔.

"That the Lord-General [Cromwell], Colonel Purefoy, Mr. Bond, Sir Henry Mildmay, Major-General Harrison, Mr. Strickland, Mr. Scot, Colonel Sydney, and Mr. Gurdon, or any four of them, be appointed a Committee, to go forth and confer with Mr. Douglas, Mr. Hamilton, Mr. Smith, and Mr. Kerr, ministers of the Scottish nation, to receive from them what they shall say by way of explanation upon what they have already spoken to the Council, concerning their engagement to live peaceably and inoffensively in Scotland, as becomes the ministers of the Gospel." [1]

The result of this conference is shown by the following minute, made at a meeting of the Council on the evening of the same day, at which there were fourteen members present, including the Lord-General, Mr. Scot, Colonel Purefoy, and Mr. Gurdon.   Sydney was not there:—

"That Mr. Robert Douglas and Mr. James Hamilton, prisoners in the Tower of London, be discharged from their imprisonment, and be at their full liberty." [2]

Now these minutes of 9th and 11th of February prove that Cromwell was acting, even so late as within a few weeks of his turning round upon them, as the (to all appearance) sincere friend and colleague of Vane, Scot, and Sydney.   They also prove that Cromwell performed his part of the business of government, as a member of the administrative council, though not as dictator or sole ruler.   If it could be shown that any attempts were made by the other members of the Council of State to deprive Cromwell of his legitimate voice and vote as a member of the Council of State, there might be some colour for what his son Henry Cromwell afterwards said to Ludlow in Ireland.

[1] Order Book of the Council of State, Friday, February 11, 1654, MS. State Paper Office.

[2] *Ibid.* Friday, at night, February 11, 1654. *Marginal note* in another hand:—"Send this warrant to the Lord Bradshaw this night, who will take care of it."

Ludlow having made this remark, that "his [Cromwell's] power [as Lord-General and member of the Council of State] was as great, and his wealth as much, as any rational man could wish to procure to himself, without raising envy and trouble," Henry Cromwell replied:— "You that are here may think he had power, but they made a very kickshaw of him at London." [1]   This, as Ludlow observes, was in fact to "acknowledge the ambition of his father." For, if the Government were to be by a Parliament and a Council of State, the Council of State being the Executive, it will be seen, from many of the minutes I have transcribed, that their Lord-General or Commander-in-Chief had no reason to complain of any undue interference with his particular department; that in all matters relating to the employment of the military forces, they acted through the Lord-General—their form of words being, " That the Lord-General be communicated with "—" That the letter be referred to the Committee, who are to confer with the Lord-General, and report their opinions to the Council,"—" That his Lordship be desired from this Council to give orders," &c.   This indeed was not a military despotism; and it seems it was a military despotism that Cromwell desired, that is, provided that he was the despot.   In fact, so far was the Council of State from making "a kickshaw of him," that they favoured him only too much.   While the pay of the rest of the army was often kept many months in arrear, we find, from such minutes as the following, that they paid special attention to the payment of " the Lord-General's regiment " —a regiment which made a return for such good treatment

---

[1] Ludlow's Memoirs, vol. ii. p. 491: 2nd edition, London, 1721.—It is astonishing, indeed, that Cromwell's conduct should ever have found defenders. Many arguments might be found in defence of Cæsar and Bonaparte, which do not apply in the least to the case of Cromwell.

by the most disgraceful act ever committed by English soldiers :—

"That a letter be written to the Committee for the Army, to desire them that the two months' pay, due to the Lord-General's regiment on Saturday last, according to the muster of 1,200 men, may be speedily paid." [1]

It appears from a petition of the Levant merchants to the Council of State that several of their ships returning from Turkey were obliged, for their security from the Dutch men-of-war in the Mediterranean, to put into harbour upon the coast of Italy, where they landed all their silks and fine goods. They were then taken into the service of the State, the English Government being in want of ships of war in the Mediterranean. For which reason, and "in regard of the present dangerousness of those seas by the Dutch," the petitioners prayed that they, bringing their goods overland to Dunquerque, might "have liberty to import them thence to England, without seizure or penalty imposed by the Act of Parliament for encouragement of navigation:" "ordered, that the case be humbly reported to the Parliament," [2] which amounted to granting the prayer of the petition.

It had now become evident that a great battle must be fought with the Dutch fleet before many days passed. On the 15th of February, 165⅔, the Council ordered :—

"That new warrants be drawn for all the messengers of

[1] Order Book of the Council of State, Thursday, February 10, 165⅔, MS. State Paper Office.—On the same day the Council ordered, "That the sum of £200 be paid out of the exigent moneys of the Council to Mr. Marchmont Needham, in consideration of his great labour and pains in the translation of Mr. Selden's book entitled 'Mare Clausum.'"—*Ibid.* same day.

[2] *Ibid.* same day.—The Order of Parliament, giving power to the Council according to the prayer of the petition, is, by a minute of March 14, referred to the Committee for Foreign Affairs.

the Council, for the enabling them to ride post, to press horses upon all roads, and also any fit vessel in any port they shall come unto, whither they are directed, in order to sail towards the fleet." [1]

On Sunday the 20th of February, the Council received a despatch from the fleet, the importance of which is shown by this order:—" That £10 be given to Mr. Symball, for his diligence in bringing a despatch from the fleet." [2]

On that Sunday there were fourteen members of the Council present, including Vane and Scot. Bradshaw was president. Cromwell was not present; neither was Sydney. Vane was on that day evidently the directing spirit of the Council, as appears from the following orders, which formed the business of that day :—

" That it be referred to the Commissioners of the Admiralty to speak with the Lord-General [Cromwell], concerning putting aboard the fleet 1,200 or 1,500 land-soldiers, upon the same terms as the other land-soldiers were sent, and to give orders therein accordingly." [3]

" That a letter be written to the Commissioners of the Navy, to let them know the necessity of having the ships now fitting forth completely ready by the 1st of March; and, therefore, that they take care of supplying them with all things necessary, and especially with men." [4]

On the following day, Monday, the 21st of February, 165¾, an order was made :—

" That the Council do sit to-morrow morning at 8 of the

[1] Order Book of the Council of State, Tuesday, February 15, 165¾, MS. State Paper Office.

[2] Ibid. Sunday, February 20, 165¾.— On March 2, there is another order respecting the payment of this messenger: " That the sum of £20 be paid to Henry Symball, messenger, in pursuance of an Order of Parliament, for bringing the letter from the Generals of the fleet, containing an account of the late action against the Dutch." —Ibid. Wednesday, March 2, 165¾.

[3] Ibid. same day.

[4] Ibid. same day.

clock; and that Mr. Thurloe do by that time make extracts of the intelligence sent to the Council, of the late fight with the Dutch, in order to report the same to the Parliament." [1]

On Tuesday, the 22nd of February, the following orders were made :—

" That the sum of £5 be paid to Edward Proctor, waterman, in consideration of his bringing a pacquet of good news to the Commissioners for the Admiralty." [2]

" That it be recommended to the Commissioners for the Admiralty to take care that physicians and chirurgeons may be forthwith despatched to Dover and Portsmouth, to take care of the sick and wounded men there." [3]

" That Sir Henry Vane do humbly acquaint the Parliament with the intelligence come concerning the late engagement with the Dutch." [4]

" That Sir Henry Vane do humbly move the Parliament to take into consideration the families of such as have been slain in the engagement with the Dutch, some whereof are already known, and further particulars expected every hour." [5]

On the 18th, the 19th, and the 20th of February, 165⅔, was fought the greatest battle that had yet been fought between the English and the Dutch fleets, which were about equal in the number of ships, each fleet consisting of about 80 line-of-battle ships and frigates. The best and largest ships of the two nations, commanded by the best admirals that the world had ever seen—on the Dutch side by Tromp, De Ruyter, Evertz, Floritz, De Wilde, on the English side by Blake, Deane, Penn, Lawson—were engaged. On board of the English fleet were also many

---

[1] Order Book of the Council of State, Monday, February 21, 165⅔, MS. State Paper Office.

[2] *Ibid.* Tuesday, February 22, 165⅔.

[3] *Ibid.* same day.

[4] *Ibid.* same day.

[5] *Ibid.* same day.

hundreds of the veteran soldiers of the Parliamentary army, men who had passed through a thousand dangers, and had been victorious in a hundred battles and sieges.

Early in the morning of the 18th of February, the English fleet being in that part of the English Channel between the Isle of Portland and Cape de la Hogue, and some five leagues distant from the English shore, the English admirals descried the Dutch fleet, consisting—" as we then judged," say the English admirals[1] in their letter to the Speaker, " and are since informed by some of their own number—of 80, all men-of-war, and some 200 [2] merchantmen," a league and a half to windward of the weathermost of their ships, and two or three leagues to windward of most of the English fleet.

Blake's ship, the *Triumph*, with the *Fairfax* (Rear-Admiral Lawson), the *Speaker* (Vice-Admiral Penn), and about twenty more ships, being nearest to the Dutch, Tromp "might probably," says the despatch of the English admirals, " if he had pleased to have kept the wind, have gone away with his whole fleet, and we had not been able to have reached him with our main body, only with a few frigates, our best sailers, which had not been likely to have done much upon them." [3]   But Tromp, seeing that the main body of the English fleet was about a league and

[1] Blake, Deane, and Monk to the Speaker, February 27, 165⅔, in Old Parliamentary History, vol. xx. p. 116.

[2] The Dutch writer of the " Life of Cornelius Van Tromp" states the merchantmen at 250. He says : " Lieutenant-Admiral Tromp, after he had cruised some time in the Channel, to wait for the ships that were to come from Holland, arrived, at the beginning of February, near the isle of Rhée, to convoy 250 merchant-ships

that were there assembled from divers parts of Europe ; and after having staid there seven days, he set out with that fleet to conduct them home to their own country. But as he came near Portland, he descried the English fleet under the command of Blake, upon which he stood directly towards them."—*Life of Cornelius Van Tromp*, p. 89.

[3] Blake, Deane, and Monk to the Speaker, February 27, 165⅔.

a half distant, at once perceived the advantage this presented to him, of attacking with a greatly superior force these twenty-three ships, forming hardly more than a fourth part of the English fleet. Accordingly, he put all his merchantmen to windward, and ordered them to stay there—" as some that we have taken have since informed us," say the English admirals[1]—" and himself, with his body of men-of-war, drew down upon us that were the weathermost ships, when we were in a short time engaged."

Nothing could more strikingly manifest the extraordinary fighting qualities of the Englishmen who manned those twenty-three ships, than the fact that those ships fought the whole Dutch fleet for two hours,[2] without that result which, under such circumstances, Lord Rodney pronounced inevitable, when he said that the officer who brings the whole fleet under his command to attack half or part of the enemy, will be sure of defeating the enemy and taking the part attacked. Tromp, indeed, did take several of the English ships in this first encounter. The English admirals, in their despatch to the Speaker, mention three by name, "and some other ships, but," they add, " we repossessed them again."

But if the Dutch had pretty hard work even with those twenty-three ships, as the rest of the English fleet came up, and " had got so far ahead, that, by tacking, they could weather the greatest part of the Dutch fleet," Tromp perceived that the tables were turned against him, and,

---

[1] Blake, Deane, and Monk to the Speaker, February 27, 165⅝.

[2] The want of clearness in the despatch might make it, at first sight, appear that these twenty-three ships fought the whole Dutch fleet till 4 o'clock in the afternoon. But a sentence brought in afterwards throws a different light on the matter : "The leewardmost part of our ships continued fighting till night separated them, being engaged *within two hours* as soon as we."

accordingly, "he tacked likewise, and those with him, and left us."[1]

On the 19th of February, as soon as it was day, the English fleet made what sail they could after the Dutch, but, it being calm, the main body of the English could not get up with the Dutch till 2 o'clock. The two fleets then fought till night parted them. The English this day took and destroyed five of the Dutch men-of-war. "The Dutch fleet steered up the Channel with their lights abroad; we followed; the wind at WNW., a fine little gale all night."[2]

The account of the English admirals agrees in the main points with the description given by foreigners of this battle. Paul Hoste, in his work on Naval Evolutions, says that in this battle, which he calls the "Combat de Portland," the two fleets met in sight of Portland; that the Dutch had the wind; that Tromp, though it appeared that he ought to avoid a battle in which he should hazard his convoy of 200 merchantmen, yet, considering that if the wind should change, he would be obliged to fight with less advantage, resolved to bear down on the enemy, after having placed his convoy to windward; that the battle on the first day was very sanguinary, many ships being disabled, sunk, or fired; that nothing was able to separate two enemies so furiously excited, but the darkness of the night, during which both parties prepared themselves to renew the combat, which had remained undecided. Hoste then says, that on the second day, Admiral Tromp found himself exceedingly perplexed; and, after many deliberations, he determined to retreat.[3]

---

[1] Blake, Deane, and Monk to the Speaker, February 27,165⅔.

[2] *Ibid.*

[3] Art des Armées Navales; ou Traité des Evolutions Navales. Par le Père Paul Hoste, Professeur de Mathématiques dans le Séminaire Royale de Toulon. A Lyon. Fol. 1696 and 1727, p. 90. Granville Penn, vol. i. pp. 481_484.

Accordingly, on the third day, Tromp drew up his fleet in the form of a half-moon or semicircle; and, as a hen covers her chickens with her wings, the Dutch admiral put his convoy of 200 merchantmen richly laden in the middle—that is, within the semicircle composed of his men-of-war, his own ship occupying the post of danger and honour; for his own ship formed to windward the extreme point of the semicircle, and the rest of his fleet extended on each side to form the segments of the semicircle which covered the convoy. In this order he retreated with the wind astern, firing to the right and left on all the English ships that approached to insult his wings. Tromp continued to fight till night, which gave him time to renew his order of retreat; and Hoste says, that though pursued the following day by the English, he entered his ports " with the glory of having, by his valour and skill, preserved for his country a rich convoy which was on the point of becoming a prey of the enemy."

How far this last statement is correct, may be judged by the despatch of the English admirals, which thus proceeds :—

"On the 20th, about nine in the morning, we fell close in with them, with some fine great ships, and all the frigates of strength, though very many could not come up that day. And seeing their men-of-war somewhat weakened, we sent smaller frigates, and ships of less force, that could get up amongst the merchantmen, which put their whole body to a very great trouble, so that many of them and their men-of-war began to break off from their main body; and towards evening we pressed so hard upon them, that they turned their merchantmen out of their fleet upon us (as is conceived), for a bait; but we gave strict order, that none of our ships that could get up to their men-of-war, and had force, should meddle with any merchantmen, but leave them to the rear. We continued still fighting with them until the dusk of the evening, by which time we were some three-and-a-half leagues off Blackness,[1] in France (four leagues W. from Calais), the wind at N.W.; we steering directly for the point of land, having the wind of the Dutch fleet. So that if it had pleased the Lord, in His wise providence, who sets bounds to the sea, and over-rules the ways and actions of men, that it had been but three hours longer to-night, we had probably made an interposition between them and home; whereby they might have been obliged to have made their way through us with their men-of-war, which at this time were not thirty-five, as we could count—the rest being destroyed or dispersed. The merchantmen, also, must have been necessitated to have run ashore, or fallen into our hands; which, as we conceive, the Dutch admiral being sensible of, just as it was dark, bore directly in upon the shore, where, it is supposed, he anchored ; the tide of ebb being then come, which was a leewardly tide. We consulted with our pilots, and men knowing those coasts, what it was possible for the enemy to do ? Whose opinions were, that he could not weather the French shore, as the tide and wind then was, to get home; and that we must likewise anchor, or we could not be able to carry it about the flats of the Somme; whereupon we anchored, Blackness being N.E. and by E., three leagues from us.

"This night being very dark, and blowing hard, the Dutch got away from us; so that, in the morning of the 21st, we could not discover one ship more than our own, which were betwixt forty and fifty, the rest being scattered,

---

[1] Cap Gris Nez, opposite to Dungeness.

and as many prizes as made up sixty in all.   We spent all this night and day, while [till] twelve o'clock, in fitting of our ships, masts, and sails, for we were not capable to stir till they were repaired; at which time, being a windward tide, and the Dutch fleet gone, we weighed and stood over to the English shore, fearing to stay longer upon the coast, being a lee-shore."

The despatch thus concludes :—

"Thus you see how it hath pleased the Lord to deal with us, poor unworthy instruments, employed in this late transaction; wherein He hath delivered into our hands some seventeen or eighteen of their ships of war, which have been by your fleet (without the loss of any one. ship save the *Sampson*) taken and destroyed; besides merchant-men, whose numbers we know not, they being scattered to several ports.

"We have many men wounded, and divers, both of honesty and worth, slain.

(Subscribed)   ROBERT BLAKE,
RICHARD DEANE,
GEORGE MONK."

"P.S.—Several of the Dutch are driven ashore in France, one without any men at all in her." [1]

In this Battle of Portland, Blake himself was wounded, some accounts say severely, others slightly.   Lord Leicester in his Journal says, "General Blake was hurt in the thigh with a crossbow-shot." [2]   Another cotemporary account says, "General Blake was slightly wounded in the neck at Portland fight." [3]   Lord Leicester says, "Van

---

[1] Blake, Deane, and Monk to the Speaker, aboard the *Triumph* in Stokes Bay, February 27, 1653, in Old Parl. Hist. vol. xx. p. 116 *et seq.*

[2] Sydney Papers, edited by R. W. Blencowe, p. 139 : London, 1825.

[3] Granville Penn, vol. ii. p. 615, Appendix M.

Tromp got home into Holland with some of his men-of-war, leaving all his merchants which he was to convoy, many whereof fell daily into the hands of the English. It is said the Hollanders lost 4,000 men, the English not above 400." [1] But the loss on both sides was probably much greater than this. In another letter the General of the fleet says, " The loss on our side is greater than was expected, for we have lost many precious commanders, besides many wounded—some having lost their legs, and others their arms." Among the slain were Captains Ball, Mildmay, and Barker, " with our secretary Mr. Sparrow, whose deaths are much lamented." [2]

On the 24th of February, the Council of State ordered a letter of thanks to be written to the Generals of the fleet. [3]

Whatever was the nature or severity of Blake's wound, it would appear that soon after the battle he was suffering from an illness which alarmed the Council of State; for on Sunday, the 6th of March, the Order Book contains the following minute, which is the only minute made on that day. The minute is headed, " Lord's Day, 6th March, 165$\frac{2}{3}$," and is as follows: " Whereas it is just now signified to the Council, that General Blake is fallen very ill at Portsmouth, It is ordered that Colonel Walton and Mr. Scot be desired to speak with Dr. Pridean and Dr. Bates; and to desire them, in the name of the Council, to take a journey to Portsmouth to contribute their advice and assistance for the restoring of him to health again, if the Lord please; and to desire them to go away this night, to which end the Council have given order for a coach

<hr/>

[1] Sydney Papers, p. 139 : London, 1825.

[2] King's Pamphlets, No. 555, Brit. Mus. Granville Penn, vol. i. pp. 479,

480, 481.

[3] Order Book of the Council of State, Thursday, February 24, 165$\frac{2}{3}$, MS. State Paper Office.

and six horses to be made ready, and a messenger to attend them for defraying the charge of their journey." [1]

On Monday, the 14th of March, there is the following order relating to the same matter: " That fifty pounds apiece be paid, out of the exigent moneys of the Council, to Dr. Pridean and Dr. Bates, in consideration of their pains in their journey to visit General Blake at Portsmouth, by the order and at the desire of the Council." [2]

On Wednesday the 16th of March, the Council made the following order, with a view to remedy the want of men to man the fleet, arising from the " great number of private men-of-war," to which Blake had called their attention in his despatch of December 1, 1652, quoted in a former page :—

" That a letter be written to the Generals of the fleet, to let them know that the Council have put a stop to the granting of any more commissions for private men-of-war, unless they shall be certified of the supply of the fleet with men; and do give power unto them, for the speedy manning of the fleet, to take men out of the private men-of-war as they shall meet with them, and as they shall find they shall stand in need of them." [3]

To enable the reader to judge of the effect of this great battle at the time, I will quote a passage from a cotemporary Dutch writer, whose efforts to prove that the Hollanders " had *not much less right* to pretend to the victory than their enemies," only confirm the truth of the English claim to the victory :—" The success of this battle made so great a noise at London, that they made no difficulty to publish abroad that Tromp, Evertz, and De Ruyter were totally routed, and that 100 merchant-ships,

---

[1] Order Book of the Council of State, Lord's Day, March 6, 165⅞, MS. State Paper Office.

[2] *Ibid.* Monday, March 14, 165⅞.

[3] *Ibid.* Wednesday, March 16, 165⅞.

and fifty men-of-war, of the Dutch were taken or sunk.
Nay, and this noise was echoed over all Europe, and was
carried into France, Sweedland, Denmark; and to render
what they affected to speak of it the more credible, the
Parliament appointed an extraordinary thanksgiving-day
to be kept on that occasion. And what seemed fully to
authorise so great a triumph, and exalt the glory of Blake,
was, that the prisoners were led in a drove to Canterbury,
under the guard of a troop of horse; and that in all the
places through which they passed, they rang the bells,
thereby to make that defeat to appear the more signal and
incontestable; though the Dutch at the same time no less
confidently *pretended* " [this word "pretended," used by a
Dutch writer, is very significant] " that the action did not
pass *altogether so much* to the advantage of the English,
that they ought to have attributed to themselves *all* the
glory of it, since, say they" [*i.e.* the Dutch], " excepting
the merchant-ships that fell into their hands, the Hollanders
had not much less right to pretend to the victory than
their enemies." [1]

The English Royalist party rejoiced at any symptom
of disaster to the Parliament of England, and affected to
disbelieve their successes. Hyde wrote thus, on the
20th of March, 1653, to Secretary Nicholas in Holland :
"We do here (Paris), notwithstanding all their brags
in England of their victory, believe the Dutch to have
absolutely the best of it." And this patriotic Englishman's joy was unbounded because Blake was unable with
thirty-seven ships, some of them commanded by captains
who were traitors to the Parliament, to contend successfully
against a Dutch fleet of ninety-five ships. On the 14th of
December, 1652, he thus wrote to Nicholas : "We are in

---

[1] Life of Cornelius Van Tromp, pp. 104, 105: London, 1697.

great hope that this notable fight at sea, in which the Hollanders have so thoroughly banged the rebels, will make a great alteration in the counsels with you and here. It is the first signal overthrow those devilish rebels have sustained, either at sea or land; and therefore must make a deep impression upon the spirits of the common people of England, who have hitherto been transported by their incredible successes." Hyde hoped to bring back by foreign arms the Stuarts, and himself with them, upon the people of England. But all the naval and military power of all the world would have been powerless to do that, but for the " self in the highest " policy of Cromwell.

The fame of the English admiral filled all the world. The testimony of his friend and cotemporary, Algernon Sydney, is fully borne out by that of his enemy and, cotemporary, Clarendon, and confirmed by the verdict in aftertimes of men most hostile to his cause—of Samuel Johnson and David Hume. "The reputation and power of our nation," says Algernon Sydney, " rose to a greater height than when we possessed the better half of France, and the Kings of France and Scotland were our prisoners. All the states, kings, and potentates of Europe most respectfully, not to say submissively, sought our friendship : and Rome was more afraid of Blake, and his fleet, than they had been of the great King of Sweden, when he was ready to invade Italy with a hundred thousand men."[1] Even according

---

[1] Algernon Sydney on Government, chap. ii. sect. 28.—Algernon Sydney was a member of the Council of State when Blake fought the great Battle of Portland. A letter in Thurloe, after giving an account of the subsequent great battle in June, thus proceeds: " The very noise of the guns, which was heard very plain for three days together in some of these parts (from Dunkirk to Ostend), hath struck a very great terror into most hearts; insomuch, that the most judicious amongst them do begin to consider, in case these two mighty potentates should join together, what would become of the kings of the earth. Doubtless Babylon is upon her fall ! "—*Thurloe*, vol. i. pp. 272, 273.

to the testimony of the Dutch themselves, "the noise of this battle was echoed over all Europe, and was carried into France, Sweden, Denmark." [1]

The exploits of Fairfax and Cromwell sink into insignificance beside those of Blake. Indeed, we should find it difficult to discover any equal portion of the lives of the greatest names in war—of Nelson, of Hannibal, of Cæsar, of Frederic, of Napoleon—so full of great achievements as this short period, perhaps the most brilliant in the history of England. Within the space of ten months, besides minor exploits, such as the destruction of the French fleet under the Duke of Vendôme, Blake fought four great pitched battles against the greatest naval armaments commanded by the greatest admirals the world had ever seen. Three of these battles he won; the defeat in the fourth battle, where Blake maintained for many hours with thirty-seven ships a fight against ninety-five, commanded by Tromp, tended rather to raise than lower his naval renown. [2]

[1] Life of Cornelius Van Tromp, p. 104.

[2] In reference to the opinion that, with such a disproportion of force, as thirty-seven ships to ninety-five or one hundred, Blake ought to have declined an engagement, Dr. Johnson says: "We must then admit, amidst our eulogies and applauses, that the great, the wise, and the valiant Blake was once betrayed to an inconsiderate and desperate enterprise by the resistless ardour of his own spirit, and a noble jealousy for the honour of his country." —*Life of Blake, Johnson's Works,* vol. xii. p. 52. Dr. Johnson, in reference to the remark of Rapin that the Dutch and Spaniards sustained a great loss of ships, money, men, and merchandise, while the English gained nothing but glory, says truly, "As if he that increases the military reputation of a people did not increase their power, and he that weakens his enemy in effect strengthens himself."—*Ibid.* vol. xii. p. 59.

CHAPTER XVI.

" *Vexilla regis prodeunt inferni* verso di noi : " [1] the Protector's colours loom in the distance, spread out by the wind, and bearing, in great golden characters, the word Emmanuel ! That one word upon that flag was indeed a talisman more potent, an ensign more formidable, a symbol of success and victory more sure, more unvarying, more infallible, than the image of any beast or bird, ancient or modern—lion, tiger, leopard, or eagle, whether with two heads or one. For there have been times when the most fortunate and victorious of those have met with reverse and disaster. But who can tell the time when that banner of Emmanuel was borne backward in battle, and beheld either in captivity or flight ? [2] God with us ! [3] What a history of

[1] Dante's *Inferno*, canto xxxiv. vv. 1, 2.

[2] It is to be observed that those troops lost their character of invincibility after Cromwell had expelled the Parliament. General Ludlow thus accounts for the result of the expedition against Hispaniola : " Those very men, who, when they fought for the liberties of their country, had performed wonders, having now engaged to support the late-erected tyranny, disgracefully fled when there was none to pursue them."—*Ludlow's Me-*moirs, vol. ii. p. 496: 2nd edition, London, 1721.

[3] " That the inscriptions which are to be put on the coin of England shall be written in the English tongue. That the inscriptions shall be these : viz., on the side on which the English arms do stand alone, this, THE COMMONWEALTH OF ENGLAND ; on the other side, which bears the arms of England and Ireland, GOD WITH US."—*Order Book of the Council of State*, April 24, 1649, MS. State Paper Office.

resistless energy—of toils endured, of dangers encountered, of fields fought and won, of towns taken by assault, of hostile armies annihilated—is written in these three magic words! More than sixty years after the great leader of those who had marched under those colours had fought his last fight, and been carried to his grave—not indeed his last resting-place, for those who came after him were not ashamed to violate even the sanctities of the tomb, and to do outrage and insult to the bones of the dead enemy before whose living face they had so often fled—a very ancient laird declared to an English officer of engineers, quartered at Inverness, that "Oliver's colours were so strongly impressed on his memory, that he thought he then saw them spread out by the wind, with the word Emmanuel (God with us) upon them, in very large golden characters." [1]

No wonder that a halo should encircle the name of the chief of those who had carried those colours to so many victories, and should so dazzle the imagination as to pervert the judgment. Nevertheless, though they are not to be met with in any great abundance, there are still men in

[1] "Oliver had 1,200 men in and near this citadel [Inverness], under the command of one Colonel Fitz, who had been a tailor, as I have been informed by a very ancient laird, who said he remembered every remarkable passage which happened at that time, and, most especially, Oliver's colours, which were so strongly impressed on his memory, that he thought he then saw them spread out by the wind, with the word Emmanuel (God with us) upon them, in very large golden characters."—*Burt's Letters from the North of Scotland*, vol. i. p. 217: now edition: London, 1815. Sir Walter Scott, in one of his notes to his edition of Dryden's Works (vol. ix. p. 20), in which he refers to the above passage, and to the writer of it as "an officer of engineers quartered at Inverness shortly after 1720," says: "The garrisons established by Cromwell upon the skirts and in the passes of the Highlands, restrained the predatory clans, and taught them, in no gentle manner, that respect for the property of their Lowland neighbours, which their lawful monarchs had vainly endeavoured to inculcate."

the world whose words can be relied on, whose idol is not " self in the highest," and who (to borrow the words inscribed on the tomb of one known to me in days long gone by), sustain the honour of their country by deeds of bravery and devotion, and the honour of human nature by an unselfish life, and by benevolence never weary of well-doing.

There were such men then, though the number of them might not be great. While the worshippers of its destroyer shower reproaches upon the broken faction, others can remember that it contained men who were willing to die, and who did die, for that cause which, in their last words on the scaffold, they called " a cause not to be repented of," [1] " a cause which gave life in death to all the owners of it and sufferers for it." [2] When the members of a legislature have been expelled from their House by armed men, even though they have not been sent off in the felon's van, the worshippers of success in all its shapes step forward, and pour forth the vials of their scorn upon " such a shattered thing; " [3] and hang it up on the gibbet of their eloquence as an object for the contempt and derision of mankind. Then the man who, when " faith was broken and somewhat else," [4] turns suddenly round upon his ancient friends and comrades, and to-day concentrates in his single person all those powers of sovereignty which but yesterday had been theirs, becomes a man-god, with slaves for worshippers; and they become " a small faction of fanatical egotists, uniting to the love of power and the fanaticism of opinions all the ridicule of helplessness, and the infatuation of pretended legitimacy." `Is it really so, O Devilsdust! worshipper of the evil spirit, and kneeler

[1] The last words of Thomas Scot.
[2] Some of the last words of Sir Henry Vane.
[3] Words also of Thomas Scot.
[4] Words of Thomas Scot.

before the burning throne? Something has been seen already from those men's acts and deeds in answer to this question. Let us now look a little farther, and try if we can see anything more.

I have said in a former page [1] that Cromwell " gradually enveloped the men who sat and talked at Westminster in net within net, like so many flies in the widespread and powerful web of a huge and active spider." I will now show, on evidence which has never been produced before, that I did not use these words without sufficient authority. The following minute, made the very day after Cromwell's meeting with some members of Parliament and chief officers of the army at the Speaker's house, namely on Thursday, the 11th of December, 1651, looms like the terrible shadow of the future, and shows that Cromwell was beginning then to draw his nets closer around his prey :—

" That it be referred to the Committee for the Affairs of Ireland and Scotland, to consider *where quarters are to be had for the regiment of foot of the Lord-General, which is ordered to the guard of the Parliament*; and to take care that the captain of the guard may be spoken to, that full and sufficient guards may be placed in Whitehall (especially in the night), upon all the gates entering into the House, and upon most of the principal passages within the House." [2]

Now let it be observed, that all the time, several years, that Fairfax was Lord-General, and even all the time that Cromwell was Lord-General—he succeeded Fairfax on the 26th of June, 1650—there had been discovered no need for appointing the Lord-General's own regiment of foot as

---

[1] Vol. I. p. 160.   State, Thursday, December 11, 1651,

[2] Order Book of the Council of MS. State Paper Office.

the guard of the Parliament.   There was no need for the
change now.   The Parliament and the Council of State
had been very sufficiently guarded hitherto by Colonel
Berkstead's regiment.   And setting the Lord-General
Cromwell's regiment of foot to guard the Parliament, was
neither more nor less than setting the wolf to guard the
sheep.   But this was not all.   On the 25th of the same
month, just a fortnight after the order last quoted, the
following order was made :—

" That twelve pence a day be allowed to the soldiers of
the two regiments appointed for the guards of the Parliament and city, to be paid out of the Lord-General's
contingencies." [1]

It here becomes necessary to ascertain, as far as possible,
the pay of the army of the Parliament :—

" Die Sabbati, Januarii 11°, 1644.—The House, according to the order yesterday made, took into consideration their armies, and proceeded first into the consideration
of the New Model."

        *   *   *   *   *   *

" Resolved &c. that each trooper shall receive 2s. per diem
for his entertainment." [2]

Neither the dragoons' nor the foot-soldiers' pay is mentioned.   But it may be inferred, from a minute of the
Council of State of the 11th of May 1649, which states
" that three private soldiers of Colonel Pride's regiment
were taken to attend Dr. Dorislaus to Holland, and agreement made they should each of them have 5s. per week,
besides a gratuity at their return," [3] that the pay of the
foot-soldiers was about 6d. a day.   For it may be con-

---

[1] Order Book of the Council of State,
Thursday, December 25, 1651, MS.
State Paper Office.

[2] Commons' Journals, Die Sabbati,

Januarii 11°, 1644.

[3] Order Book of the Council of
State, May 11, 1649, MS. State Paper
Office.

cluded that they would receive a little more than their usual pay when employed on this extraordinary service; and 1s. 6d. a week, the difference between 3s. 6d. a week and the 5s. a week above mentioned, may be taken as an addition to their pay as foot-soldiers.

Besides this pay, the troops of the Parliament were allowed money to pay for their quarters, at the rate, according to many minutes in the Order Book of the Council of State, of 6d. a day for each foot-soldier, and 1s. a day for each horse-soldier. These allowances are with special reference to the troops ordered for transportation to Ireland in 1649, " during the stay at the waterside for wind and weather;"[1] and are somewhat higher than those in the following order of the House of 29th June of the same year:—" Ordered, that this House doth approve of what the General hath done in allowing 2s. 6d. a week to each soldier and non-commissioned officer of foot, and the train of artillery, and 3s. 8d. the week to the horse, over and above the established pay, in consideration of billet-money, during such time as they did quarter within the city of London and Westminster, and the parts adjacent."[2]

It would appear, however, from the following minute, that about the beginning of the year 1652, the pay of the foot was 10d. a day; and that the 1s. a day allowed by the minute of December 25, 1651, to the two regiments appointed for the guard of the Parliament, was not double the pay of the other regiments of foot, but only 2d. a day more :—

" That 2d. per diem be added to the pay of the inferior officers and soldiers of the two regiments appointed for

[1] Order Book of the Council of State, May 29, 1649, MS. State Paper Office. Ibid. August 25, 1649. Ibid.
March 27, 1649.
[2] Commons' Journals, Die Veneris, Junii 29, 1649.

the guard of the Parliament and city, more than is allowed to the rest of the army; and that it be paid out of the Lord-General's contingencies, according to their several musters, and to begin from the 25th of December last inclusive." [1]

This additional 2*d.* a day, "to be paid out of the Lord-General's contingencies," would to the soldiers have the appearance of being paid out of Cromwell's own pocket. This, in fact, amounted to giving him a sort of Prætorian Guard. It will be seen that the two following minutes, made on the 25th of December, 1651, are to the same purpose and effect :—

"That it be especially recommended to the Committee of Parliament for disposal of the Commonwealth's houses, to cause all necessary repairs to be made at James's for the convenient quartering and accommodation of the soldiers of both regiments appointed for the guard of the Parliament and city, so as that the three companies at Syon College may be also brought to James's, and that quarter at Syon College quitted." [2]

"That £50 be paid unto Major Wiggan and Major Allen upon accompt, for fire and candles for the several guards kept by the two regiments about Whitehall, James's, and the city, and that this money be paid out of the Lord-General's contingencies." [3]

[1] Order Book of the Council of State, Tuesday, January 6, 165½, MS. State Paper Office.

[2] *Ibid.* December 25, 1651.

[3] *Ibid.* same day.—On November 4, 1652, the Council ordered, "That it be referred to the Committee for Irish and Scottish Affairs, to consider of and appoint a fit proportion of match, powder, and bullets for the use of the Lord-General's regiment for the present, and likewise to consider how they may be speedily furnished with beds; and also how they may be constantly supplied for the future with a fitting proportion of ammunition, and have some of their musquets changed for snaphances." — *Ibid.* Thursday, November 4, 1652. The body of musketeers selected by Cromwell to turn out the members of the Parliament would naturally be those supplied by

The Lord-General's regiments were just as much entitled, if they were entitled at all, to higher pay than the other regiments of the Parliament, when Fairfax was Lord-General, as when Cromwell was Lord-General. And there was no more reason for paying their extra pay and their extra accommodation and conveniences out of the Lord-General's contingencies when Cromwell was Lord General, than when Fairfax was Lord-General; at least, no more reason than this, that Fairfax was a man of whom it has been said:

> " He might have been a king,
> But that he understood
>   How much it was a meaner thing
>   To be unjustly great, than honourably good."[1]

If any man ever lived whose intellectual supremacy might so dazzle us as to make us submit without repining to a despotism, that man was Julius Cæsar. But let us look at the result. The reign of Julius Cæsar himself was short; but it prepared the way for the long reign of his great-nephew Augustus, who, though far from possessing the dazzling intellectual qualities of Julius, had still sufficient ability to govern in such a manner, that Rome enjoyed more quiet under his rule than it had done for ages; so that his rule might be considered as that sort of government called a good despotism. But the effect was to change altogether the Roman character. Before that time the Romans might be on the whole bad men. But yet they were men; not slaves—creatures, half-fiend and half-baboon; men with the courage and enterprise,

those members with snaphances—that is, with flintlock instead of matchlock muskets. Well might John Lilburne say, "Alas, poor fools! we were merely cheated and cozened."—See Vol. I. p. 158.

[1] Poem on the death of the Lord Fairfax, by George Duke of Buckingham, in vol. i. p. 135 &c. of the Works of His Grace George Villiers, late Duke of Buckingham: 2 vols. 3rd edition, London, 1715.

with the mental energy and bodily activity, of statesmen-soldiers; for it makes a vast difference, when a man's education comprehends oratory as well as military science, and when oratory is left out. The very cultivation of oratory has a twofold significance. On the part of the man who cultivates it, it implies a cultivation of the higher, though not of the highest, mental faculties. And on the part of the men to whom it is intended to be applied, it implies a Government in which there is still a certain portion of freedom. Julius Cæsar himself studied oratory under the same Greek master as Cicero; and in some of Cicero's greatest causes, he acted as that great orator's junior counsel. This education forms a set of men very different from the mere drill-sergeants and barrack-masters of a military despotism, where one man undertakes to do all the thinking of all the community, that is to have any practical result, and where real and vigorous thinking—the thinking which, to borrow the words of Mr. John Stuart Mill, " ascertains truths instead of dreaming dreams "—is totally prohibited.

We have seen an attempt recently made to prove that despots are necessary to " the progress of humanity." What sort of progress that is, is very visibly written in the records of what the Romans were before and after the Empire. In short, to quote a great modern writer, " a good despotism is an altogether false ideal, which practically (except as a means to some temporary purpose) becomes the most senseless and dangerous of chimeras. Evil for evil, a good despotism, in a country at all advanced in civilisation, is more noxious than a bad one; for it is far more relaxing and enervating to the thoughts, feelings, and energies of the people. The despotism of Augustus prepared the Romans for Tiberius. If the whole tone of their character had not first been prostrated by nearly two generations of that mild slavery, they would probably have had spirit enough left to rebel against the more odious one." [1]

The records of crime prove that when any crime (a murder, for instance, of unusual atrocity) has been committed, there is a tendency observed to a repetition of that crime. The wretched criminal's sudden celebrity appears to act on the minds of certain persons, so as to produce in them an insane desire of imitating the criminal acts which have created such a public interest. But there are certain crimes, which have relation, not to taking away the life of an individual, but to crushing out the life of a whole nation, that appear to be attended with consequences similar to, but infinitely more fatal than, those which follow the crime of a common assassin. Then the great criminal becomes a hero in the eyes of some, on the ground of his having substituted repose—the repose of death—for anarchy; in the eyes of others, on the mere ground of his force of character, his courage, his energy, and his strength of will. But these are but a small part of the disastrous consequences of the success of great criminals.

A great crime, successfully committed by a great man, has consequences that last for ages; and of such great crimes none, perhaps, produced more fatal consequences than that of Cromwell. The world saw a man, who had raised himself to supreme power by a breach of the most solemn engagements, hold himself up as the elect of God. When his old comrades heard this man tell them, as he did in his speeches—and it was almost all that was intelligible in those emanations of the kingdom of darkness—

---

[1] Considerations on Representative Government, by John Stuart Mill: London, 1861, p. 53.

that he had a key to unlock the gates of heaven, as well
as a sword to command the strongholds of the earth; that
the Everlasting and Omnipotent had adopted him as His
favourite; that the bowing the knee to him, Oliver Cromwell, was an "owning of Jesus Christ;" that he, the
Judas of his party, was to reign with Christ in heaven,
after he had betrayed the men who trusted him on earth:
and when they saw that everything prospered with him—
that he was an overmatch for those of his party who, like
Blake and Ireton, were too highminded to make use of
packed cards and loaded dice—can we wonder that a re-
vulsion took place in the minds of men?—that, if from the
apotheosis of James Stuart men sought refuge in Puritanism, and in fighting for religion and liberty, from the
apotheosis of Oliver Cromwell they should seek refuge in
slavery, profligacy, and atheism or devil-worship, which is
worse?

There is something intensely revolting in this apotheosis
of a man, who can be proved to have been the cause of
deep disgrace and innumerable evils to the English nation;
to that nation which, after having fought for its rights
and liberties as no other nation had ever fought, was, as a
consequence of the usurpation of Cromwell, again subjected to the tyranny of the Stuarts; and then to the
disgrace of having to be delivered from that tyranny by
the sword of a Dutchman.

I have said in a former page,[1] that this Parliament were
most able and energetic administrators; but that, "if they
had possessed that higher statesmanship which can employ
a comprehensive survey of the past in a wise divination
of the future, they might have seen clearly enough what
the end would be." The situation, indeed, in which they

---

[1] See Vol. I. of this History, p. 216.

stood was not a common situation. It was one of rare occurrence ; and hundreds, nay thousands, of years might not present its exact parallel. Yet there was a situation, with which all of them were more or less˙ acquainted, and which, though separated from them by near two thousand years of time, as well as by distance of place and difference in race, religion, and laws, might, if deeply pondered on and closely studied, have been of some use to them.

Gunpowder and steam may change the aspect of war. But man remains unchanged—the same moral and political agent that he was when there was neither steam nor gunpowder. The English Parliament of the year 1651 made nearly the same blunder, in regard to Cromwell, that the Roman Senate had made, 1,700 years before, in regard to Julius Cæsar. The Roman Senate committed several illegal acts, with the view of protecting themselves by keeping down Cæsar. But these acts only increased Cæsar's chances, and diminished their own. The capital blunder of the English Parliament was their persistence in not dissolving themselves. They thus put the most powerful weapon into Cromwell's hands against themselves.

In speaking of this reluctance of the Parliament to put an end to their sitting, it ought, in strict accuracy, to be noted that there were two parties in the Parliament, opposed to each other on this point. We have seen in a former chapter,[1] that in one of the divisions on the 14th of November 1651, on this subject, there was a minority of 46 to 50, in the other of 47 to 49, against entertaining the question at all of putting an end to their sitting. In both divisions Cromwell was one of the tellers for the majority for fixing a time for their dissolution. And

---

[1] Chapter XII.

this important fact gives Cromwell some solid ground
for his assertion, that there was a " corrupt party " in
the House who wished to perpetuate themselves ; and, as
will be easily seen, it greatly complicates the question
we have to deal with—a question to which we shall
have repeatedly to return in this chapter. I have used the
words " English Parliament," instead of " a part of the
English Parliament," because, though the minority of 46
or 47 were against entertaining at all the question of
dissolution, the majority of 49 or 50 put off the dissolution
too long.

It would seem that those measures of the Parliament
which most displeased and alarmed Cromwell were measures dictated by the soundest policy.   It is obvious that,
while the Government was subjected to such extraordinary
expenditure by the exigencies of the war with Holland, it
was at once their interest and their duty to diminish
their other expenditure as much as possible. The most
obvious and effective mode of accomplishing this was to
make some retrenchments in regard to their military
forces.   On the 13th of September 1652 the Council of
State made the following order :—

" That the Lord-General [Cromwell] and the General
Officers of the army be sent unto, and desired to
come to the Committee for Irish and Scottish Affairs, on
Thursday morning next, to speak with the said Committee
concerning the *retrenchment* of some forces and garrisons.' [1]

This was the hitch, which Cromwell determined to avoid
by turning out the Parliament.   And yet, what could be
more advantageous at that time to the nation, though not
to Cromwell and his " creature colonels," than to reduce

---

[1] Order Book of the Council of State, Monday, September 13, 1652, MS.
State Paper Office.

the military expenditure, when the necessary expenses of
the fleet were so great?

There are several minutes in the Order Book in the
months of September and October 1652, which appear to
indicate that the Council of State, besides the general retrenchment of their land forces and garrisons, had particularly turned their attention to the reducing of those
formidable regiments which were quartered immediately
round the Parliament, and were termed the Lord-General's
[Cromwell's], Colonel Ingoldsby's, and Colonel Goffe's regiments. On Thursday the 30th of September, the Council
of State made a minute, with respect to " taking into
consideration the reducing of the Lord-General's, Colonel
Ingoldsby's, and Colonel Goffe's regiments." [1]

On Thursday next, the 7th of October, the Council of
State ordered :—

" That the Lord-General's regiment of foot be continued,
to the number of 1,200 men, *for six weeks longer;* and that
a letter be written to the Committee for the Army, to issue
out their warrants for the payment of them to that time." [2]

There are reasons enough for these proceedings on the
part of the Council set forth in their minutes, without in the
least ascribing them to a jealousy of Cromwell—reasons
founded on the imperious necessities of their situation, on
the constant and urgent demands on the public treasury
for the Dutch war—demands which tasked for their supply
all their genius and energy as statesmen. All this is forcibly shown in such minutes as the following :—

" That Mr. Salwey be desired humbly to represent to
the Parliament the distracted state of the Treasury as it

---

[1] Order Book of the Council of
State, Thursday, September 30, 1652,

MS. State Paper Office.
[2] *Ibid.* Thursday, October 7, 1652.

now stands, the great inconveniences of which the Council find every day." [1]

One day in November 1652, Cromwell, in the course of a conversation with Whitelock, whom he had met in St. James's Park, amid some just enough objections against the Parliament, such as " their designs to perpetuate them-selves, and to continue the power in their own hands," also stated " their meddling in private matters between party and party, contrary to the institution of Parliaments, and their unjustness and partiality in these matters." Sir Roger Twysden's Journal, lately published in the " Archæo-logia Kantiana" from the Roydon Hall MSS., furnishes some corroborative evidence in support of this statement of Cromwell, as reported by Whitelock. Towards the end of his Journal, Sir Roger Twysden says:—"God of His mercy grant that, for the future, it may never see a perpetuity added to the two Houses of Parliament; nor Committees to manage the justice of the kingdom, and sit judges of men's liberties, estates, and fortunes; admitting not the law for their rule, but their own arbitrary, ambiguous, revocable, disputable orders and ordinances." In another place he says: " Certainly their severity was so notorious, and their extortions so full of scandal, as the officers of the army (who ever seemed to me more full of honour and mercy than the House of Commons) did desire, the 1st of August 1647, compositions on sequestrations might be lessened; and Cromwell, in his speech of the 12th of September 1654, told the Parliament then assembled, ' Poor men, under their arbitrary power, were driven like flocks of sheep, by forty in a morning, to the confiscation of goods and estates, without any man being able to give a reason that two of

[1] Order Book of the Council of State, Thursday, September 30, 1652, MS. State Paper Office.

them had deserved to forfeit a shilling.' " [1]   These words
would have come with much more effect from Cromwell if
his own hands had been clean, and if he had not profited
more than anyone else by the confiscations of which he
professes to complain.

But the principal feature of their proceedings, strikingly
exemplified in Sir Roger Twysden's case, was this—that if
you had any one enemy in the Committee, it was impossible to obtain justice, for " against malice there was no
fence." [2] Thus, "any leading man of a Committee maligning
another (though never so quiet a liver), as having a better
estate, seat, house, accommodation to it, than he wished
him, did find means to ruin him, under the title of his
disaffecting their courses and the present cause." [3]   Sir
Roger Twysden's own case was a striking example of this :
the harsh proceedings against him, the imprisoning himself, sequestering his estate for several years, cutting down
the timber about his mansion-house, being all brought
about by two leading men of the Committee of Kent, Sir
Anthony Weldon and Sir John Sedley.

Sir Roger Twysden mentions another remarkable case :
"To which purpose," he says, " I shall here set down
what I had from a good hand, and I believe was
true.   A powerful person of those times (Sir Arthur
Haselrig), riding by a handsome seat, well-wooded and
pleasant otherwise, in the North, enquired to whom it
belonged ; and finding it unsequestered, the owner not in
the Parliament's service, he could not contain himself
from saying he had an earthworm in his breast must have

---

[1] Sir Roger Twysden's Journal,
p. 66.—The Journal was printed in
successive volumes of the "Archæologia
Kantiana." When the successive portions of the Journal have been bound
together and paged consecutively, the
page here quoted is page 66.

[2] *Ibid.* p. 168.

[3] *Ibid.*

the estate sequestered; and never left pursuing the
owner till he got it done. The truth of this I cannot
aver, only I had it from old Sir Henry Vane, a person
of that worth and honour, I dare say he would not
have spoke it but on good grounds." [1] This story certainly tends to add weight to the charge of great rapacity
made against Sir Arthur Haselrig by John Lilburne and
others.[2]

The fact is that the Council of State, from the many
domestic and foreign enemies they had to encounter, were
driven to resort to all the means they could devise, to raise
the money necessary for the equipment and pay of their
fleets and armies. One of these means was the sequestration of the estates of those they called "delinquents,"
that is, of those who favoured the opposite party. There
are various minutes in the Order Book of the Council of
State, which, though we have not the key to unlock their
whole import, seem to have reference to this subject. I
will transcribe one of these, which certainly has the
appearance of hunting for sequestrations :—

"That power be given to the Lord-Commissioner Whitelock, and the rest of the Committee appointed to receive
a proposition for the *discovery and bringing in of money*, to
dispose of the sum of £100 in such way, and to such
persons, as they shall think fit, for the advantage of the
publique." [3]

But these things do not, by any means, amount to a
proof of universal corruption on the part of the Parliament and the Council of State. On the contrary, some of
the leading members of that wonderful band of statesmen

[1] Sir Roger Twysden's Journal, p. 168.
[2] See Vol. I. of this History, p. 195.
[3] Order Book of the Council of State, Thursday, February 12, 165½, MS. State Paper Office.

and statesmen-soldiers were of an integrity pure as the driven snow. And the solemn words uttered by Sir Henry Vane the younger, on the scaffold, were literally true of himself, of Ireton, of Blake, of Scot, of Ludlow, of Sydney, and of many others. Just before the trumpets were sounded in his face, to prevent him from being heard, Sir Henry Vane, lifting up his eyes and spreading his hands, spoke these words : " I do here appeal to the Great God of Heaven, and all this assembly, or any other person, to show wherein I have defiled my hands with any man's blood or estate, or that I have sought myself in any public capacity or place I have been in ! " [1]

There is also considerable weight in the answer made to Sir Roger Twysden, when he desired he might be charged with the breach of any law : " In these times the House could not look· at the nice observance of law." [2] It was, in fact, a time of revolutionary struggle—a time when a great change was taking place in the English Government—a change which was to make the House of Commons what it has been ever since, the supreme power in the State—a time when the great actors in the struggle must be statesmen, not lawyers. No man knew this better than Cromwell, and no man had acted more thoroughly on this principle. But it now suited him to turn round on the men with whom he had acted, and repudiate both them and his former self. Moreover, the MS. records of the Council of State prove, that while the application in private matters to the Council of State might arise from the anomalous state of the Government, the Council of State generally referred such matters to the proper legal tribunals. The following is one of many instances of the Council of

[1] Trial of Sir Henry Vane, Knight, p. 477. small 4to, 1662, p. 88. See title of this curious old volume in full, *post*,

[2] Sir Roger Twysden's Journal, p. 49.

State's declining to interfere in matters belonging to the
Courts of Justice :—

"That the petition of Mary Downes, widow, relict of
Roger Downes, Esq., deceased, be recommended to the
consideration of the Lords Commissioners of the Great
Seal, to proceed therein, according to law and justice." [1]

The following is to the same effect :—

"Upon reading the petition of the Lord Baltimore, it is
this day ordered, that the said Lord Baltimore be left to
pursue his cause according to law." [2]

It is not often that a Government has left behind them
such conclusive and irrefragable evidence as this, to rebut
the calumnies of their destroyers, and to vindicate their
memory to after-ages.

Cromwell, in the course of the conversation with Whitelock, to which I have already referred,[3] put to Whitelock
the following startling question :—

"What if a man should take upon him to be King?"

Whitelock.—"I think that remedy would be worse than
the disease."

Cromwell.—"Why do you think so?"

Whitelock.—"As to your own person, the title of King
would be of no advantage, because you have the full
kingly power in you already, concerning the militia, as
you are General. So that I apprehend less envy, and
danger, and pomp, but not less power and opportunities of
doing good, in your being General, than would be if you
had assumed the title of King." [4]

[1] Order Book of the Council of State, Monday, December 22, 1651, MS. State Paper Office.

[2] *Ibid.* Tuesday, December 23, 1651.

[3] See *ante*, p. 423.

[4] There is a concurrence of cotemporary evidence that, on Cromwell's manifesting an ambition to be King, "the enemies of Cromwell began to multiply very fast"—"that it had given him a blow at the heart, and that he will not long be anything." —Sir Edward Nicholas to Lord Culpepper, June 8, 1657: see Granville Penn's *Memorials of Sir William Penn*, vol. ii. p. 8.

Cromwell.—"What do you apprehend would be the danger of taking this title?"

Whitelock.—"The danger, I think, would be this. One of the main points of controversy betwixt us and our adversaries is, whether the Government of this nation shall be established in monarchy, or in a free State or Commonwealth. Now, if your Excellency shall take upon you the title of King, this state of our cause will be thereby wholly determined, and monarchy established in your person; and the question will be no more whether our Government shall be by a monarch or by a free State, but whether Cromwell or Stuart shall be our king and monarch. And that question, wherein before so great parties of the nation were engaged, and which was universal, will by this become, in effect, a private controversy only : before, it was national—what kind of Government we should have; now, it will become particular—who shall be our governor?—whether of the family of the Stuarts, or of the family of the Cromwells? Thus, the state of our controversy being totally changed, all those who were for a Commonwealth (and they are a very great and considerable party), having their hopes therein frustrated, will desert you."

Cromwell.—"I confess you speak reason in this; but what other thing can you propound, that may obviate the present dangers and difficulties wherein we are all engaged?"

Whitelock then represents himself as propounding a private treaty with the King of Scots, whereby Cromwell might secure himself and his friends, and their fortunes; and might put such limits to monarchical power, as would secure the spiritual and civil liberties of the nation. To this proposition Cromwell thus replied:—"I think you have much reason for what you propound, but it is a matter of so high importance and difficulty, that it deserves more time of consideration and debate than is at present allowed us. We shall therefore take a further time to discourse of it."

Whitelock adds: " With this the General broke off, and went to other company, and so into Whitehall, seeming, by his countenance, displeased with what I had said; yet he never objected it against me in any public meeting afterwards. Only his carriage towards me from that time was altered, and his advising with me not so frequent and intimate as before." [1]

The words of Whitelock's statement, " by a treaty with him you may *secure* yourself, and *your friends and their fortunes* — you may put such limits to monarchical power, as will secure our spiritual and civil liberties," are exceedingly important; and Cromwell's utter neglect of securing anybody but himself, and anything but his own power and fortune — so thoroughly bearing out the truth of John Lilburne's happy expression, "self in the highest"—leaving brave and devoted and single-hearted soldiers, such as Harrison and Hacker, who had shed their blood for him in so many battles, to die a death of torture and ignominy, has always appeared to me the worst and darkest part of his strange character.

When this conference took place between Cromwell and Whitelock, nearly four years had elapsed since the death of King Charles. During those four eventful years, the Rump of the Long Parliament had talked about resigning their power, and going out to make way for their successors; but there was a hitch somewhere in the matter of going out. Whatever arguments may be used to show

---

[1] Whitelock's Memorials, pp. 549–551.

that these residuary members of the Long Parliament
really did mean to go at last, and not to perpetuate the
supreme trust and power in their own persons, and to
debar the people from their right of elections—that they
were only waiting till the right moment should arrive—
there can be no doubt that their delays in this momentous
business were the means of putting a most powerful
weapon against themselves into the hands of a man who,
as we shall see, knew well how to make use of it for his
own purposes.   If Cromwell had made use of the expulsion
of the Parliament as really the first step for paving the
way to a new and free Parliament—if he had clearly shown
by his acts that self-aggrandisement was not his object[1]—
the reluctance to resign their power, manifested by the
Rump, might certainly serve as some justification for his
doing what he did in the first instance.   But what are we
to think of the consistency, of the morality, of the honesty
of a man, who proceeded to dispose of by his will, as if it
were a private property, the dominion of his country, after
having been a party to that Representation of the Army
already quoted, which, in the clearest terms that words are
capable of expressing, declares against " *any absolute arbitrary power, engrossed for perpetuity into the hands of any
particular person or party whatsoever* " ?.

The course pursued by Cromwell has had indeed defenders, some of whom have defended him on the ground
of his proceeding being the only available protection
against anarchy; while others have prostrated themselves

---

[1] "If he had made use of his
power to establish the just liberties of
the nation, he might live more
honoured and esteemed, have the pleasure and satisfaction arising from so
generous an action, when he died, and
leave his own family, together with
the whole body of the people, in a
most happy and flourishing condition."
—*Ludlow's Memoirs*, vol. ii. p. 567:
2nd edition, London, 1721.

at his feet, and while they have worshipped him as an object of idolatry, have been very profuse of their scorn and reprobation towards all who refuse to do the like, and particularly towards those members of the Rump who persisted in refusing to recognise his authority.

The answer to the latter class of the defenders of Cromwell, who have sought to deify Cromwell, and to heap opprobrious epithets on all who have refused to worship their idol, is shortly that, as was long ago remarked, "no man can be expected to oppose arguments to epithets;" and that, though opprobrious epithets and scurrilous jesting may pass for fine writing among barbarians, they have little weight among civilised men, who, whatever be their faults, will admit the truth of an observation of a great English writer of the 17th century, in reference to some scurrilous attacks upon himself, that "to a public writing there belong good manners."[1]

The argument of those who have defended Cromwell on the ground of his proceedings being the only protection against anarchy, is founded on an imperfect and incorrect view of the facts of the case—a view which confounds this case with another, which, though somewhat *similar*, is *not identical*; as when we see, as we constantly do, well-informed public writers asserting that a Cromwell or a Napoleon is needed to prevent anarchy. Now, though

---

[1] "And first for the strength of his discourse, and knowledge of the point in question, I think it much inferior to that which might have been written by any man living, that had no other learning besides the ability to write his mind. Secondly, for the manners of it (for to a public writing there belong good manners), they consist in railing, and exclaiming, and scurrilous jesting. And lastly, for his elocution, the virtue whereof lieth not in the flux of words, but in perspicuity, it is the same language with that of the kingdom of darkness." —*The Question concerning Liberty, Necessity, and Chance*, clearly stated and debated between Dr. Bramhall, Bishop of Derry, and Thomas Hobbes of Malmesbury: London, 1656.

Napoleon might be needed to prevent anarchy, Cromwell
was most decidedly not. On the contrary, it was Cromwell's
usurpation which caused the anarchy which, by confusion
of ideas and of facts, has been transferred from its proper
place to a place which does not belong to it—namely, from
the state of confusion caused by Cromwell's unjust usurpation, to the state of order and of good and strong government which his evil ambition destroyed.

To no Government that ever existed upon earth could
the term "anarchy" be more unjustly applied than to
that Government which existed in England from 1648
to 1653. But between 1653 and 1660 there were—as
Hobbes has shown, in a passage of his "Behemoth," with
his characteristic clearness and precision—six changes or
"shiftings" of the supreme authority. [1]   There never,
probably, has been a more complete example of confusion
of ideas, perversion of facts, and consequent illogical and
inaccurate conclusions, than is afforded by the confounding
of these historical phenomena in such a way, and to such
a degree, as to compare the Government of the Council
of State—composed of such statesmen as Vane, Scot,
and Sydney, which was destroyed by Oliver Cromwell, to be
succeeded by, first, a narrow and hard military despotism,
and then an anarchy—with that preeminently bad French
Government, which may be called the Government of the
Guillotine, and by putting an end to which Napoleon
Bonaparte may be said to have substituted a military
despotism for anarchy. In the case of England and
Cromwell, *military despotism did not prevent, it produced
anarchy*, though the contrary has been so long and so confidently asserted.

The answer, then, to those who affirm that the course

[1] Hobbes's Behemoth, pp. 322, 323 : London, 1682.

Cromwell pursued was the only course practicable under the circumstances of the case—that it was what is, in the modern German jargon, called a historical or political necessity—is that it was not a political necessity, inasmuch as, as has been already proved from the minutes of the Council of State of the Long Parliament, and can be further proved from the minutes of Cromwell's Council of State, the Long Parliament governed infinitely better than Cromwell; and, further, that to Cromwell, as to all men in his situation, there are always two paths open—the one that which has been trodden by ten thousand tyrants— the other that which has been chosen by the few men who have been able to resist the greatest temptation to crime known to mortals—by Epaminondas, by Timoleon, by Washington—the great men who, in the dispute about the value of such men in history, at least are good to show that truth, justice, and honour are not altogether extinct among mankind.   Will it be pretended that two thousand years ago, Sicilian Greeks—people of a temperament which made them such easy victims to tyrant after tyrant—could justly appreciate the magnanimity of Timoleon, when, after having delivered them from all their domestic tyrants and from all their foreign enemies, he voluntarily resigned his dictatorship; and could universally recognise in him a man who had amply earned, what Xenophon[1] calls, "that good, not human but divine, command over willing men "— " a man uncorrupted by a career of superhuman success "[2]— " a man whom everyone loved, trusted, and was grieved to offend—a man who sought not to impose his own will upon free communities, but addressed them as freemen, building only upon their reason and sentiments, and

[1] Xenoph. Œconomic. xxi. 12.
[2] Grote's History of Greece, vol. xi. p. 272.

carrying out, in all his recommendations of detail, the
instincts of free speech, universal vote, and equal laws;"[1]
and that Englishmen, living in the middle of the
17th century, would have been unable to appreciate at
its just value, and to turn to its right use, a similar act of
magnanimous justice on the part of Oliver Cromwell?
Besides the direct political consequences of such an act
and of its contrary, which are great enough, the social and
moral consequences are of unspeakable extent and magnitude.   How many a villain on a small scale has justified,
at least to himself, his career of self-aggrandisement,
through all the adroit falsehoods which make mean villains[2]
rich and prosperous, by the audacious violation of truth
and the gigantic villany of Cromwell![3]

It is observable that these three truly great men, Epaminondas, Timoleon, and Washington, were all alike exempt
from the irascible and vindictive as well as the ambitious
passions.   What Mr. Grote has said of Timoleon is applicable no less to the other two.   Timoleon "was distinguished no less for his courage than for the gentleness of
his disposition.   Little moved either by personal vanity
or by ambition, he was devoted in his patriotism, and
unreserved in his hatred of despots, as well as of
traitors."[4]   The furious transports of rage which took

---

[1] Grote's History of Greece, vol. xi.
p. 267.

[2] " No villany, no flagitious action,
was ever yet committed, but a lie was,
first or last, the principal engine to effect it."—*South*.

[3] It is one of the greatest of human
misfortunes, that the evil which great
men do is so much more apt to be imi-
tated than the good.   "Quo in genere
multum mali etiam in exemplo est.
Studiose enim plerique facta principum
imitantur : ut L. Luculli, summi viri,

virtutem, quis ? at quam multi villarum
magnificentiam imitati sunt!"—Cicero
De Off. i. 39.

[4] Grote's History of Greece, vol. xi.
p. 192.   Plutarch, Timoleon, c. 3. . .
. . . . Φιλόπατρις δὲ καὶ πρᾶος διαφερ-
όντως, ὅσα μὴ σφόδρα μισότυραννος
εἶναι καὶ μισοπόνηρος.   Condorcet
says of Turgot that, notwithstanding
the gentleness of his character he could
not dissemble his hatred for knaves,
his contempt for cowardice or baseness: but that these sentiments neither

possession at times of Cromwell, of Frederic, of Napoleon, never darkened the clear, calm, and well-tempered minds of Epaminondas, of Timoleon, of Washington. This fact alone, however, would hardly constitute the specific difference between the two classes of great men; for Julius Cæsar, who belonged in essentials to the former class, possessed as much gentleness or mildness in his political antipathies as any of the latter class.

It is also observable that each of these three men, of politically stainless name, was born and educated in an oligarchical community—a fact (however philosophers may interpret its meaning) which ought to be recorded, amid the many unfavourable exhibitions which oligarchies have presented to the world. I know no individual statesman produced in democratical Athens, or in democratical America, who can be compared to them. Socrates, who equalled them in high-souled and disinterested heroism, was a philosopher only, and not a practical politician. The very example of such men is of inestimable value. Mr. Grote considers the difference in the careers of Timoleon and Dion to be due to the fact that the person whom Timoleon selected for his peculiar model was Epaminondas, the noblest model that Greece afforded, with his energetic patriotism, his freedom from personal ambition, his gentleness of political antipathy, and the

inspired him with a spirit of injustice nor of vengeance. What Condorcet has recorded of Turgot—"that constant agreement between his conduct and his principles, his sentiments and his reason; that union of an inexorable justice with the gentlest humanity; of sensibility with firmness of character; of justness of understanding with depth and subtlety; that firm adherence to his opinions without ever exaggerating them; the sentiments all pure, the emotions all either gentle or courageous, the calm spirit full of candour and justice" (*Vie de Turgot*, p. 290, Londres, 1786)—may be well applied also to Timoleon; while in the latter were added talents for action of the highest order, forming altogether a character perhaps unparalleled in history.

F F 2

perfect habits of conciliatory and popular dealing which
he manifested, amidst so many new and trying scenes, to
the end of his career. While, on the other hand, Dion, a
member of a despotic family, and bred under the energetic
despotism of the elder Dionysius, had never learnt to take
account of the temper or exigencies of a community of
freemen. "The source from which he drank was the
Academy and its illustrious teacher, Plato—not from
practical life, nor from the best practical politicians like
Epaminondas." [1]

Ludlow says that some discerning men of the Parliament, especially those who had the management of the
war with Holland, observing the mine which Cromwell
was working, endeavoured to countermine him, by ba-
lancing his interest in the army with that of the fleet,
procuring an order from the Parliament to send some
regiments from the army to strengthen the fleet.[2] This
statement is fully borne out by various minutes of the
Council of State already given, as well as by the two following minutes of Friday the 2nd of January, 165$\frac{2}{3}$:—

"That it be recommended to the Commissioners for the
Admiralty, to take care that the supernumerary soldiers
now disbanded out of the regiments in Scotland, may, when
they come into England, be disposed to the service of the
fleet, the Council having given order for the furnishing of
money for the bringing of them into England." [3]

"The Council, finding that there is at present a great
want of men for the speedy and effectual manning out of
the ships in the service of the Commonwealth, do thereupon
order, that it be recommended to the Commissioners for the

[1] Grote's History of Greece, vol. xi.
p. 277.
[2] Ludlow's Memoirs, vol. ii. p. 450
2nd edition, London, 1721.

[3] Order Book of the Council of
State, Friday, January 21, 1652, MS.
State Paper Office.

Admiralty to consider how a fitting proportion of land-soldiers may be made use of for the present occasion for the manning out of the fleet·; and that it be recommended to the said Commissioners, to communicate with the Generals of the fleet, concerning the apportioning of the number of men which shall be judged necessary for that service." [1]

Undoubtedly the splendour of Blake's achievements, the consequent importance which the fleet acquired both in the eyes of the Parliament and of the nation, and the constant drafting of soldiers into the fleet, furnished new and pressing causes of uneasiness to Cromwell. If Blake went on fighting a few more battles like his last, besides the power and honour that would thence accrue to the Parliament itself, there would arise in Blake a man invested with at least as much of the magic that surrounds a commander, whose career has been signalised by a succession of the most brilliant victories on a large scale, as he himself had obtained; while, on the other hand, could he in time transfer the power of the Parliament wholly to himself, Blake and himself would no longer be co-ordinate powers, but Blake would thenceforth stand to him in the relation of a strictly subordinate officer. He therefore at once—with that resolute promptitude that never deserted him at a critical moment, and which seemed worth to him as much as all the strategic genius of Hannibal and Frederic (which he did not possess) was to them,—resolved that *now* was the time to strike.

It was absolutely necessary for the attainment of Cromwell's object that he should be quite sure of the army. After the death of Ireton, the two men who had most interest with the army were Lambert and Harrison. I have

---

[1] Order Book of the Council of State, Friday, January 21, 165⅔, MS. State Paper Office.

already shown how, on the death of Ireton, Cromwell had
secured the concurrence of Lambert in his plot against
the Parliament.[1]   Lambert was not a religious fanatic,
and, as a military man, he was the ablest in the army,
and popular among the soldiers; but he was weak as a
politician, and easily fell into the snare set for him by a
politician so crafty as Cromwell.   As religious fanaticism,
therefore, had not to be encountered in Lambert, all that
Cromwell had to do in his case was to create in him a
spirit of hostility to the Parliament, sufficiently strong
to induce him to agree to their destruction.   This was
completely effected by the Parliament's refusing to send
him to Ireland with the title of Deputy.

Ludlow has given a curious account of a conversation he
had with Harrison, after that enthusiast had discovered
his mistake in aiding Cromwell to turn out the Parliament.   The perfect sincerity of Harrison's delusions is
there made apparent.   Ludlow went to make Harrison a
visit at his house at Highgate, where Cromwell had permitted him to remain a prisoner, after he had been a
prisoner at Pendennis Castle.[2]   Ludlow having asked
Harrison his reasons for joining with Cromwell in turning
out the Parliament, Harrison answered that his first reason
was, " because he was fully persuaded they (the Parliament)
had not a heart to do any more good for the Lord and His
people."   " Then," said Ludlow, " are you not now con-

---

[1] *Ante*, Chapter XII.

[2] Ludlow says " Carisbrook Castle;"
but, as the author of the " Memoir of
Thomas Harrison," published in the
same volume (Family Library, No.
xxxi.) with the trial of Charles I.,
says, " Ludlow appears to be wrong,
as he occasionally is, as to dates and
details, owing to his having written

his Memoirs from memory in Swit-
zerland several years after the events
happened.   Vane was sent to Carisbrook, but Harrison was confined at
Pendennis.—*Thurloe*, vol. v. p. 407;
Godwin, vol. iv. p. 276, *Mercurious
Fumigosus*, a journal of the day, No.
306." p. 233, note 2.

vinced of your error, since it has been seen what use has been made of the usurped power?" To which he replied, " Upon their heads be the guilt, who have made a wrong use of it; for my own part, my heart was upright and sincere in the thing." To this Ludlow answered that, " Though it should be granted that the Parliament was not inclined to make so full a reformation of things amiss as might be desired, yet he could not doubt that they would have done as much good for the nation as it was then fitted to receive."

Harrison's second reason was, " because he owned a sort of men who acted upon higher principles than those of civil liberty "—the men called " saints " in his phraseology. He then cited a passage of the Prophet Daniel, where it is said " that the saints shall take the kingdom and possess it." Ludlow endeavoured to answer him, in his own style of argument, by saying that the same prophet says, in another place, " that the kingdom shall be given to the people of the saints of the Most High," and that if they should presume to take it before it was given, they would be guilty of doing evil that good might come of it. Ludlow further told him "that such proceedings are not only unjust, but also impracticable, at least for the present; because we cannot perceive that the saints are clothed with such a spirit, as those are required to be to whom the kingdom is promised; and, therefore, we may easily be deceived in judging who are fit for government, for many have taken upon them the form of saintship, that they might be admitted to it, who yet have not acted suitably to their pretensions in the sight of God or men: for proof of which we need go no further than to those very persons who had drawn him to assist them in their design of exalting themselves, under the specious pretence of

advancing the kingdom of Christ." Harrison admitted
the force of Ludlow's argument, as he well might, having
discovered that the reign of the saints, which Cromwell
had held out to him, meant the reign of Oliver Cromwell,
and having suffered and still suffering imprisonment for
refusing to own the identity of the reign of Cromwell with
the reign of the saints and their King Jesus; yet he said
he was not convinced that the texts of Scripture quoted
by him were not to be interpreted in the sense in which
he had taken them.[1]

In another place Ludlow says, that Cromwell "made
higher pretences to honesty than ever he had done before,
thereby to engage Major-General Harrison, Colonel Rich,
and their party, to himself.   To this end he took all occasions in their presence to asperse the Parliament, as not
designing to do those good things they pretended to, but
rather intending to support the corrupt interests of the
clergy and lawyers.   And though he was convinced that
they were hastening with all expedition to put a period to
their sitting, having passed a vote that they would do it
within the space of a year, and that they were making all
possible preparations in order to it; yet did he indus-
triously publish, that they were so in love with their seats,
that they would use all means to perpetuate themselves.
These and other calumnies he had with so much art in-
sinuated into the belief of many honest and well-meaning
people, that they began to wish him prosperity in his undertaking."[2]

This statement of the brave, single-hearted, and uncom-
promising soldier Ludlow, is supported in all points by
the cautious, pliant, if not obsequious lawyer Whitelock.

---

[1] Ludlow's Memoirs, vol. ii. pp. 563–   [2] Ludlow, *ibid.* p. 449.
566: 2nd edition, London, 1721.

After the entry in his Memorials or Journal of the last great victory of Blake, Whitelock says that Cromwell and some of his officers " now began to assume to themselves all the honour of the past actions, and of the conquests by them achieved, scarce owning the Parliament, and their assistance and provision for them ; but taxing and censuring the members of Parliament for injustice and delay of business, and for seeking to prolong their power, and promote their private interest, and satisfy their own ambition.   With these and many others the like censures, they endeavoured to calumniate the Parliament, and judge them guilty of those crimes whereof themselves were faulty; not looking into their own actions, nor perceiving their own defaults, yet censuring the actions and proceedings of the Parliament very opprobriously." [1]

The utter falsehood of the charge of " injustice and delay of business " is made clear as the light of the sun by the subsequent fact of the total neglect, by the Government of Cromwell, of Blake's fleet.   Blake wrote to the Admiralty, on the 11th of March 1657, setting forth, in the most urgent terms, the wretched condition of his fleet—" grown so foul, by reason of a long continuance abroad, that if a fleet outward-bound should design to avoid us, few of our ships would be able to follow them up."   " I have acquainted you often," he writes, " with my thoughts of keeping out these ships so long, whereby they are not only rendered in a great measure unserviceable, but withal exposed to desperate hazards : wherein, though the Lord hath most wonderfully and mercifully preserved us hitherto, I know no rule to tempt Him, and therefore again mind you of it, that if any such accident should for the future happen to the damage of his

---

[1] Whitelock's Memorials, p. 548 *et seq.*

Highness and the nation—which God forbid—the blame
may not be at our doors, for we account it a great mercy
that the Lord hath not given them [the Spaniards] the
opportunity to take advantage of these our damages. Truly
our fleet is generally in that condition that it troubles us
to think what the consequences may prove if such another
storm, as we have had three or four lately, should overtake
us before we have time and opportunity a little to repair.
Our number of men is lessened through death and sickness, occasioned partly through the badness of victuals,
and the long continuance of poor men at sea.   The
captain of the *Fairfax* tells me in particular that they are
forced to call all their company on deck whenever they go
to tack."—All the answer he could get was (instead of what
he so urgently asked for, " forthwith a sufficient supply of
able seamen ") that the Commissioners of the Admiralty
were sorry to hear of his illness, sorry also to hear of the
wretched state of his ships; but that they could not promise him any immediate aid, because the Lord Protector's
time was completely taken up with Parliamentary intrigues,
the great question of Kingship being then under consideration.[1]   This was not the way in which the business of
the navy was managed when Vane was Chairman of the
Committee of the Admiralty that was appointed from its
own members by the Council of State.   And yet Oliver
Cromwell had the audacity to charge those men with
" delay of business," and the folly to exclaim, in that fit of
insanity in which he turned out the Parliament, "The
Lord deliver me from Sir Henry Vane! "

Ludlow goes on to say, in continuation of the passage I
have last quoted from him, " Divers of the clergy, from

[1] Dixon's Robert Blake, pp. 344, 9304; and MS. Orders and Instruc-
345, cites Blake's Despatch, Add. MSS. tions, May 2, 1657, Admiralty Office.

their pulpits, began to prophesy the destruction of the Parliament, and to propose it openly as a thing desirable. Insomuch that the General, who had all along concurred with this spirit in them, hypocritically complained, to Quartermaster-General Vernon, 'That he was pushed on by two parties to do that, the consideration of the issue whereof made his hair to stand on end. One of these' (said he) 'is headed by Major-General Lambert, who, in revenge of that injury the Parliament did him, in not permitting him to go into Ireland with a character and condition suitable to his merit, will be contented with nothing less than their dissolution: of the other Major-General Harrison is the chief, who is an honest man, and aims at good things; yet, from the impatience of his spirit, will not wait the Lord's leisure, but hurries me on to that which he and all honest men will have cause to repent.' Thus did he craftily feel the pulse of men towards this work, endeavouring to cast the infamy of it on others; reserving to himself the appearance of tenderness to civil and religious liberty, and of screening the nation from the fury of the parties before-mentioned." [1]

Though, as has been seen from the passage of Ludlow last quoted, "divers of the clergy" prophesied from the pulpits the destruction of the Parliament as a thing desirable, Cromwell, part of whose policy was to have the clergy on his side, failed to obtain the concurrence of some of the chief of them. Cromwell held meetings with them, for the purpose of bringing them over to his views. But with some of them the millennial doctrine did not seem so be so much in favour as it was with Harrison.

A curious scene, that took place at one of these meetings, is cited by Mr. Forster, from the " Life of Henry Neville,"

---

[1] Ludlow's Memoirs, vol. ii. pp. 449, 450 : 2nd edition, London, 1721.

a member of the Council of State, and one of those who remained true [1] to their Commonwealth principles to the last—a scene which is given as from Neville's lips: "Cromwell, upon this great occasion, sent for some of the chief city divines, as if he made it a matter of conscience to be determined by their advice.   Among these was the leading Mr. Calamy, who very boldly opposed Mr. Cromwell's project, and offered to prove it both unlawful and impracticable.   Cromwell answered readily upon the first head of 'unlawful,' and appealed to the safety of the nation being the supreme law.   'But,' says he, 'pray, Mr. Calamy, why impracticable?'   Calamy replied, 'Oh! 'tis against the voice of the nation; there will be nine in ten against you.'   'Very well,' says Cromwell; 'but what if I should disarm the nine, and put a sword into the tenth man's hand; would not that do the business?'"[2]   And thus it

[1] See Ludlow's Memoirs, vol. ii. pp. 600–603: 2nd edition, London, 1721.

[2] Life of Henry Neville, p. 35, cited in Mr. Forster's Life of Cromwell, vol. ii. pp. 52, 53: London, 1839.—Neville was one of the most regular in his attendance at the meetings of the Council of State, and his name frequently occurs in the minutes. I give one instance: "That Mr. Neville and Mr. Carew be added to the Commissioners of the Council, appointed to treat with the Dutch Ambassadors."—*Order Book of the Council of State*, Thursday, June 17, 1652, MS. State Paper Office. Henry Neville, after the usurpation of Cromwell, brought an action against the Sheriff of Berkshire, for foul practices at the last return for that county. "But not being willing," says Ludlow, "so far to acknowledge the present authority as to prefer his action upon the Instrument of Government, he was advised by Serjeant Maynard, Mr. Allen of Gray's Inn, and some others, to bring his action of the case against the Sheriff.   On the day of trial, Mr. Nevil desired Sir Arthur Haselrig, Sir James Harrington, Mr. Scot, myself, and some other members of the Long Parliament, to be present in the court; when, after all the objections made by the Sheriff's counsel were overruled by the Court, and the witnesses heard on both sides, the Chief Justice (St. John) declared to the jury how heinous a crime it was that a sheriff should presume to impose upon them such members as he pleased to serve in Parliament, which was the bulwark of the people's liberties." The jury found the Sheriff guilty, and adjudged him to pay £1,500 for damages to Mr. Nevil, and £100 to the Commonwealth. The conclusion of the affair is curious and characteristic: "But now the Chief

was indeed, and only thus, that the business was done. It is not surprising, after this, that Colonel Streater should be represented, when Harrison stoutly asserted that "he was assured the Lord-General sought not himself, but that King Jesus might take the sceptre," as replying that " Christ must come before Christmas, or else He would come too late."

I have said that the capital blunder of the Parliament was their persistence in not dissolving themselves, and that they thus put the most powerful weapon into Cromwell's hands against themselves. But though the question of dissolution is stated by Whitelock to have been urged by the soldiers as of "right," "justice," and "public liberty," and though Cromwell had always shown himself eager for such dissolution, the strange part of this business is that, when the Parliament, " now perceiving" (says Ludlow), "to what kind of excesses the madness of the army was likely to carry them, resolved to leave as a legacy to the people the government of a Commonwealth by their own representatives, when assembled in Parliament, and in the intervals thereof, by a Council of State chosen by them, and to continue till the meeting of the next succeeding Parliament, to whom they were to give an account of their conduct and management, and to this end resolved, without any further delay, to pass the Act for their now

Justice, having, as he thought, sufficiently pleased the popular interest by what he had said concerning the rights of the people, began to contrive means to gratify his master Cromwell, by whose order the Sheriff had acted ; and to this end, upon the motion of the Sheriff's counsel, granted an arrest of judgment, and appointed a day in the next term to hear what could be said on each side. In the meantime the Sheriff conveyed away his real and personal estate. Endeavours were likewise used to take off Mr. Nevil, by compounding the business." But Neville had the judgment recorded for an example, " and then declared himself resolved to deal with the Sheriff as became him."—*Ludlow's Memoirs*, vol. ii. pp. 600-602 : 2nd edition, London, 1721.

dissolution," [1] Cromwell resolved not to suffer them to pass that Act, but to turn them out by military force before they could pass it.   The explanation of this strange proceeding on the part of Cromwell is, I think, that Cromwell was (as Ludlow says), " sensible of the design, and of the consequences of suffering the army to be new-moulded, and put under another conduct," [2] which the constant draughts of soldiers into the fleet tended to do; and also that he was afraid, " lest the disinterested proceeding of the Parliament—who (by dissolving themselves) were about to leave the nation under a form of government that provided sufficiently for the good of the community—might work the people into a greater aversion to his selfish design." [3]

Lord Macaulay has said of Lord Temple, that those who knew his habits tracked him as men track a mole; that wherever a heap of dirt was flung up, it might well be suspected that he was at work in some foul crooked labyrinth below.   But though Cromwell's dark and tortuous course might resemble that of a mole, his human calculation, which the mole did not possess, led him to remove the heaps of dirt which served as landmarks for the course of the mole, and thus to obliterate, in a great measure, the traces of his dark work.   His careful keeping back and, no doubt, ultimate destruction of the Bill for a New Parliament—a business to which I will advert more fully in a subsequent page of this chapter—was a remarkable example of this manner of proceeding.   In other cases, such as the following, he was unable to obliterate the marks of his tortuous course, of the crooked ways he pursued underground.

While he was making " the most solemn professions of

[1] Ludlow's Memoirs, vol. ii. p. 455:   [2] Ludlow, *ibid.* p. 451.
2nd edition, London, 1721.   [3] Ludlow, *ibid.* p. 452.

fidelity to the Parliament—assuring them, that if they would command the army to break their swords over their heads, and to throw them into the sea, he would undertake they should do it—yet did he privately engage the officers of the army to draw up a petition to the Parliament, that for the satisfaction of the nation they would put that vote which they had made, for fixing a period to their sitting, into an Act; which, whilst the officers were forming and debating, the General, having, it seems, for that time altered his counsels, sent Colonel Desborough, one of his instruments, to the Council of Officers, who told them, that they ought to rely upon the word and promise of the Parliament to dissolve themselves by the time prefixed; and that to petition them to put their vote into an Act, would manifest a diffidence of them, and lessen their authority, which was so necessary to the army. The General, coming into the Council whilst Desborough was speaking, seconded him: to which some of the officers took the liberty to reply, that they had the same opinion of the Parliament and petition with them; and that the chief argument that moved them to take this matter into consideration, was the intimation they had received, that it was according to the desires of those who had now spoken against it, and whose latter motion they were much more ready to comply with than their former." [1]

What was the cause of this alteration in Cromwell's plans? Was it that Cromwell, seeing that the Parliament had now set about their Bill for a dissolution of the present and the election of a new Parliament, and were proceeding with great energy and activity in preparing it for the final vote, saw that the reason for the petition no

[1] Ludlow's Memoirs, vol. ii. pp. 451, 452 : 2nd edition, London, 1721.

longer existed? This is the most obvious cause. But then
it involves the supposition, that Cromwell really wished
the Bill to be passed; and his subsequent proceedings
proved, in the most conclusive manner, that he did not
wish the Bill to be passed. We are then driven to seek
another cause, and to ask if he stopped the petition, lest
it might have the effect of accelerating the passing of a
Bill which he did not wish to be passed? There is, it will
be seen, a contradiction here in Cromwell's conduct, which
cannot be explained away. He had professed himself
eager to have the question of the Parliament's dissolution
settled; and when, at last, the Parliament were proceeding
to settle it, and were on the point of finishing their work,
he expelled them by military force, carried off their Bill
for a New Parliament; and then blackened their characters
by charges, some of which I can prove to be false, and
others he did not prove to be true, though he *could* have
done so if they had been true.

As Ludlow, when he states that the Parliament resolved,
without any further delay, to pass the Act for their own
dissolution, says nothing about there being two parties in
the Parliament, as shown by the divisions on the vote of
14th November 1651—one of which, a majority of 50, was
for fixing a time for the dissolution, and the other, a minority of 46 or 47, was against entertaining the question of
dissolution at that time—it may be inferred that those two
parties had both come to the conclusion that, under the
present circumstances, there should be no further delay.
There was, moreover, a third party, at least a certain number of members, who, according to Whitelock, were not
averse to the design of that part of the army, headed by
Cromwell, Lambert, and Harrison, to turn out the Parliament by force, " and were complotting with them to ruin

themselves, as by the consequence will appear." [1]   These
men appear to have been the dupes of a mistaken confidence
in Cromwell's protestations and ever ready tears, as may
be inferred from Whitelock's expression, " neither could it
be clearly-foreseen, that the design of Cromwell and his
officers was to rout the present power, and to set up themselves." [2]

About twenty members of Parliament are said, in Cromwell's declaration, dated "Whitehall, April 22, 1653,"
to have been present at the last meeting, on the 19th of
April 1653, of what is called the Council of Officers, at
Cromwell's lodgings in Whitehall ; and these twenty
members may be assumed to represent " the Parliament
men who" (Whitelock says) " complotted with Cromwell
and his officers to ruin themselves."   It is remarkable that
Whitelock was himself present, though he describes himself
and Widdrington as strongly dissenting from those who
were for " putting an end forthwith to this Parliament ; "
and expressing themselves freely to the effect that it would
be " a most dangerous thing to dissolve the present Parliament, and to set up any other Government, and that it
would neither be warrantable in conscience or wisdom so
to do." [3]   Of the opinion for putting an end forthwith to
this Parliament, Whitelock says : " St. John was one of
the chief, and many more with him ; and generally all the
officers of the army, who stuck close in this likewise to
their General." [4]   The conference lasted till late at night,
" when Widdrington and Whitelock went home weary, and
troubled to see the indiscretion and ingratitude of those
men, and the way they designed to ruin themselves." [5]

---

[1] Whitelock's Memorials, p. 552 :
London, 1732.
[2] Ibid.

[3] Ibid. p. 554.
[4] Ibid.
[5] Ibid.

It is asserted by Cromwell, in his "Declaration of the
Grounds and Reasons for dissolving the Parliament by
Force," dated "Whitehall, April 22, 1653," that the
members ("about twenty," he says) present at the conferences with the officers of the army at his lodgings on
the 19th of April, "did agree to meet again the next day
in the afternoon for mutual satisfaction; it being consented unto by the members present, that endeavours
should be used *that nothing in the meantime should be done
in Parliament* that might exclude or frustrate the proposals
before mentioned; that, notwithstanding this, the next
morning" (the 20th of April) "the Parliament did make
more haste than usual in carrying on their said Act, being
helped on therein by some of the persons engaged to us
the night before, none of them which were then present
endeavouring to oppose the same; and being ready to put
the main question for consummating the said Act, whereby
our aforesaid proposals would have been rendered void,
and the way of bringing them into a fair and full debate in
Parliament obstructed; for preventing thereof, and all the
sad and evil consequences which must, upon the grounds
aforesaid, have ensued, we have been necessitated, though
with much reluctancy, to put an end to this Parliament." [1]

The "grounds aforesaid," as far as they can be ascertained, always a very difficult matter in Cromwell's long
and dark state-papers, were that the "persons of honour
and integrity were rendered of no further use in Parliament, than by meeting with a corrupt party," and thereby
enabling by their countenance that "corrupt party" to
"effect the desire they had of perpetuating themselves in
the supreme government."

[1] Parl. Hist. vol. iii. pp. 1386–1390.

Now it is proved, by the division on the 14th of November 1651, that there was a party in the House who were against entertaining at all the question of dissolution. This party however is also proved, by the same division, to have been a minority, though a large minority, of the number present; and they were outvoted, and a day fixed for the dissolution.   It is therefore demonstrated that this assertion of Cromwell, respecting the power of a certain part of the Parliament to "perpetuate themselves in the supreme government," is unsupported by evidence.   Moreover, observe the inconsistency of his statement.   The Parliament on the morning of the 20th of April, "being ready to put the main question for consummating the Act" for dissolving themselves, "we have been necessitated to put an end to this Parliament."   That is, he (Oliver Cromwell) conceived himself necessitated to put an end to the Parliament when they were in the very act of putting an end to themselves; necessitated to prevent the consummation of an act bearing the form and having much of the substance of law, and instead of that act to do an act at once violent and utterly illegal, and at the same time to put an ineffaceable insult upon the Legislature and Government of which he was the paid servant.

In regard to Cromwell's assertion that the Members of Parliament present at the conference at his lodgings on the 19th had left the meeting with an express understanding that endeavours should be used to suspend all further proceedings on the Act for dissolution and a new Parliament till the result of the conference next day, I am inclined to think—though Whitelock makes no allusion to such a pledge having been given on the part of himself and the other members present at the conference—from the sudden anger which Cromwell is reported to have evinced, on hearing next day what the Parliament was about, that some such pledge may have been given. But if Whitelock and the other members did give such a pledge, they "did so," as Mr. Forster justly observes, "without authority, and in the absence of any means of redeeming it."[1] For the ablest as well as the most influential members of that great Parliament—those by whose unwearied industry, by whose unconquerable energy, and by whose great abilities the Dutch war had been so successfully carried on—Vane, Scot, Algernon Sydney, Bradshaw, and the Parliamentary majority they carried with them, would have considered the proposal to mould their proceedings either in Parliament or in the Council of State, according to the will of Cromwell and his creatures as a species of dictation not to be submitted to for an instant.

I have said, in a note to the preceding paragraph, that the conferences held at Cromwell's lodgings were not only unconstitutional, but illegal and even treasonable meetings;—for they were meetings at which the destruction of a Legislature and a Government was debated by its own paid servants, by its own generals and some of its military officers. Nevertheless, the singularity of the situation might not only have excused but justified those meetings,

---

[1] Forster's Life of Oliver Cromwell, vol. ii. p. 57: London, 1839.—I will add here a not unimportant note of Mr. Forster in reference to that conference on April 19, which conference, be it observed, was, in its very nature, not only an unconstitutional but an illegal and treasonable meeting. "The only sincere (however wrong-headed) republican," says Mr. Forster, "of whose attendance at these councils I can find any evidence is Sir Arthur Haselrig. That he did attend is clear from a manuscript report of a speech delivered by him in Richard Cromwell's Parliament : 'I heard, being seventy miles off, that it was propounded that we should dissolve our trust, and devolve it into a few hands. I came up, and found it so ; that it was resolved in a junto at the Cockpit. I trembled at it, and was, after, there, and bore my testimony against it. I told them the work they went about was accursed. I told them it was impossible to devolve this trust.'"—*Ibid.* p. 58, note.

if the avowed object of them had been strictly and consistently carried out—the dissolution of the present, and the election in its place of a fair and free Parliament. It is most important to carefully note that up to this day, this 19th of April 1653, the above-mentioned ground of justification of these meetings being admitted, Cromwell had committed no overt illegal act; and the meetings having, moreover, had the effect of hastening the Parliament to the very completion of their Bill for their dissolution and for a new Parliament, if Cromwell had stopped here, and allowed the Parliament to consummate their Act on the day following, that is the 20th, he would have been entitled to the credit of having acted upon the Parliament for good and not for evil and would have left to after-ages a name very different from the name which he has left.

It is very probable that Cromwell, when he went to bed after that conference, from which Whitelock went home weary late at night, had not determined on the irrevocable deed which he was to do on the following day. The last act of undertakings of that nature is apt to be, at least partly, the result of passionate impulse. Cæsar was less subject than Cromwell to such impulses. Yet Plutarch relates of Cæsar, whose farsighted intelligence could not fail to perceive, and who even " discussed at length with his friends who were present all the difficulties and *enumerated the evils which would ensue to all mankind from his passage of the river* " [1] (the Rubicon), that " at last *with a*

---

[1] Plutarch, C. Cæsar, c. 32.—The words I have marked in italics show that Cæsar himself took a very different view of the matter from that taken by certain modern writers who have attempted to prove that despots are necessary to the progress of humanity. Such men as Cæsar and Frederic II. of Prussia were not to be deceived themselves by the shallow sophistries by which inferior minds have sought to support evil deeds. Frederic, though, for form's sake, he might in manifestoes insert some idle stories about his antiquated claim on Silesia, in his conversation and memoirs pretended

kind of passion, as if he were throwing himself out of reflection into the future, and uttering what is the usual expression with which men preface their entry upon desperate enterprises and daring, ' Let the die be cast! ' he hurried to

to no more virtue than he had, and that was little enough. His own words were : "Ambition, interest, the desire of making myself talked about, carried the day ; and I decided for war." These are the words which Voltaire, in his Memoirs, says he transcribed from the work as it was when Frederic showed it to him : "L'ambition, l'intérêt, le désire de faire parler de moi, l'emportèrent, et la guerre fût résolue." In Frederic's work as afterwards published, the words are somewhat altered:—"Une armée toute prête à agir, des fonds tout trouvés, et peut-être l'envie de se faire un nom ; tout cela fut cause de la guerre que le Roi declara à Marie Thérèse d'Autriche, Reine de Hongrie et de Bohême."— *Histoire de mon Temps,* tom. i. p. 128, ed. Berlin, 1788. Voltaire's reflections on the words as they stood in the original MS. of Frederic's work, and which words Voltaire says he made the King omit when he (Voltaire) subsequently corrected his works, are well worth transcribing: " Depuis qu'il y a des conquérants ou des esprits ardens qui ont voulu l'être, je crois qu'il est le premier qui se soit ainsi rendu justice. Jamais homme peutêtre n'a plus senti la raison, et n'a plus écouté ses passions. Ces assemblages de philosophie et de déréglemens d'imagination ont toujours composé son caractère. C'est dommage que je lui aie fait retrancher ce passage quand je corrigeai depuis tous ses ouvrages ; un aveu si rare devait passer à la postérité, et servir à faire voir sur quoi sont fondées

presques toutes les guerres. Nous autres gens de lettres, poètes, historiens, déclamateurs d'académie, nous célébrons ces beaux exploits : et voilà un roi qui les fait, et qui les condamne." —*Mémoires pour servir à la vie de M. de Voltaire,* écrits par lui-même. The passage as the King has left it in his history is scarcely less conclusive than Voltaire's commentary on it. After dismissing in one word, "incontestable," the nature of his claims upon Silesia, he proceeds to expatiate upon the dilapidated state of the Austrian finances, the general disorder and weakness of the ministry and the army, and above all the youth and inexperience of the Queen Maria Theresa and her unprotected condition ; and sums up by stating that he had an army ready for action, funds provided, " et peutêtre l'envie de se faire un nom." It may be said that Cæsar, who was a philosopher as well as Frederic, also passed a judgment condemning his own actions, if we can trust Plutarch's account, given above, that he "enumerated the evils which would ensue to all mankind from his passage of the river." And as Plutarch mentions Pollio Asinius (C. Asinius Pollio) as being present when Cæsar entered into this discussion; and as C. Asinius Pollio was with Cæsar at the Rubicon and at the Battle of Pharsalia, and also wrote a history of the civil wars, which furnished materials for anecdotes about Cæsar, we may infer that Plutarch took his account from Pollio's work—a good authority.

cross the river; and thence advancing at full speed he attacked Ariminum before daybreak and took it." [1]

I have said that before the 20th of April 1653, Cromwell had committed no overt illegal act, the justification of the meetings at his lodgings being admitted. This expression must, however, be understood as applicable to the Government as then constituted. For as the Government was constituted before the expulsion by military force of the Presbyterian members of the Parliament, known as "Pride's Purge," that expulsion was undoubtedly an illegal act against the Legislature as then existing. It was an act, however, partaking rather of the nature of open war than of treachery. The Presbyterians hated the Independents, and would have destroyed them if they had had the power. The expulsion therefore of the Presbyterians from the Parliament, by Cromwell and the Independents, was an act of self-defence. But Cromwell's expulsion, on the 20th of April 1653, of the Independents who then constituted the Parliament, was an act of a totally different kind; being not an act of *self-defence against enemies, but an act of treachery against friends*—against friends who trusted him, and with whom he had acted for all the thirteen years during which he had sat with them in that great Parliament; against friends to whom, even at the very moment he was preparing to destroy them, "he made the most solemn professions of fidelity." [2] As long as truth and honour have any existence among mankind, and till a time come when those who live not merely by pillaging or overreaching other people, but by betraying their friends, shall be powerful enough to make a code of morality founded on their own practice, there can be small

---

[1] Plutarch, C. Cæsar, c. 32.
[2] Ludlow's Memoirs, vol. ii. p. 451 : 2nd edition, London, 1721.

difficulty in stamping its proper name upon the deed which Cromwell was now about to do.

For the last time in that antique chapel which formed their hall of debate, and has become more famous than any of those temples in which the Roman Senate assembled in ancient days,—sat that renowned assembly. There was Sir Henry Vane, the wildest of theologians, the subtlest and yet most practical of statesmen, with long, pale, melancholy face, and bright yet somewhat restless look, that to the superstition of that age might seem to forebode an unquiet end. There was Thomas Scot, as eloquent and almost as able as Vane, some of whose speeches, though only preserved in fragments, are among the most eloquent in the English language. There was the soldier-philosopher, Algernon Sydney, by his mother's side the descendant of Hotspur, as impatient as Hotspur himself of kingly arrogance and court arts, and like Hotspur prepared to resist them to death; with face thoughtful, like Vane's and Scot's, yet different from theirs in a certain stern, dauntless, and commanding expression, which seemed to unite the high, fierce, determined spirit of a republican soldier with the pride of a nobility of twenty generations. There too, with tall military figure, aquiline features, and bright black eyes, in which the enthusiasm that sparkled at times, and often seemed to slumber under his long dark eyelashes, gave something wild, striking, and even noble to his aspect, was the " bravest of the brave," Thomas Harrison, who, though not, like Sydney, possessing any pretensions to chivalry of lineage, carried his daring as a soldier to the most chivalrous extent; and whose religious enthusiasm took a wilder flight even than Vane's, and on this day made him the dupe to aid in digging a pitfall that was to be his own grave. For all those four men the deed that was to be done that day by their ancient friend and comrade was to lead to a terrible end. For them there will be " a darker departure " than fell to the lot of Hampden, and Pym, and Ireton. For them "the war-drum is muffled, and black is the bier." For them, amid the frantic shouts of a fickle multitude for the restoration of the Stuarts, the " death-bell is tolling," that is to herald them to the scaffold, which is destined to be their stormy and agonised pathway to the grave. Yet of all four—the statesmen and the soldiers—the deaths were to be equally without fear, and without a shadow of mistrust in their great Cause—their " good old Cause "—for which they had lived and fought and laboured, and for which they died, or, to use their own words, which they " sealed with their blood."

Early on the morning of the 20th of April, 1653, Whitelock and Widdrington went again, according to appointment, to Cromwell's lodgings, where there were but few Parliament men, and a few officers of the army. A point was again raised which had been debated the preceding night, " whether forty persons, or about that number of Parliament men and officers of the army, should be nominated by the Parliament, and empowered for the managing the affairs of the Commonwealth, till a new Parliament should meet, and so the present Parliament to be forthwith dissolved."[1]   Whitelock says he was against this proposal, and the more, fearing lest he might be one of these forty, who he thought would be in a desperate condition after the Parliament should be dissolved ; but others were very ambitious to be of this number and Council, and to be invested with this exorbitant power.[2]   During this

---

[1] Whitelock's Memorials, p. 554 : London, 1732.   [2] Ibid.

debate Cromwell, being informed that the Parliament was sitting, and "that it was hoped they would put a period to themselves, which would be the most honourable dissolution for them,"[1] immediately broke up the meeting. The members of the Parliament who were with him then left him at his lodgings, went to the House, and "found them," says Whitelock, "in debate of an act which would occasion other meetings of them again, and prolong their sitting."[2]

This statement of Whitelock, who was present— appears at first sight to be at variance with the evidence of no less than four authorities : Cromwell's Declaration, the Memoirs of Ludlow, (who, though not present, expressly says he had his information from Major-General Harrison,) the Journal of the Earl of Leicester, (who received his information from his son Algernon Sydney, who was present,) and a speech in Richard Cromwell's Parliament of Sir Arthur Haselrig, who was also present. The variation may be accounted for by the supposition that the House was for some time in debate on the Bill for settling the claims of

---

[1] Whitelock's Memorials, p. 554: London, 1723.

[2] *Ibid.* After the record of the proceedings of the 19th of April, 1653, in the printed Journals there occurs this note: " Here follows an entry, which is expunged; and against it, in the margin, is written this memorandum, 'This entry was expunged by order of Parliament, January 7, 1659.'" The Journal of that day, January 7, 1659, contains the following passage: " Whereas this House do find an entry in the Journal-Book of April 20, 1653, in these words: ' This day his Excellency the Lord-General dissolved this Parliament, which was done without consent of Parliament,' Resolved, that the Parliament doth declare, that the same is a forgery. Resolved, that Mr. Scobell be sent for to the bar of the House." Mr. Scobell, on his appearing and being shown the entry, acknowledged that it was his own handwriting, and that he did it without the direction of any person whatever. The House then ordered the entry to be expunged out of the Journal, and referred it to a Committee to consider whether the then late Act of Indemnity extended to pardon that offence.—*Commons' Journals,* January 7, 1659.

the adventurers for Ireland, and then returned to the great question of finally passing the Bill for their own dissolution, which question was ready to be put. Harrison afterwards told Ludlow—"The question for passing the Bill being to be put, Cromwell said to him (Harrison), 'This is the time, I must do it.'" And Haselrig's words are, "The question was putting for it, when our General stood up and stopped the question."

The facts then we may conclude, on the testimony of four witnesses, Cromwell, Harrison, Algernon Sydney, and Haselrig, were these. The Bill for the dissolution, with the amendments, was ready to be put to the final vote. But before proceeding to that vote the House went into a debate on a Bill for settling the claims of the adventurers for Ireland.

Now there starts up here one of those contradictions so difficult to comprehend, much less to explain, in the characters of such men as Cromwell. First, the information brought to Cromwell of the Parliament's having entered into debate on new business, and thereby raising pretexts for continuing their sitting, affords Cromwell a pretext for getting into a rage with the Parliament for not putting an end to their sitting. And secondly, when, on going to the House, he found they were actually putting the question for passing the Bill for their dissolution, he makes that a new pretext for getting into a new rage. Let those who claim for this man the perfection of human intelligence and human virtue reconcile these contradictions if they can.

"Thereupon," continues Whitelock, "Colonel Ingoldsby went back to Cromwell, and told him what the House were doing; who was so enraged thereat, expecting they should have meddled with no other business but putting a period

to their own sitting without more delay, that he presently
commanded some of the officers of the army to fetch
a party of soldiers, with whom he marched to the
House." [1]

It is remarkable that Whitelock, who was present, should
have made a statement so inaccurate as that contained in
the concluding words of the sentence [2] which .I have just
quoted down to the word "House." The sentence in
Whitelock concludes thus, " and led a file of musketeers
in with him; the rest he placed at the door of the House,
and in the lobby before it." Two of the witnesses already
mentioned, Algernon Sydney and Major-General Harrison,
distinctly state that he did not lead either a file or files

---

[1] Whitelock's Memorials, p. 554.

[2] It has been proved that the editor
of Whitelock's Embassy to Sweden
omitted some most important passages
(see Aysc. MS. Brit. Mus. 4991, p. 206,
and Brodie's Hist. vol. ii. pp. 16, note,
and pp. 43, 44, and note). There are
some circumstances in Whitelock's
account of Cromwell's expulsion of
the Parliament that seem to lead to
the supposition that the passage has
been tampered with. Besides the
gross inaccuracy mentioned in the
text, which could hardly have been
made by a man who was present, unless he had lost his senses and was
paralysed by fear, the man who has
shown this confusion of mind is represented as having also the folly to say,
" And among all the Parliament men,
of whom many wore swords, and
would sometimes brag high, not one
man offered to draw his sword against
Cromwell, or to make the least resistance against him; but all of them tamely
departed the house." Ludlow, who was
not there—being in Ireland at the
time, but who received an exact account
of what occurred from Harrison, and
others who were present—and Algernon Sydney, who was present, knew too
well, as soldiers, the folly of resistance
with the sword at such a time to make
any remark like this of Whitelock's,
which resembles the silly and malicious
imputations of cowardice which Hyde
and Mrs. Hutchinson are so fond of
making. Whitelock's remark is made
in the spirit of Jacobitism, and has
been since repeated by Jacobite
writers. For there is no mode so easy
of blackening a man or a body of men
as the charge of cowardice. How
little the mean reproach here made
was merited in the case of Vane, Scot,
and Sydney, was signally proved by
that fortitude which deliberately preferred honourable death to dishonourable submission, a fortitude beyond
the comprehension or credence of such
men as Clarendon and Whitelock.

of musketeers " in with him." Neither did the Parliament know that he had any musketeers outside the door of the House till he called them in.

As Algernon Sydney told the story to his father, " Cromwell- came into the House, clad in plain black clothes, with grey worsted stockings, and sat down as he used to do in an ordinary place." [1] After sitting and hearing the debate for some time, he called to Major-General Harrison, who was on the other side of the House, to come to him, and told him that " he judged the Parliament ripe for a dissolution, and this to be the time for doing it." The Major-General answered, " as he since told me," says Ludlow [2]—" Sir, the work is very great and dangerous, therefore I desire you seriously to consider of it before you engage in it." " You say well," replied the General, and thereupon sat still for about a quarter of an hour. Then the question for passing the Bill being to be put, he said again to Major-General Harrison, " This is the time, I must do it." Then suddenly standing up he made a speech, wherein he loaded the Parliament with the vilest reproaches,[3] charging them with not having a heart to do anything for the public good, with having espoused the corrupt interest of presbytery and the lawyers; who were the supporters of tyranny and oppression, accusing them of an intention to perpetuate themselves in power, *had they not been forced to the passing of this Act, which he*

---

[1] The Journal of the Earl of Leicester, p. 139, in Sydney Papers, edited by R. W. Blencowe, A.M.: London, 1825.

[2] Ludlow's Memoirs, vol. ii. p. 455 : 2nd edition, London, 1721.

[3] Ludlow's Memoirs, vol. ii. p. 456 : 2nd edition, London, 1721.—Lord Leicester says, "After a while, he rose up, put off his hat, and spake. At the first, and for a good while, he spake to the commendation of the Parliament for their pains and care of the public good ; but afterwards he changed his style, told them of their injustice, delays of justice, self-interest, and other faults."—*Journal of the Earl of Leicester*, pp. 139, 140.

affirmed they designed never to observe ; [1] and thereupon told them, " that the Lord had done with them, and had chosen other instruments for the carrying on His work, that were more worthy." All this he spoke with so much passion, as if he had been distracted. The cant which introduces the name of the Deity on all occasions, a cant which is offensive enough in the ordinary saints of that time, is infinitely more offensive in the mouth of a man who uses it as a cloak for his own rapacious self-aggrandisement. It is like an attempt to invest the mortal tyrant with the attributes of Immortality and Omnipotence.

Sir Peter Wentworth stood up to answer him, and said " that this was the first time that ever he had heard such unbecoming language given to the Parliament, and that it was the more horrid in that it came from their servant, and their servant whom they had so highly trusted and obliged." But as he was going on, Cromwell stept into the midst of the House, where he said, " Come, come, I will put an end to your prating.". Then walking up and down the House like a madman, and kicking the ground with his feet, he cried out, " You are no Parliament; I say you are no Parliament; I will put an end to your sitting; call them in, call them in." Thereupon Harrison went out and presently brought in Lieutenant-Colonel Worsley, who commanded the General's own regiment of foot, with five or six files of musqueteers, " about 20 or 30 " says Lord Leicester, " with their musquets ; " [2] which Sir Henry Vane observing from his place, said aloud,

---

[1] Ludlow's Memoirs, vol. ii. p. 436. —The words which I print in italics are another proof, in addition to those I will give presently, that Cromwell's assertions respecting the Act here referred to are false. -

[2] Lord Leicester's Journal, p. 140. " Six hommes font une file."—*Mémoires de Montecuculi,* I. ii. 24.

" This is not honest, yea, it is against morality and common honesty." [1]   Then Cromwell fell a railing at him, crying out with a loud voice, " O Sir Henry Vane, Sir Henry Vane, the Lord deliver me from Sir Henry Vane ! " Then looking upon one of the members, he said, " There sits a drunkard ; " and giving much reviling language to others, he commanded the mace to be taken away, saying, " Here, take away this fool's bauble ! " [2]

Cromwell, then, pointing to the Speaker in his chair, said to Harrison, " Fetch him down." Harrison went to the Speaker, and said that, " seeing things were brought to this pass, it would not be convenient for him to remain there." The Speaker, according to Ludlow, [3] answered that " he would not come down unless he were forced." But according to Lord Leicester, the Speaker sat still, and said nothing. " Take him down," said Cromwell. Then Harrison went and pulled the Speaker by the gown, and he came down. [4] " It happened that day," continues Lord Leicester, " that Algernon Sydney sat next to the Speaker on the right hand. The General said to Harrison, ' Put him out.' Harrison spake to Sydney to go out ; but he said he would not go out, and sat still. The General said again, ' Put him out.' Then Harrison and Worsley put their hands upon Sydney's shoulders, as if they would force him to go out. Then he rose and went towards the door." [5]

Cromwell then addressed himself to the members of the House, who were, says Ludlow, between 80 and 100, and

[1] Ludlow's Memoirs, vol. ii. p. 45 : 2nd edition, London, 1721.

[2] Ludlow says (vol. ii. p. 457) Cromwell said, " What shall we do with this bauble ? Here, take it away." Whitelock says (p. 554), " He bid one of his soldiers to take away that fool's bauble, the mace." Lord Leiceste

says (p. 141), " Then the General went to the table where the mace lay, which used to be carried before the Speaker, and said, ' Take away these baubles.'"

[3] Ludlow's Memoirs, vol. ii. p. 457.

[4] Lord Leicester's Journal, p. 140.

[5] Ibid. pp. 140, 141.

said to them, " It's you that have forced me to this, for I
have sought the Lord night and day, that He would rather
slay me than put me upon the doing of this work." [1]
" Cromwell," continues Ludlow, " having acted this treacherous and impious part, ordered the guard to see the
House cleared of all the members, and then seized upon the
records that were there, and at Mr. Scobell's house. After
which he went to the clerk, and, snatching the Act of
Dissolution, which was ready to pass, out of his hand, he
put it under his cloak, and having commanded the doors
to be locked up, went away to Whitehall." [2]

Lord Leicester says that, as the members were going out,
the General said to young Sir Henry Vane, calling him by
his name, that he might have prevented this extraordinary
course; but he was a juggler, and had not so much as
common honesty.[3]   Lord Leicester prefaces this anecdote
with the words "they say," and it is not mentioned either
by Ludlow or Whitelock. It is probable enough, however,
that Cromwell said something of the kind by way of retort
to Vane's exclamation, " This is not honest; yea, it is
against morality and common honesty." Which of the
two, Vane or Cromwell, was the juggler may be left to
the judgment of impartial posterity.

It has been shown that Cromwell, on this 20th of April
1653, first got into a passion when he was informed that
the Parliament were occupied with other business than
the Act for their dissolution; and secondly, that he got

---

[1] Ludlow's Memoirs, vol. ii. pp.
457, 458: 2nd edition, London, 1721.

[2] *Ibid.* p. 458.—" This villanous
attempt," adds Ludlow, "was much
encouraged by the ambassadors lately
arrived from Holland with instructions to conclude a peace, who insti-

gated Cromwell to take the power into
his own hands, well understanding
that he would soon be necessitated
to make peace with them upon what
terms they should think fit."—*Ibid.*

[3] Lord Leicester's Journal, p. 141.

into a passion with them when they were going to put the question for finally passing the Bill for their dissolution. If such conduct have something of the appearance of madness, it is madness with method in it. To do an act of treachery and perfidy with a burst of imperious anger, instead of doing it with the command of temper which is usually observed to belong to treacherous and perfidious natures, may give to such an act an appearance of daring, of grandeur, of magnanimity, which, false though it be, may yet be able to dazzle the imagination and mislead the judgment. I do not say that Cromwell had nicely calculated this effect of his passion on this occasion. I think it more probable that he found the work he had set himself to do disagreeable, and that he took refuge from the reproaches of his own mind by putting himself into a passion—a very common proceeding with many men. I also agree with Hume, that while Cromwell could descend to employ "the most profound dissimulation, the most oblique and refined artifice," he was "carried by his natural temper to magnanimity, to grandeur, and to an imperious and domineering policy." A man of this temper of mind is apt to attempt to indemnify himself for the restraint he has found it convenient to put at one time on the predominant part of his nature, by giving at another time the loose rein to his imperious passions; and, when he suddenly turns round upon his former friends, and ruins them and their cause, to seek to justify his deeds to himself, if not to others, by heaping on those, to whom he had just before given the highest commendations and made the most solemn professions of fidelity, every term of reproach and contempt which a scurrilous vocabulary can supply.

It must have been a strange sight to see the members

of that great Parliament walking away in groups of two or three, after this extraordinary scene, from the old Gothic chapel, which had witnessed their labours and their triumphs, and which, through all the ages of its famous history, has never before or since held such men as they. To the superior spirits among them—to Vane, to Scot, to Algernon Sydney, whose knowledge of the past history of mankind would give them some foresight of the future, and whom the deed done by Cromwell that day was, at no very distant time, to send to the scaffold[1]—it must have been manifest that their career as statesmen was ended; that never more for them could the Parliament or the Council of State be the great arena, where they had once so powerfully contended for liberty and empire.

Cromwell, having thus settled to his own satisfaction the expulsion of the Parliament, returned to Whitehall, where he found the Council of Officers in debate concerning this weighty affair; and informed them that he had done it, and that they needed not to trouble themselves any further about it. But Colonel Okey and some others, officers of the army, who did not come under John Lilburne's designation of "creature colonels," repaired to the General, to desire satisfaction in that proceeding, conceiving that the way they were now going tended to ruin and confusion. "To these," says Ludlow, "having not yet taken off his mask, but pretending to more honesty and self-denial than ever, he professed himself to do much more good, and with more expedition, than could be expected from the Parliament; while professions from him

---

[1] I think that, but for this deed of Cromwell—which not only ruined the cause for which the Parliamentary armies had fought, but destroyed all faith in the honesty of the Independents—the Stuarts would never have been able to return.

put most of them to silence, and moved them to a resolution of waiting for a further discovery of his design, before they would proceed to a breach and division from him. But Colonel Okey, being jealous that the end would be bad, because the means were such as made them justly suspected of hypocrisy, enquired of Colonel Desborough what his [Cromwell's] meaning was to give such high commendations to the Parliament, when he endeavoured to dissuade the officers of the army from petitioning them for a dissolution, and, so short a time after, to eject them with so much scorn and contempt; who had no other answer to make, but that, if ever he drolled in his life, he had drolled then." [1]

In the afternoon of that same day, the 20th of April 1653, in the morning of which he had thus expelled the Parliament, Cromwell came to the Council of State, who were assembled at the usual place of meeting in Whitehall. Cromwell was accompanied by those two officers whose concurrence, as has been shown, he had taken such care to procure—Lambert and Harrison. On his entrance, Cromwell said: "Gentlemen, if you are met here as private persons, you shall not be disturbed; but if as a Council of State, this is no place for you; and since you can't but know what was done at the House in the morning, so take notice, that the Parliament is dissolved." To this Serjeant Bradshaw [2] answered : "Sir, we have heard what you did at the House in the morning, and before many hours all England will hear of it. But, Sir, you are

---

[1] Ludlow's Memoirs, vol. ii. pp. 495, 460: 2nd edition, London, 1721.

[2] Bradshaw was not President of the Council for this month. "That Mr. Bond be appointed President of the Council for the month ensuing."— *Order Book of the Council of State,* Wednesday, March 23, 165$\frac{2}{3}$, MS. State Paper Office. The Earl of Salisbury had been President of the Council for the month preceding—namely, from February 23 to March 23.

mistaken to think that the Parliament is dissolved; for
no power under Heaven can dissolve them but themselves;
therefore take you notice of that." Something more,
according to Ludlow, was said to the same purpose by
Scot, Haselrig, and Love; and then "the Council of
State, perceiving themselves to be under the same violence,
departed." [1]

When a man of Cromwell's abilities sets to work to give
a particular colour to any transaction, it is no easy matter
to discover the true colour of that transaction. Cromwell's
strongest point against the Parliament was his assertion
that their Bill for a new Parliament, which they were passing through its last stages when he expelled them from
their house, contained clauses by which "these present
members were to sit, and to be made up by others chosen,
and by themselves approved of." These words are from
a "Narrative of the Manner of the Parliament's being Dismissed," published on the day after the expulsion of the
Parliament, the 21st of April, which the compilers of the new
"Parliamentary History" designate as "of equal authority
with that of the Journals themselves; being published at
the very time of action, and licensed by Mr. Scobell, Clerk
of the House." [2] But the compilers of the "Parliamentary
History," in making this assertion, must have forgotten the
vast difference between the position of Mr. Scobell on the
20th of April 1653, and his position on the following day,
the 21st of April 1653. As Antony in Shakspeare's play
said of Cæsar, we may truly say of that great Parliament:
"But yesterday their word might have stood against the
world: and now none so poor to do them reverence." The
"Clerk of the House" was no longer their servant, but the

[1] Ludlow's Memoirs, vol. ii. p. 461:   [2] Parl. Hist. vol. iii. pp. 1381,
2nd edition, London, 1721.   1382.

servant of their destroyer ; and in that capacity he could do, and did, his part to poison the very fountain-head of history.

I believe, as firmly as I believe my own existence, that at this stage of his career Cromwell made as much use of falsehood as his creature Monk afterwards did, when he was taking measures to sell his country for a dukedom and a large sum of money.   My belief is grounded on a vast mass of evidence, long and carefully weighed.[1]   Yet he took such precautions in this case, that it is impossible to *prove* that the Bill did not contain what he asserted that it contained ; for he seized it, and carried it off with him to his own house, and it was never produced afterwards. The words quoted above, if they mean anything, mean that the present Parliament, under colour of giving the people a new and free Parliament, meant to perpetuate their own power.   Now this is most distinctly denied by two witnesses, both of them credible and well-informed : the one,

[1] As one of innumerable instances of the opinions formed, by those who knew him personally, of Cromwell's honesty and veracity, I give the following : "Amongst these was a cornet, whose name was Day, and who, being charged with saying that Cromwell was a rogue and a traitor, confessed the words ; and, to justify himself, said that Cromwell had affirmed, in the presence of himself and divers other officers, that if he did oppress the conscientious, or betray the liberties of the people, or not take away tithes by a certain time *now past,* they should then have liberty to say he was a rogue or traitor.   He moved, therefore, that he might be permitted to produce his witnesses, who were then present, to the particulars before-mentioned ; but the matter was so ordered, that he and some others were fined and imprisoned for their pretended misdemeanours."—*Ludlow's Memoirs,* vol. ii. p. 605 : 2nd edition, London, 1721.   That Cromwell was quite conscious of the distrust with which his assertions were received by those he addressed, is proved by the expressions with which he interlarded his discourse, such as, "*This is very true that I tell you, God knows I lie not!*" a form of words certainly not indicative of a man of *truthful habits*—a phraseology now in use among the lowest and least veracious members of society.   A man of habitual veracity and honour would no more think of using such asseverations, than an honourable matron would think it necessary to affirm that she was "an honest woman."

General Ludlow, a member of that Parliament; and the other Mrs. Hutchinson, the wife of Colonel Hutchinson, also a member of it.

Falsehood, in the shape of calumny, has ever been and will ever be one of the most powerful weapons of those who, while they pursue their selfish ends with the ravenous fury of wild beasts or savages, find themselves compelled to pay some deference to the public opinion of their age and country. When you have done any man a deep and grievous wrong, it may appear a duty you owe to yourself and your family, to blacken the character of the man you have injured, so that what you have done may have a chance of appearing not wrong, but right. In the beginning of that 17th century, a very remarkable example of this mode of proceeding occurred in the affair which James I. called the " Gowrie Conspiracy." The Earl of Gowrie and his brother, Alexander Ruthven, were murdered by King James, who published his own account of the matter, in which he declared that he had acted in his own defence ; and everything in the shape of a defence of the Earl of Gowrie and his brother was so effectually destroyed, that not a single copy can now be met with.[1]

Cromwell, in his " Declaration of the Grounds and Reasons for thus Dissolving the Parliament by Force," dated " Whitehall, April 22, 1653," asserted that " those persons of honour and integrity amongst them, who had eminently appeared for God and the public good, were rendered of no further use in Parliament, than, by meeting with a corrupt party, to give them countenance to carry on their ends, and for effecting the desire they had of perpetuating themselves in the supreme government; for which purpose the said party long opposed, and frequently declared

[1] See Pitcairn's Criminal Trials of Scotland, vol. ii. pp. 209, 210.

themselves against having, a new representative : and
when they saw themselves necessitated to take that Bill
into consideration, they resolved to make use of it to
recruit the House with persons of the same spirit and
temper, thereby to perpetuate their own sitting.''[1]

This passage partakes, in a large measure, of the darkness
that characterises Cromwell's utterances, whether written
or spoken, when he had a case to make out.   First he
admits that there were " persons of honour and integrity
amongst them."   Then he says that " those persons of
honour and integrity were rendered of no further use in
Parliament, than, by meeting with a corrupt party, to
give them countenance to carry on their ends, and for
effecting the desire they had of perpetuating themselves in
the supreme government."   The meaning I suppose is,
though the grammar is in a state of chaos, that the persons of honour and integrity were made use of by a corrupt
party as a cloak to deceive the nation.   And in the next
passage " the said party " means the " corrupt party "
before mentioned.

Now it certainly appears, from the Journals of the 14th
November 1651, that when the question was put, " That it
is now a convenient time to declare a certain time for the
continuance of the Parliament, beyond which it shall not
sit," there was a large proportion of members, out of a
house of 96—in one division 46 to 50, in another 47 to 49—
who were against entertaining the question at all.   In
both the divisions Cromwell was one of the tellers for the
Yeas.   It was, however, four days after, on the 18th of
November, ultimately " Resolved, that the time for the
continuance of this Parliament, beyond which they resolve
not to sit, shall be the 3rd day of November 1654."   And,

---

[1] Parl. Hist. vol. iii. p. 1387.

by a subsequent resolution, the 3rd of November 1653 was appointed, instead of the 3rd of November 1654.

It may be inferred from this, that the above-mentioned minority of 46 or 47 constituted the "corrupt party," referred to by Cromwell in the passage just quoted of his "Declaration" of 22nd April 1653. So far, then, Cromwell had a colour of truth to support his assertions. But this colour will not go far. For his assertion implies that this "corrupt party" was a majority, and not, as the Journals show in the above-cited divisions, a minority, though undoubtedly a large minority. And therefore that assertion, that the "corrupt party" had so framed their Bill for electing a new Parliament, as to render it an instrument for perpetuating themselves, is unsupported by evidence.

If Cromwell could have *proved* the truth of his assertions, why did he not publish a copy of the Bill? *He could not prove* the truth of his assertions, and he took good care that the Bill should never be forthcoming. The Bill had not been printed or even engrossed. "Cromwell," as Mr. Forster says, "had seized the only copy in existence on the day of the dissolution; had carried it himself, under his cloak, to his own house at Whitehall; and was never afterwards known to refer to it in any way."[1] It was to be expected that, partly from carelessness, partly from bias against the Rump, writers such as the compilers of the "Parliamentary History" should, as has been shown, assume as true Cromwell's assertions respecting the Bill which he seized, and never produced afterwards. But it is rather surprising that Mr. Forster, who has investigated

[1] Forster's Life of Oliver Cromwell, vol. ii. p. 75: London, 1839. — Mr. Forster, in his "Life of Vane" (pp. 158-162), has collected from the Journals of the House the main provisions of the Bill, which were substantially the same as those of Ireton's Bill, called "An Agreement of the People of England," described in the First Volume of this History, pp. 27-30.

this subject with great care and ability, should have ad-mitted, or taken for granted, Cromwell's assertion that the Bill provided for the re-election, or for the continuance without re-election, of the members of the present Parlia-ment.

Besides the reasons I have already assigned for saying that Cromwell's assertion was not proved, and that his ob-ject was to make it *seem* that the Bill contained such provisions without being able to *prove* it, though, had it been *true*, he could have *proved* it at once, by printing and publishing the Bill, it is a significant circumstance, that while the *semi-official* "Narrative," already re-ferred to, issued on the 21st of April, asserts in positive words that "by the said Act these present members were to sit and to be made up by others chosen, and by them-selves approved of," the *official* "Declaration," issued on the 22nd of April, carefully avoids any such positive asser-tion, using more vague words, "recruit the House with persons of the same spirit and temper, thereby to perpetu-ate their own sitting." The craft of Cromwell is very conspicuous in this distinction. He might, and would of course, disown the *semi-official* paper when it suited him so to do. The words of the *official* paper, which he could not disown, were so chosen that they might be explained to mean, either that the present members were to continue to sit, and that persons of the same spirit and temper were to be added to them, to make up the full number of 400 ; or that the present members were either not to sit at all in the next House, or were to take their chance of re-election with the new members who were to form the new Parliament.

Add to all this evidence against the assertion of their destroyer, that the Parliament meant to perpetuate themselves, the solemn declaration of Thomas Scot, one of their most illustrious members. In a speech made in Richard Cromwell's Parliament, Thomas Scot said: "The Dutch war came on. If it had pleased God and his Highness to have let that little power of a Parliament sit a little longer,—when Hannibal is *ad portas*, something must be done *extra leges*,—*we intended to have gone off with a good savour, and provided for a succession of Parliaments; but we stayed to end the Dutch war*." [1]

"Thus," says a hostile writer, "by their own mercenary servants, and not a sword drawn in their defence, fell the haughty and victorious Rump, whose mighty actions will scarcely find belief in future generations." [2] A more modern hostile writer declares he knows not in what eyes are tears at their departure, except it be their own; and then he approvingly quotes the assertion of his veracious man-god, "my Lord-General," "we did not hear a dog bark at their going." It would, I apprehend, be somewhat difficult to detect a dog in the act of barking at the hanging of "my Lord-General" himself, and all his parasites in one rope.

Yet let not this renowned Parliament die unheard. And in the vindication of the purity of its intentions, and of the respect due to its memory—by such men as Scot and Vane, who "sealed the cause with their blood," and declared upon the scaffold, in the last words they uttered, "that it was a cause not to be repented of,"—there is a tone of deep yet manly sorrow, that must command the respect of every candid and generous mind. There is too,

[1] This speech, which was made in Richard Cromwell's Parliament, is reported in the "Diary of Thomas Burton, Esq., Member in the Parliaments of Oliver and Richard Cromwell, from 1656-1659," edited by John Towill Rutt.

[2] Roger Coke's Detection of the Court and State of England, vol. ii. p. 30.

in the words of those men, all the solemnity of death; for events were already looming in no distant future, which foreboded to them a dark and inevitable fate. Nevertheless, their courage quailed not; and in their, I might say, dying words[1]—even, as it were, from the very ashes of that great assembly, which such men as they were to make immortal—there " flashed forth a stream of heroic rays." Ay, these are the true heroes; though libraries may be written, and temples dedicated, to the Moloch-worship of successful renegades, liars, and robbers!

Thus ended that Government called "The Commonwealth," after a duration of four years and nearly three months. Though English historians have extended the name of Commonwealth to the military despotism of Cromwell which succeeded, and have thus given to Cromwell all the credit due to the good government of the statesmen of the Commonwealth, and to the statesmen of the Commonwealth all the discredit due to the bad government of Cromwell, the original records of the proceedings of both remain, to show to all ages the vast difference between that body of men who constituted THE COUNCIL OF STATE, and that body of men who constituted CROMWELL'S COUNCIL OF STATE.

[1] Scot's last words in Parliament—when some of the Presbyterians, who were in the reassembled Long Parliament, before its final destruction by Monk, moved that before they separated they should bear their witness against the execution of the King—were that, "though he knew not where to hide his head at that time, yet he durst not refuse to own, that not only his hand but his heart also was in it."—*Ludlow's Memoirs*, vol. ii. p. 864: 2nd edition, London, 1721. The words, as reported in Burton's Diary, which seem to refer to the same occasion, are these: "I would be content it should be set upon my monument—if it were my last act, I own it—I was one of the King's judges. I hope it shall not be said of us, as of the Romans once, 'O homines ad servitutem parati!'" Vane and Algernon Sydney, though neither of them approved of the King's execution, or had either "hand or heart in that affair," manifested the same lofty and intrepid spirit before their judges and on the scaffold.

The last meeting recorded in the Order Book of THE
Council of State, is on Friday, the 15th of April 1653.
No business of any particular importance is recorded in the
minutes; nor does anything appear in the minutes, giving
the least sign or foreboding of the catastrophe of Wednesday next, the 20th of April.   There were eighteen members
of the Council present, including Vane, Scot, the Earl of
Salisbury, and Sir Arthur Haselrig.   There is no record preserved of the meeting in the afternoon of the 20th of April.
And so closes the last Order Book of the Council of State.

The first meetings of Cromwell's Council of State, beginning a new Order Book, like the former Order Books in all
outward signs, is on Friday the 29th of April 1653.   The
members present of this new Council of Saints—who were,
as poor Harrison dreamt, to initiate the Millennium—were
the Lord-General Cromwell, Major-General Lambert,
Major-General Harrison, Mr. Carew, Colonel Bennet,
Colonel Sydenham, Colonel Stapeley, Mr. Strickland.   Of
these eight, six were military men.   This seems to be the
general proportion.   Thus on Tuesday, the 3rd of May 1653,
the members present were Major-General Lambert, Major-
General Harrison, Mr. Carew, Major-General Desbrough
[Desborough, Cromwell's brother-in-law], Mr. Strickland,
Colonel Sydenham, Colonel Stapeley.   This, therefore, was
a mere barrack-room Council—a Council of what John
Lilburne called the " creature colonels," whom Oliver,
assuming the style royal, might call " creatures of our
own," as Queen Elizabeth called the Earl of Leicester
" a creature of our own."   John Lilburne proved only too
true a prophet.   Never more were Vane,[1] Scot, and Sydney
to appear in that Council-room.   There was no affinity

---

[1] As to the composition of Crom-   fusal to be a member of it, see note 1,
well's Council of State, and Vane's re-   p. 479.

between the nature of Oliver Cromwell and theirs. But there was a strong affinity between Cromwell's nature and that of Monk, and of another man whose name soon after appears in the list of the members of Cromwell's Council of State. The name of that other man is an omen and, as it were, a history of what were to be the consequences of the grand perfidy of Cromwell. The name is entered on the list thus—" Sir A. A. Cooper."

It was of such men, no doubt, as Cromwell, and Monk, and Cooper, that Sir Henry Vane was thinking when, in his prayer with his family and friends, in his chamber on the morning of his execution, he used these words—" Oh ! what abjuring of light, what treachery, what meanness of spirit, has appeared in this day ! "[1]

The three men above mentioned may be designated as a triumvirate of traitors, who carried the successful practice of treachery and falsehood to a height sufficient to strike the common herd of their imitators at once with admiration and despair. And so long had this successful career lasted, with that one of the three who survived the others, Cooper or Shaftesbury (for he had rotted into a peer with that title), that it might really have seemed that the only character to be venerated on earth, where success has so much to do with veneration, was that of an adroit practitioner of treachery and falsehood. This man had been a traitor to every party, but, up to a certain point, his treacheries had always prospered. " Whether it were accident or sagacity," says Lord Macaulay, " he had timed his

[1] The Tryal of Sir Henry Vane, Kt. At the King's Bench, Westminster, June the 2nd and 6th, 1662 ; together with what he intended to have spoken the day of his sentence (June 11) for arrest of judgment (had he not been interrupted and overruled by the Court) and his Bill of Exception. With other occasional speeches, &c. Also his speech and prayer on the Scaffold. Small 4to. Printed in the year 1662, p. 83.

desertions in such a manner, that fortune seemed to go to and fro with him from side to side."[1]

Lord Macaulay has described with great force the character of Shaftesbury—with greater force than either Butler or Dryden; though the character of Shaftesbury, while still living, had been drawn by them, "two of the greatest writers of the age—by Butler with characteristic brilliancy of wit, by Dryden with even more than characteristic energy and loftiness, by both with all the inspiration of hatred."[2] And the character of Shaftesbury was a sort of archetype of the characters of the politicians who appeared in England, not only after the restoration of Charles II., but after the expulsion of the Long Parliament by Cromwell. From that time, if we except Blake—who continued to fight the foreign enemies of England, but who never, in any sense, became the creature of Cromwell[3] —none of the great spirits, whose fixedness of purpose, intensity of will, and fierce yet single-minded and unselfish enthusiasm, had fought the great fight for liberty in the hall of debate as well as on the field of battle, had borne down before them the opposition alike of adverse opinions and of hostile armies, and extorted even from enemies a reluctant admiration, ever more acted with Cromwell. Between him and them a deep and impassable gulf had been fixed. Henceforth he must seek for other instruments of his will; for those who had been his coadjutors in the advancement of the

---

[1] Macaulay's Essay on Sir William Temple.

[2] *Ibid.*

[3] Neither Blake himself, nor his brother Benjamin, nor his nephew Robert, ever set their hands to the declaration of approval of Cromwell's expulsion of the Parliament, to which Cromwell obtained the signatures of Deane, Monk, Penn, and many of the captains of the ships.—See the declaration in Granville Penn's Memorials of Sir Wm. Pann, vol. i. pp. 489–491: London, 1833. See also Dixon's Robert Blake, p. 247: 8vo. edition, London, 1852.

great work of delivering England from civil and religious tyranny—from the tyranny of Laud, as well as from the tyranny of Strafford and Charles Stuart—would never submit to be the tools of their treacherous comrade, who now sought to substitute a tyrant under the name of Cromwell for a tyrant under the name of Stuart.[1]   Whatever vices or infirmities those men might have had, they had not the vices and infirmities of slaves or cowards—of quacks, of liars, of renegades.   One who lived among them and knew them well, though he had the weakness to serve under and to eulogise their treacherous destroyer, had learned from his knowledge of them how to describe that firmness of purpose which disdained submission [2]—that fortitude which

---

[1] " With Cromwell were associated, in his Council of State, eight officers of high rank and four civilians. The last would seem to have been thrown in as a convenient screen alone; for the Council of State, so constituted, was, to all intents and purposes, a military council. It will scarcely be believed that a desperate attempt was made to secure, in the position of one of the civilians, the name and authority of Sir Henry Vane; for none knew better than Cromwell, that any damage to such a character must be self-inflicted, and none more certain than he that such co-operation, by any argument secured, would altogether avert the possibility of a popular outbreak before his plans were ripe. No argument was therefore forgotten, no inducement omitted, to achieve the services of the 'juggling' Vane. But the manner of their reception became his character. As he had treated the insult, he treated the mean submission. From Belleau, his house in Lincolnshire, to which he had at once

retired after the 20th of April, 1653, he wrote a brief answer to the application from the Council, that 'though the reign of saints was now no doubt begun, he was willing, for his part, to defer his share in it till he should go to heaven.'"—*Forster's Life of Oliver Cromwell* (vol. ii. p. 129, London, 1839) cites an intercepted letter of Mr. T. Robinson to Mr. Stoneham, at the Hague, in Thurloe's State Papers, vol. i. p. 265.

[2] On the day before his execution some of Vane's friends having attempted to persuade him to make his submission to the King, and by that means endeavour to save his life, he said, " If the King did not think himself more concerned for his honour and word than *he* did for his life, he was very willing they should take it." And when others spoke to him of giving some thousands of pounds for his life, he said, " If a thousand farthings would gain it, he would not give them ; and if any should attempt to make such a bargain, he would spoil their market:

disdained escape : [1]

> "The unconquerable will,
> And study of revenge, immortal hate,
> And courage never to submit or yield,
> And what is else not to be overcome.' [2]

In the same essay in which Lord Macaulay has so

for I think," he added, "the King himself is so sufficiently obliged to spare my life, that it is fitter for him to do it than myself to seek it."
—*State Trials*, vol. vi. pp. 189, 190.

[1] When the Restoration came, Major-General Harrison refused to withdraw from his house and escape, deeming that a desertion of his cause and principles. He was accordingly seized with all his horses and arms, at his house in Staffordshire and brought to London. He was then committed to the Tower, and his horses taken to the Mews for the King's use. I have already described Harrison's behaviour on the scaffold (Vol. I. pp. 79, 80). There is a touching simplicity and earnestness in the few words that he was permitted to speak on his trial, where he saw the faces of brass of Monk, Shaftesbury, and Holles on the bench, among the judges who condemned him to death; "I would not," he said, "offer of myself the least injury to the poorest man or woman that goes upon the earth. I did what I did, as out of conscience to the Lord; for when I found those that were as the apple of mine eye to turn aside, I did loathe them, and suffered imprisonment many years. I chose rather to be separated from wife and family than to have compliance with them, though it was said, 'Sit at my right hand,' and such kind expressions. Thus I have given a little poor testimony that I have not been doing things in a corner, or from myself. Maybe I might be a little mistaken; but I did it all according to the best of my understanding, desiring to make the revealed will of God in his Holy Scriptures as a guide to me. I humbly conceive that what was done was done in the name of the Parliament of England, and that this Court or any Court below the High Court of Parliament hath no jurisdiction of these actions."
—*State Trials*, vol. v. pp. 1024, 1025. A more sincere, honest, and single-hearted enthusiast than Harrison never existed. There is in Lincoln's Inn Library a small 4to. which contains, besides the "Trial" and "Life and Death of Sir Henry Vane" before referred to, "The Speeches and Prayers of Major-General Harrison and others of 'the late King's judges,' with several occasional speeches and passages in their imprisonment and at their execution, faithfully and impartially collected."

[2] I will give here two out of many minutes in the Order Books, showing that Milton's work was not confined to foreign tongues : "That Mr. Milton do go to the committee of the army and desire them to send to the Council the book of examinations taken about the risings in Kent and Essex."—*Order Book of the Council of State*, June 22, 1650, MS. State Paper Office. "That Mr. Milton do peruse the examinations taken by the committee of the army concerning the insurrections in Essex, and take heads of the same, to the end the Council may judge what is fit to be taken into consideration."—*Ibid.* June 25, 1650. See also Vol. I. p. 172 of this history.

powerfully delineated the character of Shaftesbury, he has made an ingenious attempt to trace the cause of the difference between the leading politicians of the Long Parliament and the leading politicians who succeeded them. The cause of that difference he considers to lie in the difference between the moral qualities "which distinguish the men who produce revolutions from the men whom revolutions produce."

If this be true—and if the moral qualities of Shaftesbury, of Danby, of Churchill, of Jefferies, of Lauderdale, of Claverhouse, were the natural fruit of the great English Revolution—why then, it may be asked, did not the American Revolution produce an equally abundant crop of such men? The answer is, that it would have produced such a crop, if Washington had acted the part which Cromwell acted; that is, if he had turned round, and made use of the military power which he possessed to ruin the cause for which he had fought, and the men with whom he had acted, and who had entrusted him with that military power. By such a proceeding he would have driven away, or imprisoned, or destroyed (as Cromwell did) all the men who had fought and acted for something higher than self; and would have let loose, as Cromwell did, all the men whose god was, like his own, "self in the highest." It was the gigantic villany of Cromwell which was the father of all the villanies of the next two generations of Englishmen—from the falsehoods and treacheries of Monk, who sold the men who trusted him, and with them his country, to Stuart, who sold it to the King of France; of Shaftesbury, who just before the Restoration declared to the Regicides that he would be damned, body and soul, rather than suffer a hair of their heads to be hurt, and just after the Restoration was one of the judges who sentenced them to death; of

Lauderdale, who sold his King, and afterwards turned round, and in the name of that King's son tortured his former friends with iron boots and thumbscrews,—to "the hundred villanies of Marlborough." And yet Cromwell himself, who did all this, was one of the men who produced the revolution, not one of the men whom the revolution produced.

Such are some of the consequences of a great crime committed by a great man. The civil wars of Rome, without the termination which the success of Cæsar gave to them, might have been productive of many bad men, but not of such fiends in human shape as Tiberius and Sejanus, as Caligula and Nero, and their courtiers. Such men were not the natural production of a revolution or revolutions, but of the act of a man who, being entrusted with military power by his country, turned that power successfully against the country which had so trusted him. As Thomas Scot said of Cromwell—"Faith was broken, and somewhat else." And when an incarnate lie is set up and enthroned as the representative of a nation, that nation cannot be pronounced to be in a very healthy or hopeful condition.

As we look mournfully on the last page of these records [1] of the labours of statesmen who, like the Roman Senate of ancient days, had destroyed empires, and shown themselves more powerful than kings; and reflect that their free and far-extending thoughts and counsels were to be succeeded but by a troop of "creature colonels," and by the statesmanship of the barrack-room, we may say of them and of their fate—Farewell the free debate, where mind meets mind, and the result is determined by the

[1] I mean the last page of the Order Books of THE *Council of State*, a very different body from *Cromwell's Council of State*.

reason of the most powerful intellect, not by the domineering will of a man at the head of a band of soldiers!—Farewell the statesman-thought, the high design, which, seeking something higher than self, commands the respect of free-born men even in its very errors; and, far more than "the plumed troop and the big wars " of him whose god is " self in the highest," " makes ambition virtue ! "

.The consequences of Cromwell's proceeding, by which he had substituted for the Council of Statesmen a barrack-room Council of " creature colonels," soon began to show themselves.   Cromwell, in the hour of his extremity at Dunbar, said, in that letter he wrote to Haselrig, " Let H. Vane know what I write ; I would not make it public, lest danger should accrue thereby."   It had not then occurred to him to pray that " The Lord would deliver him from Sir Henry Vane ! "   It was indeed in an evil hour, for himself as well as others, that he so prayed—in that fit of insanity, in which he blasphemously gave to the Evil Spirit who had taken possession of him the name and attributes of the Omnipotent.   Had the voice of that Sir Henry Vane, whom he loaded with scurrilous reproaches, been heard, as, in the days that could return no more, it had been heard in the Council of State, the expedition against Hispaniola would never have been undertaken ; or if, by any chance, it had been undertaken, it would have been placed under very different leaders from Penn and Venables.   The expedition was, in itself, a distinct departure from the policy of the statesmen of the Commonwealth, who in all their measures had observed those rules of "morality and common honesty," which Vane told Cromwell he had violated in his expulsion of the Parliament.   It was a positive violation of treaty; as unwarrantable as Frederic II.'s attack on Silesia.

Cromwell had now, however, taken up his lot with the common herd of robber-tyrants, who, provided their villanies are successful, are hailed as gods upon earth. And as one principal occupation of those lofty personages is to rob one another, Oliver Cromwell bethought him, after having so infamously cheated the English nation, of committing a robbery on a large scale on his brother and ally the King of Spain, as the best method he could devise of purchasing the freedom of the high company into which he had thrust himself. But even there Cromwell failed in establishing a parallel favourable to himself, "who," as Cowley says, "for his particular share of it, sat still at home, and exposed them so frankly abroad."[1] Cowley should have added, too, that he exposed them in a pestilential climate.[2] Napoleon Bonaparte accompanied his army to Moscow. If Oliver Cromwell wanted the glory of foreign conquest to gild over his perfidy and villany, he should have accompanied his fleet to the West Indies, and shown the world whether his genius and valour were equal to the task of averting the disgrace which in that disastrous expedition fell so heavily upon the arms of England.

Even after that disgraceful failure, the genius and valour of Blake could still gain many victories and triumphs for England, though Blake's fleets were no longer equipped and provisioned as they had been by the great statesmen of the Commonwealth; and Blake's own premature death may in great part be attributed to the

[1] Cowley's Discourse, by Way of Vision, concerning the Government of Oliver Cromwell.

[2] For a description of their sufferings from the pestilential climate, see Admiral Penn's Journal, published in Mr. Granville Penn's Memorials of Admiral Sir William Penn, vol. ii. p. 56 *et seq.*—"The fever and flux have been so general," writes Admiral Penn to Cromwell, "that 'tis rare to find a man that hath escaped either one or both of them."—Penn to Cromwell, June 6, 1655, in *Granville Penn*, vol. ii. p. 112.

culpable neglect of the usurper, who was too much occupied with the intrigues for his own further personal
aggrandisement to pay due attention to the naval affairs
of the State. For Blake's death was certainly owing
to his health's being thoroughly broken, by his being
kept at sea so long without intermission; and his ships
were rendered so foul that, under any commander but
himself, they would have been quite unserviceable.

As I have said, none of the great spirits of the English
Commonwealth ever more acted with Cromwell—except
Blake, whose strong and noble passion for the honour of
his country still led him to fight that country's foreign
enemies, and whose resistless energy, directed by the instinct of genius, was such that, wherever he led, victory was
still his companion, till he " who would never strike to any
other enemy, struck his topmast to Death." From Cadiz to
Leghorn, from Leghorn to Tunis, from Tunis to Santa Cruz,
his fleet held on its victorious course.   To him, as to his
antitype of later days, whom England delights to honour,
while to Blake she has as yet refused even a tomb :—

> To him, as to the burning levin
> Short, bright, resistless course was given ;
> Where'er his country's foes were found,
> Was heard the fated thunder's sound,
> Till burst the bolt on yonder shore,
> Roll'd, blaz'd, destroy'd—and was no more!

But the honour of the exploits of Blake belongs to himself,
and to the great statesmen of the Commonwealth, who had
first discovered his genius, and had created the powerful
navy which that genius led to victory. Very different, as
we have seen in the business of Hispaniola, was the
result when the genius of Cromwell was left to its own
resources.

Plato and Tacitus have exhausted the powers of language

in depicting those "wounds and lacerations" which the minds of tyrants would disclose if they were laid open. Some traces of those mental tortures may be discerned even on their outward aspects, and sometimes where the intellectual grandeur of the head and face renders the effect more remarkable; as in that immortal marble,[1] in that look of the great Dictator, which is so instinct at once with mind and courage, as if a more than human intelligence shone through it, strangely combined with an expression about the mouth of tremulous sensibility, and as if the mind within were so powerful as to have preserved a serenity showing no trace of all that stormy and eventful past—of years of war, of toil, of mental anxiety, of bodily suffering, of superhuman success—save something of an air, partly stern, partly anxious, partly melancholy, which may perhaps indicate remorse, and which seems to forebode, but not to fear, a terrible fate.

The great English Protector's face is a far less intellectual one than that of the great Roman Dictator, and I have never seen any portrait of it which evinces any trace of this look of anxiety observable in the bust of Cæsar to which I refer. But I have seen in the State Paper Office signatures of Cromwell's ("Oliver P.") in 1656, which, from their extremely tremulous character, betray either very great mental anxiety or very great bodily weakness. Could this be the effect of what is called remorse, or at least of that torture of the mind arising from the uneasy, the racking consciousness that he had committed a gigantic crime in vain? These signatures are strikingly different from his signatures of earlier days—even from his signature two years before, in 1654. As we look at these tremulous signatures, and remember that the writer was

---

[1] The bust of Julius Cæsar in the British Museum.

not sixty years of age, we are tempted to ask, is this the man whose adamantine nerves some ten years before, after all the toil and excitement of the day of Naseby, could still before he slept write that letter to the Speaker in such firm, bold, and distinct characters? But when he penned that letter, on the night of the 14th of June 1645, his conscience was as clear as that which enabled Vane and Scot, and Harrison and Sydney, to meet death with such intrepid serenity. To have kept such a clear conscience would have been far better for him while he lived, and a far greater honour to his memory, than a dormitory among the ashes of kings. If his saying on his deathbed, when one of his chaplains, whom he had asked if it was possible to fall from grace, answered that it was not possible, " Then I am safe, for I know that I was once in grace," is accurately reported, it proves that he was himself conscious that he had deviated from the path of rectitude, of honesty. In spite of all his long-winded and involved sophistries to his Parliaments, he could not cheat his own conscience : for his was one of those minds of which Walter Scott says that, while Fear is the scourge of cowards, Remorse is the torturer of the brave—Remorse, which the Greeks personified under the name of the Erinyes, or the Avenging Deities, and which, in the case of powerful criminals, whom no other punishment can reach, half avenges the wrongs of mankind !

INDEX.

the invasion of the Scots, ii. 163–165, and 163 *note*

rey, William, Lord, of Werke, nominated a member of the first Council of State, i. 37 ; but not re-elected in February 16$\frac{49}{50}$, i. 178

Guise, Dukes of, a branch of the House of Lorraine, their affinity to the Stuarts, ii. 4. Henry, Duke of, his concern in the massacre of St. Bartholomew, *ibid.*

Gustavus Adolphus, King of Sweden, was the first who introduced the use of the cartridge, i. 167. None of the Scots' regiments which had been in the service of, were engaged in these wars, though some officers that had served under him were in the service of the Scots' Parliament, i. 322, 323

HAMILTON, James Hamilton, Marquis of (commonly called Duke of), one of the leaders of the party of the "Engagement," i. 258 ; all of whom were brought to the Stool of Repentance, i. 269, 270. His mode of levying men for his expedition into England ; many yeomen in Clydesdale fled from their houses to Loudoun Hill to avoid being pressed, 320. Tried by a High Court of Justice and beheaded, 48

Hamilton, William (brother and heir of the preceding), was severely wounded at the Battle of Worcester, and died of his wounds four days after the battle, ii. 194

Harrington, Sir James, nominated a member of the first Council of State, i. 37. One of those who always opposed Cromwell's usurpation and tyranny, ii. 444

Harrison, Thomas, Major-General, Royalist calumny and scurrility respecting, i. 77. His wild religious enthusiasm, and his daring as a soldier, 78. His fearless demeanour on the scaffold, 79. Was to Cromwell what Murat was to Bonaparte, ii. 94. Commands the forces raised by the Council of State to oppose the Scots' army, ii. 150, 151, 153, 179. One of the members of the Inns of Court who, at the beginning of the Civil

War, composed the Earl of Essex's life-guard, ii. 244. Conversation of, with Ludlow, 438–440. The dupe of Cromwell's strong professions of honesty and saintship, 440. So that he stoutly asserted "he was assured the Lord-General sought not himself, but that King Jesus might take the sceptre," to which it was replied that "Christ must come before Christmas, or else He would come too late," 445. Cromwell's character of, "An honest man, and aims at good things, yet, from the impatience of his spirit, will not wait the Lord's leisure," 443. Refuses to make his escape at the Restoration, 480, *note*

Haselrig, Sir Arthur, John Lilburne's charge against, i. 195 and *note*. John Lilburne's charge of rapacity against Haselrig, supported by a statement of Sir Roger Twysden, ii. 424, 425. One of those who always opposed Cromwell's usurpation and tyranny, 444 *note*, and 452 *note*

Henrietta Maria, Queen of Charles I., her name connected with the Irish massacre, i. 132 ; ii. 4 and *note*. Plans of, for punishing her husband's rebellious English subjects, ii. 2

Henry III., King of France, character of, ii. 8, 12

Henry VII., King of England, employed Empson and Dudley in oppressing, "cheating," and pillaging the people of England, ii. 15, 16. Substituted for the old English nobility a nobility composed of such persons as Empson and Dudley, 17

Henry VIII., King of England, gave up to the executioner Empson and Dudley, ii. 15. But continued the work of his father in oppressing, plundering, and degrading the English nation, and in direct violation of his promise, solemnly declared in Parliament, that none of the Church property (which had become national property) should be converted to private use, but that it should be applied to the necessary expenses of government, and thus save the people from taxation, distributed it among court lackeys, cooks, and turnspits, ii. 239, 240

Heveningham, William, nominated a

LONDON
PRINTED BY SPOTTISWOODE AND CO.
NEW-STREET SQUARE

MR. MURRAY'S
LIST OF RECENT WORKS.

A NEW SERIES OF THE WELLINGTON DESPATCHES; CIVIL AND POLITICAL. Edited by HIS SON. Vol. I.—The CONGRESS of VERONA. 8vo. 20s.

EARL GREY'S CORRESPONDENCE WITH KING WILLIAM IV., from 1830, to the Passing of The Reform Act, 1832. Edited by HIS SON. 2 vols. 8vo. 30s.

MADAGASCAR REVISITED UNDER A NEW REIGN, AND THE REVOLUTION WHICH FOLLOWED. By REV. W. ELLIS. With Illustrations. 8vo. 16s.

KING GEORGE THE THIRD'S CORRESPONDENCE WITH LORD NORTH, 1768-83. Edited, with an Introduction and Notes, by W. BODHAM DONNE. 2 vols. 8vo. 32s.

OLD LONDON; PAPERS read by the following Authors at the LONDON CONGRESS of the ARCHÆOLOGICAL INSTITUTE, July 1866. With Illustrations. 8vo. 12s.

A. J. B. BERESFORD HOPE, M.P.	EDWARD FOSS, F.S.A.
DEAN STANLEY, D.D.	JOSEPH BURTT, Esq.
G. T. CLARK, Esq.	REV. J. R. GREEN.
G. GILBERT SCOTT, R.A.	GEORGE SCHARF, F.S.A.
PROFESSOR WESTMACOTT, R.A.	

ASHANGO LAND; A SECOND JOURNEY INTO EQUATORIAL AFRICA. By P. B. DU CHAILLU. With Map and 30 Illustrations. 8vo. 21s.

HISTORY OF LATIN CHRISTIANITY; including that of the Popes to the Pontificate of Nicholas V. By DEAN MILMAN. *New and Revised Edition.* 9 vols. Post 8vo. 6s. each.

A YACHT VOYAGE TO ICELAND, JAN, MAYEN, AND SPITZBERGEN. By LORD DUFFERIN. *Fifth Edition.* With Illustrations. Post 8vo. 7s. 6d.

THE WAGES AND EARNINGS OF THE WORKING CLASSES, with some FACTS illustrative of their ECONOMIC CONDITION. Drawn up from authentic and official sources. By LEONE LEVI, F.S.A. 8vo. 6s.

A COMPLETE HISTORY OF ARCHITECTURE, FROM THE EARLIEST TIMES TO THE PRESENT DAY. By JAMES FERGUSSON, F.R.S. With 1,500 Illustrations and Index. 3 vols. 8vo.

CONTINUATION OF A HISTORY OF THE CHRISTIAN CHURCH; FROM THE CONCORDAT OF WORMS TO THE DEATH OF BONIFACE VIII., A.D. 1122–1303. By CANON ROBERTSON. 8vo. 18s.

LIFE OF SIR JOHN ELIOT : 1590–1632. By JOHN FORSTER, LL.D. With Portraits. 2 vols. 8vo. 30s.

LECTURES ON THE HISTORY OF THE JEWISH CHURCH. By DEAN STANLEY. With Maps. *3rd Edition.* 2 vols. 8vo. 16s. each.

PRINCIPLES OF GEOLOGY; or, The Modern Changes of the Earth and its Inhabitants, considered as illustrative of Geology. By SIR CHARLES LYELL, BART. *10th Edition.* With Illustrations. 2 vols. 8vo. 16s. *each.*

THE ILIAD OF HOMER, rendered into ENGLISH BLANK VERSE. By the EARL OF DERBY. *5th Edition.* 2 vols. 8vo. 24s.

PLATO, AND THE OTHER COMPANIONS OF SOKRATES. By GEORGE GROTE, F.R.S. *2nd Edition.* 3 vols. 8vo. 45s.

THE HARVEST OF THE SEA; or, The Natural and Economic History of the British Food Fishes. By JAMES G. BERTRAM. With Illustrations. 8vo. 21s.

THE ZAMBESI AND ITS TRIBUTARIES, AND THE DISCOVERY OF LAKES SHIRWA AND NYASSA. By DAVID and CHARLES LIVINGSTONE. With Illustrations. 8vo. 21s.

BLIND PEOPLE: THEIR WORKS AND WAYS. With Sketches of the Lives of some famous Blind Men. By REV. B. G. JOHNS, M.A. With Illustrations. Post 8vo. 7s. 6d.

THE PRESENT STATE OF CHRISTIANITY, AND THE RECENT ATTACKS MADE UPON IT. By M. GUIZOT. Post 8vo. 10s. 6d.

BENEDICITE; or, THE SONG OF THE THREE CHILDREN. By G. CHAPLIN CHILD, M.D. 2 vols. Fcp. 8vo. 12s.

THE STUDENT'S MANUAL OF MORAL PHILOSOPHY. By WILLIAM FLEMING, D.D., late Professor in Glasgow University. Post 8vo. 7s. 6d.

JOHN MURRAY, Albemarle Street.